U.S. v. Microsoft

JOEL BRINKLEY
STEVE LOHR
THE NEW YORK TIMES

U.S. v. Microsoft

McGraw-Hill

New York St. Louis San Francisco Washington, D.C. Auckland Bogotá Caracas
Lisbon London Madrid Mexico City Milan Montreal New Delhi
San Juan Singapore Sydney Tokyo Toronto

McGraw-Hill

*A Division of The **McGraw·Hill** Companies*

1234567890 AGMAGM 09876543210

ISBN 0-07-135588-X

Printed and bound by Quebecor World, Martinsburg.

Credits for the photographs in the insert are as follows:
Judge Jackson: Paul Hosefros/The New York Times; Bill Gates: Joe Marquette/Associated Press; Jim Barksdale: Larry Downing/Reuters; John Warden: Dith Pran/The New York Times; David Boies: Tyler Mallory/The New York Times; Microsoft team: Kamenko Pajic/Associated Press; Government team: Paul Hosefros/The New York Times; Joel Klein: Doug Mills/Associated Press; William Nuekom: Tyler Mallory/Associated Press.

McGraw-Hill books are available at special quantity discounts to use as premiums and sales promotions, or for use in corporate training programs. For more information, please write to the Director of Special Sales, Professional Publishing, McGraw-Hill, Two Penn Plaza, New York, NY 10121-2298. Or contact your local bookstore.

 This book is printed on recycled, acid-free paper containing a minimum of 50% recycled, de-inked fiber.

Contents

CHAPTER 3
Microsoft Mounts Its Defense   135

CHAPTER 5

Just the Facts   *263*

CHAPTER 6

Judge and Judgment   289

Preface

The Microsoft antitrust trial captured the attention of most people who make their living in the worlds of technology, but it also stood to affect almost everyone who uses a computer. When the appeals process is complete, the case is likely to set rules that lay out the antitrust limits for the new economy—and for a robust industry that seems always to move in a dozen directions at once, expanding in one vector even as it contracts in another.

The New York Times viewed the Microsoft case as a touchstone millennial event that signaled a transition from business-as-usual at the end of the 20th century to seemingly limitless global markets at the beginning of the 21st. That is why we decided to produce this book.

Its foundation is the news coverage we produced in the course of the trial. Not all the articles published during that time are here, and many that are included have been edited to shorter lengths. To that foundation we have added material that has appeared nowhere else: background, profiles and analysis intended to add insight, coupled with reporting undertaken especially for this book. We carried out many additional interviews, studied yet more documents and examined precedents explicitly for this effort.

And yet, this book remains very much a first-draft of a history in progress. Though the trial is over, appeals are under way and are likely to continue for a year or more. No one knows how this story will end.

Still, the Microsoft trial offered an extraordinary window into the workings of one of the world's most important, influential and indisputably interesting companies—and into the often brilliant, sometimes foolish, always aggressive men who steered its ambitious course. No matter what happens on appeal, the story told here stands as a compelling courtroom account. It may change your view of Microsoft or of the government—or of both.

We covered every minute of the trial, gavel to gavel. After it ended, we gained extraordinary access to principals on all sides of the case, so we might better understand its origins and why what had once seemed a longshot for the government produced, in the end, so lopsided a conclusion. The answers we took away from interviews with the leading players on the government team and at Microsoft, and with the judge himself, proved to be surprising.

Appeals courts may or may not uphold Judge Jackson's findings of fact or his conclusions of law. The penalties, or "remedies," he handed down may or may not ever actually be imposed on the company. But even now it is clear that the very fact of the trial, the months of unflattering scrutiny of this industry giant, have already changed the rules for Microsoft and for much of the computer industry.

Joel Brinkley and Steve Lohr
July 2000

Acknowledgments

Without the help of many people we never would have been able to produce this book, especially on a rapid schedule.

Our editors, on the Business Desk and in Washington, generously allowed us the time to work on the project. Rob Fixmer, technology editor of The Times when the project started and now editor-in-chief of Inter@ctive Week, masterfully edited our work and kept us on track to complete the book on time.

Mike Levitas, director of book development at The Times, came up with the idea for the book and most ably managed the sometimes delicate negotiations between the companies, departments, news desks and individuals whose cooperation was needed.

And Nancy Mikhail, executive editor of McGraw-Hill, accommodated herself to the odd and sometimes unsettling practices of newspaper people with grace and patience.

Our thanks to all of you.

CHAPTER ▎1

Principles in Collision

They sat on opposite sides of an imposing expanse of walnut table, polished to a high gloss, on the third floor of the Department of Justice. On one side were the leaders of the Justice Department's antitrust division and representatives of 20 state governments, all of them poised to file the most far-reaching antitrust suit against an American company in a generation.

On the other side of the table in the stately conference room, sat a team of executives and lawyers for the Microsoft Corporation, the rich, powerful and widely admired dynamo of the nation's high-technology economy.

The meeting on May 15, 1998 was to begin "last rites" talks—a term of art for what amounts to a high-stakes poker game in the civil proceedings that constitute an antitrust case. The government approaches a defendant in a final attempt to reach a settlement before going to court. The corporate defendant must make one of two choices. If it settles, it must accept unpalatable changes in the way it does business, but at least the pain is known and it derives from negotiation. If the defendant does not settle, the company faces the uncertainty of a trial based on the malleable standard of antitrust. A vague declaration in defense of competition, the Sherman Antitrust Act of 1890, has been variously interpreted over the years and has been used as a forceful if unpredictable tool to restructure industries and dismantle companies—as Standard Oil, American Tobacco, Alcoa, United Shoe Machinery and AT&T could attest.

Even when the government loses or folds, the defendant does not necessarily win. A major antitrust suit by the Federal government can hobble a once-invincible corporation, distracting it, dulling its competitive intensity. The Justice Department dropped its mammoth suit against I.B.M. in 1982, after 13 years, but by then the company had been fundamentally changed by the experience. It was more cautious, more willing to share markets with companies like Microsoft, the then-tiny software company whose operating system I.B.M. chose for its personal computer in 1981, an act of extreme corporate generosity or myopia, as history would prove.

Both sides knew the stakes and the history when David Boies leaned across the conference table and looked directly at William Neukom, the general counsel of Microsoft. And everyone at the table also knew that Boies brought a special perspective to this conflict. He had been one of the principal lawyers for I.B.M. during its marathon battle with the Justice Department.

"You know, once the United States government files suit against you, everything changes," Boies recalls saying. "People are more willing to come forward and testify against you. Others are more willing to question you, resist you. The whole world changes."

The Boies comment would prove to be remarkably prescient. Yet, at the time, the Microsoft team apparently, and perhaps understandably, regarded it as a bluff from a seasoned litigator and avid gambler who visited the gaming tables of Las Vegas and Atlantic City several times a year.

As Boies recalls the moment, Neukom and the company's other lawyers looked back at him impassively, singularly unimpressed. "They didn't really respond other than to repeat what they'd been saying all along"—that the government did not understand the software industry.

The "last rites" talks collapsed the next day, and two days later, on May 18, Justice Department lawyers filed the landmark antitrust suit known as *The United States of America v. the Microsoft Corporation.*

The cross-table exchange in May 1998 established the pattern that was repeated again and again in the Microsoft case—two sides, far apart, speaking past each other, what one side finds significant, the other dismisses as irrelevant. As their investigation progressed, the Justice Department and states came to believe that the evidence against Microsoft was deep and damning, revealing predatory intent and conduct in convincing and vivid detail. For its part, Microsoft saw the long-running antitrust inquiry as largely a byproduct of successful lobbying by its rivals. The government did not understand the software business, in Microsoft's view, because what knowledge they had came from the company's competitors. But given a fair hearing, in court—or in the court of public opinion—Microsoft believed that its views would prevail.

To grasp how those opposing positions hardened, it helps to go back. And Aug. 21, 1995, is a good place to start. On that day, a brisk, even perfunctory courtroom session took place in Washington, D.C. "This hearing is going to be short and sweet, ladies and gentlemen," Judge Thomas Penfield Jackson said by way of opening. And it was. Twenty minutes later, lawyers for the government and Microsoft shook hands and filed out of the Federal district courthouse in Washington, carrying copies of a court-approved antitrust agreement known as a consent decree.

Though the two sides had agreed to the consent decree, Microsoft seemed the winner. The six-page document required the company to make some changes in the way it licensed its industry-standard Windows operating system to personal computer makers, but it did not fundamentally affect the way Microsoft did business. The government—first the Federal Trade Commission, then the Justice Department—had spent more than five years investigating the increasingly market-dominating software maker, but in the end they had barely laid a glove on the company.

On that day, Neukom, Microsoft's tall, silver-haired general counsel, known for his bow ties and manner of aristocratic reserve, was almost gloating. On the courthouse steps, he declared, "At the end of five years, we were willing to accommodate the government on some licensing matters, and the rest of our practices apparently passed muster."

For Microsoft, this was a moment to enjoy, having swatted aside a government challenge to its corporate way of life. "After all those years of investigation," Neukom later recalled, "my feeling was that that was the end of a chapter. I was pleased to have it behind us—and I thought it was behind us."

The Microsoft executive team, Bill Gates in particular, had long viewed the antitrust investigation as just another competitive hurdle. Gates even spoke of the antitrust authorities in the same tone of combative derision that he typically directed at his business adversaries. In 1992, when the FTC was pursuing Microsoft, Gates told a reporter for *Business Week*, "The worst that could come of this is I could fall down the steps of the FTC building, hit my head and kill myself."

Three years later, his lack of concern seemed justified. The consent decree had proven to have scant effect on Microsoft's business practices.

When Joel I. Klein, a prominent Washington appellate lawyer, joined the Justice Department in April 1995 as principal deputy to Anne K. Bingaman, chief of the antitrust division, his first task was to seek final approval of the consent decree. For the government, the hard lesson learned from the lengthy investigation that had resulted in the consent decree was the need for speed when dealing with fast-paced high-tech industries. It wasn't that Microsoft's business practices had passed muster—far from it, in the view of the Justice Department. But the consent decree, signed in 1994 and approved in 1995, had come too late to affect the market for personal computer operating systems.

"To really have fostered and protected competition in the operating system market, it should have been signed in 1985 instead of 1994," observed Robert E. Hall, a Stanford University economist who advised the government on the consent decree case.

When Klein became chief of the antitrust division in 1996, he refined the government's approach to antitrust enforcement in the high-tech industries. The new policy: the government must step in early, if at all.

Whatever the shortcomings of the consent decree, it did contain language that would be central to the government's sweeping suit in 1998. One provision prohibited Microsoft from tying the sale of one its products to the use of another. But in the next sentence, the decree, at Microsoft's insistence, added, "This shall not be construed to prohibit Microsoft from developing integrated products." No one could possibly have foreseen how much legal time and talent would be spent arguing the meaning of those two lines in the decree.

Microsoft, it seems, had begun flouting at least the spirit of the consent decree shortly after Klein joined the Justice Department in the spring of 1995. That July, Gates told a group of Intel executives, according to one participant's notes: "This antitrust thing will blow over. We haven't changed our business practices at all."

But other technology companies were becoming frustrated with those practices. That same year, America Online complained to Klein that Microsoft was violating antitrust law by bundling MSN, its new online service and a direct competitor to AOL, with Windows. But the department decided not to act.

In June 1996, however, Microsoft took the step that led to Judge Jackson's courtroom.

For months, James L. Barksdale, the president of Netscape

Communications Corporation, the commercial pioneer in software used to browse the Web, had been growing increasingly irritated by what he regarded as the bare-knuckle tactics Microsoft was deploying against his company. But then Microsoft did something more: it threatened to cancel Compaq Computer's license to Windows— Microsoft's industry-standard operating system, which Compaq could not survive without—because the PC maker planned to bundle the Netscape Navigator browser, not Microsoft's Internet Explorer, with its new computers.

"I'm not a lawyer, but I have more than 30 years experience in business," Barksdale recalled in early 2000. "I just knew that was something wrong." He called Microsoft's threat to cancel Compaq's Windows license "the singular act" that prompted him to take his grievances to the Justice Department. To accomplish that, he asked the company's lawyer, Gary L. Reback, to write a "white paper" detailing the problem. The 222-page paper accused Microsoft of, among other things, using its dominance in operating systems to force PC makers to take Microsoft's browser. And in August, Barksdale sent a copy to Joel Klein.

Klein said the paper got his immediate attention. "There was a big difference in my mind between MSN and this," he said. "To me, conditioning one product on another was clearly a violation of the consent decree. I authorized San Francisco to investigate."

The Justice Department's San Francisco office asked Phillip R. Malone, an up-and-coming young lawyer, to head the Microsoft investigation. And the next month, he and four other lawyers began faxing civil investigative demands to Microsoft for documents related to the Netscape charges and to Microsoft's Internet strategy. Such demands are the civil equivalent of a subpoena.

As each new request spilled out of a fax machine in Microsoft's legal department, a Microsoft lawyer would discuss the request with Malone by phone. Then the investigators simply waited. "The documents just arrived in the mail," Malone said.

Never once, he added, did an investigator have to visit Microsoft and look in file cabinets or hard drives for overlooked documents or e-mail messages. This became a point of pride at Microsoft. In a lengthy interview earlier this year at the company's corporate campus in Redmond, Wash., Neukom pointed to the document production as a rebuttal to those who say Microsoft is a corporate outlaw that can't be trusted. "Well, we produced all this information," he observed. "It is an honor system, to some degree. No one has ever accused us of withholding anything."

Microsoft's lawyers examined all the documents before they were sent off. Several government officials said these lawyers should instantly have recognized that the documents being requested meant trouble. "You can't be a lawyer and not know these documents are lethal," Klein observed.

Microsoft's lawyers later said they had understood that some of the e-mail messages could quicken a prosecutor's pulse. But they saw it as a tactical problem—the fiery communications of business aggression, which might seem incriminating at first glance—and not evidence of an antitrust violation. There simply was "no smoking gun," in the view of one company lawyer.

Even so, as the boxes of papers went out the door, Microsoft's legal troubles mounted. Remarkably, the most damaging documents—the ones that galvanized the resolve of state and federal prosecutors nationwide—were written months after that first government request arrived, months after Microsoft's leaders knew that everything they were writing was likely to wind up in plaintiffs' hands.

Judge Jackson, in one of several interviews granted to *The Times* during the trial on the condition that his comments not be used until the case left his courtroom, likened the phenomenon to the federal prosecution of drug traffickers, who are repeatedly caught as a result of telephone wiretaps. And yet, he said, "they never figure out that they shouldn't be saying certain things on the phone."

But Neukom said Microsoft had been under investigation for so long, and e-mail was so essential to the operations of the company, that managers simply could not edit every thought and continue to manage effectively. "E-mail is a big part of how we run this company," he said. "And candid, frank, open e-mail communication is a big part of our efficiency."

While Microsoft dealt with the growing federal investigation, a new group took up the chase: state attorneys general. That compounded Microsoft's problems. In time, the company would face not just the Justice Department but 20 sovereign and independent plaintiffs for the states as well.

About the time the Justice Department's first document requests arrived at Microsoft in September 1996, Mark Tobey, an antitrust lawyer in the Texas attorney general's office, read a *Time* magazine cover story about the browser war with the headline: "An epic battle is taking place between Microsoft and Netscape." Tobey, whose state is home to Compaq and Dell Computer, two companies highly dependent on Microsoft software, decided to have a look at the subject. He managed to get a copy of the Netscape white paper. With that and other information, on Feb. 9, 1997, the Texas attorney general's office issued its own civil investigative demand to Microsoft, the first formal action by a state attorney general.

In April 1997, the state attorneys general gathered in Washington for their annual spring conference, and during a meeting of the antitrust section chiefs, Tobey outlined what he had been doing, hoping to recruit allies. But his presentation on Microsoft stirred little interest—quite the opposite, in fact. Tom Miller, attorney general of Iowa, chairman of the antitrust committee, said his first thought was: "Oh my God, Microsoft? We're not going to sue Microsoft, are we?"

But through the spring and summer, Tobey argued and lobbied and eventually persuaded several of the larger states to have a look at the Microsoft documents. And, in relatively short order, the accumulating evidence persuaded other states, including Connecticut, Illinois, Massachusetts, New York and Wisconsin, to join the investigation because the documents had stunned them.

"I didn't know much about technology, or about the industry," recalled Richard Blumenthal, attorney general of Connecticut. But as he read the documents "I was really struck by the brutal, overt tactics. You rarely see things like this written down."

In the minds of almost every federal and state official interviewed, three documents stood out as the most influential. The first was a white paper that Gates wrote in May 1995, titled "The Internet Tidal Wave."

"A new competitor born on the Internet is Netscape," Gates wrote. As the leader in Web browsing software, Netscape, he added, could set the technical rules for Internet computing and thus "commoditize the underlying operating system." In other words, Mr. Gates was saying, Netscape threatened to make Microsoft Windows, which ran 85 percent of all personal computers, irrelevant.

The Gates memo, though not legally damaging on its own, pinned a motivation to what followed. Two more documents that arrived in the fall of 1997 got all the plaintiffs excited. They were e-mail messages in which James E. Allchin, a senior Microsoft executive in charge of the Windows group, expressed concern about the company's Internet strategy. Microsoft's browser, Internet Explorer, was being given away and bundled with Windows, yet it still was not catching on.

In e-mail to another senior executive written Dec. 20, 1996, and Jan. 2, 1997—more than three months after the federal government had begun obtaining documents relating to Microsoft's Internet strategy—Allchin wrote: "I do not believe we can win on our current path. Even if we get Internet Explorer totally competitive with Navigator, why would we be chosen? They have 80 percent market share. My conclusion is we have to leverage Windows more." He added, "We need something more: Windows integration."

To Microsoft, the Allchin e-mail was little more than a glimpse into one side of a product debate within the company. It was written from the perspective of a computer scientist who headed the Windows development team, not by an antitrust lawyer looking for evidence of illegal product tying. "This is one tiny slice of an honest but spirited debate within the company about what's in the best interest of customers and the company," said Neukom.

But to state and federal officials, this was the smoking gun. Allchin seemed to be clearly saying that unless Microsoft deeply embedded its browser into its monopoly product—and thus made users go out of their way to use Netscape—Internet Explorer would surely lose. When these documents arrived at the Justice Department office in San Francisco, Malone knew he had something special. He took them to Washington and discussed them with Klein and others.

"Everybody saw it; they really captured the essence of what we believed," Malone said. "They had that power."

In early October 1997, Microsoft's lawyers attended a meeting at the Justice Department to try to explain why it had integrated its Web browsing software into Windows. At the meeting, Joel Klein "held up two disks, one holding Windows and the other with the browsing software," William Neukom recalled. "He said, 'You should have consulted us. It's easy to separate these.'"

"That was the level of analysis," Neukom said, indicating he was not impressed.

But once again, at another crucial point, Microsoft misread its opponents. The federal government was feeling more confident. By the summer of 1997, Phillip Malone later recalled, "I certainly felt we had a case." The Justice Department had not only gathered hundreds of documents from Microsoft but had also interviewed dozens of industry executives, including crucial officers at Netscape. And by early fall, Klein said, "it was becoming clear to me that we had a larger case" beyond the browser question.

By now, the government's inquiry had gathered evidence that Microsoft had threatened Compaq and I.B.M., had essentially bribed America Online and had tried to hobble Sun Microsystems, among others—all to protect the Windows monopoly, as the government read the evidence.

On Oct. 20, 1997, Klein filed what proved to be an interim suit against Microsoft, accusing the company of violating the 1995 consent decree by forcing computer makers to take Internet Explorer as a condition of licensing Windows. A. Douglas Melamed, deputy assistant attorney general in the Justice Department's antitrust division, recalled later that the idea was to step in before Microsoft released a new version of Internet Explorer, which was due out soon, "rather than to let that event pass, waiting for the big case."

Judge Jackson was assigned that interim case, and in mid-December, he ordered Microsoft to offer computer makers a version of Windows that did not include Internet Explorer—even though Microsoft had argued that Internet Explorer was now an integral component of Windows. Microsoft responded that the company would offer manufacturers a choice: one version of Windows that was obsolete or another that did not work properly.

The Justice Department reacted angrily, and, as it turned out, Judge Jackson was irritated, too. Asked later what had struck him about Microsoft's defense during this case, the judge referred to this exchange in court, with David Cole, a Microsoft vice president, in January 1998: "It seemed absolutely clear to you," the judge asked him from the bench "that I entered an order that required that you distribute a product that would not work? Is that what you're telling me?"

"In plain English, yes," Cole replied. "We followed that order. It wasn't my place to consider the consequences of that."

In the end, Microsoft agreed to offer a version of Windows with Internet Explorer hidden and partly disabled, and an appeals court was due to consider the case in the spring. But the issue hardly mattered any longer. Windows 98 was due out in just a few months, and Microsoft was saying Internet Explorer would be even more tightly intertwined in this new version.

In late March 1998, the antitrust chiefs in about a dozen states agreed on a multi-state action against Microsoft. At the Justice Department, Klein still was not saying what he planned. Still, by the first week of March, anyone watching closely could have guessed that he was serious when he hired Jeffrey H. Blattner, a former chief counsel of the Senate Judiciary Committee, as special counsel for information technology.

His actual job, Blattner explained later, was chief of staff for the Microsoft case, and in preparation for his new role he read the evidence, principally the Microsoft documents. Right away, he said, "I had a very clear sense that lawyers never get to see documents like this."

Microsoft, apparently, was paying close attention, because within a few weeks the company set out on a lobbying campaign.

In late March, Dennis C. Vacco, then New York's attorney general, got a call from Fred Foreman, a former United States attorney in Chicago. They had been colleagues years earlier, when Vacco was United States attorney in Buffalo. Foreman had been hired by Microsoft, and he asked if he and representatives of his new client could come in for a talk.

A few days later, the Microsoft contingent arrived in New York, including Foreman and David A. Heiner, a Microsoft lawyer. The atmosphere in Mr. Vacco's office was friendly—until Heiner made Microsoft's pitch: Why was his company being viewed as a competitive threat, he asked. After all, he said, Microsoft holds "only 4 percent of the worldwide software market."

Microsoft certainly knew that Vacco was not particularly well informed about the software industry. But before meeting the Microsoft group, Stephen D. Houck, a lawyer in the attorney general's office, had given him a detailed briefing about the case. Houck said Vacco did not say much in response to the 4 percent remark. But Vacco later recalled that as he thought about what he had been told, "I was almost derisive." After all, he noted, the case was not about the worldwide software business; it was about the PC operating-system business, and Microsoft held about 85 percent of that market.

"I don't know if they were purposely playing me because they thought I had a lack of knowledge," Vacco said. "But I knew that was ridiculous." Microsoft's visit, he said, firmed his resolve.

That scene was replayed in many of the 12 states visited by Microsoft delegations. Asked about the 4 percent argument later, Neukom smiled and expressed surprise. "I can't imagine in what context that statement would have been made," he said. "I never made it."

Then, in April, the Microsoft team showed up at the Justice Department. During a meeting in Klein's conference room, they gave a demonstration of Windows 98 and the benefits that the company said resulted from the integration of Internet Explorer.

"The meeting was cordial," Klein recalled. "We knew all of these people. We'd dealt with them before," including "on the MSN–America Online case, when they obviously got the result they wanted."

Neukom said Microsoft spent several days preparing for the meeting. "It was absolutely in our best interests to understand their concerns," he said. But "there was very little indication of open-mindedness on the other side of the table. Their mentality was that there are two separate products that you forced together to crush

Netscape," Neukom recalled. But by then, in fact, Microsoft had given the government hundreds of documents that would provide ammunition for a much broader case.

By mid-April 1998, the Justice Department had produced a draft of its suit that Klein, David Boies and other officials took to Attorney General Janet Reno. They met with her three times over a period of several days. Reno and her staff asked many questions, but finally she gave permission to file suit. Right away, Mr. Klein asked Boies to sign a contract as a special government employee so he could serve as the lead trial lawyer. Though he had worked for the government as a consultant since December, it was only then that Boies immersed himself in the Microsoft documents.

"What most impressed me was the enthusiastic zeal with which they used their monopoly power," Boies said. "In my experience, most companies will use it, but they are nervous, uncomfortable about it. But in this case there was such clarity and baldness in the conduct. I'd never seen anything like it."

In late April, Klein and the other leaders of the antitrust division met with the leaders of Microsoft, including Bill Gates, at the Washington offices of Sullivan & Cromwell, Microsoft's law firm, where Gates made impassioned arguments against the suit. As Neukom recalled it, Gates told Klein, "What we're doing is good for consumers, good for the industry and good for Microsoft."

"Bill just felt that if he could talk to them and not through lawyers, they'd understand," Neukom added.

The government lawyers responded by laying out their allegations. They tried to get Microsoft to respond. Now the company's chairman knew firsthand that the government had a broad and potentially serious case. But "we couldn't get them to focus on the issues," Boies said. "They just kept saying they didn't have monopoly power." Once more an opportunity to avoid the suit slipped away.

In several phone calls in mid-May, including some between Gates and Klein, Microsoft appeared to be making a last offer to settle the case: The company would allow computer makers to alter the opening screen of the Windows operating system. As the case had broadened, that issue had been added to the government's growing list of concerns. The theory was that the least regulatory way to give consumers more choice would be to give PC makers more choice in the form of greater freedom to modify the Windows desktop and to offer more products that competed with Microsoft's offerings.

Because of Microsoft's apparent willingness to compromise, Klein agreed to meet with Microsoft and hold the "last rites" talks that began on May 15, 1998. Like so many aspects of this case, there are two sharply contrasting versions of precisely what torpedoed these settlement talks. But it was mainly over the "first screen" freedoms for PC makers. The government says that in Washington Microsoft was offering far less than Gates intimated in his phone calls to Klein. Microsoft says what the government wanted amounted to a giveaway of its intellectual property and relinquishing of its right to insure a consistent "look and feel" for Windows.

In Microsoft's view, it was the government that had no intention of settling the case. Neukom recalled the two days of talks ending with a senior Justice Department official telling him: "I guess we're in litigation. You have no idea how difficult we can make your lives."

Given Microsoft's performance in the trial and Judge Jackson's ruling against it, the company's refusal to settle the case that day, before the suits were even filed, can be seen as a huge mistake, perhaps the biggest misstep the company has ever made. But in another respect, the company's unyielding stance was not surprising. During a court hearing a short time later, a Microsoft lawyer approached Boies and offered the following remark, as Boies recalled it: "The government has been making the same arguments for eight years. We always give the same responses. Our side always prevails. When is the government going to leave us alone?"

Still, there is another view, one more sympathetic to Microsoft. There is arrogance and hubris in its corporate ranks, to be sure, but in this case Microsoft believed it was taking a stand of principle. It truly believed that it should have the freedom to design Windows as it saw fit, and the company believed that the nation's antitrust laws would ultimately uphold its right to do so. "This case for us is about the freedom to improve our products and to defend the integrity of our most important product, Windows," Neukom explained. "And to do that, we are willing to absorb the short-term pain from this case, which is considerable."

In the government's view, Microsoft's stance had two flaws. First, the company's notion of design freedom was to integrate anything it wanted into Windows to stifle competition. So to accept Microsoft's argument would have been to grant the company an exemption from broad swaths of the nation's antitrust law. Second, Microsoft's behavior, as shown by the evidence in the trial, amounted to consistently bullying industry partners and rivals—all of which had nothing to do with its freedom to innovate, but everything to do with hobbling any potential challenger.

On June 23, 1998, a three-judge panel of the Court of Appeals handed down a ruling overturning Judge Jackson's decision in December ordering Microsoft to take Internet Explorer out of Windows 95. The ruling said Microsoft had every right to integrate new products into Windows, if the company could make a "plausible claim" of business efficiency or consumer benefit from doing so. Neukom got a call at home that morning from Steven Holley, a Sullivan & Cromwell lawyer. His message: "It's all very good and here are the highlights." It was a day of vindication on the Microsoft campus in suburban Seattle. "There was a good deal of jubilation given all the criticism of Microsoft, Bill Gates and the legal team," Neukom recalled.

If Microsoft was jubilant, the plaintiffs, at first, were crushed. "It was a bad day, no doubt," Klein recalled.

But Boies didn't see it that way. He got a copy of the appeals court decision just as he was boarding a plane for San Francisco, where he was to meet with the Justice Department's investigative team. During the trip west, he read it and then read it again, "and by the time I got to San Francisco, I was convinced it was a good thing for us" because "it gave us a road map of what the court of appeals criteria would be." Boies could frame his case around it. Just after he landed, he tried to explain the silver lining in the appeals court ruling to the Justice Department team. "They didn't immediately recognize our tremendous good fortune," he recalled with a grin.

During the summer, state and federal officials feverishly prepared for trial, trying with little success to persuade Microsoft's supposed victims—computer makers especially—to testify. "They were afraid of Microsoft," said Tom Miller, attorney general of Iowa. "We didn't have any particular success." But over the summer, the Justice Department and states continued investigating Microsoft's dealings with other companies and came up with new evidence involving Intel, Apple Computer and others—all of it, the government said, fit into Microsoft's "pattern of behavior" intended to stifle competition.

Over Microsoft's objections, Judge Jackson permitted the new evidence. Suddenly, the focus of the case had widened well beyond the "browser wars" to a broad, multifaceted scheme by Microsoft to thwart competition.

By late August 1998, with the trial scheduled to begin in less than a month, the government was still negotiating with Microsoft over its deposition of Bill Gates. In fact, the fencing between the two sides, along with the delays, forced Judge Jackson to push back the opening day of the trial. Finally, in the last days of August, David Boies and Stephen Houck flew to Seattle for three days of videotaped deposition interviews with Microsoft's chairman. A thick pile of e-mail to and from Gates was a crucial part of the government's case. He was at the center of things, guiding the Microsoft strategy and monitoring the details. And since Gates was not scheduled to appear in court, the deposition would be his testimony for the trial.

As he set up in a Microsoft conference room, Boies said he was excited yet anxious as he got ready to face Gates. It promised to be a electrifying confrontation of its type—an interrogation of one of the nation's most brilliant business executives by one of the nation's leading litigators.

"I was expecting him," Boies recalled, "to be articulate, passionate, tough, direct, intelligent and very, very knowledgeable about everything relating to the case," just as he had been in their last meeting the previous spring. In other words, "a very effective witness."

But as soon as the deposition opened, a very different Bill Gates was on display. This one was mumbling, evasive, obdurate and unaware of anything related to the government's charges. He slouched and rarely looked his interrogator in the eye. And Boies was thrilled. He knew just what he had to do.

"You want to capture as much of that as you can," he observed later. "If you have a witness that says 'I don't know,' you want to get him to say 'I don't know' a thousand times."

Gates obliged again and again. After the first two days of deposition, there was a five-day break before the third and final day. Surely, Boies concluded, Gates' lawyers would talk to their client in the interim, explain how damaging his testimony had been.

"I was really concerned that a recharged Gates would come back," Boies said. "I had two days of him in the can, and I could see its value diminishing. I almost didn't take the third day."

But he did, and to Boies's surprise, when Gates resumed the deposition, his behavior was unchanged. When the questioning had ended, Boies knew he had a powerful weapon. The Microsoft legal team said they never expected the tapes to be used in court, only the transcripts. But after the Gates deposition, Judge Jackson modified a pretrial order, allowing the tapes to be shown in court. Had Microsoft's lawyers known the tapes would be shown in court, Neukom said, "we would have prepared our witness differently," changing the style of his presentation, but not the substance. His stilted, combative answers to seemingly straightforward questions, bickering endlessly over the definition of terms like "market share," added up to a routine deposition performance, the Microsoft lawyers insisted. Deposition witnesses are instructed by their counsel to listen carefully to questions, answer as narrowly as possible and not volunteer information or expand on an answer. "That is the way Bill testified," Neukom said.

The Justice Department, of course, viewed Gates' performance very differently. The government lawyers thought it was an extraordinary piece of evidence and a gift to the plaintiffs. They thought even the transcripts were inflammatory. Boies was determined to play part of the Gates tape on the trial's opening day, now set for Oct. 19, and as often as he could in the days following. He said he hoped it would send this message to the judge: "The chairman of the company doesn't have any credible explanation for what they did, even though he was intimately involved. If he doesn't have an explanation, then how can you credit the explanations of his underlings?"

A Fin-de-Siècle Law at the Millennium

The law is a powerful tool, but not always a precise one. Perhaps nowhere is that more true than in antitrust law. Over the years, the enforcement of antitrust has varied widely, as have theories about the economy and thinking about the proper restraints on corporate behavior. That was one of the things that made the Microsoft case so intriguing to legal scholars. This looking-glass law would be tested as never before in a fast-changing high-technology industry.

"There is enough flexibility in the doctrine and enough uncertainty in how the case law applies to this industry that the Microsoft case is a huge gamble for both sides," observed William Kovacic, a professor at the George Washington University law school, a few days before the trial began.

Mr. Sherman's 1890 Nod to Populism Has Often Been Broadly Interpreted

The legal tool the Government used in its assault on the Microsoft Corporation—the Sherman Antitrust Act of 1890—is brief, vague and malleable. The combination has meant that this bedrock statute of antitrust policy has been at turns toothless and powerful over the years, depending on the politics and economics of the day as interpreted by the courts.

Sponsored by Senator John Sherman, an Ohio Republican who was the younger brother of the Civil War general William Tecumseh Sherman, the act was passed as a nod to a popular backlash against the rise of the industrial trusts in oil, steel and railroads. Farmers, laborers and small-business owners—sizable voting groups—resented the trusts as vehicles of concentrated power. But the trusts, large national holding corporations, were viewed by many others as engines of modernization and industrialization.

Economists at the time opposed the Sherman Act, and the law that Congress passed was a vaguely worded compromise. No one knew what impact it would have, but one senator, quoted in Matthew Josephson's "The Robber Barons," explained that nearly everyone agreed that "something must be flung out to appease the restive masses."

The act's two key provisions, Sections 1 and 2, mention "conspiracy," "restraint of trade" and "attempt to monopolize." Yet while the Sherman Act is now interpreted as the Magna Carta of competition, it never uses the term. After it was passed, critics of the trusts derided the "impenetrable" language of the Sherman Act and called it the Swiss Cheese Act.

But by the early 1900's, the political climate had changed. The growing antagonism for the trusts, especially as income gaps widened, was tapped by an avowed trustbuster, Theodore Roosevelt, who became President in 1901.

"The Sherman Act has always been an elastic piece of social legislation, used to attack perceived exploitation and the aggregation of power," said Eleanor Fox, a professor at the New York University Law School.

The model trust—and the principal target of the trustbusters—was Standard Oil. Shrewdly, Roosevelt made a distinction between good trusts, which thrived because of their superior efficiency, and bad trusts, which grew not as the result of inevitable economic forces but because of unfair business practices.

Throughout the 1880's and 90's, Standard Oil's rivals had complained about the company and the business practices of its founder, John D. Rockefeller. But during those years, the price of kerosene—burned to light the nation's homes—declined steadily. So Standard Oil, it could reasonably be argued, was an "enterprising monopoly."

In the early 1900's, though, Standard Oil raised prices in the United States to prop up its profits at a time it was engaged in a price war against Royal Dutch/Shell in Europe, where Standard Oil did face genuine competition. When consumers were hurt by the Standard Oil monopoly, popular support for antitrust action against the company swelled, encouraged by Roosevelt and his successor, William Howard Taft.

The Federal suit against Standard Oil was filed in 1906, and the Supreme Court approved the breakup of the company in 1911.

Standard Oil and the Microsoft case, historians observe, have some common themes. Both were dominant companies of their day, and William H. Gates, the Microsoft chairman, has been called a modern Rockefeller.

"But there is no Presidential involvement and there is no real consumer dissatisfaction in the Microsoft case," said Ron Chernow, author of "Titan," a best-selling biography of Rockefeller.

"And Rockefeller," Mr. Chernow added, "never went through the kind of honeymoon period of widespread public adulation and favorable press coverage as Bill Gates has had."

Section 1—Every contract, combination in the form of trust or otherwise, or conspiracy, in restraint of trade or commerce among the several States, or with foreign nations, is declared to be illegal.

Section 2—Every person who shall monopolize, or attempt to monopolize, or combine or conspire with any other person or persons, to monopolize any part of the trade or commerce among the several States . . . shall be deemed guilty of a felony.

OCTOBER 19, 1998

A JUDGE FROM CENTRAL CASTING
THOMAS PENFIELD JACKSON

Thomas Penfield Jackson is a natural as a judge: a big man, white haired, avuncular. But he was not a clear natural for the Microsoft trial. Hardly a technophile, Jackson had been known to write opinions longhand, and he found e-mail a cumbersome inconvenience. What's more, the fast-moving world of technology demanded an equally fast-paced trial. Jackson had once got in trouble for allowing a trial to go on far too long—so long, in fact, that the Court of Appeals had to order him to rule.

But at the very outset, he made it clear he wanted this trial to move fast. "I wanted to stay away from disasters like the IBM and AT&T cases," he explained. "I'm a great believer in taking evidence, closing the record as quickly as you can and then shipping it upstairs" to the court of appeals. As he announced the trial schedule in the summer of 1998, he made it clear he was both aggressive and hopelessly optimistic.

"I am prepared to devote the month of September to this trial," he announced. It ended up taking nine months. But in an interview later, he explained his strategy: "I spent eighteen years as a trial lawyer" before being appointed to the bench, "and I learned that the one thing that produces a settlement, or a war, is a trial date."

The Microsoft trial was by far the most prominent and probably the most important trial Jackson had yet heard, certain to bring massive media attention to his courtroom and to him. But Jackson had tried only two antitrust cases before this one. And it was far from clear that he could handle a trial and understand evidence that dealt with APIs, OEMs and ISPs.

Yet, because Jackson had tried the earlier Microsoft case, this new one would, under the related-cases rule, automatically land in his courtroom. So, as the news media reported the progress the Justice Department and states were making toward filing their case, he watched the case coming his way with "a fair amount of trepidation." It was certain to be big, complex, possibly precedent-setting and the subject of "extraordinary public interest," he later acknowledged. And to say he knew little about technology was at best an understatement. His abiding concern: "Please don't let me screw this up!"

Even so, he said, "I thought I could do it" simply because he had a great deal of previous experience "becoming literate on esoteric topics for which I have no background." In any case, he added, judges "are very much generalists. We have to take anything that comes." But, as Jackson thought about the Microsoft case, he recalled his work as a private lawyer, trying to understand medical issues as he defended doctors accused of malpractice. In those cases, he said that after some time, "I really thought I understood it."

Before the Microsoft case landed in his court, Jackson's record suggested, if anything, a pro-business bent. In 1987, the Federal government sued General Motors, contending that its cars had dangerous brake defects. Judge Jackson sided with the automaker, dismissing the government's evidence as merely "anecdotal accounts of skidding events." And he later said that trying that case had helped him learn how to deal with subjects he didn't immediately understand.

But he did have a history with Microsoft—his trial of the earlier "consent-decree" case in the fall of 1997, when the government accused Microsoft of illegally requiring computer manufacturers to take its Internet Explorer browser as a condition of licensing the Windows operating system. In mid-December, he ordered Microsoft to offer computer makers a version of Windows that did not include Internet Explorer—even though Microsoft had insisted that Windows and Internet Explorer were a single product. Microsoft responded that the company would offer manufacturers a choice: one version of Windows that was obsolete or another that didn't work properly. Judge Jackson was not pleased.

Asked later if he had ever seen evidence of the alleged Microsoft arrogance so often described by the plaintiffs, he nodded and referred to the January 1998 courtroom exchange in which David Cole, a Microsoft vice president, had insisted that the company was distributing a version of Windows that wouldn't work because it was the only way to comply with Jackson's order.

Jackson was born in 1937 and grew up in Kensington, Md., a pleasant, leafy, upper-middle class suburb of Washington with Victorian homes and its own sense of community. His father, Thomas Searing Jackson, was a prominent Washington lawyer who had started his own firm, Jackson & Campbell.

He attended St. Albans prep school in the early grades, on a choir scholarship. But when his voice changed, St. Albans yanked the scholarship and demanded full tuition. So Jackson transferred to a first-class Montgomery County, Md., public high school: Bethesda–Chevy Chase. There he played football and was editor of the school newspaper.

He spent his undergraduate years at Dartmouth, creating a lifelong affiliation with the school. In fact, for several years he headed Dartmouth's alumni association in Washington. After graduation, he spent three years in the Navy, most of it aboard a destroyer, then attended Harvard law school. He kept up with Harvard, too. In fact, it was while reading a Harvard alumni magazine in the fall of 1997 that he ran across the name of Lawrence Lessig, an academic expert on antitrust and technology. The judge asked Lessig to serve as a special master during the government's 1997 case against Microsoft. And then in 2000, the Judge asked Lessig to write a brief on issues in the antitrust trial.

Soon after Jackson left Harvard, he joined his father's law firm as a civil and criminal litigator. Among other cases, he defended several medical organizations charged with malpractice. He was widely considered a tenacious litigator.

Eventually, he became politically active in Montgomery County, a locality so heavily Democratic that Republicans like Jackson were curiosities. But the flip side was that it was easy for Republicans to stand out and be noticed. For that reason, Jackson came to the attention of the Committee to Re-elect President Nixon, which he served as a lawyer in 1972.

In 1980, at the start of President Reagan's first term, his name was mentioned for a possible appointment to the District of Columbia Superior Court or the D.C. Appeals Court. But he was not appointed, and some lawyers then said he was passed over because of his membership in the Chevy Chase Country Club, which accepted no black members. That was no doubt viewed as impolitic for a judge presiding over trials of District residents, most of whom were black.

The Reagan White House clearly didn't care about the club membership; two years later, in 1982, Reagan appointed him to a better position, United States District Court. And, like every judge in that courthouse, he presided over his share of interesting and important cases in the following years. Among his early cases was the 1988 trial of Michael K. Deaver, the former top Reagan aide who was convicted of lying under oath during an investigation of whether he had improperly lobbied former White House associates.

But his most prominent case, before Microsoft, had been the trial of the Mayor of Washington, Marion S. Barry Jr., on drug and perjury charges. As in the Microsoft trial, he often interrupted the lawyers to ask witnesses questions of his own.

One of his more interesting exchanges with a witness in that trial was with Rasheeda Moore, the former model who had been used to lure Mayor Barry to a hotel room, where he was videotaped smoking crack cocaine. Moore had referred several times on the tape to "Jell-O." Spectators and reporters wondered if that was a code word for drugs, but neither the prosecution nor the defense thought to ask. So Judge Jackson spoke up: Was Jell-O a cipher for drugs? "No, unh-unh," she replied. Moore insisted she was merely talking about dessert.

Judge Jackson probably did not believe that. In fact he had trouble with that entire trial. A few days after it ended, he complained in a speech to the Harvard Law Forum that he thought "four jurors were determined to acquit regardless of the facts," adding that "they obviously did not tell the truth during jury selection when questioned about possible bias." Jackson went on to say that the Government had put on a very strong case.

Not long after, in 1995, the local paper *Legal Times* sent a reporter to spend a day in Jackson's courtroom, to check out reports that the judge was unusually slow moving. The reporter wrote that Jackson took a two-hour lunch and three "ten-minute" breaks that each lasted half an hour. All in all, the Judge had spent three hours and four minutes on the bench, while his breaks lasted three hours and 46 minutes.

During the Microsoft trial, Jackson scheduled a 90-minute lunch break every day that usually lasted about 110 minutes. And he had a regular break mid-morning and mid-afternoon, each of which lasted about 20 minutes. Trial opened at 10 A.M. and generally adjourned for the day at about 4:20, though he had scheduled it to go as late as 5 P.M. So, generally, Judge Jackson spent about four hours on the bench and three hours on breaks. But given the technical nature of much of the testimony, that was probably as much as his or anyone else's attention span could have handled.

In his spare time, Jackson liked to sail on the Chesapeake Bay. He and his wife spent every weekend at their home on the water in St. Mary's County in Southern Maryland. They considered that their real home, not the apartment they kept on Pennsylvania Avenue near Georgetown. Married three times, he had two grown daughters and two granddaughters. His wife, Pat, was director of development at Sidwell Friends, a private prep school in Washington.

The Microsoft trial, of course, gave the judge more exposure, more attention in the press, than he had ever experienced. Plainly not comfortable with that, he wrote a commentary in 1997 for a judicial conference that revealed his view of the news media.

"The relationship between a potentially newsworthy case and the press is roughly comparable to the relationship between a healthy organism and an infectious disease," he wrote, "The press, like all infectious diseases, is a predator. It will feed on whatever it can find, including the host if its appetite is not sated."

Opening Arguments

By 7 A.M., there was already a line forming outside the Federal courthouse in Washington. The doors wouldn't open until 8 A.M., when the line would form again on the second floor, snaking down the hall from Judge Jackson's courtroom. There were a few scattered civilians in line, but it was mostly journalists, lawyers and lobbyists. After the courtroom doors opened at 10 A.M., many were turned away for lack of seats.

The Microsoft trial was a multimillion-dollar legal chess match. Both sides had vast resources. And by the time the trial began, both sides knew what pieces their adversary possessed; it just wasn't clear how the other side would use them.

Opening statements would provide the first courtroom glimpse of the game plan of the plaintiffs and the defense. The two men who squared off, David Boies, the lead trial lawyer for the Justice Department, and John Warden, a partner at Sullivan & Cromwell, which represents Microsoft, had known each other for three decades. There was no friendship in evidence in the courtroom, as each man in turn presented the framework—and some of the fire—of the trial strategy his side would pursue.

Known for his rumpled blue suits and steel-trap memory, Boies went first for the Government, and the strategy it would pursue became clear. On large video screens, Boies showed excerpts of the taped deposition taken of Bill Gates, the Microsoft chairman and cofounder.

What appeared on screen was amazing, as if some imposter had stepped into skin of the nation's richest man. He was evasive, forgetful and unfamiliar with key decisions at Microsoft, out of the corporate loop. Yet everyone knows Gates *is* the corporate loop at Microsoft. His deposition contradicted his reputation.

Next to appear on the screen were e-mail messages to and from Gates that seemed to contradict his testimony. The Government was going to attack Microsoft's credibility, starting at the top. At one point, one of the video screens failed for about 30 seconds, but Boies kept right on "reading," though he looked ahead at the suddenly blank screen beside the judge. This, as his wife, Mary, related later, was an inadvertent display of his formidable memory. He had no notes. He had memorized the documents.

The next day, it was Warden's turn. A heavy-set man with a baritone drawl, he knew precisely what the Government was trying to do and he sought to deflect it. Tough-talking e-mail, some of it even threatening? Welcome to capitalism, Warden seemed to be saying in the language of the courts and the law.

"The antitrust laws are not a code of civility in business," he chided. And Warden was certainly not going to let assaults on the man paying his bills go unchallenged. He accused the Government of trying to "demonize Bill Gates," a national hero responsible for so many of the "benefits that society is reaping from the information age."

As Microsoft Trial Gets Started, Gates's Credibility Is Questioned

After months of noisy prelude, the antitrust trial against the Microsoft Corporation opened in Federal court this morning with a pointed personal attack on the credibility and integrity of William H. Gates, the company's chairman.

In a taped deposition, part of which the Government showed today in court, Mr. Gates said he knew little if anything about the main charges leveled against his company by the Justice Department and 20 states.

"My only knowledge is the *Wall Street Journal* article; it surprised me," Mr. Gates said of reports of a meeting in which his company was said to have offered its chief competitor in Internet software a chance to divide the market. Gazing directly at his questioner, brow furrowed, head tilted slightly to the left, he added, "I was not involved" in discussions of the key meetings.

But as the Justice Department proceeded with its opening statement over the next two hours, its lead lawyer in the case, David Boies, presented more than a dozen memos and e-mail messages written by Mr. Gates over the last three years, showing clearly that he and other senior Microsoft executives not only had known about the matters in question but had forcefully directed them.

Using memos and documents, the Government portrayed a company obsessed with crushing its competitor, the Netscape Communications Corporation, and willing to use every tool at its disposal, including threats and financial inducements, to force or persuade other companies to drop any planned or existing alliances with Netscape.

Mr. Gates told his questioner at another point in the deposition that he had not even read the Government's antitrust suit. As to the charge of an illegal collusion to divide software markets, Mr. Gates said only, "I think somebody said that was in there."

Mr. Gates also said that in 1995, "somebody came to me to ask if it made sense investing in Netscape."

Shaking his head dismissively, Mr. Gates recalled, "I said it didn't make any sense to me."

Moments later, Mr. Boies displayed on a 10-foot video screen an enlargement of a memo in which Mr. Gates wrote to Paul Maritz, a senior Microsoft executive, that over time Microsoft might have to compete with Netscape. "But in the meantime we can help them," Mr. Gates wrote. "We can pay them some money."

At the heart of this competition—and central to the case—are browsing programs used to navigate the Internet's World Wide Web. Netscape got an early lead in the market with its Navigator browser. What frightened Microsoft was that Navigator could also be used as a "platform," a layer of software on which other programs can run. This is the main function of an operating system, a market in which Microsoft has a monopoly with Windows.

Leaving the Federal courthouse this afternoon, William H. Neukom, Microsoft's senior vice president for law and government affairs, said that the Government's opening presentation was "based entirely on loose and unreliable rhetoric and snippets that were not in any reliable context." Microsoft will offer its own opening remarks on Tuesday. "None of this rhetoric even approaches proof of anti-competitive conduct," he said.

Earlier, however, Mr. Boies had told the judge: "It's competition on the merits that the antitrust laws foster. But this is not a situation of competition on the merits." Instead, he said, it was a "clear restraint of trade."

In one 1995 e-mail message relating to Microsoft's effort to push Netscape out of the market for browsers that run on Windows computers, Mr. Gates wrote other Microsoft executives: "I think there is a very powerful deal we can make with Netscape. I would really like to see something like this happen!!"

Other memos showed that Mr. Gates was continually and personally involved.

In an attempt to demonstrate a pattern of anticompetitive behavior, Mr. Boies led Judge Thomas Penfield Jackson of United States District Court through a chronology of memos and messages that seemed to show Microsoft threatening and cajoling other companies.

After a meeting with Mr. Gates in 1996, an executive with America Online, the nation's largest on-line service, wrote to other executives in his company: "Gates delivered a characteristically blunt query: 'How much do we need to pay you?' " he asked, to damage Netscape. " 'This is your lucky day.' "

In the summer of 1995, one memo showed, Mr. Gates wrote to Andrew S. Grove, chairman of the Intel Corporation, bluntly asking why Intel was doing software research that might conflict with Microsoft's plans.

"I don't understand why Intel funds a program that is against Windows," the message said. An Intel note a few weeks later said, "Gates made vague threats about support-

ing" Intel's competitors, unless Intel agreed to shut down its software research.

Intel eventually gave in, but while this standoff was under way, a Microsoft memo shows that the nation's computer makers were paralyzed while awaiting word on whether Microsoft deemed it acceptable to use certain features of a new computer chip that Intel was selling. Mr. Gates wrote: "This is good news. It means they are listening to us."

In another case, the memos indicated that Microsoft threatened to stop selling a version of the Microsoft Office suite of business programs for the Apple Macintosh unless Apple Computer stopped supporting Netscape.

A central argument in the Government's suit is that Microsoft has bundled its Web browser, Internet Explorer, with Windows to force Netscape from the market. For the last year, at least, Microsoft has argued that the browser was added to Windows only for the benefit of customers.

In court today, the Justice Department displayed numerous internal memos suggesting that the bundling had indeed been a tactical decision. The memos showed that Microsoft's leaders first wanted to sell Internet Explorer and expected it to bring in $120 million a year in sales. Then, when the plan to push Netscape out of competition with Microsoft failed, the company's leaders decided to bundle the browser with Windows instead as a means of helping it gain a majority share of the market.

In one memo, written in December 1995—in the thick of Microsoft's effort to push Netscape out of the market—Mr. Gates wrote a memo to others in the company acknowledging that Netscape was designing browser software "far better than we are."

In an interview a few months later, displayed in court today, Mr. Gates said: "Our business model works even if the Internet Explorer software is free. We are still selling operating systems. What's Netscape's business model look like in that case? Not very good."

The Government also offered several memos from computer manufacturers complaining bitterly about a Microsoft licensing restriction prohibiting them from offering Netscape if they wanted to offer Windows.

"We're very disappointed," Hewlett-Packard wrote to Microsoft last year. "This will cause significant, costly problems. From a consumer perspective, it is hurting our industry. If we had another choice of another supplier, based on your actions here, we would take it."

OCTOBER 19, 1998

The Case of Law v. Fact

A cynical old adage of trial lawyering states: If the law is against you, argue the facts. If the facts are against you, argue the law.

Each side in the Microsoft case, of course, argued emphatically that both the law and the facts were in its corner. In his opening statement, John Warden said that the charges against his client were based on fanciful accounts supplied by Microsoft's business rivals. Yet his most powerful theme was to remind the court that there is a high hurdle for proving antitrust violations, even against powerful companies like Microsoft, because of the trend of pro-defendant rulings over the last two decades.

Anticipating the quantity and tone of the Government's evidence, Warden said, in essence, that Microsoft's intemperate statements and lively e-mail flavored with capitalist aggression may not sound nice, but that did not prove the company broke the law. Warden tried to put the Government's seemingly incriminating facts, which looked bad for Microsoft, in the larger context of the law, which Microsoft believed leaned in its favor.

But intemperate statements and combative e-mail seemed to take on much greater significance when Boies decided to play portions of the Gates deposition on the first day and as often as he could in the days after. Taken together, the documents and tape suggested that the company not only was belligerent with its competitors but was antagonistic toward the court. As it turned out, the tactic played just as Boies had hoped with Judge Jackson.

"That was a very effective strategy," the judge said. "It set the tone for everything that came after. Here is the guy who is the head of the organization, and his testimony is inherently without credibility. At the start it makes you skeptical about the rest of the trial. It was a brilliant move by David Boies."

Microsoft Says Antitrust Case Is 'Fantastical'

Stinging from the Government's opening statement, a defiant Microsoft Corporation forcefully defended its chairman, William H. Gates, in Federal court today, asserting that the no-holds-barred tactics of his company are not only common in the computer industry but also good for the economy.

Microsoft's opening salvo in the sweeping antitrust suit seemed to be devised as much for public opinion as for the court. The company faces weeks of being portrayed as a predator in a highly publicized trial, which could badly tarnish Microsoft's reputation even if it wins.

The Government's case amounts to a litany of episodes of Microsoft's having used its market power to bully and bend competitors, business partners and corporate customers to its will.

Today, Microsoft's legal team sought to frame these episodes as part of rough-and-tumble capitalism.

While the way Microsoft does business may not be to everyone's liking, they suggested, it is not illegal. "The antitrust laws are not a code of civility in business," said John Warden, Microsoft's lead lawyer.

The second day of the trial came as Microsoft reported a 58 percent gain in quarterly earnings, demonstrating once again its power in the personal computer software industry.

In his two-hour opening statement, Mr. Warden angrily accused the Government of trying to "demonize Bill Gates," whom he described as "a man whose vision and innovation have been at the core of the benefits that society is reaping from the information age."

The Justice Department and 20 states suing Microsoft, Mr. Warden said, are misinterpreting routine business meetings in the computer industry as anti-competitive conspiracies.

A key charge in the suit, for example, is that Microsoft prodded Netscape to illegally divvy up the browser market in a June 1995 meeting—a charge based mainly on the accounts of Netscape executives.

"Netscape's account of this meeting was fantastical," Mr. Warden said. "None of the histrionics, shouting and table pounding occurred. It's fantasy."

In Microsoft's view, the Government's case is wrongheaded because it does not understand the computer industry, especially the necessity of cooperation among companies so that sophisticated technology products work with each other. Just as the line between one software product and another is often blurred, the company argues, so is the line between competition and cooperation; rivals in one area routinely cooperate in another.

Microsoft will try to cast doubt on several of the Government's accusations by characterizing meetings as efforts at cooperation by companies that, understandably, do not always agree.

The Government, for example, has accused Microsoft of trying to put pressure on both the Intel Corporation and Apple Computer Inc. to back off Internet software efforts that conflicted with Microsoft's plans—and to support Microsoft in the browser war.

"Those proposals and threats claimed by the Government," Mr. Warden said, "will be shown by evidence to have been garden-variety commercial discussions between companies developing complementary products. They are of no antitrust consequence."

OCTOBER 20, 1998

CHAPTER 2

The Government Presents Its Case

AT THE HELM
JOEL KLEIN

Everyone likes to attach a special motivation to Assistant Attorney General Joel Klein's pursuit of the Microsoft case.

Some colleagues insist he was interested in restoring the reputation of the Justice Department's Antitrust Division, which brought the case in collaboration with 20 state attorneys general, particularly after the division's controversial—and, in hindsight, obviously inadequate—settlement with Microsoft in an earlier antitrust case in 1995.

At Microsoft's headquarters in Redmond, Wash., however, executives like to hold Klein's personal ambitions responsible for their company's troubles. Klein wants to be the attorney general in a Gore administration, these executives say, and so he set out to knock off Microsoft to burnish his reputation as a fighter.

"He's after a star, a reward," one Microsoft executive complained.

All of that is speculation. And Klein himself says his only reason for pursuing the company was that Microsoft was an egregious violator of the nation's antitrust laws. If there's more to it than that, he has never let on. Nor would he be expected to, for Joel Klein is, by all accounts, an exceedingly intelligent man, who observes, "My style is: I'm careful."

It would be hard to imagine better qualifications for the job he holds. A magna cum laude graduate of both Columbia University and the Harvard Law School, he served as a clerk for David Bazelon, chief judge for the United States Court of Appeals for the District of Columbia—and then for Supreme Court Justice Lewis F. Powell Jr. Both were highly coveted positions.

Klein spent 20 years as a Washington lawyer, working in three law firms, eventually including his own. He came to specialize in taking on appellate cases and arguing them before the Supreme Court, appearing before the court eleven times over the years. He won eight of those cases.

Another speculation about his motivations, heard from his detractors now and then, is that Klein grew up on the poor side of the tracks and therefore got special satisfaction from swatting at the world's richest man, Bill Gates. Nothing in Klein's behavior supports that theory, though he did once remark that Gates made more money each second than he earned every year.

Klein was born in 1946 and grew up in the Astoria neighborhood of the New York borough of Queens, as well as in Bensonhurst. His father was a postman, and they lived in civilian housing that had been converted from World War II army barracks. He was senior class president of W. C. Bryant High School and a scholarship student at Columbia. As a child he became a lifelong Yankees fan. Despite his years of success as a high-powered Washington lawyer, Klein continues to live in a relatively modest Washington apartment.

In 1993, the Clinton White House invited him to help prepare its Supreme Court nominee, Ruth Bader Ginsburg, for her confirmation hearings. His long experience arguing cases before the court suggested he would be good at that. Klein had known the Clintons for years; he was a regular at the Renaissance weekends the first family attended every year at Hilton Head, S.C.

After the Clinton's close friend and deputy White House counsel Vince Foster committed suicide that same year, Klein was asked to take his position. There he remained for two years, largely staying out of trouble as the Clintons lurched from one personal and political crisis to another. In 1995, Ann Bingaman, then head of the Antitrust Division, chose him as her principal deputy. Clinton appointed him to replace Bingaman when she left in 1996, and he held the job in an acting capacity for more than a year, working his way through a difficult confirmation. His biggest problem in the Senate was that under his leadership the Antitrust Division had approved the huge merger between two local telephone giants, Bell Atlantic and Nynex, which together monopolized East Coast service from New England to Richmond, Va. Some Senators saw that as evidence he was a pushover, while some others, whose states included companies that had been targets of Klein's office, argued that he was too tough.

But he eventually won over some wavering senators and was confirmed. During his first few years on the job, his office took on dozens of cases, including high-profile suits against airlines, bankcard companies and military contractors. The division's caseload was far larger than it had been in decades.

Microsoft argued that his division had no business bringing cases against the software industry because he did not understand it. The industry plays by different rules, making the antiquated antitrust laws inappropriate, Microsoft repeatedly insisted. But Klein responded, "I don't think the principles vary in any particular way. The core truths are the same. What drives businesses is to get a big chunk of market power. The question for us is how they acquired it and how they use it."

Over time, some senators who had criticized Klein came to openly admire him. After watching Klein's performance in the Microsoft case, one detractor, former Senator Howard Metzenbaum, remarked, "I was wrong, and I have no reservation in saying I was wrong."

FOR THE UNITED STATES

DAVID BOIES

For Microsoft's witnesses, a few simple words of introduction became deeply unnerving. "My name is David Boies, and I represent the United States."

And little wonder. Time after time, Boies caught Microsoft witnesses off guard as the words from their mouths were contradicted by the statements of internal Microsoft documents or in their own e-mail. Boies would inevitably lead the witness down some path with a line of questioning, then spring his evidentiary ambush.

Veteran trial lawyers routinely tell law school students and young associates that such "gotcha" moments in the courtroom are mostly the stuff of television and movies—the real world, they explain patiently, doesn't work that way. But it did work that way with surprising regularity over the course of the trial, and David Boies (pronounced BOYZ) was the main reason Microsoft stumbled so often.

Microsoft's legal team conceded that Boies was skillful at orchestrating these dramatic moments, but insisted they were not legally significant. He was good at playing to the press gallery, they suggested, but in the serious world of litigating a case his sleight of hand did not matter. The repeated refrain heard from Microsoft lawyers and press spokesmen after each embarrassing moment in the courtroom was that Boies had left the direct testimony of its hapless witness "virtually untouched." The direct testimony for both sides was submitted in written form, under court rules intended to speed up the trial, so that court time was reserved for cross-examination and redirect questions.

The Boies approach, in the view of William Neukom, the Microsoft general counsel, was to use the "high jinks of courtroom theatrics to try to obscure the evidentiary record."

It is possible that on appeal, as the higher-court judges review the direct testimony and trial transcripts, instead of watching Boies perform, Microsoft could get some vindication if the sweeping ruling against Microsoft is pared back. But most legal experts who have followed the trial say there is little, if any, chance of a complete reversal. The reason is that Judge Thomas Penfield Jackson found the government's case, as Boies presented it, to be both compelling and convincing.

So much of the government's case centered on what had happened in private meetings involving Microsoft and other companies, some of which occurred more than three years before the trial began. In court, the two sides presented contrasting versions of what had been said at these private meetings. After poring through the written evidence and the testimony, Judge Jackson had to decide whom to believe. In almost every instance, he sided with the government.

Judge Jackson simply did not believe the Microsoft witnesses. Their credibility, as the judge saw it, was in tatters after Boies got through with them—and so was Microsoft's defense.

Though it no doubt comes as scant comfort for Microsoft, the company was beaten in the district court by a lawyer widely regarded as one of the best. In 1986, *The New York Times Magazine* did a lengthy cover story on Boies with the simple headline, "The Litigator." And it described him as "the Wall Street lawyer everyone wants." The *National Law Journal* named Boies its "Lawyer of the Year" in 1999, calling him "the Michael Jordan of the courtroom."

Boies has an uncanny record of success. His memorable wins include defending CBS in a $120 million libel suit brought by General William Westmoreland, the former Vietnam commander, a suit

Westmoreland dropped before it reached a jury. He helped the Resolution Trust Corporation win a $1 billion settlement against Drexel Burnham Lambert and its junk-bond impresario Michael Milken. He defended Westinghouse against the government of the Philippines. And he was one of the principal lawyers for IBM in its many antitrust battles both against private companies and against the Justice Department.

Nothing much about Boies could be called conventional. In court, the multimillionaire lawyer wears cheap blue suits and a Timex watch strapped on top of his sleeve, so he can monitor the time without lifting a cuff. Still, he does have some costly indulgences including expensive restaurants, fine wines and gambling trips to Las Vegas and Atlantic City. He favors craps, the unthinking, literal roll of the dice.

He has scant interest, though, in high culture. His third wife, Mary Boies, describes his television viewing tastes as "anything in color that moves," though he has a particular fondness for "Star Trek" reruns.

His personal life, too, took some unconventional turns. Boies decided to marry his high school sweetheart in Fullerton, Calif., a marriage that immediately disqualified him from a scholarship to Antioch College. Instead, he spent nine months as a construction worker, then as a bookkeeper. He also started playing tournament bridge, and his winnings nearly matched his bookkeeper's salary. He enrolled in the University of the Redlands, a small school in California that was Baptist at the time, raced through that school and won a scholarship to the Northwestern University law school. Boies, divorced at the time, began dating another student, who happened to be married to a professor at the law school. It became a minor scandal at Northwestern, and Boies transferred to the Yale law school.

After Yale, Boies joined Cravath, Swaine & Moore, a leading New York law firm. At 31, he was named a partner, the youngest in the firm. Samuel Butler, then Cravath's presiding partner, told *The New York Times Magazine* that Boies was "kind of the eccentric genius here." At one time, IBM had three secretaries working separate eight-hour shifts to keep up with his regimen and odd hours.

Boies left Cravath in 1997, when he chose to stay with client George Steinbrenner, the owner of the New York Yankees, who had sued Time Warner, one of Cravath's most lucrative clients. Not everyone at Cravath was sad to see him go. Many there had tired of what they regarded as his prima donna ways, his arrogance and his press coverage, which struck them as hagiography.

Boies formed a boutique law firm, Boies & Schiller, with a long-time friend and Washington lawyer, Jonathan Schiller. So he was available when Joel Klein, head of the Justice Department's Antitrust Division, first called him in November 1997. The next month, Boies signed on as a consultant to the government, and in April 1998, he began working full time on the Microsoft case.

The Boies working style—unpredictable hours, a tendency for being hard to find and keeping his plans to himself until the eleventh hour—were a source of irritation to the lawyers at the Justice Department and for the states. Yet, as at Cravath, Boies was given a lot of leeway. Joel Klein's edict to his subordinates: "If it has to do with the trial, ask David."

The ingredients that account for his courtroom performance include thorough preparation, plenty of backup from other lawyers on his team and a remarkable memory. He starts from a script but, far more than most lawyers, he varies from it. In the Microsoft trial, he would let a witness make a rambling speech and then, seizing on a spoken sentence or two, he would recall the document among the thousands in evidence that would refute the witness's testimony.

His formidable memory helps him overcome the fact that he is dyslexic. A late reader as a child, he still reads with difficulty. "He overcompensates with an overwhelming memory," observed Mary Boies, who is also a lawyer.

But he has other talents as well. One is an ability to cut through all the minute, often distracting, detail in a case, and see its underlying argument or narrative. Both in writing a complaint and in presenting a case in court, it is essential, Boies said, to "lay out a forceful story."

"It's not hard to learn an area of law," Boies said. "I know how to communicate, read cases, organize facts. That is what a lawsuit is all about."

In the courtroom, though, Boies also apparently has a rare conceptual sense of where a cross-examination is headed—the legal equivalent of an athlete who seems to sense beforehand where the ball is going to go next. In *The New York Times Magazine* piece in 1986, Thomas Barr, Boies's mentor at Cravath, observed, "The one talent of David's that stands out is his ability to lay out a course of action that would take into account any sort of complicated facts and develop a far-reaching scenario. It's a chess-player's sense: If I do this, the following 15 things are going to happen, and if step 11 goes so, I'll do this rather than that. It's a fantastic game-playing ability."

As a lawyer, Boies is a craftsman, not a moralist. To him, the Microsoft case was a stimulating challenge—an opportunity to play the game of antitrust litigation at the highest level—rather than the righteous crusade it seemed to be for some in the plaintiffs' camp.

In a lengthy interview earlier this year in his offices in Armonk, N.Y., Boies talked about his craft and the Microsoft case. Had Microsoft approached him before the government, Boies said he might well have represented the defendant. If he had, Boies said his advice to William Gates, the Microsoft chairman, would have been to settle the case in early 1998 before the suit was filed. He would have advocated this Microsoft posture: "Were there mistakes? Yes. Did we overreach? Yes. But the offending behavior was on the margins, and we're willing to accept remedies that fit the violations."

"Had Microsoft done that," Boies noted, "a lot of what we later found out we never would have found."

His compensation, based on a fixed government contract and the hours he put in, worked out to an hourly rate of about $35 an hour—a tiny fraction of his usual $500 an hour rate. Yet Boies was certainly not complaining. "If someone had told me that Sullivan & Cromwell, which I believe is one of the great law firms, and Microsoft, which is a great company, would put on a case that gave me the opportunities that this did, I would have paid them to let me do it," he said.

He described his general strategy for cross-examination: "You want your first plays set and you want to have your last plays set. You want to end on a strong note. In between, you need themes that work. You want to find a handful of themes and work them."

A part of the litigator's art is editing. He credited the Justice Department's excellent staff from its San Francisco office for much of his success in the trial. They worked with witnesses, culled the evidence and prepared page after page of suggested questions. Still, he estimated that he used only about 30 percent of the questions, so as not to stray from his themes, his story.

After all that time immersed in Microsoft's documents and in questioning its executives, what had Boies come to think of the subject of this trial? The language of Microsoft's e-mail and some of its dealings with other companies, Boies observed, seemed to come "almost from a different era in terms of business conduct."

Boies said he didn't really know, but he speculated that Microsoft's antitrust problems were mainly a matter of immaturity. "A lot of it, I think, has to do with the newness of the company and the industry. It is a very new company to have become so big and so powerful so quickly, in a new industry with new people. Microsoft had not absorbed the corporate culture of established corporations. And, of course, that is part of what made it great, made it innovative. But there were certain rules of the road that got lost along the way."

FOR THE STATES

THOMAS MILLER

A state attorney general is both a politician and, in most instances, a law enforcement official—two professions that do not necessarily fit neatly into one personality. For many state attorneys general, the politician comes first, and the resulting impression is of an anxious aspiring governor, eager to latch onto any populist cause that can generate headlines. But Thomas Miller, the Iowa attorney general, who played a lead role for the states in the Microsoft case, has a very different style.

A tall man with graying blond hair, Miller is soft-spoken, deliberate and low-key. In early 1997, when the possibility of a case against Microsoft was first discussed at the national meeting of attorneys general, Miller was not enthusiastic. At the time, he recalled thinking, "Oh my God, Microsoft? We're not going to sue Microsoft, are we?"

Miller had taken the lead among the states in their successful campaign against tobacco companies. But going after Microsoft had none of the populist appeal or potential payoff of the tobacco litigation. When the last check was sent, payments from the tobacco settlement would add about $2 billion to the Iowa state treasury. In the tobacco litigation, politicians had spoken movingly of friends and relatives who smoked and died of lung cancer or heart disease. Miller's father, Elmer, was a smoker who died of heart disease in 1964 at age 64. Miller told The Des Moines *Register* that he was convinced that if his father had known of the effects of smoking in the 1950's, he would have quit and lived longer.

The Microsoft case was never going to generate the support and emotion of the tobacco litigation. Before the suit was filed, and even after Judge Thomas Penfield Jackson ruled against the company, Microsoft and Bill Gates were widely admired by most Americans, according to public opinion polls. People might complain about Windows crashing their computers, but Microsoft simply did not rank high among the things that worried most Americans.

"State AG's march in parades and go to Rotary club lunches," observed James Tierney, the former Maine attorney general who helped coordinate that states' efforts in the Microsoft case. "This was not a popular issue, and they knew that."

But Tierney, a friend of Miller, added: "There was a growing sense among the AG's who took part in this case that no company should have this much power, and there was a real unease about how Microsoft used its power."

No attorney general became as deeply involved in the Microsoft case as Miller did. As chairman of the antitrust committee of attorneys general, Miller started to review the documents that had been acquired in the early stages of the states' investigation in 1997. "At some point," he said, "it became clear in my mind that someone had to stand up to them."

Miller was born and bred in Dubuque, Iowa. Elmer Miller was not educated, having dropped out of school to help support the family. But he passed the exam to become a county assessor, and thereafter instilled in his son the belief that working for the government was public service, a worthy vocation.

Miller was an outstanding student, graduating at the top of his class of 325 from Dubuque Wahlert High School. He stayed in Dubuque for his undergraduate education, attending Loras College, an all men's school at the time. After Loras, he went to the Harvard law school.

Miller was elected attorney general in 1979 and served until 1991, when he stepped down to run for governor. He lost in the Democratic primary, in part because he opposed abortion, not a popular stance in a fairly liberal Midwest state. Miller, a Catholic, has since altered his position on abortion, saying such decisions should be matters of private conscience instead of government policy. In 1994, he regained the office of attorney general.

Like David Boies, Miller came to believe that Microsoft's antitrust problems stemmed from a corporate myopia that might, oddly, have been a byproduct of its rapid rise and enormous commercial success. Its corporate behavior and actions, Miller said, were fine for the scrappy entrepreneurial upstart that Microsoft once was, but became inappropriate after it had become a dominant force in the industry. "What Microsoft did not recognize," he observed, "was that it had crossed the line to become a monopolist, so its behavior had to change."

The Witnesses

As the trial unfolded, qualitative differences between the witnesses produced by the government and those produced by Microsoft became apparent. While the company would defend itself primarily through the testimony of its own executives, the Justice Department relied heavily on witnesses from the computer industry and academia. But perhaps the more telling difference would be in the level of preparation the witnesses seemed to have received from lawyers on either side. Those testifying for the government were seldom caught off guard in cross-examinations by Microsoft lawyers, while witnesses appearing for the company frequently found themselves tangled in attempts to reconcile often contradictory statements in testimony and the documents in evidence, especially e-mail.

Jim Barksdale was seen as the person who brought "adult credibility" to the upstart Netscape. And as the leadoff witness for the prosecution, Barksdale was being asked to

James Barksdale

NETSCAPE

lend the government's case against Microsoft a voice of maturity and trustworthiness. The Justice Department's case began with Netscape and revolved around Netscape. And Netscape's chief executive seemed an impressive first witness for the government. Beyond the details of his testimony, he was there to establish the credibility of the government's case.

The government was making this implicit message with Barksdale: Sure, he is Microsoft's enemy. But this is not your standard Silicon Valley hothead nerd with no perspective. This guy has been around. He's 55 years old, and he worked for IBM, Federal Express and McCaw Cellular before joining up with Netscape. Microsoft itself tried to hire Barksdale as its president and chief operating officer in 1994, though he decided against it because working with Bill Gates and Steve Ballmer meant, "I wouldn't be captain of my own ship." So Judge Jackson, look at this guy and listen to him. This guy knows business up, down and sideways. He knows that what he saw Microsoft doing crossed the line.

A Southerner, born and raised in Jackson, Miss., Barksdale is laconic of speech, fond of homespun one-liners populated by snakes, dogs, chickens and country porches—speech known as Barksdaleisms at Netscape. His personal style is not a familiar one in the software business, a hyperkinetic industry where people typically try to win arguments by simply talking faster than anyone else.

Not everyone was charmed by Barksdale. Some in Silicon Valley regarded his plain-folks style as merely an act and said that, while he may have been a skilled manager and a charismatic leader, he lacked the deep knowledge of technology an Internet software startup needed to compete with Microsoft head to head. But the dissenters were a minority. All things considered, Netscape had done well to survive, given the money and armies of engineers Microsoft dedicated to its battle against the fledgling company. And it did more than survive, being sold to America Online in a stock-swap deal valued at $4.2 billion when it was announced in November 1998 and $10 billion when it closed in March 1999, as America Online's share price rose sharply. Many, many former Netscape engineers—not just Barksdale and his management team—walked away from the experience very wealthy indeed.

When John Warden cross-examined Barksdale, there was plenty of verbal combat. In his questioning, Warden tried hard to pretend that the word "browser" had no place in the courtroom. But Barksdale gave no rhetorical ground. To explain, Microsoft was trying to argue that Internet Explorer, the company's browsing software, was simply a feature of the Windows operating system, not a stand-alone program. To concede otherwise might reinforce the government's accusation that Microsoft had rolled Internet Explorer into Windows mainly to undermine the market for Netscape's browser.

So as Warden questioned Barksdale, he repeatedly called the software by one of several tautological tongue twisters, such as "Internet Explorer technologies" or "browser functionality." He refused to utter the word "browser" by itself.

When Warden asked Barksdale a question about "Internet Explorer technologies," Barksdale shot back, "Oh, you mean the browser?"

No, Warden answered, he meant "Internet Explorer code, Internet Explorer technologies."

"It's a browser," Barksdale retorted.

Warden refused to take the bait. Through another five minutes of questioning, he resorted to one circumlocution after another to avoid using the word. But finally the questions grew so awkward that he had to alter his tactic. So he began putting questions this way: "Is it possible to separate what you call Internet Explorer from Windows 98?" Later, Warden asked about the "functionality in Windows that you call the browser."

Barksdale didn't back down either. "The browser itself is not a part of Windows," he insisted, "but it is called into play by Windows when browser functions are needed."

To speed up the trial, Judge Thomas Penfield Jackson had ordered that direct testimony from witnesses from both sides be submitted beforehand in writing. So all courtroom questioning of witnesses began with cross-examination. The direct testimony from a witness varied from a couple dozen pages to hundreds of pages. It was typically released to the press and public at 4 P.M. on the day before the witness was scheduled to take the stand.

In his 127 pages of written testimony, Barksdale asserted that Microsoft's control of the personal computer operating system market "and Microsoft's ability to improperly exercise the power associated with that control, allow Microsoft to cripple or cut off altogether innovative products that will benefit consumers if Microsoft deems those products to be too competitive with Windows or Microsoft's other software products."

He added that the first time he really recognized the "effectiveness" of Microsoft's market power and its "determination to use it" came in the late spring of 1996. Compaq, he said in his written testimony, had just decided to use Netscape's Navigator browser on one line of its computers. Shortly afterward, he was told that Microsoft had threatened to cancel Compaq's license for Windows 95 if it put Netscape's browser on its machines instead of Microsoft's browser.

Barksdale also testified that he was told that Compaq had reversed its decision and would no longer ship the Netscape browser on its machines. "Thus," Barksdale wrote, "Microsoft was able effectively to destroy the value of Netscape's browser-distribution contract with Compaq, one of the world's largest PC manufacturers."

And in his direct testimony, Barksdale characterized the June 21, 1995, meeting between Microsoft and Netscape as an unambiguous attempt by Microsoft to divide the browser market. "I have never been in a meeting in my 35-year business career in which a competitor had so blatantly implied that we would either stop competing with it or the competitor would kill us," he stated. "In all my years in business, I have never heard nor experienced such an explicit proposal to divide markets."

Later in the meeting, Barksdale asked if Netscape's ability to obtain technical information from Microsoft was conditioned on Netscape's accepting the proposal. Barksdale quoted Dan Rosen, a Microsoft manager, as saying, "It certainly isn't independent." Any technical information Netscape was seeking could be obtained, Barksdale quotes a Microsoft executive as saying, "depending on how we walk out of this room today."

Earlier in the year, Barksdale told *The New York Times* in an interview that the Compaq threat was the "singular act" by Microsoft that prompted him to go to the Justice Department and complain. "I knew that was against the law," he had said. (Netscape said that earlier communications with the Justice Department, including the letter after the June 1995 meeting, were mainly in response to the Government's inquiries—though Microsoft did not think so.)

Barksdale, to be sure, is no lawyer. So it is not necessarily a contradiction that it was Microsoft's pressuring of Compaq that led to his going to the Justice Department, even though that episode came a year after the meeting at which Microsoft made "the most explicit proposal to divide markets" that he had ever heard. The 1998 written testimony made the 1995 proposal sound clear-cut. But was it? The apparent discrepancy was intriguing at least, suggesting that the trial testimony from both sides tended to be presented with a clarity that may or may not have been evident at the time. It is perhaps a bit cynical to say that Judge Jackson's dilemma was to decide which side's revisionist history he found most persuasive, but doing so was certainly part of his task.

At the trial, Barksdale took the stand for the first time in the afternoon session following Microsoft's opening statement. Below is the portion of that day's story that dealt with the beginning of his cross-examination.

Antitrust Case Relies Heavily On Events at a 1995 Meeting

With James Barksdale on the stand, Microsoft's legal tactics soon became apparent. John Warden, 57, a heavyset man and a detailed, methodical interrogator, sought to portray Netscape as a Microsoft rival that went running to the Justice Department as a business tactic.

His questions also tried to lead Mr. Barksdale into acknowledging that all software makers are constantly adding features to their products and that many companies enjoy large shares of their markets without being branded as monopolists. Both are central themes of Microsoft's defense.

Mr. Barksdale, a lean, craggy 55-year-old who speaks with the accent of his native Mississippi, proved an elusive and often entertaining witness. Mr. Warden asked him about the early years of his career when he was a salesman for IBM from 1965 to 1972—years when that company faced the kind of antitrust scrutiny Microsoft faces today.

Mr. Warden asked Mr. Barksdale if he had believed at the time that the then-dominant IBM was a monopolist.

"I don't know if I believed it," Mr. Barksdale replied, "but we were trained to behave as if we were a monopoly because we were operating under a consent decree," as Microsoft is today.

Mr. Warden then asked Mr. Barksdale if he did not believe that the dominant computer product of that day—the IBM mainframe— was not a so-called bundled product as hardware and software that customers had to buy together.

The question relates to the current case because the Government contends that Microsoft's Windows operating system and its Internet Explorer browser are in fact two products bundled together for the purpose of forcing customers who want its industry-standard operating system to also take its browser. Microsoft says the browser is a feature of Windows, and thus that browser and operating system are a single product.

To the mainframe question, Mr. Barksdale replied that IBM mainframe hardware and software had once been sold as a bundle but that a 1968 consent decree forced IBM to sell them separately—a solution very similar to the unbundling remedy the Government is seeking in the current case.

"That forced unbundling gave rise to a whole new industry of hardware companies like Amdahl that made mainframe machines that run IBM mainframe software," Mr. Barksdale said.

To try to show that Netscape viewed a Government suit as a competitive tactic, Mr. Warden repeatedly questioned Mr. Barksdale about his meetings with Justice Department officials.

Mr. Warden produced a document for presentation at a Netscape strategy meeting, titled "Project Rocket Launch Plan." At the meeting, held early this year, one of four items under the heading "The Situation" was "DOJ and court actions create opportunity for Netscape."

Mr. Warden then asked Mr. Barksdale whether he viewed a Justice Department suit as a "key" opportunity for his company. Not a key one perhaps, Mr. Barksdale replied, but he did view a Government antitrust suit against Microsoft as "a way of protecting an opportunity to keep the playing field open for Internet software."

OCTOBER 20, 1998

Grand Theater and Jurisprudence

Producing dramatic moments is part of the courtroom craft. When cross-examining witnesses, trial lawyers try to undermine a witness's testimony by surprising him with contradictory evidence of any kind—his own prior statements or documents, for example. In a corporate antitrust case, the documents of your colleagues can be equally damaging. Each side wants to present the court a clearly delineated story line: We're the good guys, they're the bad guys. We're telling the truth, they're lying.

Life or business affairs are never quite that neat. Microsoft would be on the receiving end of most of the embarrassing moments in the trial. In its defense, it would argue that even if true, the government's seemingly incriminating evidence was merely embarrassing, not damaging to its defense.

At the least, the e-mail from James Clark, Netscape's cofounder, to a Microsoft executive, showed that Netscape's business plans had evolved over time. Clark considered cooperating with Microsoft in late 1994 and tried to encourage Microsoft to consider that approach—a collaboration that might have included investing in Netscape. Later, in a rare instance in which it found itself on its heels, the Justice Department said, yes, it was a titillating courtroom moment, but the Clark e-mail had nothing to do with the case—the specific anticompetitive acts committed by Microsoft.

Microsoft Uses E-mail From Netscape To Contest Antitrust Case

Trying to refute a central accusation in the Government's antitrust case, the Microsoft Corporation produced a secret e-mail message today from the chairman of the Netscape Communications Corporation seeking Microsoft's cooperation, offering to stay out of its way and suggesting that Microsoft invest in Netscape.

The e-mail, written on Dec. 29, 1994, was introduced to suggest that it was Netscape, not Microsoft, that initiated some of the elements of what the Government portrays as an illegal offer by Microsoft in June 1995 to divide with Netscape the market for software used to browse the Internet's World Wide Web.

The e-mail message, written by James Clark, the chairman and cofounder of Netscape, was submitted in court today by Microsoft as part of its defense in the sweeping antitrust suit filed by the Justice Department and 20 states. It was perhaps the most surprising piece of evidence produced during a second day of often combative cross-examination of the Government's leading witness, James Barksdale, the president and chief executive of Netscape.

Throughout the morning and afternoon sessions, John Warden, Microsoft's lead lawyer, frequently tried to goad Mr. Barksdale to concede key points in Microsoft's defense—namely, that Netscape's browser is widely distributed despite Microsoft's allegedly unfair business practices, and that Microsoft's Internet Explorer browser only began gaining market share against Netscape's Navigator in the fall of 1996, because Explorer had been significantly improved, not because of predatory conduct on the part of Microsoft.

Mr. Barksdale made few concessions, repeatedly replying, "No, I don't agree."

In the e-mail memo to Dan Rosen, a Microsoft executive, Mr. Clark wrote, "We have never planned to compete with you."

Later, Mr. Clark wrote: "We want to make this company a success, but not at Microsoft's expense. We'd like to work with you. Working together could be in your self-interest as well as ours. Depending on the interest level, you might take an equity position in Netscape, with the ability to expand the position later."

Mr. Clark concluded his e-mail appeal by noting, "No one in my organization knows about this message."

Mr. Barksdale said he did not know about the e-mail until recently and that the first time he saw it was in court today. He said that Mr. Clark told him about his December 1994 proposal to Microsoft this summer when Netscape executives were being deposed by Microsoft's legal team in preparation for the trial.

"He said that he made an offer to them including some of this and that it was rejected," Mr. Barksdale testified.

On the witness stand today, Mr. Barksdale sought to portray the December 1994 e-mail from Mr. Clark as a freelance overture that did not represent corporate policy. "He never discussed it with the board, and he never discussed it with me," Mr. Barksdale said.

Because Mr. Clark's offer was quickly dismissed by Microsoft, the Government asserts that its introduction in court by Microsoft is mainly an effort by the defense to try to "change the facts and change the subject," in the words of David Boies, the Justice Department's lead trial lawyer.

The December 1994 e-mail is not related, the Government contends, to the June 1995 meeting in which the Justice Department says that Microsoft made its illegal offer. According to the Government, Microsoft offered to make an investment in Netscape and to give Netscape's software developers crucial technical information about the Windows operating system if Netscape would agree not to make a browser for the Windows 95 operating system, which Microsoft released two months later.

Mr. Clark sent his e-mail during Netscape's precarious start-up phase, before the company had yet begun to make a lot of sales and with Mr. Clark watching his $5 million investment in the company dwindle. In his testimony, Mr. Barksdale tried to dismiss the memo as a sales ploy, perhaps made in desperation, as opposed to a genuine business plan for Netscape.

Mr. Warden asked Mr. Barksdale of Mr. Clark, "Do you regard him as a truthful man?"

After pausing, Mr. Barksdale replied, "I regard him as a salesman."

"I'm not going to touch that," Mr. Warden responded.

Microsoft also introduced a portion of Mr. Clark's pretrial deposition to try to prove that as early as the fall of 1994 Netscape was aware of Microsoft's intention to bundle its browser with its Windows operating system. This is potentially significant because the Government says that Microsoft's principal reason for folding the browser into the operating system was as an anticompetitive tactic to undermine Netscape. In the fall of 1994, Microsoft asserts, Netscape had not yet produced its first product.

In his deposition, Mr. Clark testified that he first heard William H. Gates, the chairman of Microsoft, talk of bundling the browser and the operating system at an industry conference in October 1994.

Mr. Clark, asked if he had a personal conversation with Mr. Gates about this, said no, instead recalling it as a vaguely threatening comment made to the conference audience.

"All he said was: I hope no one plans to make money on browsers because they will be bundled into the operating system," Mr. Clark said.

In his cross-examination, Mr. Warden also tried to establish that Netscape had long viewed all-but-free distribution of its browser as part of its business plan. This assertion relates to the case because Microsoft's decision to distribute its Internet Explorer browser free is characterized in the Government's suit as one of several extraordinarily aggressive steps Microsoft took to try to undercut Netscape.

To make this point, Mr. Warden introduced as evidence portions of the manuscript from a new book, "Competing on Internet Time: Lessons from Netscape and Its Battle with Microsoft" by Michael Cusumano, a professor at the Sloan School of Management at Massachusetts Institute of Technology, and David Yoffie, a professor at the Harvard Business School.

The book, based on extensive interviews with present and former Netscape executives, quotes Marc Andreessen, a cofounder and executive vice president, as describing browser marketing as "free but not free."

The concept refers to the notion that many individuals and corporations downloaded browser software from Netscape's Web site without paying for it. Still, free distribution is valuable because it encourages companies to adopt Netscape's technology, and Netscape bases its business on selling large software packages for hub computers, or servers, that feed data to many personal computers in a network.

Mr. Warden raised the issue to suggest that Netscape's business model did not vary much from what Microsoft did. When asked about that, Mr. Barksdale replied, "I have never heard this term 'free but not free.' I have not heard it, I don't espouse that, and that was not our strategy."

OCTOBER 21, 1998

Back and Forth and Back Again

Because Netscape was the starting point and the centerpiece of the Government's case, James Barksdale spent the most time on the stand under fierce cross-examination from Microsoft and was then taken over the same ground yet again by the Justice Department to try to bolster his original testimony. At times, it was the courtroom version of blood sport.

Microsoft Disputes Netscape Meeting Account

In his third day cross-examining James L. Barksdale, Microsoft's lawyer, John Warden, suggested that the market-division accusation stemmed from anger on the part of Netscape executives when they learned at that meeting that Microsoft intended to bundle its own browser with its Windows operating system.

"Is there really anything going on here other than a difference of opinion between you and Microsoft on where the line is" between a browser and an operating system? Mr. Warden asked.

At that Mr. Barksdale—normally a calm and unerringly polite witness—exploded. "We feel strongly that a browser is a separate application," he said, "and a manufacturer that controls 90 percent, plus, of the world's operating systems and pulls the browser into it has stepped across that line!"

"That's your objection?" Mr. Warden asked. "You disagree with them building it into the operating system?"

"I do, I do, I do," Mr. Barksdale said.

In court today, Microsoft presented memos and e-mail messages suggesting that Netscape had eagerly sought the June meeting. Mr. Barksdale acknowledged that he had written memos to other Netscape executives in early June 1995 in which he had enthusiastically reported that in an earlier meeting,

Microsoft had shown an interest in investing in his company.

"No, they didn't do anything as rash as trying to buy us (yet) but they did suggest that they wanted to invest in us," Mr. Barksdale wrote to another employee three weeks before the meeting. "It was a good session."

Another memo from Mr. Barksdale to several senior Netscape employees reported that Microsoft had been "very friendly, non-threatening" and had congratulated Netscape on having "done a great job."

As Mr. Barksdale's e-mail recounted it, the Microsoft executives had added, "How can we work together? Discussion done with Bill's blessing," a reference to Mr. Gates.

With that as a prelude, Mr. Warden, Microsoft's lead counsel in the case, produced several other e-mail messages and memos suggesting that Netscape and Microsoft had both plunged into planning for the June 21 meeting.

Mr. Warden used each to cast further doubt on the Government's accusations. One piece of documentary evidence indicating that Microsoft did propose dividing the browser market are notes that Marc Andreessen, a co-founder and executive vice president of Netscape, took on his laptop computer during the meeting.

A copy of those notes was released today by the court.

Mr. Andreessen wrote that Microsoft had issued a "threat that Microsoft will own the Windows 95 client market, and that Netscape should stay away."

Another piece of evidence is the memo from Mr. Rosen to Mr. Gates, written the day after the meeting. Mr. Rosen quotes another member of the Microsoft team as telling the Netscape executives: "We need to understand if you will adopt our platform," Windows, "and build on top if it, or if you are going to compete with us."

The memo continued, "They understand that we are going to incorporate into the platform technology that they provide today." The Microsoft executives, according to Mr. Rosen's memo, told Netscape's leaders that their intention was to "suck most of the functionality of the current Netscape browser" into Windows.

But Mr. Rosen's memo did not indicate that the Netscape executives had reacted negatively to this. The memo was introduced into evidence today, but not referred to in court.

In fact, summing up his conclusions after three days of testimony, Mr. Warden said, "I suggest to you, Mr. Barksdale, that if you look at the whole record of events leading up to June 21, the only fair conclusion that can be reached is that Mr. Andreessen imagined or invented the proposal to divide the markets, and that you and your company signed onto it in order to assist in this prosecution."

"I absolutely disagree with that," Mr. Barksdale retorted. "It's absurd. I was in the meeting. I know what I know."

"I was there," he said. "You weren't."

OCTOBER 22, 1998

Microsoft Says Key Meeting Was a Setup

Opening a new line of defense in its antitrust trial, the Microsoft Corporation today portrayed a meeting that is a focal point in the Government's case as a "setup" orchestrated by its Internet software rival, the Netscape Communications Corporation.

Microsoft based that claim on the fact that the Justice Department issued a civil subpoena to Netscape the day after the meeting, on June 21, 1995, and that two days later Government lawyers received a reply from a Netscape lawyer.

Microsoft obtained the previously undisclosed letter from the Netscape lawyer to the Justice Department only two days ago—an omission that Microsoft called a "flagrant" breach by the Government of the rules of pretrial document discovery.

In his fourth day cross-examining James L. Barksdale, the president and chief executive of Netscape, John Warden, Microsoft's lead lawyer, asked the question that framed what he called the "setup" defense.

"Isn't it a fact," Mr. Warden declared, "that the June 21, 1995, meeting was held for the purpose of creating something that could be described as a record to be given to the Justice Department to spur them on to take action against Microsoft?"

Mr. Barksdale replied, "That's absurd."

David Boies, the Justice Department's trial counsel, said the subpoena for information was issued to Netscape in connection with another inquiry into Microsoft that the Government was already conducting at the time. Mr. Boies said that Microsoft's effort to portray the June 1995 meeting as a Netscape conspiracy suggested that Microsoft's lawyers were straining to try to discredit a powerful allegation in the Government's case. "Any time a defendant says, 'We were set up,' I think that tells you how a trial is going," Mr. Boies said.

The subpoena issued by the Justice Department the day after the Netscape-Microsoft meeting did refer specifically to a separate matter that the Government was investigating at the time: Microsoft's plan to bundle its on-line service, Microsoft Network, or MSN, with its new operating system, Windows 95, which was shipped two months later, in August 1995.

In the end, the Justice Department took no action to prevent Windows 95 from being shipped with a link to Microsoft Network.

Nonetheless, the June 23, 1995, response by Gary L. Reback, then a Netscape lawyer, to the Justice Department's subpoena for information in the MSN investigation focused mainly on the meeting two days earlier.

Mr. Reback's four-page letter states that at the meeting, Microsoft said it would not provide Netscape with necessary technical information unless "Microsoft gets an equity interest in Netscape, a seat on Netscape's board of directors, and otherwise controls Netscape's ability to compete against Microsoft."

Later, Mr. Reback, a partner at Wilson Sonsini Goodrich & Rosati, wrote that Microsoft had made it clear that if Netscape was going to compete with Microsoft "in any way," then Microsoft "will competitively harm Netscape."

Later today, Microsoft introduced documents and memos from Netscape's files suggesting that the company had lost an important corporate customer to Microsoft largely because of Netscape's own failings, not because of predatory behavior by Microsoft.

In 1996, Intuit Inc., maker of Quicken, the popular personal-finance software, asked Netscape to provide a customized version of Netscape for use with Quicken. The Netscape documents suggest that the company could not provide the new software for many months.

One slide from an internal Netscape presentation shown in court today included the heading "We offered, but did not deliver" the five custom modifications to the program that Quicken had wanted.

"While you were trying to figure things out," Mr. Warden said, "Microsoft had already offered" a customized version of its browser.

Mr. Barksdale acknowledged that Netscape had made errors, but added, "I don't think that was the primary reason we did not get the business." Microsoft offered Intuit special inducements that Netscape could not match, he said, including free software and special coding in Windows that made Quicken easier to run.

After four full days of cross-examination, Mr. Warden closed the questioning of Mr. Barksdale this evening by entering into evidence a note that had been written in jest by several employees for display on Netscape's internal computer network.

"Next Monday Netscape will release two or three more bug-ridden beta versions" of Netscape Navigator, the note began, adding that the program "is faster than a dog with no legs, if the dog's up to his waist in treacle. And dead."

Mr. Barksdale explained: "We allow our employees to let off steam this way. Mostly they complain about the food in the cafeteria."

OCTOBER 26, 1998

The Apple Factor

The Justice Department decided it had seen enough of having its leading witness badgered by Microsoft. It released documents including a lurid account of a threat by Microsoft as recounted in a note sent by a top Apple executive to Barksdale. The Justice Department also released the pretrial deposition testimony of a senior executive of America

Online, who described his company's March 1996 contract with Microsoft. Microsoft agreed to give America Online a prominent link to its Windows first desktop screen, and in return America Online was required to make sure that more than 85 percent of all browsers it shipped to subscribers be Microsoft's Internet Explorer. A dry business contract perhaps, but many legal experts believed that the America Online deal—an exclusionary distribution contract with the nation's runaway leader as an Internet service provider—may have been where Microsoft most clearly overstepped the antitrust standards of legal behavior.

Microsoft Refrain: Who Was Harmed?

The Microsoft Corporation's defense in the antitrust trial that began last week boils down to one question: Where's the harm?

John Warden, Microsoft's lead lawyer, never quite uttered those words. But he nonetheless posed the question in hundreds of ways in his raspy baritone drawl during the three days that he cross-examined the Government's lead witness, James L. Barksdale, the president and chief executive of the Netscape Communications Corporation.

Microsoft stands accused by the Justice Department and 20 states of being a new-age monopolist, bullying other companies so that it could stifle competition in the Internet software market. Netscape, the early leader in the market for software used to browse the World Wide Web, was the main target of Microsoft's illegal campaign, the Government contends.

Mr. Warden used his combative cross-examination of Mr. Barksdale as a forum for trying to make Microsoft's case. With his pointed questions, Mr. Warden sought to establish that while Microsoft was assuredly aggressive and powerful, there was scant evidence that its behavior resulted in the effects that classic antitrust doctrine deems illegal—namely, raising prices or restricting output so that consumers suffer.

The Government contends that Microsoft bundled its Internet Explorer browser with its industry-standard Windows operating system and gave the browser away free to crush Netscape.

Microsoft replies that it folded its browser into its operating system as a convenience to consumers. Mr. Warden tried to drive home the point with a sarcastic question: "Mr. Barksdale, do you think consumers would be better off if Microsoft had not given the browser away free, in your hypothetical world?"

Mr. Barksdale replied that in the long run he thought consumers would benefit if Microsoft had not made the browser free because the move had eliminated the incentives for other companies to enter the browser market with innovative products.

Still, Mr. Warden made his point: to side with the Government, a court must favor a would-have-been world of hypothetically greater innovation instead of the present, which has not yet created widespread consumer dissatisfaction. Where's the harm?

From every imaginable angle of interrogation, Mr. Warden hit the same theme. The Government has contended that through exclusionary deals with computer makers and gateway services to the Internet like America Online, Microsoft made it more difficult and expensive for Netscape to distribute its browser. Microsoft's power to engage in this exclusionary behavior, the Government adds, derives from the "choke-hold" monopoly the company enjoys because 90 percent of all personal computers run the Windows operating system.

But isn't it true, Mr. Warden asked pointedly, that 26 million copies of Netscape's browser were downloaded over the Internet during the first eight months of this year? "I wouldn't dispute the number," Mr. Barksdale replied.

Mr. Warden then introduced internal Netscape documents showing that the company plans to distribute 159 million copies of its browser over the next 12 months. He asked Mr. Barksdale for an estimate of the number of Web sites from which computer users can download Netscape software, and Mr. Barksdale replied that there were said to be more than 20,000 such Web sites.

Mr. Barksdale replied testily, and reasonably, that most people don't take the time and trouble to download software. That, he said, gives Microsoft a big advantage because of its deals making Internet Explorer the main browser offered by leading personal computer companies and America Online, which are the key distribution channels to home users.

Still, Mr. Warden's point was made. Microsoft's monopoly appears to be a pretty leaky choke-hold, at least when it comes to software distribution in the Internet era. Where's the harm?

And Mr. Warden got personal with Mr. Barksdale. Microsoft's strategy against Netscape may have been to "cut off their air supply," in the memorable phrase of one senior Microsoft executive. And competing with Microsoft has been difficult, but the result could scarcely be characterized as financial ruin for Netscape and its leaders. Mr. Warden asked Mr. Barksdale to calculate the value of his Netscape shares. More than $100 million, he replied. Where's the harm?

With this line of defense, antitrust experts say, Microsoft is playing a strong hand. As William E. Kovacic, a visiting professor at the George Washington University Law

School observes: since the mid-1970's, when the United States began facing more global economic competition, Federal courts have tended to view big companies as engines of innovation and economic efficiency that should be left alone, unless their behavior can be proved to harm consumers.

The judgment of the courts, Mr. Kovacic notes, has been that the antitrust laws should not be used to put "saddlebags on thoroughbreds."

But in its case, the Government is asking the court to weigh considerations beyond the current welfare of consumers and health of the industry that Microsoft dominates.

"The Justice Department is saying that we want the race of modern capitalism to be a fast one, but we also want to make sure that the winner succeeds because he is the fastest runner not because he tripped the guy next to him," said Carl Shapiro, a professor at the University of California at Berkeley and a former senior official in the Justice Department's antitrust division.

The Government has contended that in specific meetings with Netscape, Intel and Apple Computer, for example, Microsoft sought to intimidate rivals and bully its partners to help it curb competition. Look closely at what Microsoft did, the prosecutors say, and the picture that emerges is of a monopolist at work, illegally using its market power to squelch competition.

Microsoft's strategy for refuting these contentions is twofold: fiercely dispute the Justice Department's evidence by mustering any available e-mail or snippet of deposition testimony that can be used to undermine the Government's interpretation of events, and constantly return to the theme that even if Microsoft behaved badly, there is little evidence to show that the economy or consumers were hurt as a result.

The linchpin of the Microsoft defense is that, yes, the company may be big, powerful and even nasty at times—"the antitrust laws are not a code of civility in business," Mr. Warden reminded the court but the company presides over a sector of the economy for which it is hard to argue that the "dead hand of monopoly" is at work. In other words, Microsoft is asking: Where's the harm?

OCTOBER 26, 1998

In Its Case Against Microsoft, U.S. Now Cites Note From Apple

After four days spent watching lawyers for the Microsoft Corporation attack its key witness, the Justice Department today introduced a host of new documents, videotaped depositions and fresh testimony to strengthen its antitrust case and undermine Microsoft's defenses.

Among the new evidence potentially most damaging to Microsoft was a handwritten note describing what the Government portrays as strong-arm tactics Microsoft successfully employed to force Apple Computer Inc. to ship Microsoft's Web browser, Internet Explorer, with Macintosh computers.

The new evidence came as David Boies, the lead Government lawyer, got his turn to question his own witness, James L. Barksdale, the president of the Netscape Communications Corporation, who today completed his fifth day of testimony in Federal court here.

The Apple evidence consisted of a note from Fred D. Anderson Jr., Apple's chief financial officer, to Mr. Barksdale, explaining why Apple had agreed to use Internet Explorer on Macintosh computers.

Mr. Anderson said Microsoft had "threatened to abandon Mac" if the company did not make Internet Explorer the default browser.

Specifically, Mr. Anderson said, Microsoft had threatened to stop developing its word processor, Microsoft Word, and other crucial programs for Macintosh computers—a threat that if carried through, would mean "we were dead," Mr. Anderson wrote.

"I was mad as stew when I got that," Mr. Barksdale testified.

Microsoft said that Apple agreed to opt for its browser as part of broad agreement that included a $150 million investment by Microsoft, cross-licensing of patents and settlement of an old legal case—not just because of Microsoft's commitment to continue making business software for the Macintosh.

In testimony given last month but first made public today, a senior executive of America Online Inc. said that his company chose Microsoft's browser over Netscape's in return for Microsoft's placing a prominent link to America Online from the main screen, or desktop, of Microsoft's Windows, the operating system shipped on more than 90 percent of all new computers.

David M. Colburn, a senior vice president of America Online, the nation's largest on-line service, stated that Microsoft's willingness "to bundle America Online in some form with the Windows operating system was a critically important competitive factor that was impossible for Netscape to match."

Testifying for the Government, Mr. Colburn also said that his company's March 1996 contract with Microsoft required that more than 85 percent of all browsers America Online shipped to its members had to be Microsoft's Internet Explorer. In the battle for browser market share, America Online's millions of subscribers were perhaps the biggest prize in the industry.

In an October 1996 promotional agreement, Microsoft agreed to pay America Online 25 cents for each America Online subscriber converted to Microsoft's browser from a rival, presumably Netscape, and to pay a $600,000 bonus for doing it quickly. During his negotiations with Microsoft executives, Mr. Colburn stated, "I was told that Microsoft had no limitations on what it could spend to gain market share for Internet Explorer."

In a statement, Microsoft disputed Mr. Colburn's assertion that the crucial factor in its deal with America Online was the offer of a link on the Windows desktop—the most valuable real estate in cyberspace.

"Microsoft and Netscape competed for the America Online contract, and Microsoft won on the merits of its technology," the statement said.

In questioning Mr. Barksdale, Mr. Boies displayed several documents from Microsoft's files intended to strengthen the Government's accusation that Microsoft made an illegal offer to Netscape to divide the market for browsers in a meeting on June 21, 1995—an offer that Netscape did not accept.

During cross-examination of Mr. Barksdale last week, John Warden, Microsoft's lead lawyer, suggested that Marc Andreessen, a co-founder and executive vice president of Netscape, had "imagined or invented the proposal to divide the markets." Mr. Andreessen took notes during the June 21 meeting; they later became a key piece of Government evidence.

After Mr. Boies produced several internal Microsoft e-mail messages in which senior executives seemed to be openly discussing such a deal, Mr. Barksdale said, "This seems to corroborate exactly what we have been saying."

Mr. Boies also displayed part of a transcript of the questioning last summer of Chris Jones, a Microsoft executive who attended the 1995 meeting. The Justice Department asked Mr. Jones if dividing the market for browsers had been a topic of discussion.

"Oh, I believe there was a discussion of that nature," Mr. Jones said.

The Government also submitted an internal Microsoft sales document, suggesting how much importance the company placed on insuring that personal computer makers bundled its browser with its operating system—which was required by Microsoft contracts and done, the Government contends, to stifle competition in the browser market.

"It came on my machine, is the #1 reason people switch to Internet Explorer," the Microsoft sales presentation from May 1998 declared.

To which Mr. Barksdale responded, "It just shows what I've been saying here for a week is true—and Microsoft knew it."

OCTOBER 27, 1998

As a senior vice president for America Online, the largest on-line service, David Colburn, a confident executive in his forties, was responsible for negotiating and implement-

David Colburn

AMERICA ONLINE

ing significant new contracts. Through two days on the stand, he refused to yield an inch, deflecting every attempt by Microsoft's legal team to discredit his perception of events with a simple but firm no—even when, in a few cases, documents raised questions about his positions.

Colburn's testimony was a crucial element of the government's charge that Microsoft used its operating system monopoly as a powerful tool to disadvantage competitors. Back in 1996, AOL had agreed to make Internet Explorer the default browser used by its millions of members—in return for Microsoft's agreement to place a prominent link to America Online on the Windows 95 desktop.

That was particularly important to AOL because prominently displayed on the desktop of every copy of Windows 95 that shipped was an icon for the Microsoft Network, or MSN. the online service the Microsoft had created as direct competition to AOL.

Colburn had joined AOL in 1995 after practicing law in Silicon Valley. By the time he came aboard, the service had already established itself as a somewhat unlikely superpower in the computer industry. When America Online was established in 1985, CompuServe was the undisputed king of online services, the neighborhood of cyberspace where the true "digerati" lived at a time when the Internet was still available mostly to a limited number of academics and military personnel. To build a business, AOL positioned itself in an unglamorous side of the business, competing with consumer online services like Prodigy, which were designed to attract people who didn't have a great deal of knowledge about computers. It gained market share by designing software that made getting online simple, then mailing millions of copies in a blind, shotgun fashion to addresses nationwide—a practice known in the industry as "carpet bombing." Most recipients considered the ubiquitous disks junk mail and promptly threw them away. But every month, thousands more people popped them into home computers and signed up for the service.

When the Internet started becoming an important force, in the mid-90's, AOL became the first of the online services to offer its members access, introducing millions of everyday consumers to true e-mail and, more importantly, to the World Wide Web. In fact, while CompuServe and Prodigy dragged their feet in offering access to the Internet—a delay that would ultimately prove fatal to both—AOL embraced the global network swiftly and enthusiastically. In a matter of months, it established itself as the world's largest gateway to the Internet. But while members seemed happy enough with AOL's e-mail, they complained constantly that the Web browser the service had built into its software beginning in 1995, was inadequate, unable to do read the fancy formatting and perform all the graphical tricks that many of them were beginning to experience at work using Netscape's Navigator browser. By early 1996, it had become clear that

AOL would have to offer a third-party browser, and most users assumed it would be Netscape's. Instead, the company announced that it would offer both Navigator and Microsoft's Internet Explorer browser—but that IE, as Explorer was universally known, would be the default browser, the one AOL's software installed automatically. If members wanted Netscape, they would have to find it on the service, download it and install it—a complicated, time-consuming process that did not appeal to the vast majority of AOL's members, the perennial "newbies" of the Internet.

By the time Colburn testified in early 1999, AOL had signed up 16 million members. And while it had never won much respect from the elite of the computer industry, it controlled more Internet traffic than Microsoft or any other Internet provider. It had become a giant and a force to be reckoned with.

U.S. Describes Microsoft Fight To Secure Ally

Firsthand testimony from a senior executive at America Online and new documents introduced in court provided an extraordinarily detailed portrait of the Microsoft Corporation's campaign to thwart a planned partnership between the nation's largest on-line service and the Netscape Communications Corporation, Microsoft's rival in the Internet software market.

Microsoft's main weapon in the campaign, the Government contends in its antitrust suit, was offering America Online a prime place on the desktop of its industry-standard Windows operating system. That deal, the Justice Department contends, is an example of how Microsoft illegally used the market power derived from its monopoly in operating systems to stifle competition in the market for the browser software used to navigate the World Wide Web.

In the fall of 1995, America Online and Netscape, the browser pioneer, were eager to forge a strategic alliance to fight Microsoft, which they saw as "the common enemy," according to an internal document written by Stephen M. Case, the chairman of America Online. In the internal e-mail, a draft document circulated among senior America Online executives before being sent to Netscape, Mr. Case said he agreed wholeheartedly with a recent message from Marc Andreessen, one of Netscape's founders, urging the two companies to "use our unique respective strengths" to resist "the Beast from Redmond that wants to see us both dead."

Microsoft's Internet Explorer browser competed against Netscape's Navigator, which was then the industry-leading Web software, and its MSN on-line service was seen as an important challenger to America Online.

Yet by March 1996, the planned America Online-Netscape alliance had been abandoned and America Online chose Internet Explorer as its main browser—a big lift for Microsoft in the browser market, as its software was soon used by millions of America Online subscribers.

During dogged cross-examination by John Warden, Microsoft's lead lawyer, David M. Colburn, a senior vice president at America Online, held firmly to his assertion that the pivotal consideration for choosing Internet Explorer was that Microsoft eventually agreed to put a start-up button for America Online in a folder on the Windows desktop—"a critically important competitive factor that was impossible for Netscape to match."

In court today, Mr. Warden repeatedly sought to argue that America Online chose Microsoft's browser largely because Microsoft's software was technically superior—and he introduced internal documents from America Online engineers who preferred Microsoft's technology.

But when he asked if that was so, Mr. Colburn simply replied, "No."

The Government entered into evidence e-mail messages intended to support Mr. Colburn's answer—including one written on Jan. 8, 1996, in which William H. Gates, Microsoft's chairman, described to four of his executives a recent telephone conversation with Mr. Case of America Online. Mr. Case "views us technically as behind Netscape but credible enough to do a very good job," Mr. Gates wrote, adding, "I said integration with Windows will be great for his users."

An internal e-mail message from Mr. Case to several members of his executive team a few weeks later suggests hard bargaining with Mr. Gates—and that Microsoft's technology was neither inferior nor the only consideration. "From a pure technology standpoint, it does look like Microsoft may win this one," Mr. Case wrote on Jan. 24, 1996. "Couple that with their distribution (OS) muscle, then Netscape clearly faces an uphill battle."

"OS" referred to Microsoft's operating system, Windows, which is loaded on more than 90 percent of personal computers sold today.

After introducing the Case e-mail in court, Mr. Warden asked Mr. Colburn if it did not suggest that Microsoft had won the America Online deal mainly because of its superior technology.

Mr. Colburn gave little ground, saying that he would focus more on the second sentence of the Case e-mail, which referred to "distribution muscle." And, Mr. Colburn added, "In the first sentence he says Microsoft may win, which is hardly a ringing endorsement."

Mark Murray, a Microsoft spokesman, said today that America Online had "played Microsoft and Netscape off against each other, and in the end Microsoft won fair and square."

Mr. Warden used his cross-examination to question America Online's motives for testifying on the Government's behalf. He noted that proposals for an alliance with

Netscape in 1995 called for America Online to pull back from some software development efforts and for America Online to handle the programming for Netscape's popular Web site, now called NetCenter.

A central allegation in the Government's case against Microsoft is that it illegally proposed dividing up the browser market with Netscape in June 1995. In an attempt to turn the tables on that charge, Mr. Warden asked, "In your dealings with the Justice Department to defeat the 'Beast from Redmond,' did you disclose that you had proposed a market-division agreement with Netscape?"

Mr. Colburn replied, "Those are your words, not mine."

After the day's court session,

David Boies, the lead trial lawyer for the Justice Department, said that the Microsoft defense team's focus on a proposed arrangement between Netscape and America Online was another attempt by Microsoft to "change the subject."

"The antitrust rules are different for a company with monopoly dominance like Microsoft," Mr. Boies said.

"In the case of Netscape and America Online, neither one of them had monopoly power."

At the time the deal was being negotiated, however, America Online was four times as large as its nearest competitor, and Netscape had an estimated 84 percent of the browser market.

OCTOBER 29, 1999

Microsoft Defends AOL Deal

Back for a second day, Mr. Colburn stood firm as Mr. Warden tried to portray Microsoft's dealings with its business partners and competitors as standard practice in the industry.

The Government said that Microsoft had used its monopoly power in personal computer operating systems to persuade America Online, the largest on-line service, to agree to an exclusionary deal that stifled competition in the market for software used to browse the World Wide Web. Microsoft's main rival in the browser market is the Netscape Communications Corporation.

Microsoft replied that there was nothing exclusionary or illegal about

its contract with America Online. To further his "everybody does it" defense, Mr. Warden focused on America Online's contract with Netscape for a so-called instant-messaging feature within its on-line service. Instant messaging allows two computer users who are on-line at the same time to exchange typed messages with each other immediately—equivalent to a typed version of a telephone conversation.

The language of the September 1997 contract between Netscape and America Online prohibits America Online from promoting software from Netscape's major rivals on its instant-messaging screens.

"Why," Mr. Warden asked, "are these prohibitive provisions in the agreement?"

Mr. Colburn replied that as part of the deal, Netscape wanted to make sure competitors' products were not promoted—precisely the kind of conduct Microsoft is accused of doing illegally.

When he got his turn with the witness, Mr. Boies sought to point out that business practices that are legal for most companies often are not legal for a company with monopoly power, as the Government contends Microsoft possesses.

Mr. Boies also asked Mr. Colburn whether its instant messaging feature was a method for distributing browser software.

Not ordinarily, Mr. Colburn replied. Typically, he said, "a user who comes to the instant messaging area already has a browser."

Mr. Warden finished by asking Mr. Colburn whether it was not true that although Microsoft's Internet Explorer is the default browser shipped with the on-line service's software, "America Online subscribers have the free and unfettered opportunity to use Netscape's browser if they so choose?"

"Yes," Mr. Colburn replied, "if they can figure out how to get it. It's not easy."

OCTOBER 30, 1999

The Luddite Learning Curve

John Warden and David Boies may have been among the nation's premiere antitrust lawyers, but as the trial entered its second week, during the interrogation of Colburn, it became clear that neither was particularly conversant with computers. Nor was Judge Jackson.

Through the first few days, the Justice Department—not known to be the foremost votary of advanced technology—put on a high-tech word- and light-show to display the memos and e-mail the government has gathered from Microsoft's files.

Working with an assistant who manipulated the documents with sophisticated presentation software, David Boies was able to point to a quotation in a long memo projected onto a video screen so that his assistant could blow it up in a pull-out box, then highlight it in yellow—all within a few seconds. Even with the usual glitch or two along the way, the presentation was quite effective, no matter how each viewer might have felt about the message.

Then came Microsoft's turn. Microsoft, of course, sees itself as the world's vanguard of high technology, and the company's PowerPoint software for public presentations of this sort is the industry standard.

But when Microsoft's lead attorney, John Warden, got ready to put a key memo up for display, the first thing the judge and audience saw was his beefy hand sliding a ragged sheet of paper onto an overhead projector—the sort of image many viewers might have recalled from a high-school science class. The relevant passage had been colored over by hand with a highlighter.

In arguments during the first week, Microsoft's lawyers had described the government's case as "the return of the Luddites," an allusion to the English workers who first tried to stop the advance of industrialization in 1811 by smashing new machines that were being used to manufacture socks.

Yet, Mr. Warden looked like something of a Luddite himself, standing there with that overhead projector. In truth, however, he might simply have felt more comfortable with this approach. After all, when he described the advance of computer technology over the last few decades, he concluded by telling the judge that even with all this progress, "There are a few of us, including me, who still use a fountain pen and a legal pad."

The judge nodded and smiled. Still, within a week or so, Microsoft had assembled staff to produce fancy presentations that were at least equal to those of their opponents.

As the trial began, Microsoft's legal team certainly knew that Justice Department investigators had obtained thousands of e-mail messages from the company's files. But they were visibly stunned by the effective use the government made of them in court. In fact, as soon as Boies completed his opening statement, William H. Neukom complained that the one- or two-sentence e-mail excerpts were "loose and unreliable rhetoric and snippets that were not in any reliable context."

And in court, Warden told the judge, "I urge your honor to view with considerable skepticism the crazy quilt of e-mail fragments that seemingly forms the core of the government's case."

The Justice Department legal team met that complaint with a smile and a shrug. Right away, they offered to make all the documents public in their entirety immediately so the so-called "snippets," could be seen in context.

But as it turned out, Microsoft did not like that idea at all, and as the Justice Department jubilantly noted, the company blocked the release. The documents used in the opening statement had not been entered into evidence, Microsoft explained, and "we wanted to draw a clear line between what was admitted and what wasn't," said Mark Murray, a Microsoft spokesman. As for the public relations contradiction this presented, Murray said, "I think we are more focused on winning the case"—an assertion his own actions would soon belie.

Avadis Tevanian
APPLE COMPUTER

Avadis Tevanian Jr. was a close lieutenant of Steve Jobs, Apple's co-founder, who had in 1997 staged a triumphant return as chief executive of the company that had exiled him for more than a decade. By the time Tevanian testified, Jobs was Apple's acting chief executive, but he had originally returned as a board member when Apple bought NeXT, the company Jobs had founded after leaving Apple, in November 1997. Among the assets acquired with NeXT was Tevanian, who had been NeXT's vice president of engineering.

By the time he took the stand as a witness for the government, Tevanian was a senior vice president for Apple. While he did not possess the strong, confident bearing that Colburn had demonstrated, he made his case effectively.

Like every witness in the Microsoft trial, Tevanian had submitted his direct testimony in advance and in writing, a procedure Judge Jackson had imposed to speed the trial. Thus, when each witness took the stand, he faced immediate cross-examination by the opposing legal team. Most of the government's witnesses consulted with Justice Department lawyers as they prepared their testimony, but they wrote it on their own.

In its opening statement, Microsoft insisted it was "more focused on winning the case" than on public relations. But very quickly Microsoft spun out an elaborate public relations strategy that dwarfed anything the government tried to do. Among its tactics was the release of lengthy responses to each witness's direct, written testimony. The intent was to ensure that reports that day and the next in the news media carried the company's point of view, even as the Justice Department was presenting its case.

Trial rules required that the written testimony be made public the evening before the witness took the stand. And with these early witnesses, Microsoft's public relations staff began delivering written responses to reporters simultaneous with the release of the direct testimony, a practice that continued through the trial. Typically, these were several pages of single-spaced, typed text with key points highlighted with boldface text and underlining. A standard precede on each cautioned, "The information and responses outlined in this document are NOT, by any means, Microsoft's full response to the testimony, but they do serve to set the record straight on some of the issues prior to a more detailed response via cross examination."

The "partial Microsoft response" to Tevanian's written testimony was, on the whole, more temperate than many such documents that followed in later weeks. It stressed that Microsoft and Apple were friendly competitors. But the response quickly devolved to a tone more typical of Microsoft, accusing Tevanian of issuing "twisted facts," "distorted allegations" and assertions that were "completely false."

Apple Executive Testifies About Threats and Bullying by Microsoft

Avadis Tevanian Jr. recalls that shortly after he joined Apple Computer Inc. as a senior executive last year, a software developer warned him that if Apple did not stop selling its highly successful QuickTime multimedia software product, "Microsoft would take any necessary action to drive Apple out of business."

Eighteen months later, "I appreciate the prophetic import of his words," Dr. Tevanian said in written testimony as a Government witness in the antitrust trial against the Microsoft Corporation.

In his direct, written testimony, Dr. Tevanian accuses Microsoft of threatening and bullying Apple to drop support for the Netscape Communications Corporation's browser for navigating the World Wide Web and instead to favor Microsoft's Internet Explorer browser. If Apple refused, he said, Microsoft executives, in several discussions with Apple, threatened to stop developing and supporting crucial Microsoft business software for Apple's Macintosh operating system.

Dr. Tevanian testified that Microsoft had also repeatedly pressured

Apple to drop out of the multimedia software market, in which Apple's QuickTime program for playing audio, video and animated graphics files is a de facto industry standard. When Apple refused, he said, Microsoft rigged the Windows operating system so that in many circumstances QuickTime would not work on Windows computers.

Apple's Macintosh line of personal computers and its operating system, Mac OS, stand as the only real competition to Microsoft, though Apple now has less than 5 percent of the market. Almost every other personal computer in the world runs Microsoft's Windows operating system.

Responding to Dr. Tevanian's testimony, Microsoft released a statement today asserting: "Microsoft and Apple continue to be great partners after more than 17 years of both competing and cooperating in the software industry. Microsoft today reiterates its strong support for the Macintosh and our Macintosh customers."

In many ways, Dr. Tevanian's testimony echoes that of the man who preceded him on the witness stand, David M. Colburn, a senior vice president at America Online. In his testimony, Mr. Colburn described how Microsoft had used its Windows monopoly to thwart a planned deal in which America Online was to distribute Netscape's Navigator as its default browser, that is, the browser distributed with America Online's software.

By offering America Online an icon on the Windows desktop, the most valuable real estate in cyberspace, Microsoft was able to persuade the on-line service to abandon Netscape and to make Internet Explorer its default browser.

Similarly, Dr. Tevanian said that while Apple offered both the Microsoft and Netscape browsers, it had originally chosen Netscape as its default browser. But Dr. Tevanian testified that when William H. Gates, Microsoft's chairman, learned of that choice, "he became very upset," and that over the following months Microsoft used a variety of threats and entreaties to persuade Apple to make Internet Explorer the default browser.

Finally, in mid-May 1997, Dr. Tevanian testified, Microsoft told Apple that it would pull the plug on application programs for the Macintosh operating system if Apple refused to adopt Microsoft's browser and declined to settle several other disputes "on terms acceptable to Microsoft."

Among the programs Microsoft threatened to quit supporting were its Macintosh versions of Word and Excel, industry-dominating word processing and spreadsheet programs. Both are also part of Microsoft Office, which has more than 90 percent of the market for business applications suites.

As a result of that domination, Dr. Tevanian said, Apple "desperately needed to maintain support for Microsoft Office for Macintosh."

At the time of the threat, which Dr. Tevanian called "extremely disturbing," Microsoft, he said, "had made a substantial investment getting Office 98 for Macintosh ready for market," yet was "willing to risk an outright loss of that entire investment to force Apple to terms."

Apple gave in and made Internet Explorer the default browser and agreed not to promote Netscape's browser. As Dr. Tevanian describes it, Microsoft sweetened the deal by making a $150 million investment in Apple and agreeing to settle some patent disputes. By the time the deal was announced in August 1997, Apple had lost $1.7 billion over the previous seven quarters.

Dr. Tevanian testified that Microsoft also used threats to persuade Apple not to market QuickTime for Windows computers. At one point, he testified, Microsoft offered to let Apple continue writing software tools for creating multimedia files— a tiny market consisting mostly of professional developers—if Apple would cede the far larger market for software that plays such files on all computers.

The business tactics he describes echo the central testimony last week of James Barksdale, the chairman of Netscape, who said that Microsoft offered to let Netscape sell browsers to the far smaller pool of non-Windows computers if the company would cede the Windows browser market to Microsoft.

Dr. Tevanian quotes one senior Microsoft executive at a meeting as saying: "We're going to compete fiercely on multimedia playback, and we won't let anybody play back in Windows."

Soon after that, he said, Apple's multimedia program stopped working well on Windows computers.

Microsoft's statement says: "While Dr. Tevanian alleges that Microsoft has somehow intentionally disabled his company's product, the facts show that Apple's engineers did not properly author the Quick-Time set-up program for Windows. Despite Dr. Tevanian's accusations, the only known interoperability issues affecting QuickTime were caused by Apple, not Microsoft."

The statement echoes Microsoft's response when the chief executive of RealNetworks, Rob Glaser, told the Senate Judiciary Committee last summer that Microsoft had engineered the Windows Media Player to "break" his company's industry-leading multimedia software for the World Wide Web. Microsoft also blamed bad programming by Real-Networks for that problem.

OCTOBER 30, 1998

Microsoft's Witness Protection Plan: William H. Gates

Microsoft's lawyers worked so hard to protect their employer, Bill Gates, that as the company's cross-examination of government witnesses plodded on and on, journalists and

opposing lawyers came to believe that Microsoft was filibus-
tering, trying to stave off as long as possible the playing of "the
Gates tape," the 20-hour deposition, videotaped at Gates's
office in Redmond, Wash., over three days in August 1998.

That may have been true at the time. But as the trial
wore on through the following months, it also became clear
that Microsoft's cross-examination of almost every witness
was long and plodding.

Though he was not scheduled to appear in person, Gates
was the trial's absent star, and everyone wanted to see the
tape. In its opening session, the government played a few
minutes, showing Gates, clearly uncomfortable, saying he
had not been involved in planning the moves Microsoft made
in the Internet software market that the Justice Department
was asserting were illegal.

Even that small taste made it clear that Gates's elusive
and obdurate deposition performance would hurt Microsoft's
case, despite the company's brave efforts to portray it otherwise. "What you will see is a witness that doesn't let the government put words in his mouth and a witness who
repeatedly defends Microsoft's right to innovate," Mark
Murray, a company spokesman, gamely told reporters who
were asking what the tape would show.

David Boies spun it slightly differently. "We think the
videotape offers a pretty fair opportunity to judge Mr. Gates's
credibility," he said.

When a lengthy excerpt was finally played, the damage
deepened, and Microsoft worked hard to persuade reporters
that deposition witnesses were supposed to behave as Gates
had. Microsoft even hired Joseph diGenova, a former United
States attorney, as a legal consultant, and one of his jobs was
to stand on the courthouse steps at the end of the day and tell
journalists that "a lot of time-consuming jousting goes on in
depositions" in the normal course of events. "A deposition is
fundamentally an ugly thing."

But other antitrust lawyers had a different point of view.
They noted that the vast majority of antitrust cases never go
to trial because they are settled before the trial begins. And
in those cases, deposition witnesses are advised to be uncooperative and adversarial, as Gates had been. However, the
situation is entirely different, they added, when it seems
likely that the case will go to trial—meaning that the deposi-

tion, particularly one on videotape, could well be seen by the judge or a jury and eventually by the general public.

"Where a case goes to trial, the credibility of a witness can be strongly and successfully attacked if he couldn't remember significant events at his deposition that any reasonable person would have remembered," said Gary Naftalis, a partner in the law firm Kramer, Levin, Naftalis & Frankel in New York.

In the Microsoft case, a trial date had already been set before the Gates deposition was taken. What's more, several news organizations, including *The New York Times*, had filed a motion with the court for public access to the deposition under a 1913 law that required it. So Microsoft's lawyers should have had little doubt that the Gates deposition would be seen by Judge Jackson and the general public.

Still, "it's possible that the lawyers preparing for the case did not focus on the fact that they might be playing the video at trial," said Moses Silverman, a partner with the law firm Paul, Weiss, Rifkind, Wharton & Garrison in New York. "It may be that they were thinking of a paper record, not a video record. On paper you can't tell how long someone paused before giving an answer."

As it turned out, Gates's performance bothered the most important viewer, Judge Jackson. During a conference with lawyers for both sides, he remarked, "It's evident to every spectator that for whatever reasons, in many respects Mr. Gates has not been particularly responsive to his deposition interrogation." Speaking directly to Microsoft's lawyers, the judge added, "Everyone at your table has reflected skepticism as the testimony is presented."

In a later interview, Judge Jackson was blunter. Playing the Gates tape was "ingenious," he said. "In effect, you put this adverse witness on the stand, and you are saying: If you can't believe this guy, who else can you believe? I can't conceive of Bill Gates being allowed to testify like that on deposition."

The conference with Judge Jackson was a result of a request by Microsoft's lead trial lawyer, John Warden, that Justice Department lawyers be required to play the whole tape at once, not in bits throughout the trial. Jackson turned down the request, saying, "If anything, I think the problem is with your witness, not the way in which his testimony is being presented." The judge added that he found the government's approach of playing short, relevant passages of the tape before new witnesses took the stand "very effective."

A few weeks later, in his first public response to criticism of his performance, Gates blamed the government, saying the real problem was with the questions he was asked, not with the answers he gave.

"I had expected Mr. Boies to ask me about competition in the software industry," Gates said, "but no, he didn't do that." Instead, Gates said, Mr. Boies was just "badgering" him "to give yes or no answers when he knew the questions were ambiguous."

Asked about the judge's criticism of his testimony, Gates said, "I answered every question, but Mr. Boies made it clear that he is out to destroy Microsoft and make us look very bad."

Antitrust Case Is Highlighting Role of E-Mail

The outcome of the Microsoft antitrust case may be a long way off, but one thing is already clear: this is the first major E-mail trial.

The Government's prosecution and the Microsoft Corporation's defense, to a striking degree, are legal campaigns waged with electronic messages. The human testimony often pales next to the E-mail evidence. On the stand or in videotaped testimony, the people being questioned shrug, mumble and forget. The E-mail is alive with ideas and competitive zeal, punctuated with profanity and exclamation points.

The second week of the trial ended with the prosecutors frus-trated because a lengthy cross-examination by Microsoft's lead lawyer left no time for the Government to show several hours of a videotaped deposition of William H. Gates, the Microsoft chairman. With a new witness, an executive of Apple Computer Inc., taking the stand today, it is uncertain when the Gates tape will be played.

The Justice Department and the 20 states suing Microsoft say they believe that the tape will strengthen their case because it shows Mr. Gates saying he was not involved in what the Government contends were illegal steps to stifle competition in the Internet software market. The Gates videotape, said David

Boies, the Justice Department's trial lawyer, offers an "opportunity to judge Mr. Gates's credibility."

But the Gates credibility gap, if there is one, becomes an issue not because of the videotape, but because his taped remarks can be compared and contrasted with the E-mail he wrote and received. The E-mail record, the Government insists, shows Mr. Gates waist-deep in plotting the anticompetitive deals and bullying tactics that he denies or professes to have never heard of in his taped deposition.

If his machinations are central to the Government's case, why not summon Mr. Gates to the trial? "The Government does not need to put Mr. Gates on the stand, because we have his E-mail and memoranda," Stephen Houck, a lawyer for the states, told the court.

The Microsoft legal team has for months been preparing its E-mail defense. First, Microsoft argues, anything that looks damaging is taken out of context. "I urge your honor," John Warden, Microsoft's lead lawyer, told Judge Thomas Penfield Jackson, "to view with considerable skepticism the crazy quilt of E-mail fragments that seem to form the core of the Government's case."

But Microsoft has also mounted an E-mail counterattack, culled from the millions of messages obtained by subpoena from competitors in pretrial discovery. Mr. Warden's cross-examination ritual is to present a Government witness with an internal E-mail from his company and then pose a declaration as a question. The interrogations have two refrains: Isn't it true your company does exactly what you are accusing Microsoft of doing? Isn't it true that Microsoft prevailed not because it is a predatory monopolist but because of its superior technology?

Microsoft is accused of trying to prod companies to stay out of its way. So last week, for example, Mr. Warden produced E-mail from Stephen Case, the chairman of America Online, suggesting a partnership with the Netscape Communications Corporation in which both companies would focus on their respective strengths. That division of labor, Mr. Case wrote, would be the best way to achieve the goal that Marc Andreessen, Netscape's cofounder, described in an earlier E-mail as beating "the Beast From Redmond that wants to see us both dead"—a reference to Microsoft's headquarters in Redmond, Wash.

Printouts of E-mail are just another form of written communication. By the 1920's, as typewriters became common, typed memoranda started being used in court cases. From the 1950's through the 1980's, legal experts say, there was an explosion of documentation fueled by the new technologies of electric typewriters, photocopying and fax machines and then personal computers. And E-mail, they add, has played an important role in legal inquiries for years, like the Iran-contra case in the 1980's when E-mail found in Oliver North's computer proved crucial.

But the Microsoft case is the

result of a sweeping Government antitrust investigation of a high-technology company where E-mail has supplanted the telephone as the most common instrument of communication.

"E-mail has just revolutionized investigations of this kind," one senior Justice Department official said.

While under investigation, Microsoft has handed over to the Government an estimated 30 million documents, mostly E-mail. In the trial, the two sides have submitted about 3,000 exhibits, mainly E-mail.

And in their E-mail, people often communicate more frankly and informally than when writing a letter or a report—tap it out, punch a button and it's gone into cyberspace. But E-mail communication is documentary evidence, which in legal cases provides a rich, contemporaneous record of what people were thinking and planning at the time.

It can be a sharp contrast to formal oral testimony, so often coached by lawyers and influenced by selective memory. "The E-mail record certainly makes the I-don't-recall line of response harder to sustain," said Robert Litan, a former senior official in the Justice Department's antitrust division who is now at the Brookings Institution. It can also be powerful ammunition for pointing to contradictions in testimony. And that is what the Government will do in attacking Mr. Gates's credibility with his videotaped deposition, taken over three days in August.

The Government offered a glimpse of that strategy on the first day of the trial. It showed a few brief clips of a point in the deposition when Mr. Gates was asked about a meeting on June 21, 1995, at which, the Government contends, Microsoft offered to divide the browser market with Netscape and to make an investment in the company, which is its chief rival in that market. In the taped deposition, Mr. Gates says he recalled being asked by one of his subordinates whether he thought it made sense to invest in Netscape. He said that he was asked about it after the June 1995 meeting and replied, "I didn't see that as something that made sense."

But in an E-mail on May 31, 1995, Mr. Gates urged an alliance with Netscape. "We could even pay them money as part of the deal," he wrote, "buying a piece of them or something."

The contradiction between Mr. Gates's deposition and his E-mail, though, does not of itself speak to the issue of whether Microsoft made an illegal offer to Netscape.

To be sure, it is what Microsoft did—not what it said in E-mail communications—that counts most. "But once the E-mail that looks bad gets in the record, you end up doing what Microsoft's lawyers are going to spend much of this trial doing—trying to explain it away," said Stephen M. Axinn, a leading antitrust litigator with the firm Axinn, Veltrop & Harkrider in New York.

NOVEMBER 2, 1998

Gates on Tape: Scant Memory Of Key Details

The William H. Gates on the courtroom screen this afternoon was evasive and uninformed, pedantic and taciturn—a world apart from his reputation as a brilliant business strategist, guiding every step in the Microsoft Corporation's rise to dominance in computing.

In two hours of videotaped questioning selected by Justice Department lawyers from their 20-hour deposition of Mr. Gates last summer, Microsoft's chairman professed ignorance of key meetings and strategies that lie at the heart of charges in the Government's antitrust suit against his company. These included purported plans to bully competitors like Apple Computer Inc. and the Netscape Communications Corporation into abandoning Internet software markets that Microsoft sought to dominate.

When presented with e-mail messages he had written, he often said he did not recognize them or did not recall the discussions surrounding them. To question after question, he responded, "I don't remember using those words," or "I'm not sure what you're trying to say."

In some cases, Mr. Gates's answers were so uncooperative that even Thomas Penfield Jackson chuckled and shook his head. Asked once, "Who was at the executive staff meeting" where a key discussion had taken place, Mr. Gates said simply, "Probably members of the executive staff."

Microsoft asserts that the few hours of taped excerpts shown today, by far the largest portion of his deposition yet made public, were often taken out of context, selected by Government lawyers merely to embarrass Mr. Gates and Microsoft, with little direct bearing on the case. Mr. Gates, Microsoft said, was obviously not going to cooperate with prosecutors trying to put words in his mouth.

For the most part, both Mr. Gates, the world's wealthiest man, and his questioner, David Boies, the Justice Department's trial lawyer, remained civil and polite. Mr. Boies, however, did show a flash or two of irritation at Mr. Gates's plodding evasions. At times, Mr. Boies pointedly reminded Mr. Gates that he was under oath.

The pile of e-mail offered as evidence today vividly showed the round-the-clock pace at Microsoft, a pace set by Mr. Gates. Messages sent to him at 4 A.M. were answered a few hours later.

Still, through two hours of thrusts and parries, Mr. Boies never quite succeeded in trapping Mr. Gates, and Mr. Gates was generally unable to discredit Mr. Boies's assertions.

Dressed in a hunter green suit with a brown striped tie, sitting at a plain conference table at Microsoft's headquarters next to his lawyer, Mr. Gates seldom smiled but never raised his voice. Long pauses—some more than 20 seconds—hung between many questions and answers.

Microsoft's chairman seldom looked his questioner in the eye, gazing down at the table instead. As he read documents that were handed to him, he sometimes rocked back and forth in his chair.

For the last week, the Government has been trying to play its selections of the Gates deposition in court, but drawn out cross-examinations of Government witnesses by Microsoft's lawyer, John Warden, had left no time. The announcement that it would be played today came as a surprise.

During the deposition, taped over three days in August, Mr. Gates was confronted again and again by e-mail—his own and messages sent to him by Microsoft executives. The Government's case, in its broadest terms, is that Microsoft has used its market muscle to fashion a network of relationships designed to insure that the rise of the Internet did not weaken its dominance. It began with trying to divide up the market for software used to browse the World Wide Web—that meeting, the Government said, took place on June 21, 1995, with its main rival, Netscape.

In his deposition, Mr. Gates said that during the period around June 1995 he had "no sense of what Netscape was doing."

Microsoft documents often contradict Mr. Gates's professions of ignorance. For example, in an internal document titled "The Internet Tidal Wave," written on May 26, 1995, Mr. Gates gives an authoritative analysis of Netscape's strategy.

He calls Netscape a "new competitor 'born' on the Internet," whose goal was to "commoditize" the value of the personal computer operating system.

The Government asserts that Microsoft unfairly used its market muscle to force Apple to choose Microsoft's Internet Explorer instead of Netscape's Navigator as the main browser on Apple Macintosh computers. A key weapon in that campaign, the Government said, was to threaten to cancel developing the Macintosh version of its industry-standard Office productivity suite—word processor, spreadsheet and presentation software. This threat, Mr. Gates was informed in an e-mail from a subordinate, "is certainly the strongest bargaining point we have, as doing so will do a great deal of harm to Apple immediately."

On June 23, 1996, Mr. Gates sent an e-mail to two of his senior aides, Paul Maritz and Brad Silverberg, saying one of his "two key goals" in Microsoft's relationship with Apple was to "get them to embrace Internet Explorer in some way."

In August 1997, Microsoft and Apple did announce a deal in which Apple agreed to make Internet Explorer the default browser on its Macintosh machines. But Microsoft says that the Government is presenting a skewed portrait of the deal, which included a $150 million investment in Apple and a separate payment estimated at $100 million.

The main element in the deal, Microsoft said, was settling a long-running patent dispute in which

Apple had demanded first $1.2 billion and then "several hundred million dollars" at two points in 1997. Apple contended that Microsoft had stolen its intellectual property.

At another point, Mr. Boies, referring to Sun Microsystems, asked Mr. Gates whether he tried to "get Apple to agree to help you to undermine Sun?" He showed Mr. Gates an e-mail written on Aug. 8, 1997, to Mr. Maritz, a senior executive at Microsoft, and others. In dealing with Apple, Mr. Gates wanted to get "as much mileage as possible" in competing against other Internet software companies. "In other words," he writes, "a real advantage against Sun and Netscape."

He concluded the e-mail by asking his aides, "Do we have a clear plan on what we want Apple to do to undermine Sun?"

Mr. Boies asked Mr. Gates what he meant when he asked that question. Pausing and staring down at his own brief message, Mr. Gates eventually replied, "I don't know."

The Government accuses Microsoft of repeatedly using its market power for anticompetitive ends, prodding partners and competitors to divide with Microsoft—or stay out of—markets that Microsoft wanted to dominate. When asked generally about these allegations, Mr. Gates gave his most unequivocal reply.

"Are you aware," Mr. Boies asked, "of any instances in which representatives of Microsoft have met with competitors in an attempt to allocate markets?"

Mr. Gates replied: "I'm not aware of any such thing. And I know it's very much against the way we operate."

Mr. Boies pushed further: "It would be against company policy to do that."

"That's right," Mr. Gates said.

NOVEMBER 3, 1998

Microsoft Defends Tactics In 1997 Talks With Apple

Microsoft argued in court today that it had every right to tell Apple Computer last year that it would stop producing word processors and other software for Macintosh computers unless Apple adopted Microsoft's Internet browser as the default choice on all its computers.

"Suppose Microsoft simply decides not to offer a product," said Theodore Edelman, a Microsoft lawyer. "Do you have a problem with that?"

"Yes," replied Avadis Tevanian Jr., the Apple senior vice president being cross-examined. "I have a problem with them doing it when they are using it as a threat to get us to do something we didn't want to do."

Several e-mail messages written by Microsoft executives disclose that the company intended to use the threat as "a club," as one message put it, to force Apple into line. Microsoft Office is so dominant—it has more than 90 percent of the market for business applications suites—that Apple executives worried that their company would be crippled if their customers could not buy it.

In the end, Apple gave in and made Microsoft's Internet Explorer the default browser and agreed not to promote Navigator, which had been the default browser on Macintosh computers. Dr. Tevanian disclosed in court today that at Microsoft's insistence, the Netscape browser is not even installed on Macintosh computers when an owner first loads a new computer with software from the installation CD-ROM—unless the new owner chooses a custom installation option. Hardly anyone does that, Dr. Tevanian said.

Mr. Edelman, a partner in the Sullivan & Cromwell law firm, argued that however Dr. Tevanian chose to describe Microsoft's bargaining tactics, the company had every right to decide which products to develop—and which to drop.

Among other attempts to impeach Dr. Tevanian's testimony, Mr. Edelman suggested that Apple brought a threat of its own to the negotiations last year, saying that it would file a $1.2 billion lawsuit con-tending that Microsoft had infringed on Apple patents.

"Didn't you personally tell Microsoft that if no deal was reached, Apple would sue Microsoft for more than $1 billion?" he asked.

No, Dr. Tevanian said, Apple had told Microsoft that it owed Apple $1.2 billion in royalties but had not said anything about filing suit.

As Microsoft had done with a previous witness, from America Online, Mr. Edelman tried to show that a user could easily install Netscape's browser on a Macintosh computer, even if the computer came with Internet Explorer as the default. On video monitors in the courtroom, Mr. Edelman showed seven sequential photographs of the Macintosh screens a user would have to navigate to change the default browser.

As he did that, Dr. Tevanian found himself in the position of having to criticize his own company's product to support his testimony. He told the lawyer that the process was not really as simple as he was making it seem. The menus were counterintuitive, Dr. Tevanian said; it would be easy to get confused.

In fact, when Mr. Edelman finished, Thomas Penfield Jackson, the United States District Court judge who is hearing the case, remarked: "It certainly doesn't tell me how to do it."

NOVEMBER 5, 1998

A New Perspective on an Old Deal

Glimpsed through the prism of all the surrounding evidence presented during the trial, Avadis Tevanian's testimony provided a very different perspective on an announcement a year earlier that had been seen as a startling development in the computer industry.

At the MacWorld trade show in August 1997, Steve Jobs had disclosed that Microsoft was investing $150 million in Apple and creating a partnership in several areas. At the time, analysts and others in the computer industry saw this as an effort by Microsoft to prop up an important customer for the company's application software, including Word and Excel, and keep the entire industry healthy and thriving.

"Apple is important, and this is good for the computer industry," Eric Schmidt, chairman and chief executive of the Novell Corporation, said on the day the deal was announced.

With the new Microsoft investment, Apple is "still in the tunnel, but at least we can see the light," declared Charles Wolf, an Apple financial analyst at Credit Suisse First Boston.

Jobs encouraged that view. With a huge image of Bill Gates on the video screen behind him, he told the MacWorld crowd, "We want to let go of this notion that for Apple to win, Microsoft has to lose. We'd better treat Microsoft with a little gratitude."

Microsoft undoubtedly found it useful to prop up a customer—and it was certainly happy to settle a simmering patent dispute between the two companies as one part of the deal.

But another part of the deal got little attention at the time, because in 1997 no one had the benefit of all that the Justice Department's investigation of Microsoft would turn up. As part of the deal, Apple agreed to drop support for Netscape and make Internet Explorer the default browser on all Apple computers.

The announcement was greeted with boos at the MacWorld event, and given everything else Microsoft was doing at the time to promote Internet Explorer and squash Netscape, the browser agreement seems to have been more than an incidental part of the Microsoft-Apple pact.

Judge in Microsoft Case Cuts Through Jargon as He Questions Witness

Exhibiting increasing frustration with the slow pace of the trial and with the sometimes incomprehensible techno-jargon, the presiding judge stepped forcefully into the courtroom proceedings today. Judge Thomas Penfield Jackson repeatedly rebuked Microsoft's lawyer and finally asked the witness, Avadis Tevanian Jr., of Apple Computer Inc., a long series of questions that went directly to the heart of the case.

Judge Jackson, of United States District Court, is both judge and jury in this case, and he has made clear over the course of the trial that he is not a technophile. He has also shown impatience with Microsoft's long and often tedious cross-examination of Government witnesses.

Mr. Tevanian, a senior vice president of Apple, is the first witness who is an engineer, not a businessman, and Judge Jackson took the opportunity to ask for explanations on several key points.

Microsoft's lawyer, Theodore Edelman, was nearing the end of his cross-examination of Dr. Tevanian this afternoon, when Judge Jackson stepped in, asking first that Dr. Tevanian explain the difference between bundling software with an operating system and fully integrating it into the operating system.

Microsoft argues that Internet Explorer is a fully integrated and inseparable part of the operating system, not simply a "bundled" product that can be removed. To take the browser out of Windows, Microsoft says, would "break" Windows.

Apple makes Mac OS, the only major operating system for personal computers that competes with Windows, and for a while Apple included its own Web browser, Cyberdog, with its Mac OS. Mr. Edelman was trying to demonstrate that Apple, like Microsoft, saw advantages in combining the browser and operating system, when the judge interrupted and asked, "From a technological perspective, what are the technical advantages of integrating a browser, as opposed to bundling it?"

Dr. Tevanian said Apple had made a study of this question, had tried integration instead of bundling but had found that it resulted in "confusion, extra overhead, and there were easier ways to do it."

The judge asked, "You don't think there is a benefit in any way, and there may even be a detriment?"

Dr. Tevanian responded: "That's right. We have found that we are able to achieve what customers want by bundling browsers." As Judge Jackson continued his questioning, Dr. Tevanian testified that Apple could remove the browser from Mac OS without harming the operating system.

The questions and answers cut to the heart of Microsoft's key defense. Dr. Tevanian is a Government witness, so it was not surprising that he gave answers that supported the

Government's case. But he is also a top executive of the only company other than Microsoft that makes a commercially viable operating system and thus the only other company with experience in combining operating systems and browsers.

Mr. Edelman stood by silently as Judge Jackson's questioning capped a day marked by increasing friction between the lawyer and the court. Several times during the day Judge Jackson criticized Mr. Edelman for asking "misleading" questions and "mischaracterizing" what Dr. Tevanian was saying on the stand.

Once, when Mr. Edelman tried to question Dr. Tevanian about a complex technical document that the witness had never seen, a Government lawyer objected, and Judge Jackson told Mr. Edelman, "I think you'd better go on to something else."

As the day ended, Microsoft introduced testimony to rebut one of Dr. Tevanian's allegations, namely that Steven Decker, a senior executive of the Compaq Computer Corporation, had told another Apple executive that Compaq would not license Apple's popular multimedia player, QuickTime, because "that would upset Microsoft."

Mr. Edelman played part of a videotaped deposition in which Mr. Decker said that Compaq had decided not to license QuickTime simply because Apple wanted to charge too much for it. The subject of Microsoft never came up in the discussions, Mr. Decker said.

Earlier in the day, Dr. Tevanian elaborated on his charge that Microsoft had tried to force Apple to stop developing its QuickTime software for use on Windows computers. He said that Microsoft had bluntly described this demand as "knifing the baby."

This threat, he said, was made in a meeting in August 1997, when two Apple executives met with two executives from Microsoft. Dr. Tevanian said this was merely the most graphic expression of Microsoft's efforts to use its market muscle to dominate the fast-growing market for the multimedia software used to play audio and video transmitted over the Internet.

Mr. Edelman, portraying Apple's allegations of Microsoft's threats as vastly overstated, introduced internal Apple e-mail and strategy documents showing that Apple had hoped to try to get Microsoft to adopt QuickTime as a standard for Windows.

"The e-mail record shows that Apple wanted Microsoft to adopt its technology, which is what the Government is accusing Microsoft of doing as an illegal act," said Mark Murray, a Microsoft spokesman.

With all three of the Government witnesses who have testified so far, Microsoft has introduced evidence intended to suggest that the three companies they represented—the Netscape Communications Corporation, America Online and Apple—all employed complaints to the Justice Department's antitrust division as a competitive tactic against Microsoft.

To that assertion, Dr. Tevanian testified: "When someone is threatening to use monopoly power against you, it is a perfectly reasonable recourse to go to the Department of Justice. Our goal was to get Microsoft to play fair."

The conflict between the two companies over multimedia software continued even after they had reached an agreement in 1997 that included settlement of a patent dispute, a $150 million investment in Apple by Microsoft and Apple's adoption of Microsoft's Internet Explorer as the preferred browser on Macintosh computers.

The subject was still a sore point on Feb. 3, when Steven P. Jobs, Apple's acting chief executive, e-mailed William H. Gates, Microsoft's chairman. Even with the improving relationship between the two companies, Mr. Jobs said "there is one thing that threatens to be quite divisive"—the behavior of Microsoft's multimedia executives.

"They are really going out of their way," Mr. Jobs wrote, "to say that they intend to kill QuickTime, and they are being quite threatening and rude about it."

Mr. Jobs added that he hoped Apple's "honest and proper effort" to make QuickTime competitive did not meet with "down and dirty tactics" from Microsoft.

NOVEMBER 6, 1998

A Skeptic on the Bench

Microsoft representatives never talked about it openly as the trial was under way, but later some acknowledged that from the very beginning they had not been entirely happy that Judge Jackson was hearing the case. Jackson had presided over the Justice Department's previous antitrust case against Microsoft a year earlier, in which the government had tried to force Microsoft to separate Internet Explorer from Windows 95. Judge Jackson had ruled forcefully against Microsoft after exhibiting open skepticism of some of the company's arguments and assertions. At one point he even acquired a new personal computer, and with the help of an assistant, removed Internet Explorer—something Microsoft had said could not be done. Actually he had only deleted the icon and a small number of files, but to the judge, that experience demonstrated that some of Microsoft's arguments were sheer hyperbole. In his questioning of Tevanian, Jackson used a gentle, non-judgmental tone. But the questions showed he was curious at the least, skeptical at most, of Microsoft's arguments in this case, too. After all, the areas he was probing with Tevanian were the very ones on which he had heard testimony and issued a strong ruling in the previous case. And in that case, he had ordered Microsoft to unbundle Internet Explorer and Windows 95. The following summer, an Appeals Court had overturned that ruling, infuriating Judge Jackson, who called the appeals ruling "wrong-headed." But it had also noted that Judge Jackson hadn't been presented with any real evidence in that case, just statements by lawyers from both sides.

Now, Jackson was gathering an evidentiary record, and from this moment forward, nearly all his questions and remarks in court seemed to favor the government's case over Microsoft's defense.

But in discussions outside the courtroom, the Judge demonstrated that the perceptions about him were wrong. He was surprisingly respectful of Microsoft, even as he was ruling against the company. At one point he said, "Microsoft is a large and important company, innovative and admirable in a lot of ways."

Spinning on the Courthouse Steps

As the trial advanced, more and more damaging evidence against Microsoft was played in court, causing the company to worry that it would suffer grievous public relations damage even if it ultimately prevailed. So Microsoft began holding frequent out-of-court news conferences, usually early in the morning before the court session opened.

One of these occurred in one of the last days of Avadis Tevanian's testimony. Expecting the government to play a damaging videotape in court that day (it had been mentioned in testimony the previous week), Microsoft summoned reporters to an 8 A.M. news conference at a hotel near the Capitol to offer an advance rebuttal in the form of their own videotape.

The government's videotape, Microsoft feared, would attempt to demonstrate that Microsoft had—in the words of an Apple Computer executive—"sabotaged" Apple's QuickTime multimedia player. So Tod Nielsen, a Microsoft executive who oversaw the company's relations with outside software developers, played another videotape and offered an abundance of technical details that showed, he said, how

Apple's own programmers were to blame for the fact that the latest version of QuickTime did not work well with Windows.

The idea was that the news media would have this in mind as they watched Tevanian's tape later that day. The only problem was that the government never played Tevanian's tape, making Microsoft's videotape moot. When Philip R. Malone of the government's legal team got his turn to question Tevanian, he never even referred to the QuickTime problem. Instead, he used e-mail messages and memos to reinforce the government's assertion that Microsoft had threatened to stop producing its market-leading Office suite of business software for Apple's Macintosh computers unless Apple adopted Microsoft's Internet Explorer as the default browser on its computers.

Microsoft argued that in an August 1997 deal in which Apple agreed to make Internet Explorer its default browser while Microsoft agreed to produce its Office suite for the Macintosh, invest $150 million in Apple and settle several patent disputes, the patent disputes were the truly important issue resolved. To reinforce that point in court, Theodore Edelman, a Microsoft lawyer, played a tape showing Jobs announcing the Microsoft deal at the 1997 MacWorld convention.

But like the early morning videotape, the Jobs videotape backfired. Jobs did point out that important cross-licensing agreements had been part of the deal, but the tape showed that when he mentioned Apple's patent disputes with Microsoft, the crowd broke into raucous, derisive, laughter. Apple partisans have long asserted that Microsoft stole the basic look and feel of Windows from Apple's operating system, Mac OS.

The tape also showed that Jobs' announcement that Internet Explorer would become the default browser on Macintosh computers brought a sustained chorus of boos and catcalls from the audience.

The videotape was only about five minutes long, but through it all, everyone in the courtroom—including Judge Jackson—was laughing loudly.

The computer industry is filled with bright eccentrics, and Steven McGeady of Intel is certainly one of them. A soft-spoken, bearded

Steven McGeady
INTEL

software expert, McGeady proved particularly irritating for Microsoft. He was a vice president of Intel, Microsoft's natural ally, the other half of the "Wintel" duopoly—the industry shorthand for the dominant software company and the dominant chip maker in computing. Yet there he was on the stand testifying against Microsoft, a traitor to his corporate class.

Intel was coy about McGeady's appearance. The company—and McGeady—insisted that he was testifying as an individual in the trial. Still, the twin powers of personal computing have had their share of family spats, and Microsoft suspected that McGeady was there with the blessing of Andrew Grove, Intel's chairman.

McGeady took his stance of independence seriously, though. The witnesses on both sides of the Microsoft trial generally fit into two categories—veteran expert witnesses and executives of well-heeled companies. The expert witnesses were seasoned courtroom performers, while the executives were trained and rehearsed by their legal counsel. But McGeady declined to even talk to the Justice Department's lead trial lawyer beforehand.

McGeady had been deposed by staff lawyers in the Justice Department's San Francisco office, who had told Boies that they felt McGeady would be a powerful witness. For McGeady, appearing in court was not a good career move. He was motivated to testify because he believed it was the truth, the San Francisco staff told Boies, not because he wanted to protect the value of his stock options. Yet Boies was still uneasy about McGeady, not wanting to risk unpleasant surprises from an unpredictable witness. "The first time I talked to that SOB was when he took the stand," Boies recalled.

Intel Executive Testifies of a 'Credible And Fairly Terrifying' Threat by Microsoft

The Microsoft Corporation repeatedly threatened its key ally in the computer industry, the Intel Corporation, as part of its campaign to stifle any challenge to its business posed by the rise of the Internet, an Intel executive testified in court today.

Steven McGeady, an Intel vice president, testified that Microsoft had threatened to pull back from supporting new Intel microprocessors unless Intel shelved its own software efforts and favored Microsoft over Internet software rivals like the Netscape Communications Corporation and Sun Microsystems Inc.

Each new generation of its microprocessor—the electronic brain in about 85 percent of personal computers—represents a huge investment by Intel. And to work well, a new chip requires that Microsoft refine its Windows operating system. So the prospect of any cooling in Intel's hand-in-glove relationship with Microsoft is a serious concern for Intel.

"It was clear to us that the threat was credible and fairly terrifying," Mr. McGeady testified at the Microsoft antitrust trial.

The Government backed up Mr. McGeady's testimony by introducing internal e-mail from Intel and Microsoft. It also showed more excerpts from the videotaped deposition of William H. Gates, the Microsoft chairman. The Justice Department's intent was to portray Microsoft as using its market muscle to retain its tight grip on the industry and to insure that the pace of innovation was set by Microsoft.

"Basically," Mr. McGeady said, "Microsoft was concerned that things would get out of its control."

On the tape shown today, David Boies, a Government lawyer, asked Mr. Gates if he was aware of work by Intel on Internet software. Mr. Gates said, "I can't think of any."

On the stand today, Mr. McGeady told of a meeting on Aug. 2, 1995, at Intel's headquarters in Santa Clara, Calif., attended by senior executives from Microsoft and Intel including Mr. Gates and Andrew S. Grove, the Intel chairman. Mr. McGeady attended the meeting and briefed Mr. Gates and the other Microsoft executives on the work Intel was doing on Internet software—mainly programming intended to make audio and video sent over the Internet play faster and more smoothly.

Mr. Gates, Mr. McGeady said, became "very enraged." He added, "His view was that we were competing with Microsoft."

The Justice Department also introduced an internal Intel memo that Mr. McGeady wrote after the meeting, which said that Mr. Gates was "livid" about Intel's "investments in the Internet and wanted them stopped."

Microsoft asserts that the Justice Department is presenting a distorted picture of the Intel–Microsoft relationship and that Mr. McGeady is a disgruntled Intel executive whose pet software projects were tabled for good business reasons.

"We did not threaten to withhold support for Intel's new microprocessors, and we did not do it," said Carl Stork, general manager of the Windows division.

"Intel and Microsoft are pretty honest with each other, and when we think Intel is doing something stupid we say so," Mr. Stork said. "But the defining characteristic of the Microsoft–Intel relationship is close cooperation to expand the personal computer business for our mutual benefit and to benefit consumers."

Still, today's evidence also shed light on tensions in the relationship during 1995 and 1996, when the Internet seemed to promise a revolution in the software industry and Microsoft appeared to be a laggard.

In 1995, a rift developed over Intel software called "native signal processing," or N.S.P. It was part of an effort to improve the multimedia performance of personal computers—to make "PC's sing and dance," as Mr. McGeady put it. N.S.P. was intended as a layer of software that ran beneath the operating system and on top of multimedia hardware devices.

Microsoft did not like N.S.P. And after one meeting with Microsoft executives, Gerald Holzhammer, an Intel executive, reported in an e-mail, "They are upset with us being in 'their' operating system space."

In July 1995 Mr. Gates met with Mr. Grove and in a subsequent e-mail informed his senior executives about the meeting. "The main problem between us right now is N.S.P.," he wrote. "We are trying to convince them to basically not ship N.S.P."

Later, Mr. Gates wrote that a point he "kept pushing to Andy is that we are the software company here, and we will not have any kind of equal relationship with Intel on software." When Mr. Grove asked why Microsoft had not yet agreed with Intel on a framework for sharing intellectual property on a new chip, code-named Merced, one reason Mr. Gates offered was, "We

were distracted by the N.S.P. crisis—making sure no one ships that pile of problems."

Microsoft says that N.S.P. was not really tailored to work properly with Windows 95, the operating system that it was about to release in August 1995. In his deposition, Mr. Gates, with his trademark bluntness, stated, "Intel was wasting its money by writing low-quality software."

Initially, PC makers were enthusiastic about N.S.P. But after Microsoft opposed it, the computer makers—known as O.E.M.'s, for original equipment manufacturers—grew leery and Intel backed down.

After the N.S.P. rift, Intel agreed to give Microsoft advance word of its software work, and PC makers became reluctant to follow anyone's lead but Microsoft's. In e-mail to his senior executives on Oct. 18, 1995, Mr. Gates wrote, "Intel feels we have all the O.E.M.'s on hold with our N.S.P. chill." He noted that Hewlett-Packard was unwilling to do anything to optimize its new PC's for Intel's new MMX chip or "the new audio software Intel is doing using Windows 95, unless we say so. This is good news because it means the O.E.M.'s are listening to us."

Tensions in the Intel-Microsoft relationship continued over Internet software. For example, Intel felt that Sun Microsystems' Java, an Internet programming language, was destined to become an industry standard. So Intel had technical programs to support Java, which could theoretically become a threat to the dominance of Windows someday.

After a meeting with Paul Maritz, a Microsoft executive, Frank Gill, an Intel executive, wrote in an internal e-mail, "Java remains a major controversy."

Intel's support for Java, Mr. Gill wrote, was viewed by Microsoft as "supporting their mortal enemy."

NOVEMBER 9, 1998

Gates Quoted As Seeing Case 'Blow Over'

William H. Gates, the chairman of the Microsoft Corporation, confidently told a group of industry executives in 1995 that the Government's antitrust investigation of his company would "blow over" with scant effect, an executive who attended the private meeting testified in court today.

And although Microsoft had signed a consent decree with the Government a year earlier agreeing to alter its software licensing deals with personal computer makers, Mr. Gates was also quoted as saying that the company had not really changed its business practices.

"This antitrust thing will blow over," Mr. Gates said, according to the handwritten notes of an executive of the Intel Corporation that were introduced today in the trial of the Microsoft antitrust case.

"We haven't changed our business practices at all," Mr. Gates was quoted as telling a group of Intel executives at the meeting on July 11, 1995, at Intel's headquarters in Santa Clara, Calif.

The notes were taken by Steven D. McGeady, a vice president of Intel, who is a witness for the Government.

Mr. Gates's comments about not having altered Microsoft's business practices could be significant because they might suggest that the company was not complying with the legally binding consent decree.

If the Government wins the antitrust case, legal experts say, Mr. Gates's comments could help the Justice Department argue that sweeping remedies—perhaps even breaking up the company—are required to restore competition in the computer software business.

The Justice Department, these experts say, could point to the Gates remarks as evidence that Microsoft had shown no restraint even when operating under an agreement with the Government. A Federal court approved the consent decree in 1995, but Microsoft had agreed to its strictures when it signed the agreement in 1994.

Microsoft viewed the Government's pointed focus on the Gates comments as a "further personal attack on Bill Gates" and "another example of the Justice Department's tactic of "trial by excerpt,"" said Mark Murray, a company spokesman.

Mr. Murray pointed to other comments quoted by the Intel executive—that the computer business was "unbelievably competitive" and "healthy"—as evidence Mr. Gates was speaking in the broader context of an industry leader who was optimistic the Justice Department would eventually agree that Microsoft's business did not require Government intervention.

Besides, Mr. Murray added, Mr. Gates's remarks probably focused mainly on the Justice Department's inquiries in 1995 about whether to allow Microsoft to bundle a new on-line service, Microsoft Network, with Windows 95.

The notes of Mr. Gates's comments were introduced during the second day of testimony by Mr. McGeady, the Government's fourth witness in the trial. Late this morning, Microsoft began cross-examining him.

Steven Holley, a lawyer for Microsoft, used internal Intel e-mail and the videotaped deposition of another Intel executive to try to raise doubts about Mr. McGeady's assertion that Microsoft had forced Intel to shelve some multimedia and Internet software development work and to curb its support for such Microsoft software rivals as Sun Microsystems Inc. and the Netscape Communications Corporation.

Much of the cross-examination focused on an Intel software initiative called "native signal processing," or N.S.P., which was intended to improve the ability of personal computers to play high-quality audio and video. Mr. McGeady was deeply involved in the development of N.S.P., a program that was sharply pared back after Microsoft protested in 1995.

In court, Microsoft argued that Intel began marketing N.S.P. to personal computer makers and did so when Microsoft was focused on bringing out Windows 95, even though N.S.P. was tailored for an earlier version of the operating system, Windows 3.1.

When asked why Intel had not given Microsoft more advance notice of its work on N.S.P., Mr. McGeady replied that Intel's software engineers had feared that Microsoft would try to "stomp it out of existence." And, he added, "It was the fear that was eventually realized."

Yet under cross-examination, Mr. McGeady admitted that in retrospect "it was a mistake" to target its multimedia software for Windows 3.1 instead of Windows 95. The reason, he explained, was that Intel thought that the release date for the next-generation operating system might well slip into 1996.

Microsoft also showed parts of a taped deposition from Ronald J. Whittier, an Intel executive who was Mr. McGeady's boss. Mr. Whittier said that pressure from Mr. Gates to table N.S.P. was "a factor" in Intel's decision not to ship the software. But, he said, Intel was mainly "looking out for our own best interests" because if N.S.P. slowed the adoption of personal computers using Windows 95, that could damage Intel's main business—microprocessor sales to PC makers for use in new machines.

Viewing the tape, Mr. McGeady said, "I'd say Microsoft helped enlighten us about what our best interests were."

NOVEMBER 10, 1998

Microsoft Tries to Discredit Intel Executive

Lawyers for the Microsoft Corporation made a broad and aggressive attempt today to discredit an Intel executive who has emerged as an important Government witness, portraying him as a resentful employee and introducing testimony from his own supervisor that differed from his memory of events.

In testimony early this week, Steven McGeady, an Intel vice president, said William H. Gates, Microsoft's chairman, and other Microsoft executives, had threatened Intel's leaders in 1995 as part of a successful effort to push them out of the software-development business.

Ron Whittier, a senior vice president for Intel and Mr. McGeady's supervisor at the time, attended some of the meetings where the threats were purportedly made, and in his deposition he said he did not remember hearing them.

But Mr. McGeady was unbowed, by this or any other bit of evidence introduced today intended to contradict his account. "I'm sure Ron's telling the truth that he doesn't remember," he told Steven Holley, a lawyer for Microsoft.

Later, when David Boies, the Government's lead attorney, got another chance to question Mr. McGeady, he played longer portions of Mr. Whittier's deposition intended to show that his failure to remember the events in question should not be surprising. The longer passages showed that Mr. Whittier could not remember much of anything about that period.

Mr. McGeady completed his testimony this evening, as the Government's antitrust trial against Microsoft ended its fourth week. Microsoft lawyers presented a voluminous and detailed attack on Mr. McGeady, portraying him as an arrogant, difficult Intel employee who held a strong personal animosity toward Microsoft—even though he knew that Intel's leaders were intent on maintaining a good relationship with the software giant.

Notes from one meeting showed that another manager had told Mr. McGeady that he was a "prima donna." But that did not seem to bother Mr. McGeady. "I've been called far worse," he said with a slight smile.

As the morning advanced and the attacks grew sharper, Judge Thomas Penfield Jackson asked Mr. Holley: "What is the point of this? What are you trying to accomplish? Are you just trying to embarrass him?"

Mr. Holley said he did not want to respond in public.

But at the end of the day, Microsoft's attacks seemed to have had some effect. Mr. Holley had worked to show that Mr. McGeady was a disgruntled employee out of the Intel mainstream. And after both sides had finished asking their questions of Mr. McGeady, Judge Jackson asked the witness if he was speaking for Intel, or just for himself.

Mr. McGeady said the answer was complicated; he was here because the Government had subpoenaed him to testify. But, he added, he was a senior executive directly involved with the issues in question during 1995 and 1996, when the threats were reportedly made. Sitting in the courtroom audience all this week were a senior Intel spokesman and corporate lawyer who had been sent to support him. And it seemed clear that while the company wished it could stay out of this case, once an executive was subpoenaed, Intel's leaders would back him.

Still, by the end of the day, it was clear that Mr. McGeady was no fan of Microsoft. In one internal memo he wrote in August 1995, Mr. McGeady noted that Microsoft had bought rights to the Rolling Stones song "Start Me Up" to promote Windows 95. Mr. McGeady wrote that "Sympathy for the Devil" might have been a more appropriate choice.

And in an electronic mail message to Andrew S. Grove, Intel's chief executive, in December 1996, he wrote that he had "long taken the position that anything that weakens Microsoft without indirectly weakening us is good for Intel."

Asked to explain, Mr. McGeady said, "Anything that could bring more competition to the software industry is good for Intel."

But then Mr. Holley ended his cross-examination of Mr. McGeady by reading another passage in the note to Mr. Grove. In that one, Mr. McGeady wrote that perhaps "Microsoft could be goaded into doing something really stupid and anti-competitive, finally enraging the apparently placid antitrust police."

With a smile, Mr. McGeady observed that his prediction had come to pass.

NOVEMBER 12, 1998

Glenn Weadock, an author of computer books including "Windows 95 Registry for Dummies" and an independent consultant, made a brief appearance at the trial. He was there

Glenn Weadock
AUTHOR

as a stand-in for consumers, in this case corporate users of software. The Government's original witness list had a technical executive from Boeing, but he was pulled before the trial began and Weadock was inserted instead. The lack of a corporate customer willing to stand up and say it was harmed by Microsoft's practices seemed a weakness in the Justice Department's case. Weadock arrived instead, with a survey of a handful—and perhaps handpicked—selection of corporate customers.

On the witness stand, Weadock was a yawn compared with the witnesses that had gone before. Sensing that, the government showed more excerpts of the videotaped deposition of Bill Gates.

Whatever the legal merit of this tactic, it certainly made for good courtroom theater.

Microsoft Is Said to Irk Some Big Users

Some of the nation's largest companies, including Citibank and Federal Express, view the Microsoft Corporation's strategy of integrating Internet software with the Windows operating system as a costly inconvenience with few benefits, according to an independent consultant serving as an expert witness in the Government's antitrust suit against Microsoft.

Microsoft's decision to tie its Web browser to the operating system lies at the core of the Government's lawsuit. The company argues that integrating software for browsing the World Wide Web is a natural evolution for personal-computer operating systems—and a vital competitive step.

But the Government charges that it is a cynical and illegal tactic chosen only to give Microsoft a lopsided advantage in its competition with the Netscape Communications Corporation, maker of the principal competing browser.

Whatever the truth, Glenn E. Weadock, president of Independent Software Inc., and the next witness in the case, says many corporations are not happy about Microsoft's strategy. Mr. Weadock is scheduled to testify starting on Monday, the fifth week of the trial.

In written testimony made public this evening, he said: "No corporate PC manager, in fact no one outside of Microsoft, has ever described a Web browser to me as operating system software. Organizations typically consider browser software as applications software, like e-mail or word processing."

Many managers want all of the companies' computers to run the same software, he adds, and do not appreciate the additional trouble and expense of trying to remove access to Microsoft's browser, if the company has decided to use another one.

In a statement issued this evening, Microsoft said, "Mr. Weadock's testimony is a collection of opinions, not fact." Other companies such as Dell, Monsanto, Siemens, Nabisco and Toyota, the statement said, have "embraced the Windows platform" and "realize the benefits of integration every day."

Working for the Justice Department, Mr. Weadock—an author, teacher, consultant and speaker on the subject of personal computer software since 1982—interviewed technology managers at 13 large corporations, including J. C. Penney, Morgan Stanley Dean Witter and the U.S. Steel Group. The companies were chosen by the Department of Justice. Among them were some that had expressed interest in the Government's case, and others that were chosen randomly, Mr. Weadock's testimony said.

In every case, the technology

managers said they wanted the ability to choose Web browsers on their own and therefore found it inconvenient that Microsoft had tried to make the choice for them.

Microsoft often notes that computer users are free to install Netscape's browser or any other if they choose. But Mr. Weadock said the technology managers told him they did not like having two browsers on their computers because duplicative software wasted space on the computer systems and held the potential to create "conflicts with other applications and with company developed" software.

Mr. Weadock found that the quandary had cost Microsoft some business because "some companies are resisting or electing not to use Windows 98 largely or in part because it would force them to have a two-browser desktop." He mentioned only one such company by name: Chrysler.

But Mr. Weadock found that Microsoft's strategy is having the company's desired effect in other cases. For example, he quotes an unidentified Boeing executive as telling a Justice Department investigator that the company decided to begin using Internet Explorer principally because "we do not have a choice."

"The integration between Internet Explorer and the operating system cannot be fully disabled," the Boeing executive was quoted as saying. "Our only choice is whether we install two browsers or just install Internet Explorer."

In its statement, Microsoft argued that "the Government has picked companies and individuals which support its claim that the integration of Internet Explorer technologies into Windows is bad for customers." By choosing only these people, the statement adds, "the Government handed Mr. Weadock a stacked deck."

NOVEMBER 13, 1998

On Tape, Gates Seems Puzzled By Words Like 'Market Share'

William H. Gates, the chairman of the Microsoft Corporation, stubbornly debated the meaning of words like "we" and "concern" during an hour of his videotaped deposition shown in court today. Even "market share" seemed a curiously alien term to a man whose company owns just about all of the market in major product categories of the personal computer software business.

Most significant for the antitrust case against his company, Mr. Gates said that he did not recall what he was thinking or what he meant when he wrote in a January 1996 e-mail to top aides, "Winning Internet browser market share is a very, very important goal for us."

The Government used the Gates tape—the third excerpt from his deposition shown in the Microsoft trial—to attack Microsoft's defense that it decided to fold Internet browsing software into its Windows operating system to improve its centerpiece product, Windows.

Microsoft said today that the Government's tactic of repeatedly showing portions of the taped deposition is turning the trial into a "sideshow"—a personal attack on Mr. Gates, the nation's richest person.

But the Government argues that the Gates tapes provide important context for its case by showing what Mr. Gates, the central actor at Microsoft, did and what he said about it.

Microsoft's legal advisers say that in his deposition, Mr. Gates was merely taking a characteristically competitive and combative approach to what deposition witnesses are supposed to do—to try to narrow the questions asked, fence with interrogators and avoid broad or responsive answers.

"A lot of time-consuming jousting goes on in depositions," said Joseph diGenova, a former United States Attorney who is a Microsoft legal consultant. "A deposition is fundamentally an ugly thing."

Still, Mr. Gates's determined resistance to the questions asked by David Boies of the Justice Department at his deposition apparently struck even legal veterans as unusual. Judge Thomas Penfield Jackson chortled and shook his head at some of Mr. Gates's replies. Microsoft's lawyers laughed a few times. Even Mr. Gates flashed a tight smile, once or twice, as he seemed to be enjoying the give-and-take when he felt confident he was giving nothing.

Mr. Gates paused before answering questions for even longer periods, up to 30 seconds or so, than he had in the earlier excerpts shown. At times, he played a waiting game with his interrogator.

At one point, Mr. Boies asked, "Do you understand the question, Mr. Gates?"

"I'm pausing to see if I can understand it," Mr. Gates replied.

At another point, Mr. Boies said he would ask another question, since Mr. Gates did not have an answer to his previous question. "I have an answer," Mr. Gates replied quickly. "The answer is I don't remember."

Later, Mr. Gates was asked about his e-mail on Jan. 5, 1996, in which he wrote that increasing browser market share was a "very, very important goal for us." Mr. Boies asked, "So you don't remember what you were thinking when you wrote it and you don't remember what you meant when you wrote it; is that fair?"

Leaning forward and grinning, Mr. Gates replied, "As well as not remember writing it."

The verbal fencing over terms like "market share" relates to the antitrust case because the Government is trying to demonstrate that regardless of Microsoft's courtroom arguments the company regarded its Internet Explorer browser as a separate product, marketed separately and measured separately.

Microsoft says that Internet Explorer is a "feature" of its Windows operating system, and not a separate product. Indeed, a Federal appeals court ruling in a related case agreed that Microsoft should be free to determine what software is included in its operating system as long as there is some consumer benefit from the integration.

After the Gates deposition, the Government's fifth witness, Glenn E. Weadock, a computer consultant, took the stand to be cross-examined by a Microsoft lawyer, Richard Pepperman. Mr. Weadock's testimony, submitted in written form last Friday, is that many companies, like Boeing, find Microsoft's practice of tightly folding its browser into Windows to be a costly inconvenience. This is especially true, he testified, if corporate customers want to use the Netscape browser with Windows since Microsoft's browser software is deeply embedded into recent versions of Windows.

Under questioning, though, he did say that there is plenty of debate within the industry about what should and should not be in an operating system.

Mr. Weadock also said some companies undoubtedly find having

the browser integrated into the operating system to be an advantage. The issue, he said, was whether consumers had a choice.

"Nowhere in my testimony," Mr. Weadock said, "did I say there are no companies that find the integration of Internet Explorer appealing. But there are those who don't, and they can't get rid of it."

In court yesterday, the Government also introduced many new documents into evidence. For example, one internal e-mail from Gateway Inc., a large personal computer maker, described a conversation with a Microsoft executive in February 1997, suggesting that Microsoft used its market muscle to force PC makers to adopt Internet Explorer.

The Microsoft representative, according to the Gateway executive, mentioned Microsoft marketing and sales campaigns to promote Gateway machines, but "they won't do it if they see Gateway is anything but pro-Microsoft" on the browser.

NOVEMBER 16, 1998

John Soyring had been with IBM since 1976, in a good position to watch as IBM plucked Bill Gates from obscurity and helped start his little company, Microsoft, down the road to dominance of the software industry. And for much of the last decade, Soyring had held a job that allowed him to work closely with Microsoft during a time when the relationship between the two companies deteriorated and, eventually, fell apart. Soyring was in charge of the office that developed IBM's OS/2 operating system.

John Soyring
IBM

IBM gave Microsoft its big break by choosing the company's MS-DOS from among several competing products as the operating system for the first IBM Personal Computer in 1981—and by allowing Microsoft to license its operating system to other personal computer makers. From that serendipitous beginning, Microsoft grew by the 1990s to hold a monopoly in personal-computer operating systems.

Paradoxically, IBM also started Microsoft down the road that had led Gates and his company to this antitrust trial. It was Microsoft's relationship with IBM that first drew the attention of federal antitrust authorities.

In November 1989, on a hot afternoon at a computer industry convention in Las Vegas, Gates looked as if he'd been dragged to a news conference with a senior executive from IBM—which at the time still dominated Microsoft and the entire computer industry. The two companies were collaborating on the design and marketing of OS/2, a name that stood for Operating System 2, which was to be the successor to MS-DOS. But Microsoft was also beginning to sell a competing product, a piece of "shell" software called Windows that hid MS-DOS behind a graphical user interface, or GUI. The industry trade press was full of worried articles: Which system was going to become the new standard?

With Gates standing uncomfortably at his side, James A. Cannavino, an IBM division president, said that the two companies wanted to "clear the air." OS/2 was the future, he said. As for Windows, he added, it would remain a niche product for less-powerful computers. Windows, he asserted, would never receive all the advanced features of OS/2.

Gates certainly did not look happy. But he did not disagree. The news conference got little attention, just a few articles deep inside newspapers and trade publications. But a few weeks later, Norris Washington, a senior antitrust lawyer with the Federal Trade Commission, happened to read one of those articles, in Byte magazine. The FTC shares jurisdiction for antitrust enforcement with the Justice Department. "IBM and Microsoft have now defined their unified vision of graphical operating environments," the article said, "and it looks sort of like a U.S. economic model," divided into lower-, middle- and upper-class products.

As Washington saw it, IBM and Microsoft were colluding to divide the operating system market—a potential violation of antitrust law. Soon the FTC staff opened an investigation of Microsoft and IBM. And since that small first step, Microsoft had been under unrelenting scrutiny from Federal antitrust investigators delving into a constantly evolving series of allegations and charges, month after month, year after year, culminating with the landmark antitrust trial.

Microsoft Hampered OS/2, IBM Official Tells Court

A senior IBM executive accused the Microsoft Corporation today of imposing contract restrictions on software developers that prevented OS/2, IBM's computer operating system, from effectively competing with Microsoft Windows. John Soyring, the director of network computing software for the International Business Machines Corporation who took the witness stand this afternoon, he was in charge of developing OS/2 in the early 1990's.

For part of that time, OS/2 was being jointly developed by IBM and Microsoft as a replacement for MS-DOS, the Microsoft operating system that preceded Windows. In written testimony, Mr. Soyring largely blamed Microsoft for OS/2's tiny 6 percent market share. Though the suit does not include complaints about Microsoft's monopoly hold over personal-computer operating systems, its competitive business practices are central to the case.

Mr. Soyring testified that Microsoft provides certain programming tools that software developers use to write programs that run on Windows machines. Developers rely on those tools, he said, but Microsoft forbids their use in writing software for other operating systems.

As a result, Mr. Soyring said, if a developer wanted to create a version of, say, a word processing program for OS/2 computers, it would have to "re-create much of the application from scratch," making it difficult to "justify the cost of offer-ing the application on OS/2." Microsoft, in a statement today, said, "IBM made decisions with its OS/2 operating system that were not well received by consumers and did not make it easy for developers to make great applications for their platforms."

In November 1989, when IBM and Microsoft were still collaborating on OS/2, they designed it to run only on expensive computers with more memory than was typical at the time. Until hardware caught up, the companies said, customers could use Microsoft's new product, Windows. But eventually, the computing world turned to Windows, and Microsoft ended its partnership with IBM.

The Government also played a short clip from the 20-hour deposition last summer of William H. Gates, the chairman of Microsoft, in which he was asked about Microsoft's relationship with IBM. In an e-mail message last November, Mr. Gates wrote that he was unhappy with IBM because "the Java religion coming out of the software group is a big problem."

Java is the programming language created by Sun Microsystems that can be used on any operating system. As in previous parts of the deposition shown in court, Mr. Gates said he did not recall much about his e-mail message or about other topics on which he was questioned.

Mr. Gates did volunteer that he had wanted IBM to stop criticizing

Microsoft, adding that he had "talked about rhetoric being lowered on both sides."

Mr. Soyring—like a previous witness, Glenn Weadock, who ended his testimony today—also said IBM saw no advantage in integrating a Web browser with the company's operating system. "Indeed," he said, "integration could be inefficient and disadvantageous to customers" because it could "increase the size of the operating system and therefore the size of the hardware required to run it effectively."

As Mr. Weadock finished his testimony earlier in the day, the Government showed memorandums and played deposition excerpts from executives of several large corporations—including Boeing, Packard

Bell NEC and Gateway—who offered similar sentiments.

"Generally, Gateway wants to have flexibility on anything associated with the Internet," Jim Von Holle, a Gateway executive, wrote in an internal company memo last April. "We want Microsoft to provide us with the technology, not make decisions and choices for us or our customers."

Jon Kies, a Packard Bell NEC executive, said in a videotaped deposition that "it wouldn't make sense to have two very large programs installed"—Microsoft's browser and another that a user might choose to use instead—"taking up hard disk space and potentially confusing customers."

Microsoft Says IBM Tried To Enlist Rivals in Collusion

In a series of attacks in Federal court today, the Microsoft Corporation accused IBM of engaging in many of the same practices that had led the Federal Government and 20 states to file antitrust charges against Microsoft.

While cross-examining Soyring, a Microsoft lawyer produced an e-mail message in which John M. Thompson, IBM's software chief, last year proposed to the leaders of Sun Microsystems Inc. and the Netscape Communications Corporation a strategy for a joint campaign against Microsoft.

Mr. Thompson urged the others to help him enlist Oracle and Novell in the effort "to put Microsoft on

the defensive." The e-mail was written in response to a plan by Microsoft to establish its own version of the Java programming language.

On Tuesday, a Federal judge in California gave Microsoft 90 days to make its version of Java compatible with the standards set by Sun, which invented and licenses the language.

But in court today, Microsoft's lawyer, Steven Holley, used Mr. Thompson's memo to contend that IBM had been attempting collusion with several other companies to disadvantage Microsoft.

"We must clearly explain to our customers that Internet Explorer is Microsoft's primary weapon to kill 100 percent pure Java," Mr. Thompson wrote. Internet Explorer, Microsoft's Web browser, uses Microsoft's own version of Java—not the "100 percent pure" version authorized by Sun.

Mr. Holley asked Mr. Soyring, "Do you think it is appropriate for five of the leading computer companies in the world to meet and collude" against Microsoft?

Mr. Soyring said he had not been involved in the discussions and knew nothing about them. But the disclosure was potentially useful to Microsoft because the Government's suit accuses Microsoft of illegally colluding with several other companies, including America Online and Apple Computer, to the disadvantage of Netscape, Microsoft's chief competitor in the market for Internet software.

Several times during the trial, Microsoft has used the tactic of accusing its accusers of similar practices. The company argues that the computer industry plays by different rules than the rest of corporate America and that Federal prosecutors do not understand those rules.

But Justice Department lawyers say the argument means nothing; if other companies are violating the law, they should be prosecuted, too.

Today, Mr. Holley tried to make the case that IBM was "integrating" its own browser, WebExplorer, with IBM's personal-computer operating system, O/S2 Warp. A key charge in the suit is that Microsoft illegally integrated Internet Explorer in the Windows operating system in an attempt to disadvantage Netscape. As part of his argument against IBM, Mr. Holley introduced into evidence the packaging for commercial copies of OS/2. Advertising copy on the box states, "IBM's WebExplorer is built in," and "Internet access has been integrated into OS/2 Warp."

"Why does it say that?" Mr. Holley asked.

Mr. Soyring replied that the phrases were marketing language, not an accurate technological description. Unlike Internet Explorer, he added, WebExplorer can be loaded into an OS/2 computer, and taken out again, without impairing the functioning of the operating system.

Still, Mr. Holley's questions, and similar questions he asked an Apple Computer executive early this month, may prove useful in showing that many other companies believe that including a Web browser along with an operating system is a useful and even essential marketing step.

NOVEMBER 19, 1998

Steven Holley, one of several Microsoft lawyers who cross-examined government witnesses, is a bright young attorney who carries himself

Steven Holley
CROSS-EXAMINING FOR MICROSOFT

with the arch, stiff-shouldered assurance of a man who regards himself as a captain of his profession. And, like all the lawyers trying this case, he had figured out what the judge knew, and what he didn't know, leading him to ask questions that anyone with any knowledge of the computer industry might regard as ridiculous.

For example, a principal assertion in Soyring's testimony was that OS/2 failed to gain acceptance from consumers because IBM could not persuade software companies to rewrite their programs for it. All the companies had written their software for Windows, and it would cost too much money to write a new version for OS/2. To succeed, IBM would need to use the Windows software development tools so that developers could offer the Windows version of their programs for OS/2. But Microsoft's contracts, Soyring noted, forbade that.

To that, Mr. Holley said with a leading tone to his voice, "IBM never approached Microsoft to find out whether it would agree" to give IBM those software development tools.

Soyring said he was not aware of any such approach. What he did not say was that it would be ridiculous to think that Microsoft would give that kind of help to IBM, a company that was trying to offer real competition to Windows. But the way the question was posed gave no hint of that, and it was not clear that the judge knew enough to draw that conclusion.

Later in the day, Holley threw another gratuitous question at Soyring: "So, you started in late '93, as I understand your testimony, to promote OS/2 Warp 3 to consumer users, and you quit in 1996. You didn't give it a very long effort, did you?"

By 1996, Windows 95 was firmly entrenched, and Microsoft owned more than a 90 percent share of the personal-computer operating system market. Certainly IBM could have continued trying to sell OS/2 to consumers, but that probably would have been expensive folly. As Mr. Soyring dryly put it: "It wasn't in the best interest of our customers to keep spending money and taking them down that path."

Live Testimony by Gates Would Pose Risks For Both Sides at Antitrust Trial

Since the case is about digital technology, it seems apt that the most heated debate in the Microsoft trial is about the virtual witness— William H. Gates on videotape.

The Billathon continued last week with the Government using more taped excerpts of its deposition of Mr. Gates, the chairman and co-founder of the Microsoft Corporation. By now, with repetition, the Gates tapes have lost much of their punch to shock or amuse. The subject may vary, but each excerpted section is much the same. Hunched forward, staring down, like a student being punished in the principal's office, Mr. Gates comes off as forgetful, evasive and endlessly quibbling over the meaning of the simplest business terms like "market share."

The joke making the rounds in the industry is that it was the word "share" that Mr. Gates found confusing.

But the real issue surrounding Mr. Gates now becomes whether the virtual witness becomes a real one. Putting Mr. Gates on the stand presents a real risk for both sides.

A convincing, disciplined performance by Mr. Gates—who, according to opinion polls, remains an entrepreneurial hero to most Americans—could bolster Microsoft's defense, legal experts say. Yet Microsoft's defense could be undermined if Mr. Gates proved a volatile witness, arrogant and unresponsive, coming off as a man with something to hide, legal experts agree.

He is not on the 12-person witness list of either Microsoft or the Government, but either side could call him. Each side is permitted to call two rebuttal witnesses. And Judge Thomas Penfield Jackson, who limited the witness lists in the interest of speeding the trial along, has indicated that his ground rules are flexible.

Surely, Mr. Gates would be welcome on the stand in the Federal District Court in Washington.

But if he is to be a witness, it seems, it will have to be Microsoft that calls him. The Government is certainly inviting the Microsoft legal team to take that risk. In his remarks during the daily news conferences on the courthouse steps last week, David Boies, the lead trial

lawyer for the Justice Department, was just short of taunting. Asked whether he would call the Microsoft chairman as a witness, Mr. Boies said dryly, "We have a deposition that we're very comfortable with."

Mr. Gates appears to be irritated at the reaction to his deposition tapes. At the Comdex computer trade show in Las Vegas, Nev., he told The Associated Press that the prosecutors' use of the tapes was "more about Government P.R. than the substance of the case," and he accused Mr. Boies of trying "to put words in my mouth" during the deposition.

In Washington, Mr. Boies replied that Mr. Gates "seems to be indicating more and more that he wants to come." Strongly suggesting that the Gates tapes are hurting Microsoft and that the company is losing the case, Mr. Boies added: "It wouldn't be unusual to change the game plan if the present game plan isn't working. Maybe that's what you're seeing."

Microsoft says that all this is "spin" and that Mr. Gates's deposition performance was a triumph of stonewalling. "The substance of his deposition testimony has not helped the Government's case," said Charles F. Rule, a former senior official in the Justice Department's antitrust division who is an adviser to Microsoft.

The legal advice Mr. Gates received going into his deposition was clearly to give his adversaries little or nothing to work with. He may have done that to a fault, because he appears to be a cipher, almost lifeless.

The problem with the Gates tapes—whether a legal one or not—is that Mr. Gates does not come across as Bill Gates, brilliant, passionate about the technology he has championed and thoroughly in command of Microsoft. And that would seem to raise a credibility issue in the case.

That view of the Gates tapes, Microsoft says, is uninformed, the reflex impression of people unschooled in the intricacies of the legal process. Depositions involve a lot of jousting over words and nit-picking.

Still, with the Microsoft trial moving into its sixth week, six Government witnesses have been cross-examined by Microsoft's lawyers. There has been plenty of pausing and parsing of words, but none of the witnesses has displayed the kind of white-knuckle resistance that Mr. Gates has demonstrated.

Last Thursday, in a meeting in Judge Jackson's chambers, John Warden, a Microsoft lawyer, protested the repeated showing of excerpts of the Gates tapes mainly "for the purpose of creating news stories day after day after day," according to a transcript of the meeting.

The judge disagreed. "If anything," he said, "the trouble is with your witness." Later, he added, "I think it's evident that, for whatever reasons, in many respects Mr. Gates has not been particularly responsive to his deposition interrogation."

Still, as much as the Justice Department lawyers seem to be inviting Mr. Gates to show up, his appearance would be a risk for the Government. There has been a difference of opinion between Mr. Boies and Stephen Houck, the lead trial lawyer for the 20 states that are suing Microsoft with the Justice Department. Mr. Houck has suggested that the Government call Mr. Gates, but Mr. Boies, colleagues say, has said that is a risk for Microsoft to take. "You don't call someone who is brilliant and totally committed to beating you," Mr. Boies was quoted as saying.

"The Government's nightmare," said William E. Kovacic, a visiting professor at the George Washington University Law School, "is that he comes on like Bill Gates, a guy with a deep conviction that what he is doing is right." What Mr. Gates did not do in his deposition, Mr. Kovacic said, was play the time-honored game of politicians, which is to "sidestep the question and present your vision of the issue."

Judge Jackson has given the other witnesses plenty of leeway for lengthy yes-but answers. "The judge would have to let Gates give speeches because he has let everyone else do it," Mr. Kovacic said. "If he didn't, Microsoft would clearly have a bullet to use on appeal, unmasking the judge's bias."

Other antitrust experts, however, advise Microsoft to stay with its nine lower-level Microsoft witnesses and leave Mr. Gates out of the trial. "I think it would be a mistake, especially with a litigator and cross-examiner as skilled as David Boies," said Stephen Axinn, a partner of Axinn, Veltrop & Harkrider. "If Microsoft calls Gates, they're crazy."

NOVEMBER 23, 1998

Antitrust cases are a blend of law and economics. In an antitrust trial, the economists called in as expert witnesses sketch out a context for the court. The experts for the Justice Department and the states explained why the acts in question were anticompetitive, while Microsoft's expert economist spelled out why the company's practices were pro-competitive. Without any firsthand knowledge of the industry, they paint pictures of absolute certainty, though they are totally opposed visions. One side says it's day, and the other side says it's night.

Frederick R. Warren-Boulton
ECONOMIST

And at the rates these expert economists are paid—from $600 to more than $1,000 an hour—why wouldn't they come up with a clear, closely reasoned argument to support the stance taken by their client? That is precisely what the economic experts at the Microsoft trial did. So the courts always take expert testimony with several grains of salt and due skepticism. Still, weighing the economic testimony was crucial to the outcome of the trial. They focused on the central issue in the trial: Is Microsoft a monopoly or not? And how do computer software markets work? The economists dealt, often in boringly minute detail, with defining the "relative market." Does Microsoft price its product like a monopoly? Did it exclude rivals from distributing its product? Are consumers harmed by Microsoft? Always, the answers were rendered in statistics and charts.

The first economist to take the stand was Frederick Warren-Boulton, who had served as chief economist for the antitrust division of the Justice Department during the Reagan years, a period of little antitrust enforcement. Warren-Boulton, a partner in an economic consulting firm, was a witness chosen by the states. His selection was seen by some antitrust experts as a shrewd signal by the prosecutors that even people of conservative pedigree believed that Microsoft was guilty. Yet, the fundamental fact is that professional expert witnesses like Warren-Boulton are guns for hire. Their implicit motto—to paraphrase the title of a popular television series in the 1960's—is "Have economic theories, will travel."

Warren-Boulton was cross-examined for five days, and even Judge Jackson got tired of the at-times mind-numbing review of economic detail. He first urged the Microsoft lawyer handling the interrogation to hurry along. Later, the judge seemed to lose patience altogether and told the lawyer in no uncertain terms, "This has got to stop!"

Microsoft Says Proposed
Netscape Deal Supports Its Case

The Microsoft Corporation argued in Federal court today that the proposed acquisition of the Netscape Communications Corporation by America Online seriously undermined the Government's antitrust suit against the software giant.

"From a legal standpoint, this proposed deal pulls the rug out from under the Government," William Neukom, Microsoft's senior vice president for legal affairs, said this morning on the courthouse steps.

The reasoning behind this assertion, Microsoft says, is that the proposed deal demonstrates that Netscape and the larger software industry are healthy and vibrant—even with all of the illegal and anticompetitive practices charged in the Government's suit.

But David Boies, the Government's lead attorney, said all of that was irrelevant. "Whatever the deal ends up being—if there ends up being a deal—is not going to remove any of the obstacles that Microsoft has placed in the path of competition in this industry," he said.

Michael Lacovara, a Microsoft lawyer who was questioning a Government witness, the economist Frederick R. Warren-Boulton, suggested to him during the trial today that the proposed acquisition undermined his argument that Microsoft seems headed toward obtaining a monopoly in Internet browser software to match the one it apparently holds in operating systems. After all, about 22 percent of Americans who use the Internet reach it through America Online. And at present America Online uses Microsoft's Web browser, Internet Explorer, as the service's default choice. In exchange for that, Microsoft places an America Online advertisement and Internet link in Windows 98.

Mr. Lacovara asked the witness whether, once America Online's service contract expires in January, "would you expect AOL to continue to distribute Microsoft software?" Yes, Mr. Warren-Boulton responded. "It is not at all clear to me that AOL's incentive to do this is changed by this proposed merger with Netscape." He noted that America Online officials had said their need to be among the on-line services featured in Windows forced them to accept Microsoft terms—establishing Internet Explorer as the default choice.

Mr. Lacovara then asked him the question that lay under his entire cross-examination of the witness—and Microsoft's larger assertion today about the proposed Netscape–America Online deal. "Surely this combination," he asked, 'tells you something about the nature of competition in the software industry?"

Mr. Warren-Boulton's answer was probably not the one Mr. Lacovara had been after.

"To the extent that this potential merger is the result of Microsoft's actions with these exclusive contracts and other actions," he said, "it

is unfortunate to see the disappear-
ance of a firm like Netscape, the
brightest, newest star." Mr. Warren-
Boulton's purpose on the stand for
the Government is to establish that
Microsoft does have a monopoly in
operating-system software; more
than 90 percent of the world's computers use a Microsoft operating
system. That is the foundation
under most of the Government's
case since Federal antitrust law forbids certain behavior by a monopolist that would be legal for a firm
that faces healthy competition.

Through repeated, often circum-
locutious questioning, Mr. Lacovara
tried to make the case that Microsoft's overwhelming market share
was ephemeral. The software industry is so vibrant and fast moving, he
suggested, that Microsoft could be
toppled from its position at any
moment—a point of view the company encourages among its employees.

On Friday and today Mr. Lacovara repeatedly pointed out that
other companies are placing other
operating systems on the market,
and some software companies—
principally Microsoft's greatest
rivals—are writing software for
these new systems. But Mr. Warren-
Boulton argued that "the existence
of these fringe competitors in the
operating system market does not
mean in any way that Microsoft
does not have monopoly power."

This afternoon Mr. Lacovara
made an issue of the success the
Apple Computer Company is having
selling its new iMac computer. He
entered into evidence an Apple
news release issued last month
showing, among other things, that
12.5 percent of the people buying Apple's new iMac computer
had previously owned a Windows
machine. Apple computers use a different operating system, Mac-OS.

NOVEMBER 24, 1998

Tactics and Strategies in P.R. War

Microsoft believed that the America Online–Netscape
deal was a godsend—proof that its business was too fast-
paced for antitrust enforcement to keep up with. Just how
eager Microsoft's senior public relations officers were was
evident from their e-mail exchanges on a Sunday in
November, the day before the deal with officially announced. Their eagerness became apparent only months
later, when the Government entered into evidence a long
string of e-mail messages in which the PR officers worked
out their strategy.

A small, speculative note about the negotiations, the
first public notice of the proposed AOL-Netscape deal, ran
on the Dow Jones news service on the morning of Nov. 22.

Jim Cullinan, a Microsoft public relations executive, spotted it that day at 12:14 P.M.

Cullinan's initial instinct was to keep the response low key. "We don't comment on rumors," he wrote to his colleagues via e-mail. "We remain mum." But very quickly, hotter heads prevailed. By lunchtime, reporters started calling asking for comment, and Greg Shaw, a more senior public relations officer, offered the observation, "This deal certainly underscores the fact that competition is vigorous in this industry." It was a point, Mr. Shaw said, that the company should try to get raised in every news article, saying, "this undermines the core of the case."

With that, Mark Murray, the point man in the company's public relations effort in the antitrust case, got busy and drafted a detailed plan of attack for "the next 24–48 hours." Seldom one to mince words, Mr. Murray opened his strategy memo by saying, "This deal blows an enormous hole in the Government's case." He added, "The Government should hire a contortionist to explain why they're suing Microsoft, in the face of such powerful competition."

Murray then laid out the public relations strategy and assigned workers to each of a dozen or so tasks. First, he wrote, Microsoft's lead lawyers would make comments to the cameras on the federal courthouse steps the next morning, just before the trial opened. A Microsoft worker was assigned to "assemble B-roll and radio sound bite packages of the courthouse step comments and disseminate to all media."

Government affairs specialists "should call sympathetic columnists," Mr. Murray added. And they should "outreach to Congressional state/local officials and our core supporters." Meanwhile, Charles F. Rule, a Microsoft lawyer, "should call the top 10–12 antitrust 'experts' who get quoted on our case, and try to sell them on the idea that this fundamentally undermines the Government's case," Mr. Murray wrote.

After some additional back and forth, Brad Chase, a senior Microsoft marketing executive, weighed in at 9:10 P.M. and issued the following instruction: "In all seriousness, if any form of this deal happens, we need all of our friends in politics to go nuts. This gives them an opening to drive a truck through, and they should be let loose."

Asked about this months later, Mr. Murray said he could

not see how the e-mail messages had anything to do with the legal case. "I am sure there were frantic e-mails at the Justice Department that day," Mr. Murray said. "They were probably tearing their hair out about what this would do to their case."

James Gosling was easily the most physically striking figure at the Microsoft trial. The 43-year-old computer scientist arrived looking like

James Gosling
SUN MICROSYSTEMS

an extra from a Viking movie who had slapped on a jacket and tie and marched into the courtroom. He stood about six-feet-four, with a thatch of unruly reddish hair that fell to his shoulders and a similarly colored beard. He approached the trial with what seemed to be a sense of amused irony, a half-grin on his face, as if he were enjoying some private joke.

Gosling is the personification of the technological threat to Microsoft. He was the lead engineer behind Java, an Internet programming language developed by Sun Microsystems. And Java was intended to allow applications to run on any operating system—a cross-platform language, in computing parlance.

In some ways, Java—more than the browser alone—was the real nightmare for Microsoft, the "commoditization" of the operating system that Bill Gates warned of in his 1995 "Internet Tidal Wave" memo. Netscape's business plan, working closely with Sun Microsystems, had been to use the browser to distribute Java, and the two in combination could in the future run software applications on any underlying software system—Windows, Unix, Linux, even OS 390, IBM's mainframe operating system.

Gosling is that rare computer programmer who is also extremely articulate in English. A native of Calgary, he came to the United States to attend graduate school at Carnegie Mellon University in Pittsburgh. After getting his Ph.D. in 1983, he talked to one of Sun's founders and was offered a job, but he declined. "I had also been talking to some friends at the IBM research labs, and they had all this really cool stuff, and I was just convinced that IBM was going to really crush Sun completely," he recalled.

A few years at Big Blue was all Gosling needed to change his mind. The project he worked on at IBM, he said, was a "political monstrosity" and the machine that resulted was "just horrible." A year later, he left for Sun.

The technology case—as opposed to the legal one—against

Microsoft is that it slows the pace of innovation with the chokehold that results from its control of the personal computer operating system. New technology comes to market at the pace Microsoft decides, these critics say, because it must run on Windows, using Microsoft's technology. In addition, they note, placement on the Windows desktop is a uniquely powerful channel of distribution—and another instrument of Microsoft's control. The PC operating system, they say, is the essential utility of computing, and Microsoft gives access to compliant allies and denies access to any real challengers.

Among software engineers in Silicon Valley, like Gosling, the real resentment against Microsoft is that programs used by most of the world would be better if Microsoft were not slowing things down. "Microsoft has this basic strategy they call 'embrace and extend' which some people call 'disgrace and distend,' " said Gosling. "But it's all about making it easy so that people can get on to the Microsoft platform. And then they screw around with it so that going the other direction is really hard."

More Gates Tape and More Spin

Even as Gosling testified, Bill Gates once again took center stage. The government played new excerpts from his deposition, and in them Gates professed general ignorance of his company's legal battles with Sun over the company's Java programming language. That brought more media coverage that Microsoft saw as exceedingly negative. So a few days later, Microsoft decided to fight back. The company called a news conference featuring Gates by satellite, displayed on two big-screen TVs.

Gates complained about Boies's interrogation, saying Boies had been "badgering" him "to give yes-or-no answers when he knew the questions were ambiguous." But he spoke for only a few minutes, after which Microsoft's supporting cast took the podium to assert that the government was attempting to try the case in the news media.

"They are trying to turn this into a P.R. spectacle," said Charles F. Rule, a former head of the Justice Department's antitrust division and a Microsoft legal consultant. As he spoke, Rule was flanked by the leaders of Microsoft's legal team and the large video monitors for Gates's appearance. "Our focus is in the courtroom," Rule said, "but we cannot and will not stand by without responding."

In the Microsoft trial, to be sure, the news cycles favored the government. The Justice Department made a host of newsworthy allegations about how Microsoft had bullied an entire industry, time after time. On defense, Microsoft was left with the unenviable task of trying to explain why the things the company had done were not as bad as they seemed.

And the Microsoft P.R. machine worked overtime, though generally with little effect. Microsoft had been holding one or two briefings each week, while regularly issuing position papers and news releases. At this event, for example, the company distributed a 21-page report, entitled "A Case of Trial in Error: The Microsoft Antitrust Suit," that largely repeated legal and political arguments the company had already made several times.

Responding to later in the day to Microsoft's event, the Justice Department did issue a one-sentence statement: "Microsoft's latest press statements are another public relations effort to distract attention from the overwhelming evidence introduced in court showing that Microsoft has illegally used its market dominance to block competition from innovative technologies that threaten its operating system monopoly."

As Microsoft staged its odd news conference, the company had won another small victory. South Carolina Attorney General Charles M. Condon, one of the 20 state attorneys general who filed their own antitrust suit against Microsoft, surprised the other attorneys general by announcing that he was dropping out of the case.

Condon was generally considered to be the most conservative among the 20 attorneys general. He explained that "over the last year, it has become clear that the government's case has been about Internet competitors, not consumers."

But in an interview earlier in the year, as he was getting ready to join the lawsuit, Condon had a different perspective: He was worried that by stifling competition in general, Microsoft was hurting the nation's high-technology economy.

"My concern," he said then, "is that there is in fact very active competition, the possibility of entry by other companies, in this very important area. The economy is booming, and I am certain that a large part of that is new technology. I want it to keep going."

When he announced he was pulling South Carolina out of the suit, he denied that Microsoft had persuaded him to do so. But it became clear over the following weeks that Microsoft had heavily lobbied many of the attorneys general—and candidates for the office in the fall elections—trying to peel more of them away. The others held firm, however, including newly elected attorneys general who took office a few weeks later.

New York was the lead state among the 19 states that remained involved with the suit. Marc Wurzel, a spokesman for Attorney General Dennis Vacco, called Condon's decision "a non-event; it will have no impact on the case. And in the context of multi-state efforts like this, it's not at all unusual for states to come in and drop out as the matter proceeds."

Testimony on Microsoft's League of Its Own

At an industry meeting in February 1997, an official of the Microsoft Corporation vowed that his company "wouldn't be cowboys" by altering the Java programming language on its own, an executive of Sun Microsystems Inc. said in testimony released today. Seven months later, he testified, Microsoft did just that, in an effort to eliminate "the threat posed by Java technology to Microsoft's operating system monopoly."

In direct written testimony made public today, Dr. James A. Gosling, a vice president of Sun and the chief scientist of its Java software division, opened a new line of attack by the Justice Department in its antitrust lawsuit against Microsoft: the company's move to tailor its version of Java for its Windows operating system, making it incompatible with the standard Java language developed by Sun.

Microsoft's changes to Java are also the subject of a private contract suit in California in which a Federal judge two weeks ago ordered Microsoft to make its version of Java compatible with Sun's version within 90 days.

In the antitrust trial, the Government contends that Microsoft's Java strategy is part of a pattern of anticompetitive practices that the company took to stifle competition and maintain its dominance in the market for personal computer software. The Government asserts that the combination of Java, an Internet programming language, and the browser software used to navigate the World Wide Web, which was pioneered by the Netscape Communications Corporation, posed a potent threat to Microsoft.

The essence of that threat was the promise that programs written in Java could run on any operating system. Traditional software runs on only one operating system, and because on more than 90 percent of personal computers that operating system is Microsoft's Windows, software developers have long written mainly for Windows. That tends to lock in the company's dominance.

In his 35 pages of testimony, Dr. Gosling said that he created the Java programming language in 1991 to free programmers from the limitation of "platform-specific software." But in September 1997, Dr. Gosling said, Microsoft introduced an upgraded version of its browser software, Internet Explorer 4.0, that was linked to Windows "in ways to undermine the cross-platform promise of Java technology."

An expert programmer whose resume includes a dozen patents, Dr. Gosling testified that what Microsoft had done to the Java programming language was "analogous to adding to the English language words and phrases that cannot be understood by anyone else."

Microsoft says that the Government and Sun are misrepresenting both its actions and its motives. Its changes, Microsoft says, were introduced to overcome the shortcomings of standard Java and make it run better on Windows. Sun's motto for Java, "Write Once, Run Anywhere," has proved a wonderful marketing slogan but not a real-world description of the language's capabilities, Microsoft insists.

Indeed, many programs written in Java today do have to call directly on a specific operating system to work properly. But Sun has one way of enabling these "native" calls on the operating system, while Microsoft has another. That difference is the crux of Sun's California case and of the Government's claim that Microsoft has tried to "pollute" Java.

James Gosling was not the focus of attention during his first day on the stand. Instead, Bill Gates—the overarching, if physically absent, presence at the trial—was once again the target of the Government's assault. This time, the courtroom presentation zeroed in on the contrast between the shrug-and-mumble Gates of his videotaped deposition, who seemed unconcerned by Java, and the Gates of his e-mail, who took the Java threat very seriously indeed.

DECEMBER 1, 1998

Gates Testifies He Knew Little About Microsoft-Sun Legal Battle Over Java

In excerpts from a videotaped deposition played in Federal court today, William H. Gates, chairman of the Microsoft Corporation, professed general ignorance of his company's legal battles with Sun Microsystems Inc. over Sun's Java programming language.

Asked under oath on Aug. 29 if he was familiar with a civil lawsuit that Sun had recently filed accusing Microsoft of violating its contract to use Java, Mr. Gates paused for nearly 30 seconds before replying, "Not really." Later he said with a shrug, "I read something about it on our Web site four days ago."

The questioning in August was in the form of a sworn deposition taken by the Justice Department for the Government's lawsuit accusing Microsoft of predatory business practices that violated antitrust laws.

The trial turned today to the company's difficult relationship with Sun, which created and owns Java, a programming language that could in theory threaten the domination by Microsoft's Windows of the market for personal computer operating systems. Microsoft licensed Java from Sun three years ago but then wrote its own version of the language, which is in some ways incompatible with Sun's original.

The Government is trying to show that Microsoft's battles with Sun are part of a broad pattern of illegal, predatory behavior intended to protect its Windows operating system monopoly.

Through a long day of testimony, live and videotaped, Microsoft presented two faces. On videotape, Mr. Gates seemed largely unconcerned by Sun, though at one point he said that Java "might be evolved in the future" into a competitive threat. But in live questioning, a Microsoft lawyer, Tom Burt, tried to force James A. Gosling, the Sun executive who created Java, into saying that Sun intended to mount a deadly threat against Microsoft.

Mr. Burt displayed memos and e-mail from Sun executives describing ambitions to challenge Microsoft using Java.

"Charge! Kill Hewlett-Packard, IBM, Microsoft and Apple all at once" using Java, Sun's chief executive, Scott G. McNealy, wrote in one e-mail message, according to a newsletter entered into evidence.

Bill Joy, another Sun executive, wrote in 1995 that "Java gives Sun a chance to break away from the Microsoft monopoly."

But Dr. Gosling seemed amused by that and other exuberant statements by Sun executives over the years. And when Mr. Burt asked him if Sun wanted to take over "100 percent of the computer market," Dr. Gosling chuckled before responding, "I think we would be happy if we achieved two orders of magnitude less than that," or 1 percent.

In contrast to Mr. Burt's strategy, however, Mr. Gates seemed wholly unconcerned by Sun and Java. At one point in the Aug. 28 deposition,

David Boies, the Government's lead lawyer, asked Mr. Gates, "Did you ever try to find out what Microsoft is charged with, what they're alleged to have done wrong?"

In a casual tone, Mr. Gates responded that he had asked Paul Maritz, a senior Microsoft executive: " 'Do I need to learn about this lawsuit? Do I need to spend a lot of time on it?' He said, no, he's focused on it, and I can focus on other things."

But then Mr. Boies presented e-mail to Mr. Gates from others in his company last year showing that they were quite concerned with Sun and Java—particularly since Java was a significant component of the World Wide Web browser made by the Netscape Communications Corporation, Microsoft's chief competitor in Internet software. And in an e-mail entered into evidence earlier in the trial, Mr. Gates once remarked that Java "scares the hell out of me."

In one e-mail introduced today, Mr. Maritz wrote to Mr. Gates: "If we looked further at Java being our major threat, then Netscape is the major distribution vehicle."

Mr. Gates said he could not recall that e-mail, adding that "Maritz may or may not have agreed" with the notions he was describing.

In another message to Mr. Gates last year, a Microsoft executive, Tod Nielsen, wrote, "We are proactively trying to put obstacles in Sun's path and get anyone that wants to write in Java to use J/Direct," Microsoft's version of the language for Windows.

Mr. Gates said he did not recall

the message, adding, "I don't know what it means."

Microsoft issued a statement today defending Mr. Gates's responses and criticizing the Government for playing the video of the deposition.

"Mr. Gates's performance reflects his adherence to the instructions lawyers routinely give their clients who are being deposed," it said.

DECEMBER 2, 1998

A New Tack Is Taken By Microsoft

Microsoft's lawyers sought to show in Federal court today that Sun Microsystems Inc., a tough competitor in the software industry, was guilty of the same sort of anticompetitive behavior that had prompted the Federal Government and 20 states to file an antitrust suit against the Microsoft Corporation.

With a Sun executive, James A. Gosling, on the stand, a Microsoft lawyer, Tom Burt, introduced internal e-mail in which Sun executives two years ago described meetings with the Netscape Communications Corporation at which it appeared that the two companies were working toward an agreement not to compete in Internet software.

One memo summarizing Sun's goals, said, "Unify browser efforts; stop competing."

At that point, Netscape had a commanding market share in the browser software used to navigate the Web, while Sun was creating another browser, called Hot Java, written in Sun's Java programming language.

A key charge in the Government's case against Microsoft is that the company threatened to crush Netscape if it did not cede to Micro-soft the market for browsers written for Microsoft's Windows operating system. Microsoft denies that charge and says its discussions with Netscape were unremarkable.

In court today, Mr. Burt asked Dr. Gosling about the Sun-Netscape meetings. "It's not at all unusual for companies to get together and talk about how technologies ought to evolve, is it?" he asked.

Dr. Gosling said, "That's correct." But a few moments later, he added, "I do not recall any kind of decision to back away from browsers because of any agreement with Netscape." Sun decided not to begin selling Hot Java, he said, simply because the company could not figure out how to make money with it when Microsoft was giving away its browser, Internet Explorer.

In some ways, Microsoft's tack today appeared to counter its earlier strategy. On Wednesday, Mr. Burt presented a case that Sun, a power in the software industry, planned to use Java to mount a challenge to Microsoft's dominance of the PC operating system market. This line of attack was designed to convince Judge Thomas Penfield Jackson that Microsoft was facing such strong competition that it could not be considered a monopoly under the law.

But today, Mr. Burt introduced numerous documents and testimony to suggest that Sun's version of Java was actually a slow, bug-ridden, poor-performing programming language that was the object of ridicule in the industry. Given those facts, he suggested, it was perfectly reason-able for Microsoft to create its own, superior version of Java.

That tactic was intended to counter Government evidence that Microsoft created a partly incompatible version of Java to cut off any competitive threat posed by Sun's version. Mr. Burt never addressed the seeming contradiction.

DECEMBER 3, 1998

Trial Reviews Dispute With Sun Over Java

The antitrust trial against the Microsoft Corporation today offered an inside view of the software giant's relationship with Sun Microsystems Inc. that resembled two wary, distrustful scorpions circling each other.

The corporations shared an interest in Internet software and a programming language called Java, developed by Sun. Two years ago, Microsoft signed a license agreement with Sun to use the Java technology, but as testimony and e-mail evidence chronicled, there was always more antagonism than cooperation between the two companies.

"Our view was that when Microsoft was holding out its hand, there was a knife in that hand and Microsoft was asking us to grab that knife," said James A. Gosling, a Sun vice president and a creator of Java.

The Government introduced documents and e-mail today showing that Microsoft regarded Java as a serious threat. One internal Microsoft document said that a "strategic objective" for the company was to "kill cross-platform Java" by expanding the "polluted Java market"—an apparent reference to Microsoft's altered version of Java.

An e-mail dated July 14, 1997, from Paul Maritz, a senior Microsoft executive, to a group of company executives including William H. Gates, Microsoft's chairman, identified Sun's Java technology as "our major threat."

Microsoft acknowledges that it regarded Java as a threat, but says that its response was to build a superior version of Java technology.

"What we saw in court today is that competition between Microsoft and Sun is strong and vigorous," said John Warden, Microsoft's lead trial lawyer. "Microsoft competed hard and got ahead of Sun, and Sun is understandably unhappy about that."

Microsoft hit that theme repeatedly today in its cross-examination of Dr. Gosling. Afterward, Federal District Judge Thomas Penfield Jackson asked Dr. Gosling a question that suggested the Microsoft legal team might have made some headway.

The drift of Microsoft's cross-examination, Judge Jackson said, was that "Microsoft recognized the significance of what you did and ran with it." He went on: "They produced a better product and couldn't wait for you to catch up. What's your response to that implication?"

"Their version of better was tied to the Windows platform," Dr. Gosling replied.

Later, he added that Microsoft's Windows-version Java seemed intended to "completely destroy our goal for Java—to make it run on many platforms."

Dr. Gosling also testified that Sun's objective with Java was to "break the coupling between software applications and the underlying operating system, effectively decoupling these two markets."

Microsoft, to be sure, has a huge vested interest in making sure that the markets for applications and operating systems remain tightly coupled. Its dominant position in work-related applications like word processing and spreadsheets and the dominance of its Windows operating system reinforce each other.

With Windows running on more than 90 percent of personal computers sold, Microsoft is a crucial partner, even for rivals like Sun.

In an e-mail on Sept. 12, 1996, after visiting Microsoft executives, Eric Schmidt, who was then Sun's chief technology officer, urged that Sun collaborate with Microsoft on Java.

Mr. Schmidt, now chairman of Novell Inc., offered a simple rationale: "They will ship 50 million-plus copies of Java next year."

DECEMBER 10, 1998

David Farber, a 64-year-old computer scientist from the University of Pennsylvania, is inevitably described as "an Internet pioneer." It is

David Farber

UNIVERSITY OF PENNSYLVANIA

true, literally, since he, along with Vint Cerf and others, did the pioneering work on distributed computing in late 1960's and 1970's when the Internet was mainly a government-supported research network connecting universities and Federal laboratories, when the people using it were members of a small, close-knit community.

But Farber also personifies the original Internet culture with its belief in the virtues of decentralization, openness and freely distributed information. Today, he remains an influential figure among the Internet's elite, thanks to his Internet mailing list sent out to 25,000 people who qualify as what he calls, IP, for "interesting people."

The digerati following the trial felt that justice was served by having an Internet luminary take the stand. Esther Dyson, editor of *Release 1.0,* an industry newsletter, observed, "The trial has centered on the Internet, but it's all been about the corporations of the Internet. It was nice to finally have the users and creators represented in the courtroom as well."

Farber was no professional expert witness. Tweedy and bald, he has a tendency to round his R's into W's, so even friends affectionately compare him to Elmer Fudd. Yet what he may have lacked in practiced polish, he made up for with his deep knowledge of computer software in making his basic point for the government—that software is "infinitely malleable" and that there were no obvious technical or user benefits to Microsoft's decision to fold its browser into the Windows operating system.

Farber found being a witness to be hard work. When he returned home, his first e-mail message to his IP list said, "I have never felt so drained." Then, he headed for a 10-day vacation in Hawaii to a resort with "no phones, no TV and no e-mail."

Expert Disputes Efficiency Claims In Integrated Browser

This evening, the Government made public the direct, written testimony of the next witness in the case: David J. Farber, a computer-science expert at the University of Pennsylvania who takes the stand on Tuesday.

In his testimony, Dr. Farber disputes Microsoft's assertion that bundling Internet software with the Windows operating system improves the efficiency of both products. In its suit, the Government accuses Microsoft of bundling the two products as a tool to put Netscape, its chief rival in the market for Web browsers, at a disadvantage.

"These same efficiencies can be achieved without bundling of the Web browser software with what Microsoft calls its Windows operating system," Dr. Farber testified. "This is because there are no techni-cal barriers that prevent Microsoft from developing and selling its Windows operating system as a stand-alone product separate from its browser software."

He added: "There are no technical efficiencies for users achieved by combining Microsoft's browser software with the remainder of the software sold as Windows 98 that could not be achieved by writing two programs in a manner that later could be loaded and 'integrated' " by manufacturers or consumers.

Responding in a news release this evening, Microsoft said: "Mr. Farber has provided nothing more than an opinion piece on how he thinks Microsoft could have or should have designed Windows. But in our market economy, Government consultants don't get to redesign software products."

DECEMBER 7, 1998

At the Microsoft Trial, a Day for Parrying

A lawyer for the Microsoft Corporation failed today to shake a computer-science expert from his argument that Internet software should not be included as part of Microsoft's Windows operating system.

Central to the Government's antitrust suit against Microsoft is the charge that the company bundled Internet browser software with Windows largely as a tactic to put competitors at a disadvantage.

"In general, designers have a huge amount of flexibility in how to package these files, the same way you have a large amount of flexibility in how you put things in a grocery bag, as long as you don't crush stuff," said David J. Farber, a senior computer-science professor at the University of Pennsylvania who is a Government witness. "Software is infinitely malleable."

Steven Holley, a lawyer for Microsoft, contended that—no matter how all those files got into Windows—outside software developers now depend on them when they write programs for Windows.

To that, Dr. Farber countered that "there is no absolute efficiency given just because this is the way Microsoft has chosen to put all of this together."

Toward the end of the day, Mr. Holley got down to the level of individual program files. He displayed a large poster listing 13 major files that testimony had shown were invoked when a computer user sought an Internet address using Internet Explorer, Microsoft's browser.

Then he asked Dr. Farber if each file could be deleted without damaging Windows. When the witness answered no to the first two, Mr. Holley pasted large red "no" stickers to the board, to reinforce Microsoft's argument that Explorer is an inseparable, integrated element of Windows.

The theatrics fizzled, though, when Dr. Farber told him that the questions made no sense. Several files in question, he said, were key parts of the operating system invoked by all sorts of programs, not just Explorer.

By asking those questions, the professor told Mr. Holley: "You're asking me if I've stopped beating my wife." A moment later, Federal District Judge Thomas Penfield Jackson, who is hearing the case, asked Mr. Holley, "Can we move on to another subject?"

Judge Jackson showed interest in the discussion of individual computer files. He heard similar testimony last year, when he was deciding on the Government's request for an order barring Microsoft from bundling Internet Explorer with Windows 95. Early this year, Judge Jackson ordered Microsoft to offer Windows 95 in a form that hides access to Explorer. But a court of appeals panel overturned his ruling last summer.

When the discussion today turned to one file used by Windows and Explorer, the judge interrupted Mr. Holley to ask the witness, "If that code were part of Windows, is there any reason that Internet

Explorer, as an application, could not invoke it?"

No, there was no reason, Dr. Farber answered. The very question troubled Microsoft executives, who have labored since the trial began to convince Judge Jackson that Internet Explorer is not a stand-alone application and never has been.

Mr. Holley later asked Dr. Farber about a section from the appellate court ruling, which is central to Microsoft's defense. The panel ruled that it would be "absurdly inefficient" to require consumers to stitch computer code together, a possible result if Explorer were removed from Windows.

Dr. Farber mumbled for a moment, suggesting that he had trouble with the appellate court's language, but then explained, "I don't want to criticize the court."

To that, Judge Jackson smiled and said, "Oh, go ahead."

DECEMBER 8, 1998

At Trial, Some Language Parsing And More on Java

The Microsoft trial focused today on an esoteric issue that is crucial to the outcome of the antitrust case: What is a computer operating system?

The answer is important because the Government contends that the Microsoft Corporation illegally tied its software for browsing the World Wide Web to its industry-standard Windows operating system to stifle competition in the Internet software market. Microsoft says that its browser is not a separate product unfairly tied to Windows but merely a feature of its operating system.

For hours, Steven Holley, a Microsoft lawyer, battered away at the Government's expert witness, David J. Farber, a computer science professor at the University of Pennsylvania, asking him arcane questions about fine distinctions in programming files.

Clearly, the questioning was intended to try to get Mr. Farber to concede that drawing a neat, sharp line separating the operating system—which controls a computer's basic operations—from other software is tricky, if not impossible.

For the most part, Mr. Farber held his own, batting away the challenges to the central tenet of his testimony, which is that there is no obvious technical or user benefit to integrating the operating system and the browser as Microsoft did.

Microsoft apparently has had its own difficulties in defining just what an operating system is. The Government offered into evidence a dictionary of computer terminology published last year by Microsoft. The entry for operating systems made no mention of Internet software or anything related to it. And the definition for a Web browser seemed squarely at odds with Microsoft's courtroom contention that its Internet Explorer browser is an inextricable element of Windows rather than a separate software product, or application.

The Microsoft dictionary stated that a Web browser is an "application that allows users" to navigate the Internet.

And Microsoft, it seems, had some trouble finding a distinguished expert witness to agree entirely with its view of the operating system and the browser. In September, when Microsoft initially named its 12 witnesses, the list included Mi-chael L. Dertouzos, director of the computer-science laboratory at the Massachusetts Institute of Technology. He was listed as Microsoft's technical expert.

But Dr. Dertouzos was soon dropped from the Microsoft witness list after giving a deposition in the case, part of which was entered into evidence today. When asked, "Is a browser an application?" Dr. Dertouzos responded, "Historically and today, it is the case that browsers are treated as applications."

DECEMBER 9, 1998

Without any question, Edward Felten, a computer scientist from Princeton University, was the most aggressive, dogmatic and unshak-

Edward Felten
PRINCETON UNIVERSITY

able witness to take the stand. The government hired him to do a job—take Internet Explorer out of Windows—and he had done that on his own terms.

He created something he called the prototype removal program, which disabled Internet Explorer and removed any obvious means to see or use it.

When a Microsoft lawyer argued that his approach didn't make sense because nearly all the files that make up Internet Explorer were still there, Felten simply spat back that the lawyer was wrong. Felten had never served as an expert witness before. His expertise was operating systems, and over the years he had served occasionally as a consultant for Microsoft. But he had no strong ties to the company or to its rivals—an important reason he had been chosen.

Getting him ready for trial, Justice Department lawyers had set up a mock courtroom, complete with a judge, and had pretended to cross-examine him. Looking back on that, Felten said, they had done a better job than Microsoft's lawyers would later do in court.

"That day on the stand, it took me a long time to figure out what happened," Felten said. "I felt like I was, as athletes like to say, 'in the zone'—fully in control of the situation. And they didn't ask me anything I wasn't prepared for."

A typical courtroom exchange went like this:

Question: Are you denying here this morning that the Internet Explorer 4 Web browsing software remains in Windows 98 after the prototype removal program is run?

Answer: When the prototype removal program has been run, the user is no longer able to browse the Web. The Web browsing is gone.

Question: Right. The software is disabled?

Answer: Gone.

But Microsoft was certain that Felten was full of bunk, that all he had done was hide the Web browser. So the lawyer continued badgering Felten through the afternoon, finally angering the judge. And so it went as Microsoft pursued this part of the case.

From the first day of the trial until the last, Microsoft insisted that the tying case—that is, illegally bundling the browser with the operating system—was already dead; a federal appeals court panel had already ruled the previous summer that Microsoft was entitled to tie programs with Windows if the combination benefited consumers. Nonetheless, Microsoft's legal team continued to argue the tying case vociferously in court, even though, time and again, the arguments got the company in trouble.

In fact, when Microsoft attacked Felten's removal program head on later in the trial, while Microsoft executive James Allchin was testifying, the strategy backfired, giving Microsoft another bad week in court.

A Justice Department official called Microsoft's arguments about Internet Explorer "just a shell game—they can move the shells around however they want, whenever they want." By this, he meant that Microsoft could at any time argue that one feature of Windows or another was really Internet Explorer, or vice versa, so that no one could ever pull the two apart to Microsoft's satisfaction.

U.S. Witness Says Browser Split Is Feasible

A computer science expert from Princeton University says he has done what the Microsoft Corporation insists is impossible: extricated Microsoft's Internet Explorer Web browsing software from its Windows operating system.

The expert, Dr. Edward W. Felten, who will take the stand in Federal court on Monday as a witness for the Government in its antitrust suit against Microsoft, was asked by the Justice Department to puncture a central argument in Microsoft's defense—namely that browser and operating system are inextricably integrated.

In direct written testimony made

public this evening, Dr. Felten said that "Microsoft could have produced a version of Windows 98 without Web browsing in a way that did not adversely affect" users or developers of other software programs.

Microsoft, in a statement issued this evening, said that Dr. Felton did not actually remove Internet Explorer from Windows. "He only hid some of the functionality it provides, which does not benefit consumers," the statement said. "You can surgically remove someone's right arm, but the arm was certainly a useful part of the person's body before it was removed."

If the company can convince the judge that Internet Explorer is not a separate program, he will be unable to find that Microsoft illegally tied the browser to the operating system.

Dr. Felten, an assistant professor of computer science with a Ph.D. in computer science and engineering, said he had studied the programmers' original instructions, or source code, for both Windows 95 and Windows 98 with two graduate-student assistants.

He and his students found that Internet Explorer was "hard wired" to the operating system so that it was invoked in many circumstances, even if the user had designated another program as the computer's default Web browser. So they wrote what he called a "prototype removal program" that deleted some files and altered others to clip the "hard wired" connections so that users could not gain access to Internet Explorer by any means.

Microsoft says that removing Internet Explorer will "break" Windows 98. But Dr. Felten testified: "The prototype removal program does not prevent Windows 98 from booting properly, nor does it affect the stability of Windows 98 under ordinary use. Microsoft could have produced a version of Windows 98 without Web browsing in a way that did not adversely affect the non-Web browsing features."

After running the removal program, Dr. Felten said, he installed the major competing Web browser, the Netscape Communications Corporation's Navigator. "A computer that has undergone these procedures suffers no apparent loss of stability or functionality and provides the user the full Web browsing experience offered by Navigator," he wrote.

At the Government's request, Dr. Felten also studied the versions of Internet Explorer that Microsoft had developed for other operating systems, including Apple Computer's Macintosh Mac OS and Sun Microsystems' Solaris, a Unix operating system. Microsoft has stated that these other versions of the browser are completely different programs and, as such, their existence does not bolster the assertion that Internet Explorer is a stand-alone application that is distinct from Windows.

Dr. Felten, however, testified that his review of other versions of Internet Explorer "leads me to the conclusion that the user's Web experience with each version is substantially similar to the other versions."

Microsoft asserts that all the professor really did was to delete one small "stub" file whose only purpose was to trigger the other internet Explorer files scattered through the Windows program.

Dr. Felton acknowledged that most of the "shared program libraries" from which programs call features and functions from Windows were "left substantially unchanged" by his removal program. He could have deleted program code for Internet Explorer from some of these files, he said, but decided not to "because the limited changes performed by the prototype removal program achieve the same results."

Microsoft, in its statement, warned that the scenario Dr. Felten described would lead to a world in which consumers would have to choose among "dozens or hundreds of incompatible versions of Windows." But Dr. Felten testified that his purpose was to show that Microsoft, despite its arguments to the contrary, could have produced a version of Windows that allowed users to choose which Web browser they wanted to install.

DECEMBER 12, 1998

Microsoft Accused of Sabotaging Witness's Computer Program

A Princeton University computer-science expert today accused the Microsoft Corporation in Federal court of sabotaging a computer program he had written to demonstrate a key point in the Government's antitrust suit against the software giant.

Judge Thomas Penfield Jackson, who is trying the case in District Court here, became visibly angry at the idea that Microsoft might have taken advantage of information it acquired through the court to sabotage the Government's case.

At the Justice Department's request, the expert witness, Edward W. Felten, devised a small program last spring that was able to extricate Microsoft's Internet Explorer Web browsing software from its Windows 98 operating system—something Microsoft had said was impossible.

The question is central to the case because the Government contends that Microsoft illegally tied Internet Explorer to its industry-standard Windows operating system to stifle competition in the market for Web browsers, while Microsoft asserts that its browser is not a separate product but an integrated feature of its operating system that cannot be removed.

Testifying as a Government witness, Dr. Felten said several computers on which Internet Explorer had been removed with his "prototype removal program" worked smoothly through the summer, even when used to visit a special Microsoft Web page for updates to Windows 98.

But then in September, Dr. Felten testified, he gave Microsoft a copy of the source code for his removal program as part of a pretrial discovery request. After that, he said, "Microsoft modified the software" behind the company's update Web page "to make it incompatible" with computers that had been altered by his removal program.

At that, Judge Jackson's eyes widened, and he leaned toward the witness as he asked, "Are you telling me that as part of discovery, you gave them this code in September, whereupon it appears that there were product changes by Microsoft?" Dr. Felten affirmed that, and the judge glowered at the Microsoft lawyers' table.

Later, outside the courtroom, Microsoft told reporters that there was an innocent explanation: When the company put an early beta, or test version, of its yet-to-be released Internet Explorer 5.0 on the Web site early this month, the program had been inadvertently set up to be downloaded into a directory that Dr. Felten's program had deleted.

"This was not a change we have made to undermine the removal program of the Government," a Microsoft spokesman, Mark Murray, said.

But even beyond that incident, Microsoft had a frustrating day in court. Dr. Felten, the most assertive, combative witness who has taken the stand since the trial began two months ago, gave not an inch.

The cross-examination was so wearying and, apparently, fruitless, that Microsoft abandoned it early this afternoon, though the company had expected to continue questioning Dr. Felten into Tuesday, at least.

An official associated with the Government's case said, "If you are punching away at someone, and he punches back harder every time,

why would you want to keep punching him?"

But John Warden, Microsoft's lead lawyer, said: "This witness didn't really have much to say. He said 10 times that Microsoft could have designed Windows 98 this way or that."

During the cross-examination of Dr. Felten, a Microsoft lawyer, David Heiner, asserted that the witness had not really removed Internet Explorer from Windows at all; he had simply removed the user's access to it.

"Isn't it true," Mr. Heiner asked, "that your version of Windows is 99.9 percent as large as the Microsoft version because you really didn't take anything out?"

Dr. Felten said that was irrelevant: The code he left behind is used by other programs, not just Internet Explorer, and so it made no sense to classify it as part of Explorer.

Mr. Heiner kept pushing Dr. Felten to identify which lines of code belonged to Internet Explorer. Dr. Felten refused, at one point saying: "No that's not the right characterization. It doesn't make sense to say that just because files are used by a program, it means that they are a part of the program."

Finally the judge cut Mr. Heiner off, saying: "You're playing word games. He's told you a dozen times" that code can have multiple functions. "To continue to pursue this I don't think is appropriate cross-examination. You are simply inviting him to make a careless mistake."

At the end of the day, Mr. Warden declared that it was the Government that had a bad day. "This witness was unable, when asked, to enumerate what code constitutes the Web browser, or Internet Explorer, that we are alleged to have illegally tied to Windows," he said. "It's now been a year since we demanded that the Government do that, and they still have not done that."

Microsoft representatives tried to argue, at the end of the day, that their lawyers hadn't really cut short Dr. Edward Felten's cross examination early, even though before he took the stand they had said the cross examination would last two days. A Justice Department lawyer interpreted events this way: "If you are punching someone, and they punch you back harder every time, why would you want to keep punching?"

But Mark Murray, the Microsoft spokesman, had a different view later as he stood on the courthouse steps.

"This fellow didn't really have much to say. He said 10 times that Microsoft could have designed Windows this way or that way," Murray said. Then, gesturing behind him, Murray went on to add: "I suppose they could have designed these steps with 65 steps instead of 63."

Judge Jackson's face had visibly darkened after Dr. Felten accused Microsoft of sabotaging his program. The Judge had never seemed so angry. So toward the end of the day, John Warden told him that Microsoft wanted to explain what happened. Judge Jackson gave him permission to do that.

A few days later, Microsoft's written explanation arrived in Federal Court. The problem was, Microsoft's explanation didn't explain what happened. The company only denied any involvement.

At issue was on-line updates, a feature introduced with Windows 98 in June. It enabled users connected to the Internet to receive a "critical update" message whenever they are connected to the Internet. Microsoft issues these updates whenever the company has fixed some bug or made some improvement to the operating system. By clicking a button, the user downloads the new code from a special Microsoft Web site, and it is installed automatically. Felten said that Microsoft had made changes to its Windows 98 update site that seemed designed to thwart his removal program.

In its explanation, Microsoft said the site was updated regularly, roughly every two weeks, adding that one update was first posted on Nov. 4 and modified slightly on Dec. 4 "by a single developer working under the supervision of another developer." These were near the dates when Felten said he first noticed the problem.

"Neither of these developers," the company said, "had access to Dr. Felten's program, and neither was involved in any way with Microsoft's testing of his program. The Dec. 4 change had nothing whatsoever to do with Dr. Felten or his program. Microsoft knows of no reason why the change should have affected Dr. Felten's program and believes it had no such effect."

Felten and the Justice Department decided not to say anything at all about Microsoft's explanation.

DECEMBER 15, 1998

Trial Reviews More Microsoft Tactics

When employees of the Microsoft Corporation discuss the company's Windows operating system, their language can be extravagant, even imperial. In documents and depositions presented in Federal court today, one described Windows as "our one unique and valuable asset." Another called it "the crown jewel."

As the Government's antitrust suit against Microsoft entered its third month today, the Justice Department continued to concentrate on evidence that Microsoft used its monopoly position in operating-system software to have its way in all manner of competitive challenges. In court, the Government offered new charges that Microsoft had cajoled or threatened companies that for the most part posed no obvious threat to Microsoft or Windows. The subjects of those efforts, the Government contended, ranged from IBM and MCI to the Walt Disney Company.

The Government presented this evidence in the form of videotaped depositions from William H. Gates, Microsoft's chairman, and executives from companies who felt they had been bullied.

Last year, the Government contended, Microsoft felt that Disney was getting too cozy with the Netscape Communications Corporation. Steve Wadsworth, a Disney vice president, said that Microsoft threatened to pull Disney's logo— an easy link to the company's Web site—from its Windows channel bar.

Disney was "being roughed up by the 1,000-pound guerilla of the industry," Mr. Wadsworth testified in a taped deposition. "These guys have all the cards. I felt like we were being, you know, leveraged."

In the end, Disney reduced the level of its involvement with Netscape, afraid to lose its position on the Windows desktop.

Regarding IBM, the Government showed that in March 1994, a Microsoft executive, Joachim Kempin, addressed Mr. Gates's apparent concern over IBM's growing relationship with Lotus—a Microsoft competitor in business software—by stating in an e-mail that the company needed a "hit team to attack IBM as a large account, whereby the O.E.M. relationship should be used to apply some pressure."

By that, Mr. Kempin apparently meant that Microsoft should take advantage of IBM's need, as an original-equipment manufacturer, to install Windows on the personal computers it sold. Eventually, IBM bought Lotus.

Asked in a videotaped deposition played in court today about Mr. Kempin's e-mail, Mr. Gates said that "hit team" was a not-uncommon term for Microsoft salesmen.

Mr. Gates was also asked about an e-mail he had received from another Microsoft executive, Russell Siegelman, in 1994. In that message, Mr. Siegelman said he opposed a request by MCI to have a link to its Internet server on the Windows desktop, referring to "the

Windows box" as "our one unique and valuable asset."

Asked about that, Mr. Gates seemed perplexed and said, "The Windows box is a piece of cardboard."

Microsoft complained about the playing of videotapes today, particularly further use of the tape of Mr. Gates's deposition, several parts of which had already been shown. At one point, the Government played a brief clip in which David Boies, the Government's lead trial lawyer, entered the deposition room as the camera focused on Mr. Gates, who was scowling down at the table.

"Good morning, Mr. Gates," Mr. Boies said. Mr. Gates did not look up or answer.

"What is the legal significance of whether Bill Gates says 'Good morning' to his inquisitors?" Microsoft asked in a news release, one of two documents the company handed out today to reporters, offering 24 pages of counterarguments. "The Government's reliance on edited videotaped depositions underscores the weaknesses in the Government's

case by taking out of context assertions from Microsoft's competitors and amplifying" them, the company asserted.

But Mr. Boies told the judge that 80 percent of the final tape played today was shown at Microsoft's request.

That deposition was of Brian Croll, a Sun Microsystems executive asked by a Microsoft lawyer about Sun's inclusion of its Hot Java Web browser with Solaris, Sun's operating system for server computers.

Unlike Microsoft, Mr. Croll testified, Sun let users remove its browser from Solaris and install another.

Mr. Gates, asked in his deposition to name Microsoft's rivals for PC operating systems, listed IBM, Sun and five smaller companies.

But IBM executives testified earlier that the company could not compete with Microsoft and had stopped marketing its OS/2 operating system to consumers. Mr. Croll of Sun testified that the PC operating system business "is closed to us" because of Microsoft's monopoly.

DECEMBER 15, 1998

Microsoft Is Denied Access to Scholars' Tapes

Denying the Microsoft Corporation access to the research of two business school professors, a Federal appeals court in Boston ruled unanimously yesterday that scholars should be granted First Amendment privileges similar to those of journalists.

Microsoft sought the unpublished

notes and tapes of interviews conducted by the professors for use in its defense in the antitrust suit brought by the Government. The suit contends that Microsoft used its market power illegally to thwart competition from its main rival for Internet browsing software, the Netscape Communications Corporation.

The two companies' rivalry is the focus of "Competing on Internet Time: Lessons From Netscape and Its Battle With Microsoft," a new book by Michael A. Cusumano, a professor at the Massachusetts Institute of Technology's Sloan School of Management, and David B. Yoffie, a professor at the Harvard Business School.

Microsoft wanted the authors' notes and tapes from interviews with Netscape executives to help show that the Internet pioneer's struggles were due to its own missteps and not a result of Microsoft's predatory tactics.

But the authors argued that they had conducted interviews with the understanding that the Netscape executives would speak freely but could ask that sensitive information remain confidential.

Courts routinely recognize that kind of confidentiality agreement between journalists and the people they interview. In its 24-page decision, a three-judge panel of the Court of Appeals for the First Circuit said: "Just as a journalist, stripped of sources, would write fewer, less incisive articles, an academician, stripped of sources, would be able to provide fewer, less cogent analyses. Such similarities of concern and function militate in favor of a similar level of protection for journalists and academic researchers."

The court's ruling, said Jeffrey Swope, a lawyer for M.I.T., was a "signal step in recognizing the validity of confidentiality in this kind of academic research."

The ruling, which Microsoft could appeal to the full appeals court or to the Supreme Court, could be particularly significant for business school research, which often depends on the trust of industry executives who share sensitive information with professors. Mr. Cusumano said that he and Mr. Yoffie "both felt that our livelihoods—and the work of scholars at business schools across the country—were at stake."

DECEMBER 16, 1998

Playing The Price Is Right *With Windows*

If the Microsoft Corporation is the predatory monopolist that the Government claims it is, why isn't the price of its monopoly product—its industry-standard Windows operating system—higher?

That question is a central focus of a new study of Microsoft and the Government's antitrust suit against the company by Robert E. Hall, an economist at Stanford University's Hoover Institution. Mr. Hall helped draw up the Justice Department's 1995 consent decree with Microsoft.

The 48-page paper, "National Policy on Microsoft: A Neutral Perspective," written with Mr. Hall's son, Chris Hall, an independent software developer, is being published this week and will be available on the Internet at www.netecon.com.

The paper says the Government's evidence puts it on solid ground in challenging some of Microsoft's contracts as violations of Section 1 of the Sherman Act, which condemns contracts that restrain trade. In an interview, Mr. Hall pointed in particular to Microsoft's pacts with America Online and other Internet service providers. These contracts require the service providers to guarantee that 75 percent or more of their customers use Microsoft's browser software, crimping the opportunity for its main rival in the browser market, Netscape Communications. For a company with so much market power, a clause like that "shows that Microsoft really does push the limits," Mr. Hall said.

On the pro-Microsoft side of the ledger, the Halls find little merit in the march of Government witnesses confidently proclaiming that operating systems and browsers are distinct products, and that Microsoft fused them only to squelch competition. "Given the complete malleability of software," the authors wrote, "this is a debate at about the intellectual level of trying to decide if the Gulf of Mexico is part of the Atlantic Ocean."

The Halls' paper focuses most sharply on the contentious subject of Windows pricing. They say "the low price of Windows looks nothing like a monopoly price," amounting as it does to less than 5 percent of the total price of a personal computer.

The "low" price of Windows is a theme that will be forcefully presented by Richard Schmalensee, an economist at the Massachusetts Institute of Technology, when he takes the stand as a witness for Microsoft. Mr. Schmalensee has been making the argument since the early 1990's, when he prepared a paper expounding the low-price thesis for the Federal Trade Commission, which investigated Microsoft before the Justice Department did.

The Windows-pricing issue is crucial to the outcome of the case and, if the Government wins, to the remedies it can seek from the court. A narrow victory under Section 1 of the Sherman Act would probably yield merely a court order that Microsoft must make its contracts less restrictive. The Justice Department did not sue Microsoft to accomplish so little.

But to win a broader, Section 2 victory, the Government must prove, among other things, that Microsoft has a monopoly, that its exclusionary conduct against potential rivals like Netscape has a "dangerous probability" of preventing a challenge to its monopoly and that its conduct has caused substantial harm to consumers. Only then will stronger remedies—including, perhaps, breaking up Microsoft—move onto the agenda.

To try to show gouging of consumers, the Government produced in court an internal Microsoft document showing that from 1990 to 1996 the average price it charged personal-computer makers for licensing Windows rose to $49.40 from $19.03. Its share of the PC's total price grew fivefold, to 2.5 percent.

The Justice Department also produced an E-mail written on Dec.

16, 1997, by Joachim Kempin, a senior Microsoft executive, to William H. Gates, the chairman, and other company executives on the subject of Windows prices charged to PC makers. "While we have increased our prices over the last 10 years," Mr. Kempin wrote, "other component prices have come down and continue to come down."

The Justice Department says Microsoft's ability to raise Windows prices is strong evidence that the company is overcharging. The Halls are not convinced. Given Windows' 250 million users and market share of more than 90 percent, the authors wrote, PC makers would want it even if it cost "twice or even 10 times as much."

Microsoft contends that the Windows price is restrained by a sense that some competitive threat, though not yet in sight, is behind the next corner—a fearful perspective that is all over parts of the December 1997 memo. In it, Mr. Kempin wrote that a big manufacturer like Compaq Computer, or a coalition of PC makers, could finance development of a competing operating system. Or, he wrote, if the chip maker Intel enters "our business, it will get ugly." (Compaq, incidentally, is sending an executive to testify in Microsoft's defense.)

For his part, Mr. Hall does not believe that the seemingly low price of Windows is explained by competition, real or feared. Instead, he suggests that the Windows price is part of Microsoft's broader strategy of making Windows PC's as cheap as possible, hooking new users and making them steady repeat buyers, not only of future generations of Windows but also of higher-priced Microsoft products like its Office suite of word processing, spreadsheet and data base software.

"The Government has to make an argument as to why Microsoft keeps the price of Windows low as part of its monopoly strategy, which harms consumers over all," Mr. Hall said. "It's possible, but the Government hasn't done it yet."

JANUARY 3, 1999

At the time he took the witness stand, William Harris, chief executive of Intuit, was the most senior industry executive from a company other than Netscape to have testified. Harris

William H. Harris
INTUIT

carried himself like a chief executive, with the poise and confidence of a man who heads a company that Microsoft has been unable to catch in the sizable market for personal finance software, led by Intuit's Quicken and TurboTax programs.

Microsoft, like the government, often asked witnesses questions about parts of the case that had nothing to do with their immediate testimony. The idea was to gather quotes to bolster important arguments from anyone whose opinions carried weight. Harris was no exception. An issue in the trial was the allegation that Microsoft had raised prices on Windows, while computer-industry prices for most other software and hardware had fallen precipitously in recent years. That was important because one measure of whether a company holds a legal monopoly is whether it can raise prices without fear of competition because there is no comparable product available to consumers. Yes, the cost of Windows has gone up, Warden said during his questioning of Harris, but "Microsoft has added many new features and functionality to Windows. You agree with that, don't you?"

Mr. Harris responded: "Yes I do—just as every other software vendor, including Quicken, has added features and functionality to their applications over the years. That's a normal part of the software business." Nonetheless, he added, Quicken's price has declined. With that and similar answers, Harris offered a voice of authority to his testimony that many other witnesses could not match.

Prophylactic Questions

By this point in the trial, so much dirt had been turned up about Microsoft's business tactics that the company worried that it might be blamed for anything unfortunate that happened to anyone. As a result, Microsoft's lawyers found themselves quite often asking prophylactic questions that would have sounded incongruous to anyone stepping into the courtroom for the first time—just to be sure no one assumed Microsoft had caused whatever problem was being discussed.

While Harris was on the stand, for example, he spoke about the difficulty his company had experienced trying to reach a business deal with Netscape. So, out of the blue during cross-examination, Warden asked, "Intuit's and Netscape's failure to reach agreement since April is not due to anything, any action taken by Microsoft; isn't that correct?"

"Yes, that's correct," Harris obligingly responded.

In reference to another complication Harris described, Warden blurted out, "Has Microsoft instigated that in some fashion?" No, Harris once again agreed.

These unexpected questions left courtroom observers with a disturbing impression: Microsoft must have worried that the judge or the public had begun to see the company as the devil behind all manner of problems, even when no such evidence was being offered in court.

Intuit's Chief Urges Division of Microsoft

A senior computer industry executive, testifying in Federal court today, urged the judge to divide or limit the Microsoft Corporation so that the company could not use its market-dominating Windows operating system to promote its other products.

"It seems to me reasonable for the court to make a distinction between operating systems and other applications," said William H. Harris, the chief executive of Intuit Inc., which makes Quicken, the market-leading personal finance software. "To the extent that the operating system is an essential service," one that consumers have no choice but to use, "such market power should not be used to leverage into other markets," he said.

Mr. Harris, the second-to-last Government witness, is the first to promote specific remedies, or penalties, should the court find that Microsoft engaged in illegal monopolistic practices. Though he did not say so specifically, Mr. Harris's prescription sounded like a call to break up Microsoft.

"Without such a broad remedy," he said in written testimony, "Microsoft's ability to control consumer access will continue to increase."

That testimony apparently took Microsoft by surprise. A company lawyer, John Warden, opened his cross-examination of Mr. Harris this morning by chastising him for offering this testimony without giving Microsoft any warning. Then Mr. Warden asked him whose idea the discussion of possible remedies had been—his or the Government's.

"It was my idea," Mr. Harris said. "In the context of discussing the importance of the operating system to the industry" he added, it was only natural "to look for actions, or solutions." If Microsoft is found to have violated antitrust laws, the Justice Department will propose remedies to the judge, leading to a new round of courtroom arguments. Mr. Warden intimated today that Mr. Harris's suggestion would lead to Government regulation of the industry.

"Are you suggesting that we bring back the people on the Interstate Commerce Commission and make them the Interstate Operating System Commission?" Mr. Warden asked.

No, Mr. Harris said.

Then Mr. Warden asked him: "You modify your software in response to technological advances in the industry don't you? Microsoft should have the same ability, shouldn't it?"

Yes, Mr. Harris answered, but he

added that there was a distinction between Quicken and Windows. Unlike Quicken, he said, "the operating system is an essential service that customers must avail themselves of." He added that Microsoft's power was growing because the company was beginning to use Windows as a "choke point" for access to the Internet.

A good part of Mr. Harris's testimony dealt with the exclusionary contract Microsoft forced Intuit to sign so that Microsoft would include a link to Quicken's Web site on the "channel bar," an advertising box that used to appear automatically on the opening screen of Windows but is now optional. The contract forbade Intuit to deal with the Netscape Communications Corporation, maker of the principal competing Web browser.

Mr. Warden defended the contract but also pointed out that Microsoft had canceled the restrictive provisions in April, a few weeks before the Government's antitrust suit was filed. And he argued that Intuit had chosen to include Microsoft's Web browser with Intuit products instead of Netscape's because Microsoft's was technically superior, not because of any pressure from Microsoft.

JANUARY 5, 1999

Intuit Executive Is Questioned About Microsoft Deal

This morning, Microsoft ended the cross-examination of William H. Harris, the chief executive of Intuit Inc., and the Government played excerpts from the taped deposition in which William H. Gates, the chairman of Microsoft, was questioned last August about the company's dealings with Intuit.

Though Mr. Gates professed no knowledge of any of the interactions with Intuit at issue in the case, the Government introduced e-mail messages in which employees had briefed him on the negotiations in exhaustive detail.

Shown one such message and asked if he had been informed of its subject, Mr. Gates said, "In the sense that one of the e-mails that may have come into my mailbox might have related to that, I don't doubt it."

Much of the questioning of Mr. Harris centered on Intuit's interest in becoming an even larger player in Internet commerce. Microsoft's lead trial lawyer, John Warden, asked him about America Online's proposed purchase of Netscape, a deal that Microsoft argues is proof of healthy competition in the software industry.

"Doesn't that change the entire landscape of the Internet industry?" Mr. Warden asked.

"No, I don't believe so," Mr. Harris said. "There's a great deal of merger activity in this industry. Microsoft is rumored to be in discussions for acquisitions. I don't think the AOL-Netscape deal will be the last one we hear of."

JANUARY 6, 1999

Franklin Fisher, an avuncular 64-year-old economist from M.I.T., is the doyen of expert witnesses in antitrust trials. In the last major

Franklin Fisher
MASSACHUSETTS INSTITUTE
OF TECHNOLOGY

antitrust face-off between the Justice Department and a major computer company—the IBM case, which the government dropped in 1982, after 13 years—Fisher was on the other side of the aisle, as the chief economic witness for IBM. This time, Fisher was testifying on behalf of the Justice Department and he was being questioned by David Boies, who had also been on the IBM defense team, as a partner at Cravath, Swaine & Moore.

There was a special edge to Fisher's courtroom performance because his counterpart on the defense, Microsoft's chief economic witness, was a former student, Richard Schmalensee. Fisher was Schmalensee's thesis adviser at M.I.T. The student was a success, rising to become a professor and dean of M.I.T.'s Sloan School of Management. This brought a personal dimension to the testimony of the two men, with Fisher characterizing Schmalensee's pro-Microsoft positions as "ridiculous" and "incredulous," while Schmalensee termed his former teacher's ruminations on consumer harm likely to be caused by Microsoft's practices as "sheer speculation."

Pricing at Issue As U.S. Finishes Microsoft Case

The Government called its last witness in the Microsoft trial today after presenting 110 pages of his written testimony that amount to a summation of—and economic justification for—the Justice Department's sweeping antitrust suit against the software giant.

Much of the testimony by the witness, Franklin M. Fisher, an economist at the Massachusetts Institute of Technology, was a detailed review of major allegations in the Government's case. But he also sought to advance the case and strengthen the argument for strong sanctions

against Microsoft with his analysis of Microsoft's pricing tactics.

Mr. Fisher asserts that Microsoft commits predatory pricing by giving away its Internet Explorer browser. The doctrine of predatory pricing—defined as a monopolist selling goods below cost—has been generally rejected by courts in recent years on the theory that it is difficult to prove both the practice and any resulting harm to consumers.

But Mr. Fisher argued that Microsoft decided to give away its browser software only to thwart the threat to its dominance posed by its main rivals in Internet software, the Netscape Communications Corporation, developer of the Navigator Web browser, and Sun Microsystems Inc., creator of the Java programming language.

Besides, he added, the tricky matter of trying to determine if a price is below some technical definition of its cost to produce does not apply because "Microsoft distributes its browser at a zero price," though it has spent more than $100 million a year since 1995 on browser development.

"Classifying Microsoft's pricing as predatory and anti-competitive," he stated, "does not require reaching the difficult questions that are usually faced in predatory pricing cases."

Mr. Fisher also provided a preemptive rebuttal to an M.I.T. colleague and former student, Richard Schmalensee, who will testify next, as Microsoft's expert witness on economics. In his own report to the court, which has not been released, Mr. Schmalensee argues that the price of Microsoft's industry-standard Windows operating system is too low for Windows to be legally classified as a monopoly. The comparatively low price of Windows— less than 5 percent of the total cost of an average personal computer—has been cited by many economists as inconsistent with the Government's allegation of an enduring monopoly.

But Mr. Fisher contends that such analysis means only that Microsoft's management is taking the long view of monopoly. "The proper conclusion from Schmalensee's argument cannot be that Microsoft lacks

monopoly power," Mr. Fisher wrote in his testimony. "If any conclusion can be drawn, it would be that Microsoft is not maximizing its short-run profits."

Microsoft's product pricing, Mr. Fisher testified, should be viewed as part of a "broader campaign to eliminate Netscape's browser and Java as sources of potential competition to Microsoft's operating system monopoly—a campaign characterized by actions by which Microsoft lost money in order to raise rivals' costs and exclude them from the market."

In court today, a Microsoft lawyer, Michael Lacovara, opened his cross-examination of Mr. Fisher with more than an hour of detailed challenges to the methodology Mr. Fisher used to determine the market shares of competing Web browsers. Mr. Lacovara also introduced criticisms of Mr. Fisher by judges in previous cases in which he appeared as an expert witness.

Microsoft's lawyers say the company is being attacked by Mr. Fisher for being much the kind of company IBM was when he was defending it. "Monopoly profits are earned through high prices and inferior products," Mr. Fisher wrote in a 1983 book about the IBM case. "The notion that acts showing a pattern of lower prices and better products are the behavior of a monopolist is a confusion of the workings of competition with its opposite—monopoly."

Microsoft said in a statement that "Professor Fisher's testimony would give readers of his 1983 book whiplash."

JANUARY 5, 1999

Microsoft Presses Its View About Rivals' 3-Way Deal

In its antitrust trial today, the Microsoft Corporation made its most concerted effort yet to convince a Federal judge that the recently announced deal that brings together three of its rivals—America Online Inc., the Netscape Communications Corporation and Sun Microsystems Inc.—seriously weakens the Government's case.

In a three-way deal announced in late November, America Online agreed to buy Netscape for $4.2 billion and made a side agreement to buy and jointly develop technology with Sun. Last month, Judge Thomas Penfield Jackson, who will decide the outcome of this non-jury trial, expressed the view that the deal "might be a very significant change in the playing field as far as this industry is concerned."

During today's cross-examination of the Government's last witness, Franklin M. Fisher, an economist, Microsoft's legal team presented as evidence comments made by executives of the three companies who characterized the deal as sure to strengthen their competitive muscle in software used to browse the World Wide Web, in electronic commerce and in Internet technology—all areas of head-to-head competition with Microsoft.

A Microsoft lawyer, Michael Lacovara, repeatedly tried to get Mr. Fisher to concede that the triumvirate of rivals with ambitious plans for the future did indeed pose a genuine threat to Microsoft's dominance in the personal computer software business. At times, Mr. Fisher would give an inch or two, saying, for example, that moves planned by the three companies were a "hopeful sign" that they might some day be a counterweight to Microsoft. But each time he was challenged, Mr. Fisher returned to his view that Microsoft has a monopoly in the personal computer operating system market with its Windows family of products and that it has illegally used its market power to defend that monopoly.

"None of this," Mr. Fisher replied at one point, "affects my conclusions."

Mr. Lacovara prodded Mr. Fisher repeatedly to admit that the emerging technology championed by the group—the combination of Sun's Java software, an Internet programming language, and Netscape's Web browser—could pose a serious challenge to Microsoft in the long run. Mr. Fisher allowed that it was difficult to predict what might happen.

Yet any such challenge will not come soon, he said, adding, "I don't think it will happen at all if Microsoft is permitted to go on as it has."

Microsoft insists that the America Online-Netscape-Sun deal fundamentally changes the competitive landscape and undermines a linchpin claim in the Government's case: that Microsoft has a resilient monopoly.

"This deal was the shot heard around the world, in the industry, by the public and in this courthouse," said William H. Neukom, the Microsoft senior vice president for law and corporate affairs.

Today, Judge Jackson gave another signal that he is weighing the impact of the three-company deal on the case. He interrupted the cross-examination of Mr. Fisher to directly ask his opinion about a column this morning on the Op-Ed page of The Washington Post by David Ignatius, based largely on an interview with Stephen M. Case, the chairman of America Online.

In it, Mr. Ignatius quotes Mr. Case as saying that the deal is not intended to mount a challenge to Microsoft's mainstay, the Windows operating system, which controls the basic operations of more than 90 percent of personal computers sold today. "AOL's merger with Netscape has no bearing on the Microsoft case, as nothing we're doing is competitive with Windows," Mr. Case was quoted as saying. "We have no flight of fancy that we can dent in any way, shape or form what is a monopoly in the operating system business."

After reading the quotations, Judge Jackson asked Mr. Fisher if he agreed with that view of the deal. "I certainly do," Mr. Fisher replied.

JANUARY 6, 1999

Prosecution Almost Rests In the Microsoft Trial

As Microsoft finished its cross-examination of the Government's final witness today, the two sides argued over the issues of bundling and free distribution of Microsoft's browser.

The questioning turned unusually testy as Michael Lacovara, a Microsoft lawyer, asked Franklin M. Fisher, an M.I.T. economist, about the costs associated with giving away the Internet Explorer. Mr. Fisher said that while it might be easier for computer makers and consumers, "this case is not about being easy."

"If Henry Ford had a monopoly, we'd all be driving black cars," he said, his voice slowly rising. "That's not what competition is about. That's not what helping consumers is about. If Microsoft forced upon the world one browser, that would be really simple."

"Now you seem agitated," Mr. Lacovara said.

"I am agitated," Mr. Fisher shot back. "I feel strongly on this point. We're going to live in a Microsoft world. It may be a nice world. But it's not a competitive world."

JANUARY 6, 1999

Issue du Jour at Microsoft Trial: Are Consumers Harmed?

An economist testifying for the Government conceded today that there was scant evidence consumers had been harmed by practices that are central to the Justice Department's antitrust case against the Microsoft Corporation.

In antitrust doctrine, the damage to consumers from anticompetitive conduct is generally measured in higher prices and fewer choices of products. When asked whether consumers were being harmed by Microsoft's practices in the Internet software market, Franklin M. Fisher, an economist at the Massachusetts Institute of Technology, replied that the question was difficult to answer. But after hesitating for a moment, he added, "On balance, I'd think that the answer is no, up to this point."

Microsoft quickly seized on the comment by Mr. Fisher, the last Government witness, as support for the contention that the Justice Department and 19 states suing the company have been unable to show that consumers are being damaged by Microsoft's actions. William H. Neukom, the senior vice president for law and corporate affairs, said the Government's case was inspired by Microsoft competitors and based on the "raw speculation" that consumers might be harmed in some distant future if the company was not reined in.

But the Justice Department argues that it is sound public policy to intervene early in fast-moving high-technology industries when the predatory acts of a monopolist threaten to stifle innovation and consumer welfare in the long run— and such, it contends, is the case with Microsoft.

With the prosecution case about to close, Joel I. Klein, the Assistant Attorney General in charge of the Justice Department's antitrust division, appeared on the courthouse steps today to declare that the Government had presented "compelling evidence that Microsoft has engaged in a pattern of practices to crush any threat to its operating system monopoly."

In the afternoon, Mr. Fisher elaborated on his earlier remark about the effect of Microsoft's practices on consumers. He said consumers might suffer now from reduced choice because Microsoft's contracts make it more difficult for a rival's software to be distributed.

Still, the real problem, he argued, lies in the future, because Microsoft's monopoly in operating systems—its Windows is shipped with 90 percent of all computers sold— makes it a de facto gatekeeper on new technology in the personal computer market.

"Microsoft has shown that it will decide how innovation takes place in this industry," Mr. Fisher testified. The lesson from examining Microsoft's conduct in the browser market, he said, is that rivals "will be squashed."

Then, Mr. Fisher testified, "I don't think that's good for consumers, but those effects have only just begun."

The difficult-to-measure danger, he said, is largely prospective. "It won't be a consumer-driven society," Mr. Fisher declared. "It will be a Microsoft-driven society."

Under questioning from David Boies, the Justice Department's lead trial lawyer, Mr. Fisher sought to explain what some economists regard as an unanswered question in the Government's case: why the price of Windows is not higher.

Mr. Fisher replied that Microsoft was taking its "monopoly profits" not solely from the pricing of Windows but also from increased sales of Microsoft products that run on the Windows operating system—its Office suite of business software, including word processing and spreadsheets, for example. The Windows pricing, he added, can also be explained as a discount to increase sales and thus strengthen the Microsoft monopoly.

At one point, Judge Thomas Penfield Jackson interrupted to ask whether it was a "valid concept" that a monopolist might logically pursue a pricing strategy of "delayed gratification" to maximize its long-run gains.

"Oh, I think so," Mr. Fisher replied.

The trial resumed in June, with each side presenting three rebuttal witnesses. Each side gets a second chance to patch up the soft spots in its own case and to once again attack what it regards as the weaknesses of its opponents. Fisher was the leadoff witness for the Government in the rebuttal phase of the trial.

JANUARY 12, 1999

CHAPTER 3

Microsoft Mounts Its Defense

AT THE HELM
WILLIAM H. NEUKOM

In the courtroom every day, from the first moment of the trial until the bitter end, Bill Neukom sat at the head of the Microsoft lawyers' table, facing the judge. It was an unusual sight. Neukom was Microsoft's senior vice president for law and corporate affairs, and corporate general counsels usually leave most of the courtroom work to the litigators, stopping in only occasionally to wave the flag. But Microsoft's spokesmen called Neukom the legal team's "field marshal," and Richard Urowsky, a senior member of Microsoft's legal team from the Sullivan & Cromwell law firm, said Neukom "participates in every significant decision." In the end, that may have been part of Microsoft's problem.

From the outside, it was hard to know how closely he directed the company's defense. Judge Jackson recalled that Neukom never said a word during chambers conferences. But he was the sort of man who would not have sat there day after day unless he was in fact heavily involved. And if Microsoft's defense suffered from any one thing, it was from hubris—the certainty that its leaders knew far more than anyone else about the issues at hand, and that therefore their point of view was inarguable. Neukom suffered no shortage of hubris himself.

"We have 12 very powerful witnesses to tell our side of the story," he said in December, standing ramrod straight in front of the court-house, an air of absolute certainty in his voice. This was just before Microsoft began presenting its side of the case, and nearly all of the witnesses to which Neukom referred were Microsoft employees. As it turned out, they were the ones David Boies most often ripped to shreds. But like every member of the Microsoft team, Neukom could not have been more confidant that his own people would save the day. "On the merits of the case, it's going very well," he said.

A tall man, with a thick mane of silver hair and a courtly manner, Neukom was fully possessed of the Microsoft state of unwavering self-confidence and a certainty of view that often seemed to spill over into arrogance. That should hardly have been surprising since by 1999, he had been working for Microsoft for 20 years, almost since its founding—long enough that he might actually have helped create the Microsoft mindset. All that time with the company, including some before Microsoft's initial public offering of stock, had made Neukom a multimillionaire many times over. He clearly no longer needed to work at Microsoft, or anywhere else. But like so many Microsoft exec-utives, he believes in the company—that it is not only a great com-pany but also a force for good in the American economy. Before joining the company full time, he ran for Washington state attorney general in 1980. But as a liberal Democrat, he was trounced in the Ronald Reagan Republican landslide. "I came in a bad second," he likes to say. Still, he remained active in American Bar Association politics and served on the boards of a wide range of community orga-nizations.

He grew up just outside San Francisco, attending public high school in San Mateo. There he was chosen chief justice of the student supreme court. He went on to Dartmouth, where he was president of his fraternity, Chi Phi, and majored in philosophy. Next came Stan-ford law school. He graduated in 1967. His work as a litigator attracted the notice of a Seattle lawyer, William H. Gates II, father of the one-day software mogul. Gates brought Neukom into his firm.

Neukom got his start with Microsoft in an offhand, serendipitous manner. In 1978, Gates's son, Bill, ran a little company called Micro Soft that was moving its headquarters (probably too grand a term, actually, for an outfit with just 12 employees) from Albuquerque to Seattle. Gates Sr. asked Neukom to help young Bill negotiate a lease for office space in the Seattle suburb of Bellevue. The most challeng-ing part of that assignment, Neukom would later recall, was persuad-ing the landlord to give young Bill and his scruffy-looking colleagues access to the building 24 hours a day so they could indulge the round-the-clock zealotry that was the company's hallmark even then. Little did Neukom know then that soon he would be a captive of that very culture.

As the company grew—particularly after 1981 when it won the contract to supply the operating system for IBM's new PC—so did its legal needs. Soon, Neukom was leading a small staff of lawyers at the firm who were working on Microsoft issues more or less full time.

Finally, in 1985, he moved over to become a full-time Microsoft employee, bringing with him one lawyer and one paralegal assistant. Now his office has more than 300 employees. Most of the legal work, then as now, involved contracts and licenses—the very things that got Microsoft in so much trouble during the antitrust trial. But starting in 1989, when Federal antitrust investigators began taking notice of Microsoft, defense work also became a full-time occupation for Neukom and his legal team.

The first time the company learned that it was a target of an investigation by the Federal Trade Commission, the natural reaction on the Microsoft campus was "to take out nuclear arms and start shooting," a former company executive told *The Seattle Times*. Neukom was often described as a calming influence, but that is a relative term. After the Justice Department took jurisdiction of the Microsoft case in 1993, Neukom was often described as so irritated by the inquiry that he ended up in table-pounding sessions with government lawyers. His views of antitrust have not changed over the years. At the time, Neukom was quoted as saying, "It is not the job of antitrust law to control the economy and ensure that there is an absolute level playing field in all markets. Some companies will bring certain advantages to certain areas. That may not be fair, but that's business." That remains his stance today.

Neukom carried that attitude forward to the new case. Early in 1998, as the government was preparing to file suit, Gates testified before a hostile Senate Judiciary Committee. Neukom was disdainful.

Of the Senate hearing, he said, "We should get credit just for showing up. Bill tried his best to bring information to the discussion. But this was not a fact-finding exercise. It was a spotlight, limelight sort of thing."

His acerbic remarks displayed not just a certain hubris but also a surprising political naivety. Neukom seemed generally surprised that the Senate hearing had not been an antiseptic, factual discussion of technology. But Microsoft, he added, would go forward with a political and legal strategy based on the company's view of the way things should be—not of the way things were.

Neukom may hold a secret ambition to help set things right in the legal world. In 1994 he told the *National Law Journal* that as he contemplated what he might do next, "the judiciary is a possibility that occurs to me."

FOR THE DEFENSE
JOHN WARDEN

In antitrust circles, John Warden is famous mainly as the author of a brilliant brief for Eastman Kodak in a case that, for a number of reasons, gave Microsoft comfort in its legal campaign.

In the 1970's, Kodak had been sued by in a private antitrust case by Berkey Photo. The main allegation was that Kodak had illegally tied its 1972 110 Pocket Instamatic camera to its monopoly product, film. In 1977, Berkey won an $87 million jury verdict against Kodak. The trial had gone horribly for Kodak, the low point being the admission by a partner for the law firm representing the company that he had perjured himself. He had stated in a deposition that important documents had been destroyed, when in fact, it was shown during the trial, that they had been withheld.

Kodak brought in a new firm, Sullivan & Cromwell, for the appeal, and Warden was the partner assigned to the case. In 1979, a Federal appeals court reversed the lower court decision against Kodak, and set an important antitrust precedent. What the jury determined had been an illegal tying of two products the appeals court deemed to be innovation, an economic stimulant best left beyond the reach of judicial tampering. "Innovation is clearly tolerated by the antitrust laws," the appeals court declared.

Subsequently, the Kodak ruling has made it difficult for plaintiffs to prevail on tying claims. And the appeals brief written by John Warden not only gave Kodak a remarkable legal recovery but also steered the appeals court toward a lasting, very pro-defendant standard in tying cases. The Warden brief, legal experts say, was a masterful piece of appellate advocacy.

In the Microsoft case, as with Kodak, the company's hopes would eventually rest on appeal, and a ruling on the tying of products would be a key finding necessary for Microsoft to win a reversal and avoid drastic remedies.

Warden, who led the Sullivan & Cromwell team representing Microsoft, figured to play an important role in the appeal. For Microsoft, as for Sullivan & Cromwell and Warden himself, things could only improve at the appeals stage from the rout it would suffer in Judge Jackson's courtroom.

The lawyers at the elite Sullivan & Cromwell firm, legal analysts said, were generally known as outstanding brief writers or "paper lawyers," better at working from a script than at the extemporaneous art of trial work. Warden was often regarded as an exception, an excellent litigator. Still, he seemed strongest working from his script— though, of course, in the Microsoft trial Warden suffered, as would nearly any trial lawyer, by comparison with David Boies.

Warden's opening statement was an eloquent, powerful argument to frame the evidence and the issues to give Microsoft the benefit of the doubt. The nation's antitrust laws, he said, were "not a code of civility in business." The government's selected excerpts from video-taped deposition of the Microsoft chairman, Warden declared, amounted to a transparent effort to "demonize Bill Gates." Competitors' accounts of Microsoft's alleged arm-twisting, he added, were "fantastical," which Microsoft would show to be nothing more than "garden-variety commercial discussions between companies." They were of "no antitrust consequence," he insisted.

In his cross-examination of the government's witnesses, Warden drew blood occasionally—but, Judge Jackson would later observe, not often enough to really dent their credibility.

A heavyset man, Warden's resonant baritone carried an indeterminate accent that journalists found elusive, with descriptions ranging from "Southern drawl" to "Midwestern growl." In fact, Warden was born in Evansville, Ind., and grew up in Cairo, Ill., two towns along the Kentucky border. He met his wife, Phillis, when he was eight years old.

As a teenager, Warden worked selling parts at his father's auto dealership. Even in high school, he was an intellectual. His recreational reading included Dickens and Tolstoy. He attended Harvard University as an undergraduate and then went on to law school at the University of Virginia, before joining Sullivan & Cromwell.

Unlike David Boies, who enjoyed chatting and joking with reporters during breaks in the trial, Warden was more formal and aloof. Besides, things weren't going well for Warden. Yet though he was prickly, he had a playful streak as well. During one break midway through the trial, Warden found himself standing next to a *Times* reporter. Warden, an inveterate and excellent bridge player, mentioned that he was a dedicated reader of the paper. "Not for your trial coverage," he noted wryly. "I try to skip that. I turn straight to Alan Truscott," the paper's long-time bridge columnist.

Richard Schmalensee cut a very different figure than his former teacher Frank Fisher, who was testifying for the government. Fisher

Richard Schmalensee
MASSACHUSETTS INSTITUTE OF TECHNOLOGY

was stooped and seemed a bit frail, wearing suits that appeared permanently rumpled. Schmalensee stood tall, erect and broad shouldered, and he wore finely tailored suits. In a phrase, he looked corporate, as befits the dean of a business school, M.I.T.'s Sloan School of Management.

Still, despite differences in appearance, Fisher and Schmalensee were both polished courtroom performers, men who had spent thick portions of their professional lives being expert witnesses for hire. Schmalensee was the newer model. Later in the trial, the Justice Department would try to make an issue of the fact that Microsoft was paying him $800 an hour for his trial work and in all may have paid him as much as $250,000 in 1998 for his services. It was, of course, sheer grandstanding for the news media. Attacking an expert witness for being handsomely paid recalls Claude Rains's Vichy police chief in "Casablanca" saying, "I'm shocked, shocked, to find out there's gambling going on here."

Schmalensee got the Microsoft job because he was a blue-chip economist for hire. He had been a member of the President's Council of Economic Advisers during the Bush administration and a consultant to many corporations and public agencies over the years, including the Justice Department and the Federal Trade Commission.

And he had his work cut out for him in the Microsoft case. In his more than 300 pages of direct testimony, he took the shrewd tactic of leaving Microsoft's most controversial defense for last—that it is not a monopoly, and that further, even if it were a monopoly none of its business practices were violations of antitrust law. He focused mainly on the question of whether consumers had been harmed—a potential vulnerability in the government's case: If you can't prove current consumer harm or very likely consumer harm in the near future as a result of Microsoft's behavior, lay off. Schmalensee then proceeded to the heavy lifting, arguing that Microsoft was not a monopoly, by giving a lot of theoretical and statistical ornamentation to the company's familiar theme: We're under constant competitive threat from all quarters. Pay no attention to that 80 percent-plus share of the PC operating system market.

Both sides in the trial said that what happened in the courtroom was what counted, and that they didn't much concern themselves with the daily media coverage. Yet the coverage was closely reviewed each day by both the Government and Microsoft. It was a fleeting, unguarded moment involving Schmalensee that captured that fact. One evening, well after the trial session had ended for the day, he walked out a side door of the courtroom, down an all-but-deserted hallway, flanked by two colleagues,

"Well," he said to one of them, "we'll see how it spins."

Microsoft Puts Its First Witness On the Stand

The Microsoft Corporation began its defense in the Government's anti-trust lawsuit today with an economist from the Massachusetts Institute of Technology bearing a massive tome of written testimony with a simple message: Microsoft's business practices are good for consumers, and any Government meddling with the software industry would likely do more harm than good.

The 328-page testimony by Richard L. Schmalensee of M.I.T. is a sweeping rebuttal to the Justice Department's two-and-a-half-month attempt to prove that Microsoft used its monopoly in personal computer operating system software to thwart competitive challenges posed by the rise of the Internet.

The Government's case, Mr. Schmalensee wrote in his direct testimony, amounts to "speculation" based on a "morass of e-mails" from Microsoft executives that at first glance may seem damaging, but are not.

Forget the atmospherics, he tells the court, and focus on the outcome—what he insists is a lack of measurable harm, current or future, to consumers from Microsoft's business practices.

"Proper economic inquiry into whether a company is engaged in anticompetitive conduct should end if it concludes that consumers have not been harmed by the conduct at issue and are not likely to be harmed in the future," Mr. Schmalensee wrote.

High and rising product prices are typically the litmus test of whether a monopolist has the power to punish competitors and gouge consumers. The Government's evidence shows that Microsoft has increased the price it charges personal computer makers for its Windows operating system in recent years, even as the prices of other components of computer systems have declined. Still, the cost of Windows accounts for less than 5 percent of the price of a typical personal computer—not really evidence of the kind of price–gouging normally associated with a monopolist, as some economists have noted.

In his testimony, Mr. Schmalensee describes the suit by the Justice Department and 19 states as "fundamentally inconsistent."

The Government asserts, he notes, that Microsoft has an enduring monopoly because its Windows operating system controls the basic operations on more than 90 percent of personal computers sold, and that barriers to entry in that market are high. On the other hand, he adds, the Government says that Microsoft invested hundreds of millions of dollars because it was scared of losing its dominance to an upstart maker of Internet browser software, the Netscape Communications Corporation.

"What is striking about the late-night e-mails and the almost frantic concern over competitive threats is that they show that Microsoft itself was extremely insecure about its leadership in operating systems," Mr. Schmalensee said.

David Boies, the Justice Department's lead trial lawyer, replies that Microsoft was indeed deeply worried and "did work to improve its software, but it also had its thumb on the scale."

The Government has made several allegations against Microsoft, but a central one is that the company used its market power to prod personal computer makers, Internet service suppliers and Internet programmers to enter into "exclusionary" contracts that limited the distribution and promotion of Netscape's rival browsing software.

The Microsoft defense, again, is that the outcome in the marketplace shows that Netscape could and did widely distribute many millions of copies of its browser despite Microsoft's purportedly anticompetitive business practices. In the last two years, Mr. Schmalensee notes, Netscape has gained an additional 14 million users of its browsing software.

But to gain these 14 million users, the Government replies, Netscape distributed about 200 million copies of its browsing software at considerable extra cost, even as Microsoft gave away its browser for free and bundled it with Windows.

Such Microsoft tactics, the Justice Department asserts, are part of a pattern of predatory practices intended to stifle competition. Mr. Schmalensee counters that Microsoft's contracts requiring personal computer makers to ship the company's browser with Windows "offer more choices to consumers" and are "therefore pro-competitive."

His testimony is an advocate's brief, so Mr. Schmalensee, like the 12 prosecution witnesses, seems to interpret the evidence to suit his argument. For example, when the experience of America Online Inc. supports the Justice Department, Mr. Schmalensee refers to the leading on-line services company as "Microsoft's fickle partner and bitter rival."

But roughly 200 pages later in his testimony, Mr. Schmalensee cites America Online's success against Microsoft's MSN on-line service as proof that bundled placement on the Windows desktop screen—an advantage MSN enjoyed since 1995—does not thwart rival products from being distributed. America Online, Mr. Schmalensee writes, "skillfully exploited the many distribution channels open to it (or any other competitor) to beat MSN."

Far from being the most valuable real estate in cyberspace, Mr. Schmalensee declares, the Windows desktop is not an "even particularly important channel of distribution"—a view not held by Microsoft executives, according to several internal e-mail messages in evidence.

Mr. Schmalensee also attacks the Government's case for trying to apply outdated "textbook models of competition" and "chalk board theories" to the fast-changing facts of the software industry.

The Government replies that the economist's stance amounts to trying to get an antitrust exemption for Microsoft and the software business. "He is very close to saying you should never intervene in dynamic, high-technology industries," said Daniel Rubinfeld, a senior economic adviser to the Justice Department's antitrust division.

JANUARY 11, 1999

M.I.T. Economist Sees Microsoft Market Under Siege

In the Microsoft trial today, a Justice Department lawyer opened cross-examination of the company's first witness by asking him to concede that Microsoft held a monopoly in personal-computer operating systems.

But although the witness, Richard L. Schmalensee, an economist at the Massachusetts Institute of Technology, had submitted 328 pages of written testimony addressing every aspect of the Government's antitrust case, he said he had never studied the market for personal-computer operating systems, because "I didn't see any particular purpose in investigating that question."

Mr. Schmalensee depicted Microsoft today as a company striving to hold onto a fragile lock on the market, at one point even suggesting that the operating system used in the Palm Pilot personal organizer posed a serious potential threat to Microsoft's Windows.

That prompted incredulity from Mr. Boies, leading Mr. Schmalensee to say: "Is it a significant competitor today? No. But it is a germ of a potential competitor."

Mr. Schmalensee has served as a paid consultant and expert witness for Microsoft since 1992, leading Mr. Boies to suggest that he was Microsoft's "house economist." Mr. Boies offered excerpts from Mr. Schmalensee's testimony in a previous case as evidence, attempting to show that Mr. Schmalensee offered whatever position best served the case at hand.

Testifying last fall in a suit in

which Bristol Technology, a software company based in Danbury, Conn., was trying to establish that it competed with Microsoft, Mr. Schmalensee had said: "In that view of the world, essentially everybody that is writing software is competing with everybody else. And I just don't think that's useful."

That apparent contradiction stirred Judge Thomas Penfield Jackson to tell the witness, "What I'm trying to determine here is whether what you say here is consistent with what you said in that case."

Mr. Schmalensee said it was consistent because the issues were different. Bristol, he said, made a program for software programmers that did not compete with Windows.

But Mr. Schmalensee listed two small niche operating systems that he argued posed a threat to Microsoft: Linux and Be-OS.

"I think these are important not because they are a competitive threat today, but because they show that entering the operating system market is possible," he said. "And there will be others."

The judge then asked him if the tiny companies that make these systems were making any money. "I would be stunned if they were making any serious money," Mr. Schmalensee responded.

In his written testimony, Mr. Schmalensee said: "A firm with monopoly power over the operating system would charge at least 16 times over what Microsoft charges."

Under that formula, Microsoft would charge computer makers about $800 for each copy of Windows—the price of entire computers systems with Windows today.

JANUARY 13, 1999

Microsoft Witness Attacked For Contradictory Opinions

A Justice Department lawyer produced several prominent academic papers today that he said showed that the Microsoft Corporation's first witness in its antitrust trial had written opinions contradicting views he has offered in expert testimony for the software giant.

In a broad attack on the witness, Richard L. Schmalensee, an economist at the Massachusetts Institute of Technology, David Boies, the Government's lead trial lawyer, produced evidence that a survey cited by Mr. Schmalensee in his testimony actually appeared to be a publicity tool ginned up by Microsoft's chairman, William H. Gates.

In Mr. Schmalensee's direct testimony, he wrote that in a recent survey of software developers, "85 percent predicted that Microsoft's integration of Internet functions into Windows would help their company, and 83 percent predicted it would help consumers." He cited the figures to support his own advocacy of those positions.

"Did you ever look at that survey, find out what its purpose was?" Mr. Boies asked. When Mr. Schmalensee said he had not, Mr. Boies

Judge Thomas Penfield Jackson knew little about technology and had presided over only two antitrust trials before the Microsoft case landed in his courtroom. But he proved to be a fast learner and won plaudits for his handling of the trial.

William H. Gates, Microsoft's chairman, was the unseen director of his company's defense. His sullen and obdurate peformance during a videotaped deposition that was played during the first day in court set the stage for the rest of the trial, raising credibility questions in the judge's mind for the rest of Microsoft's witnesses.

Jim Barksdale, Netscape's chairman, got the government
investigation of Microsoft going in 1996. Angered by Microsoft's
attempts to squeeze Netscape out of the market, he asked a
company lawyer to prepare a white paper describing Microsoft's
tactics. That paper led to the opening of a Justice Department
investigation of Microsoft.

John Warden, a partner at the elite New York law firm Sullivan & Cromwell, was the lead trial lawyer for Microsoft. He called the government's use of excerpts from the videotaped deposition of the Microsoft chairman a transparent effort to "demonize Bill Gates."

David Boies said he'd never had a case that gave him as many opportunities to embarrass hostile witnesses as the Microsoft case presented. He so thoroughly discredited Microsoft's witnesses that, when it was all over, Judge Jackson said he found them unbelievable.

Microsoft's legal team was unable to keep up with the cascading series of failures and embarrassments in court. From left to right were lawyers David Heiner and Richard Urowsky, spokesman Jim Cullinan, lead counsel William Neukom, spokesman Mark Murray and lawyer Steve Holley.

Attorney General Janet Reno, left, gave approval to file suit against Microsoft in April 1998. In the middle, Joel Klein, head of the Justice Department's antitrust division, was in charge of the federal case. On the right is Tom Miller, attorney general of Iowa, who was more involved in the case than any other state attorney general.

When Joel Klein got Netscape's white paper saying Microsoft was forcing computer makers to take Internet Explorer along with Windows, he said he realized immediately that the alleged problem was bigger than had turned up in recent years. "To me," he said, "conditioning one product on another was clearly a violation of the consent decree."

William Neukom, Microsoft's chief counsel, saw nothing but empty charges from competitors in the government's suit. In court, he sat at the head of the defense table every day, and he presided over the company team during settlement negotiations. He called the last proposal for conduct restrictions "way over the top."

asked, "Did anyone ever tell you that the purpose was to give Mr. Gates helpful information to use at a Senate hearing" early last year?

Then Mr. Boies produced an e-mail message in which Mr. Gates wrote last February, "It would HELP ME IMMENSELY to have a survey showing that 90 percent of developers believe that putting the browser into the operating system makes sense," adding, "Ideally we would have a survey before I appear at the Senate on March 3rd."

In a subsequent string of e-mail messages, Microsoft employees laid out how they would pose the questions to get the responses Mr. Gates wanted.

Mr. Schmalensee said that had he known the origin of the polling information, he would have cited the figures in his testimony anyway, though he might have added "an explanatory phrase."

On Wednesday and today, Mr. Schmalensee argued at length that Linux, a free Unix-based operating system, posed a significant near-term threat to Windows, the Microsoft operating system that is shipped on more than on 90 percent of all new computers. He said he came to this conclusion largely from reading newspaper and magazine articles, particularly the computer trade press.

With that, Mr. Boies introduced into evidence an article from *PC Week On Line* last June in which Mr. Gates, in an interview, said that Linux posed no threat to Windows.

"I've never had a customer mention Linux to me," he said.

Mr. Schmalensee said Mr. Gates's statement "is at least interpretable as a marketing statement."

Mr. Schmalensee testified that the small competitors nipping at Microsoft's operating system business should be considered serious threats. And he said that their existence showed that the barriers to entry into the operating system market were not high, so Microsoft should not be viewed as a monopoly power.

But in an article in the Antitrust Law Journal in 1997, Mr. Schmalensee wrote: "A clear signal of low barriers to entry is provided only by effective, viable entry" into the market "that takes a nontrivial market share. There is a substantial difference between toehold entry and substantial entry that provides real pressure on established firms' profits."

Mr. Schmalensee acknowledged under questioning that no competitor to Microsoft had ever met that test. Still, he argued, Microsoft had behaved and spent research and development money as if it did face competitive threats, particularly from the International Business Machines Corporation, which introduced the unsuccessful OS/2 operating system almost 10 years ago. That, he suggested, put pressure on Microsoft's profits, meeting one of his tests.

"I discussed this with Mr. Gates," he said. "He told me about the time when cooperation between Microsoft and IBM ended; IBM said effectively: 'We will bury you.' He took that threat very seriously."

JANUARY 14, 1999

Browsers and Borders Are Argued
At the Microsoft Trial

In the Microsoft antitrust trial, the Government spent most of today attacking the company's central defense—that its Internet browsing software is a seamless feature of its Windows operating system and not a stand-alone product. The Government is trying to prove that the browser and operating system are wo products, illegally bundled together mainly to stifle competition.

But the Justice Department and 19 states suing the Microsoft Corporation face an uphill struggle to confirm that allegation. In a related case, a Federal appeals court ruled last June that Microsoft had virtually unlimited freedom to include anything it wanted in its products. The decision pointedly noted the "undesirability of having courts oversee product design."

In the current trial, Judge Thomas Penfield Jackson of United States District Court is not necessarily bound by the appeals court ruling. But it does suggest that the Government must make some very convincing arguments to prevail.

David Boies, the lead trial lawyer for the Justice Department, spent hours today trying to show that Microsoft's position on the issue was contradicted by the company's own internal documents and by common sense. Using other products as examples to illustrate his point, Mr. Boies insisted that it was possible to do what Microsoft says is nearly impossible—draw a bound-ary line in software code, separating one product from another.

Microsoft, Mr. Boies said, could do the same thing with its popular word-processing program, Word, as it did with its Internet Explorer browser. "But the mere fact that two programs share some software code—and a company can make it difficult to disentangle that code"— by no means proved that they were a single product, Mr. Boies said.

Mr. Boies directed question after question at Microsoft's first witness, Richard L. Schmalensee, an economist who is the dean of the Sloan School of Management at the Massachusetts Institute of Technology.

The Justice Department lawyer noted that even Michael Dertouzos, the director of M.I.T.'s Computer Science Laboratory—who was initially on Microsoft's witness list but was later dropped—had testified in a deposition that he considered the browser an application program, separate from the operating system.

Mr. Schmalensee held his ground, however, cautioning the court against immersing itself too deeply in software code. "One thing this industry teaches is that the borders between products vary over time as technology advances," he said.

At another point, he explained that he did not give "any particular weight" to the testimony from expert witnesses that the browser and operating system were separate products. "Testimony as to the way things are," Mr. Schmalensee said, should not be binding in determining "guidelines that are going to affect the evolution of this industry"—a nod to the expectation that whatever the verdict for Microsoft, the case will have a far-reaching effect on the nation's high-technology economy.

The Government argues that Microsoft's decisions to bundle its browser with Windows and to place contract restrictions on personal computer makers add up to anti-competitive behavior.

Pursuing that line, Mr. Boies asked Mr. Schmalensee if Microsoft had bundled its browser with Windows in part to increase the distribu-

tion of its browser. "It certainly had that effect," the witness replied.

Next, Mr. Boies asked if one purpose for the bundling was to make it more difficult for a Microsoft rival, the Netscape Communications Corporation, to distribute its browser.

"Yes," Mr. Schmalensee replied, "but that would have happened anyway. Competition would have plausibly raised Netscape's distribution costs."

"Competition on the merits can raise rivals' costs," he added, "but that says nothing about anticompetitive effects."

JANUARY 19, 1999

U.S. Presents Documents In Case Against Microsoft

The Government presented documents and e-mail in the Microsoft trial today as evidence for its allegation that the big software maker had imposed contract restrictions on personal computer makers to thwart competition.

The contracts imposed strict limits on Windows' opening "desktop," the screen that computer users see when they turn on their computers. These limits clearly upset some manufacturers who wanted to use the desktop to display their own brands or to feature factory-installed software—often made by Microsoft's competitors.

In a memo to the Microsoft Corporation, an executive at the Hewlett-Packard Company complained about the restraints and

concluded that if his company had any alternative to loading Microsoft's Windows operating system, "you would not be our supplier of choice."

Microsoft began imposing the restrictions in 1996, saying it had the legal right to do so and adding that the curbs helped consumers by insuring a "uniform Windows experience." But 1996 was also when Microsoft was struggling to catch up to the early leader in the Internet software market, the Netscape Communications Corporation, which pioneered the browser software used to navigate the World Wide Web.

At one point in court today, the Government also addressed the fact that on Tuesday, Microsoft reported a 75 percent jump in quarterly earnings, well ahead of expectations on Wall Street. David Boies, the lead trial lawyer for the Justice Department, mentioned the earnings report in his cross-examination of the company's leadoff witness and asked if consistently high profits were an indicator of monopoly power.

The witness, Richard L. Schmalensee, an economist and dean of the Massachusetts Institute of Technology's Sloan School of Management, conceded that persistently high profits suggest "some impediment to competitive alternatives." But such a barrier, he added quickly, could well be a very valuable asset, protected by intellectual property rights, like Microsoft's industry-standard Windows operating system.

"You simply cannot infer monopoly power from profits," Mr. Schmalensee said.

The Government contends that Microsoft's contracts were mainly intended to unfairly damage Netscape, not to benefit consumers. Microsoft used its monopoly power in the operating system market, the Government charges, to force computer makers to restrict how they could promote Netscape's browser.

To make that point, the Government cited a number of documents, including a Jan. 5, 1996, e-mail memo in which William H. Gates, the Microsoft chairman, stressed that increasing the company's browser share was a "very, very important goal." He also complained that some PC makers were displaying competing browsers on their machines "in a FAR more prominent way" than Microsoft's Internet Explorer.

Later that month, an executive review of Microsoft's sales to PC makers during the previous six months noted that one of its missed opportunities was failing to impose "control over start-up screens."

Yet by May 1998, Microsoft was weighing dropping the contract curbs on some major PC makers in response to their complaints, and it later did. An internal e-mail written by Brad Chase, a Microsoft executive, however, noted that the reaction from the company's "antitrust team was negative." He continued, "Changes like this undermine our whole defense of Windows Experience."

Asked later about the profit margins Microsoft enjoyed on its operating system sales, Mr. Schmalensee replied that was difficult to determine precisely and that the company's internal accounting systems were not all that sophisticated.

Microsoft, he said, records "operating system sales by hand on sheets of paper." Since that struck many in the courtroom as odd for a leading producer of data-base and financial-spreadsheet software, people laughed aloud in the courtroom. Later, Microsoft executives said Mr. Schmalensee probably misspoke.

"What you saw in there," said William Neukom, Microsoft's senior vice president for law and corporate affairs, "was a trial lawyer looking for an exit line."

JANUARY 20, 1999

Microsoft and the Question of Monopoly

The judge in the Microsoft antitrust trial asked the company's expert witness on economics a series of skeptical questions today, suggesting that the Microsoft Corporation may have a difficult time with one of its defenses—that it does not have a monopoly in the market for personal computer operating systems.

Judge Thomas Penfield Jackson interrupted when a Microsoft lawyer was questioning Richard L. Schmalensee, an economist and dean of the Massachusetts Institute of Technology's Sloan School of Management, about the price Microsoft charges for its industry-standard Windows operating system.

Mr. Schmalensee was explaining his view that the modest price Microsoft charges for Windows, typically less than 5 percent of the cost of a personal computer, indicated a company concerned about current and potential competition instead of the predatory monopolist the Government has tried to paint for the court.

But Judge Jackson cut in to ask if there could be sound business reasons that even a monopolist might charge less today "in search of larger glory at some later date."

To illustrate his point, the judge spoke of the hypothetical case of a cigarette company that might keep its prices low to hook generations of future smokers and customers.

"There isn't any indication," Mr. Schmalensee replied, "that Windows is that kind of addiction."

Judge Jackson seemed unconvinced. "Do you have kids?" he asked Mr. Schmalensee.

Yes, the M.I.T. dean replied, "but not all kids use Windows, Your Honor. Some use Macs," a reference to Apple Computer Inc.'s Macintosh machines, which run the Mac operating system.

The judge's occasional questions are scrutinized by both sides as a possible clue to his thinking. This is not a jury trial, so at least at the Federal district court level, Judge Jackson will determine the outcome of the case. Legal experts say that queries from the bench do not foreshadow a verdict but do suggest the issues a judge is focusing on when weighing testimony.

Whether Microsoft has a monopoly in the market for personal computer operating systems is not directly at issue in this case. The Justice Department and 19 states are not suing Microsoft for having a monopoly but for illegally using its market muscle to defend and extend the reach of its monopoly.

Still, if Microsoft can convince the court that it is not a monopoly, the Government's case collapses.

Under questioning from Richard Urowsky, a Microsoft lawyer, Mr. Schmalensee explained that his key assumption in explaining the company's business practices—its pricing, investment spending and deals—is that it lives in an industry characterized by "dynamic competition."

Unlike old smokestack industries, Mr. Schmalensee said, the software business requires even the incumbent leaders to move quickly, to keep prices low and to innovate continually. "Microsoft is constantly concerned with being displaced as a leader," he said.

The Government argues that Microsoft's behavior is that of a modern monopolist. It is in a fast-moving high-technology business, the Government concedes, but its monopoly position is nonetheless resilient partly because of the reluctance of consumers to switch operating systems once they have taken the time and trouble to figure out Windows, which runs on more than 90 percent of personal computers sold. This kind of self-reinforcing dependency—"high switching costs," in economic terms—was what Judge Jackson was alluding to with his cigarette-monopoly example.

The Justice Department has introduced documents showing that some PC makers complained when Microsoft imposed new contract restrictions in 1996 that limited their freedom to do as they please with the first desktop screen that appears when users turn on their machines. The PC makers would prefer a free hand in selling that valuable commercial real estate to software makers, including Microsoft's rivals, to load their icons.

But Mr. Schmalensee testified that those restrictions were mostly modest, such as limiting the size of icons that can be displayed. Microsoft, he added, typically uses for its own software seven of the available 49 spaces for desktop icons.

"There is lots of room for PC makers to put on other icons, so Microsoft does not limit software distribution through the desktop," Mr. Schmalensee said.

JANUARY 21, 1999

Paul Maritz was the most senior Microsoft executive to take the stand at the trial, and in a sense, he was the company's lead character witness. At the time, Maritz, a group vice president,

Paul Maritz
MICROSOFT

was regarded as the Number 3 executive at Microsoft, after Bill Gates and Steve Ballmer. Neither Gates nor Ballmer testified in court, so it fell to Maritz to defend the company in the trial.

He was an appropriate choice, a central character in many of the decisions under dispute in the case, an executive whose name was on so much of the e-mail submitted as evidence. "The key products in this case were directly under his control, and Paul Maritz knew exactly what was happening," observed David Yoffie, a professor at the Harvard business school and coauthor of "Competing on Internet Time," a book cited as evidence by both sides in the trial. "Maritz is the person who executed the Internet strategy. He is the man."

Microsoft has been called an "irony-free zone," but the burly,

43-year-old Maritz was an exception. Born in Zimbabwe (then Southern Rhodesia), he was raised on his family's cattle ranch, which did not have electricity 24 hours a day. He was educated in South Africa, then at the University of St. Andrew in Scotland. With his family background and British-influenced education, Maritz acquired a delightfully sardonic, dark sense of humor.

In a conversation in Washington the day before he took the stand, Maritz, who once handled his company's contentious partnership with IBM, said he admired the way Big Blue had remade itself after its travails in the early 1990's—then quickly added, "Of course, as Dr. Johnson said, there's nothing like the sight of the gallows to focus the mind."

In July 1999, Maritz announced he was stepping down as a group vice president to spend more time with software developers and to go back to writing code himself. How long he would stay at Microsoft was uncertain. Many of Microsoft's leading executives had felt the tug of other interests in their 40's. For Maritz, the years at Microsoft, which he joined from Intel in 1986, had been rewarding indeed. In the fall of 1999, Forbes estimated his net worth at $650 million.

Executive's Testimony Attacks Accusers

The most senior executive of the Microsoft Corporation to testify at its antitrust trial delivered an unflinching defense of the company's practices today and an attack on the testimony of industry executives who appeared as Government witnesses.

In 160 pages of written testimony, Paul Maritz, a group vice president at Microsoft, described the software industry as one of fierce competition and relentless change, creating wealth and benefiting consumers. And he warned of the danger of Government meddling.

It would set a "very bad precedent," he wrote, "if a rule were established, ostensibly with the objective of promoting competition, that actually impeded efforts to compete through product improvement."

But Mr. Maritz reserved his most forceful and detailed testimony for trying to discredit the courtroom accounts of executives from the Netscape Communications Corporation, the Intel Corporation and Apple Computer Inc.

In the case of Intel, Mr. Maritz described the relationship between the two companies as a highly productive partnership of equals, with occasional disputes that "become intense from time to time."

The intense disputes in the antitrust case involved mainly Intel's work on Internet and multimedia software and its support for Netscape, Microsoft's rival and the pioneer in software used to browse the World Wide Web. Intel's main business is producing microprocessors, the brains of PC's, but it also develops some software.

The Justice Department and 19 states say Microsoft bullied Intel into shelving software work that conflicted with Microsoft's plans and to curb its support for Netscape's technology.

To bend Intel to its will, the Government charges, Microsoft threatened to withhold software support for a new generation of Intel microprocessors. Because more than 90 percent of PC's run Microsoft's Windows operating system, any threat to withhold Windows support for a microprocessor could severely damage Intel.

In his testimony, Mr. Maritz describes Intel's software work as second-rate development that "often falls below the high quality standards of Microsoft software." The temporary delay in support for Intel's MMX chip in 1995, Mr. Maritz says, was actually Intel's fault, resulting from what Microsoft regarded as the chip maker's overly zealous approach to intellectual property claims.

Mr. Maritz also attacked the credibility of Steven McGeady, the Intel executive who appeared as a Government witness. Mr. McGeady testified that in a private meeting in September 1995, Mr. Maritz described Microsoft's strategy toward Netscape as seeking to "cut off their air supply"—by giving away free the

Microsoft browser, while Netscape's business depended on selling its browser.

In his testimony, Mr. Maritz wrote, "I never said, in the presence of Intel personnel or otherwise, that Microsoft would 'cut off Netscape's air supply' or words to that effect."

Later, Mr. Maritz characterized Mr. McGeady as having a deep-seated bias against Microsoft—a witness whose accusations "speak volumes about his attitude toward Microsoft and the credibility of his testimony."

The personal assault on Mr. McGeady's testimony could be risky, some legal experts say, by inviting the court to choose whom to believe—the Intel executive or Mr. Maritz. If Mr. Maritz seems less convincing, the credibility of his own testimony is in doubt.

In one e-mail already in evidence, Mr. Maritz wrote that Mr. McGeady posed a problem in getting Intel to curb its support for a competing Internet technology, adding, "Unfortunately he has more I.Q. than most there."

Mr. Maritz strongly disputes the Government's allegation that Microsoft forced Apple to make Microsoft's Internet Explorer its main browser by threatening to stop developing its Office productivity programs for Apple's Macintosh systems.

The reluctance to continue developing word processing, spreadsheet and other programs for the Macintosh, Mr. Maritz wrote, was that in 1996 and 1997 Apple seemed on the verge of failure. Many within the company, including Mr. Maritz, believed that Microsoft's software developers could be better used writing programs that promised higher sales.

Mr. Maritz cites an e-mail written in November 1996 by the head of Office development to William H. Gates, the Microsoft chairman. The Macintosh "is perceived as in decay," the testimony quotes from the e-mail. "There is broad resistance within the ranks to doing this release," which was Mac Office 97.

Another source of friction between the two companies, Mr. Maritz wrote, was a long-running patent dispute. At the time, Apple's management contended that Microsoft's Windows and other programs used intellectual property protected by Apple patents and sought $1.2 billion to settle the matter—a contention Microsoft regarded as outlandish, Mr. Maritz wrote.

But soon after Steven Jobs took over as interim chief executive in July 1997, the patent claims, the Office development issue and others were settled. On Aug. 5, 1997, Microsoft announced a deal in which it invested $150 million in Apple, the patent issue was settled for an additional undisclosed payment, Microsoft agreed to develop Mac Office and Apple agreed to make Internet Explorer its preferred browser.

Internet Explorer, Mr. Maritz testified, was not viewed as a key part of the Apple-Microsoft pact.

JANUARY 22, 1999

At Microsoft Trial, Accounts Differ on Dealings With Apple

The Justice Department's lead lawyer in the Microsoft antitrust case clashed today with the company's highest-ranking witness as the Government charged that the software maker had used its market power as "a club" in its dealings with Apple Computer Inc., while the Microsoft executive countered that his company was responding to a threat of "patent terrorism" from Apple.

The conflicting accounts of how Microsoft convinced Apple to make Microsoft's Internet software the preferred choice over that of its browser rival, the Netscape Communications Corporation, was the main focus of the Government's early cross-examination of Paul Maritz, a Microsoft group vice president, who took the stand this afternoon.

But David Boies, the Justice Department's lead trial lawyer, also questioned Mr. Maritz sharply on what he said to an executive of the Intel Corporation and about Microsoft's intentions toward Netscape.

After weeks of dry testimony from economic experts for both sides, the trial shifted into a higher gear, taking on the some of the feel of a legal prize fight. Mr. Boies is a leading trial litigator, and Mr. Maritz is the stand-in at the trial for his boss, William H. Gates, the

Microsoft chairman. Both sides, it seemed, scored a few points this afternoon in a cross-examination that will continue on Tuesday.

Throughout the trial, the Government has shown excerpts of Mr. Gates's videotaped deposition, taken last year, showing him to be combative, evasive and forgetful. Mr. Maritz presents a different face of Microsoft, answering questions in his deep baritone, directly, with clipped precision.

Put simply, he contends that there is nothing in evidence that really shows the company did anything other than compete vigorously to bring consumers better products.

In his cross-examination, Mr. Boies is seeking to discredit Microsoft's story and to raise doubts about the credibility of its leading corporate witness.

Mr. Boies introduced a series of internal Microsoft e-mail to try to show that the company's current account of its thinking in negotiating a deal with Apple is very different from the language of its own documents in 1996 and 1997.

The Government contends that Microsoft used the threat of no longer developing its Office productivity software for the Macintosh—the most widely used applications software on Apple machines—as a way to insure that Apple favored Microsoft's Internet Explorer. Microsoft replies that the main consideration in an August 1997 deal with Apple—which continued Office development and gave Microsoft's browser preferential status—was to settle a lingering patent dispute with Apple.

Mr. Boies presented Mr. Maritz with a series of e-mails, including one from Mr. Gates to Mr. Maritz on June 23, 1996, identifying "two key goals" in dealing with Apple. One was to keep a high share of the market for applications software on Macintosh machines, and the second, Mr. Gates wrote, was to "get them to embrace our Internet Explorer in some way."

Mr. Gates did mention the patent issue in the e-mail, but only as an aside later in the message.

Mr. Maritz replied to that e-mail, and other similar messages, by saying that resolving the patent issue was an underlying theme in all negotiations with Apple. "He didn't have to tell me," he said of one message from Mr. Gates. "It was a constant refrain that unless we settle the patent issue nothing else goes forward."

For years, Apple had contended that Microsoft's industry-standard Windows operating system and Office programs violated Apple's patent rights. With Apple's fortunes declining sharply, Mr. Maritz said, Microsoft feared that Apple would try to cash in with a desperate patent suit, possibly seeking an injunction to stop Microsoft from shipping its main products, Windows and Office.

"We were concerned what in the industry is called patent terrorism," Mr. Maritz testified. "You're dealing with a company in danger of going out of business, and there is no way of using your patents in defense because they essentially have no business left."

Mr. Boies also questioned Mr.

Maritz sharply on whether he ever told a group of Intel executives that Microsoft's plan for competing with Netscape was to "cut off their air supply" and that "everything they're selling, we're going to give away for free."

Earlier in the trial, an Intel executive testified that Mr. Maritz had made that statement in a meeting with Intel executives in September 1995. But in his written trial testimony, released last Friday, Mr. Maritz denied ever saying any such thing.

Mr. Boies presented Mr. Maritz with his deposition testimony taken last October. When asked about the comment, Mr. Maritz replied that "it's possible but I just don't recall."

Mr. Maritz said he sharpened his denial after reviewing the matter in preparation for his trial appearance. Mr. Boies replied that the quotation appeared in an article in The New York Times in January 1998, long before his deposition was taken.

Yes, Mr. Maritz replied, but added that back then it was not attributed to him but only to "a Microsoft executive." In fact, the article in The Times, on Jan. 12, 1998, quoted an Intel executive who attributed the remark to Mr. Maritz by name.

JANUARY 25, 1999

Microsoft Official Says Company Sought Cooperation

A senior executive of the Microsoft Corporation testified today that his company tried to convince its main rival in the Internet software market to become less of a head-on competitor.

Paul Maritz, the highest-ranking executive appearing as a witness at the Microsoft antitrust trial, portrayed the discussions with the Netscape Communications Corporation in 1995 as mainly an effort to find "common ground" between the two companies.

David Boies, the Justice Department's lead trial lawyer, presented several Microsoft e-mails written shortly before the Netscape meeting saying that Microsoft wanted to make sure Netscape's software for browsing the World Wide Web did not become a technology "platform" for which software programmers would write applications—making it a potential alternative to Microsoft's industry-standard Windows operating system.

In a June 1, 1995, e-mail, one Microsoft executive identified key goals as "move Netscape out" of Internet browser software for future versions of Windows and to "avoid a cold or hot war with Netscape," adding, "Keep them from sabotaging our platform evolution."

When asked to comment on this e-mail and others, Mr. Maritz replied, "We clearly had an agenda for making certain technologies common in the industry."

But in some of the sharpest questioning since the trial began last

October, Mr. Boies persistently asked an elusive Mr. Maritz about the implications of Microsoft's proposal. If Netscape had agreed to shift its focus away from software that Microsoft deemed mainstream to its strategic interests, he asked, would Netscape have become a "less significant platform threat?"

That, Mr. Maritz conceded, was partly true. "At one level, yes," he said. But he noted Microsoft was mainly trying to get Netscape to agree to Microsoft's preferred set of basic Internet technologies and nothing in their talks would have prevented Netscape from competing in other Internet-related software, including multimedia software, groupware and Java, an Internet programming language.

The result, he said, could have been that Netscape would have become an even more formidable rival. If Netscape had focused less on the browser and more on software and services that compete less directly with Microsoft, for example, Mr. Maritz said Netscape might have a "much more entrenched position within large corporations today."

In short, Mr. Maritz said the result of Microsoft's proposal might have been to reduce competition in certain niches of the software business, but not to diminish competition overall.

William H. Neukom, Microsoft's senior vice president for law and corporate affairs, said words matter less than actions in antitrust law. "After that meeting," he said, "there was full-fledged competition between Microsoft and Netscape."

Yet the Government replies that the head-to-head competition occurred only after Netscape rejected Microsoft's proposal. After the afternoon court session, Mr. Boies said, "It is significant for our case that Microsoft has admitted seeking to persuade Netscape not to engage in platform competition."

In the morning, the Government tried to raise questions about the credibility of Microsoft's current legal stance by accusing the company of engaging in a "concerted effort" to alter the words used to describe Internet software internally and in its public statements to suit the company's legal stance.

The Government pointed to company e-mail from early last year that said Microsoft had to make sure that the word "browser" was no longer used in referring to its Internet browsing software and that the "legal staff" be brought in to check the language.

The wording plays a role in the case because the Government contends that the software maker bundled its Internet Explorer browser into its Windows operating system to thwart competition in the Internet software market.

Microsoft replies that since the rise of the Internet the company had always planned to fold the software used to browse the World Wide Web into its operating system. The browser, Microsoft insists, is merely a feature of the operating system and not a stand-alone product.

In an e-mail in February 1998, a Microsoft executive, wrote that "saying 'put the browser in the OS' is already a statement that is prejudicial to us," and went on, "The name 'browser' suggests a separate thing." (OS stands for operating system.)

In another e-mail in February 1998, a Microsoft executive reported "good progress" in cleaning up the wording used on the company's Web site. "We don't refer to it as a product or even a browser," he wrote. "It's browsing software."

By early 1998, Microsoft was already being sued by the Justice Department in a related case concerning a 1995 antitrust consent decree. Mr. Maritz emphasized that the change in the approved corporate vernacular was mainly to clearly explain the consumer benefits of tightly integrating the browser with the operating system.

Still, Mr. Maritz said the legal environment also played a role, necessitating the use of "more precise language" as "this set of events was heating up."

JANUARY 26, 1999

As he stepped onto the stage, Jim Allchin seemed like Microsoft's dream witness—nonthreatening, soft spoken, a gentle looking man, tall with prematurely white hair and a disarming smile. Allchin, a very senior executive, just didn't fit the bullying monopolist image in which the government had cast Microsoft.

James Allchin
MICROSOFT

Allchin ran the division that produced the Windows operating system. Windows wasn't just Microsoft's most important product; it was at the heart of every allegation in the government's case. Windows was the glue that held Microsoft together—and the invincible weapon, the plaintiffs charged, that Microsoft wielded whenever it faced a competitive challenge.

Unlike many in his profession, Allchin held a doctorate in computer science. He graduated with an undergraduate degree in that discipline from the University of Florida in 1973 and worked for a few years at Texas Instruments, developing a general-purpose computer operating system. He earned a master's degree in computer science from Stanford and his doctorate from the Georgia Institute of Technology. He also helped design a network operating system at Banyan Systems before joining Microsoft in 1990, bringing clear expertise in computer operating systems.

Microsoft said Allchin was one of the executives who forced Bill Gates and others to focus on the Internet in the mid-1990s. And he was a member of the eight-man executive committee that ran the company. In the reorganization announced in the spring of 1999, Allchin was once again given a senior position.

Unfortunately for Allchin and his employers, the high hopes that accompanied him to the witness stand were quickly dashed.

Microsoft Official Defends Company's Strategy at Trial

A senior executive of the Microsoft Corporation delivered a forceful defense of the company's actions in the Internet software market today, saying it had acted mainly in the pursuit of a "Holy Grail of software development" by making its products more powerful, easier to use and seamlessly integrated.

The executive, James Allchin, the second company official to appear as a witness at the Microsoft antitrust trial, also argued that other software makers have done what the Government says is anticompetitive in Microsoft's case, and he presented a detailed history of his company's product plans for the Internet.

In his 139-page written testimony, Mr. Allchin repeatedly struck the theme that the Justice Department and the 19 states suing Microsoft are making an ill-advised effort to tamper with innovation and product design in a leading high-technology industry.

"I am not a lawyer or an economist," Mr. Allchin wrote, "but I do not understand how a company's efforts to improve its products can ever be 'anticompetitive.'"

The testimony of Mr. Allchin, a senior vice president in charge of the technical development of the company's Windows operating system, is a salvo in Microsoft's legal fight with the Government over how the lawsuit is framed, which is crucial to the outcome of the case.

Microsoft says its decision to bundle its Internet Explorer browser with its industry-standard Windows operating system and give the browser away free was a straightforward product-design decision that benefits consumers.

But the Government contends that those moves represent the abuse of Microsoft's monopoly power to thwart competition.

Most antitrust experts say that Microsoft's strongest defense is to frame the case as a debate over its product decisions. Indeed, in a related case, a Federal appeals court ruled last June that Microsoft had the right to bundle its browser with Windows, warning of "the undesirability of having courts oversee product design."

But the Government views Microsoft's bundling decision as simply one step in a pattern of what it regards as predatory business practices intended to stifle competition.

The prosecution case, according to antitrust experts, is strengthened by framing the courtroom debate around Microsoft's business practices and contracts.

JANUARY 28, 1999

U.S. Pushes to Get a Microsoft Defense to Boomerang

The Microsoft Corporation set out in Federal court this morning to demonstrate that computer users gain numerous benefits from the company's decision to integrate a Web browser with the Windows operating system, but by this afternoon the demonstration appeared to have backfired.

On cross-examination, James Allchin, a senior Microsoft executive, readily acknowledged that nearly all of the same benefits would be available to users who bought a version of Windows with no browser included and later installed Microsoft's browser separately.

For the Government, the acknowledgment seemed a landmark in the trial, since the foundation of Microsoft's defense rests on the assertion that Windows and Internet Explorer are one inseparable product.

David Boies, the Government's lead lawyer, clearly jubilant outside the courtroom this evening, said: "What we demonstrated today is that you don't have to weld the two together to get these benefits. You get exactly the same experience by combining two products, if that is what the customer wants, but the customer gets a choice."

Not surprisingly, Microsoft had a different take.

"Point by point, we demonstrated the facts that the Court of Appeals found when it ruled in our favor last year," said Mark Murray, a Microsoft spokesman. "And that is that consumers reap major benefits that cannot be achieved by simply adding Netscape on top of the operating system."

Ruling in a separate but related case last June, a three-judge panel for the United States Court of Appeals for the District of Columbia Circuit said Microsoft had the right to determine what features and functions to include in its operating system—as long as the combination "offers advantages unavailable" if a consumer purchased separate software products and combined them to achieve similar capabilities. Mr. Boies said today that he showed that Microsoft could meet the court's test by selling Windows and the browser separately.

"I think there is no benefit that we did not debunk today," he added.

As soon as Mr. Allchin, a senior vice president in charge of the technical development of the company's Windows operating system, took the stand this morning, Microsoft played several hours of videotaped demonstrations that Mr. Allchin had prepared. They carefully laid out the benefits that users gain from the inclusion of Web browsing software in Windows 98, hewing closely to the test that had been laid out in the Court of Appeals decision.

Among these advantages are the ability to look through files on the computer's hard drive and Internet Web pages, using the same software window, as well as the ability to call up Web pages from numerous places in Windows and display them as background on the computer screen.

These and other benefits are "capabilities that are only available through the deep integration of Internet technologies into the Windows operating system," one of the presenters on the videotape said. Among them, he noted, is one that allows users to get help on line, while users of older systems might have to "dig up documentation from the pile in the back of the closet."

But when the tapes had ended and Mr. Boies began cross-examining Mr. Allchin, he asked whether Microsoft offered its Web browser separately to people still using older versions of Windows 95 that did not come with the browser included.

Yes, Mr. Allchin said, and by loading this separate software package, "it becomes almost Windows 98."

Then Mr. Boies led Mr. Allchin back through his videotape, asking him point by point, 19 times, whether each benefit of integration could be obtained by buying Windows 95 with no browser installed, then separately acquiring the browser software and loading it on top.

Yes, Mr. Allchin acknowledged each time. "But you are playing semantic word games here," he said. "You are replacing core operating system files when you do this."

Mr. Boies then asked: "But it is entirely practical to deliver these two pieces of functionality separately, isn't it? All you're doing is offering a competitive product, and some consumers would choose it and some consumers would not."

Mr. Allchin did not get a chance to respond directly. But through the questions, he did doggedly maintain that "all you are doing is taking two pieces of Windows and putting them together."

FEBRUARY 2, 1999

Shadows of Higher Courts

While the Justice Department saw Jim Allchin's concessions about Windows 95 and Internet Explorer as terribly damaging, Microsoft doggedly maintained that David Boies's questions were meaningless. All the questions dealt with Windows 95 and the Internet Explorer upgrade that had been offered in 1997—the very products that were the subject of the previous Justice Department suit, filed against Microsoft in the fall of 1997. At that time, the government

am sure I would not have nailed the Allchin testimony as forcefully as I did if I had not known what the Court of Appeals had in mind."

He must have thought there was at least a reasonable chance that Judge Jackson would contradict Microsoft's favorite ruling.

U.S. Attacks a Microsoft Videotape as Misleading

In one of the most sensational moments since the Microsoft antitrust trial began, the Government accused a senior Microsoft executive in Federal court today of offering a misleading videotape into evidence and using it to try to discredit an important Government witness.

Initially, James Allchin, the Microsoft executive, was embarrassed and said that his staff had made an error.

"Mr. Allchin," said the Government lawyer, David Boies, "you do understand that you came in here and you swore this was accurate?"

Mr. Allchin replied, "What I'm seeing here is that they filmed the wrong system."

Later in the day, Microsoft said it had actually shown the correct videotape; it said an unexplained problem with the computer used in the taped demonstration had created a mistaken impression.

"Microsoft's demonstration was completely accurate," a company spokesman, Mark Murray, asserted on the courthouse steps at the end of the day.

In any case, Mr. Boies said the episode raised questions about Microsoft's credibility. "The court has to evaluate the credibility of the witness," he said.

At issue in the conflict today were videotaped demonstrations that Microsoft presented on Monday. One tape was an effort to debunk the testimony of Edward W. Felten, a Princeton University professor who devised a program that he said extricated Microsoft's Web browser, Internet Explorer, from the Windows operating system.

The issue is crucial because the Government contends that Microsoft's decision to combine Windows with a Web browser was an abuse of monopoly power to thwart competition. Microsoft maintains that it was merely providing an integrated product offering a benefit to consumers.

Microsoft said that Dr. Felten's program had merely hidden the browser and that all the browser's programming code remained. Microsoft also maintained in the demonstration tape played on Monday that Dr. Felten's program had

wanted to force Microsoft to unbundle Windows and Internet Explorer.

In the Appeals Court ruling that Microsoft regarded as its salvation from all challenges, the judges had offered the view, as Microsoft now put it in a press release, that the company "has the right to determine what features and functions to include in its operating system as long as the end product offers 'plausible consumer benefits.' The Court ruled that Microsoft's integration of Internet Explorer and Windows meets that test. The Court also said that the method by which Internet Explorer is distributed, and whether installation is done by customers or computer manufacturers, is irrelevant."

All that was true, but no one really knew how important the Appeals Court ruling would be on this issue. The court had carefully noted that its ruling was based on an exceedingly thin evidentiary record. When this case landed in the court, it would be accompanied by as rich an evidentiary record as anyone could imagine. Further, no one knew if this case, on appeal, would be heard by the same three-judge panel—or another group of judges. And even one member of the previous three-judge panel had forcefully dissented, writing that, "in effect, the majority has fashioned a broad exemption from antitrust law for operating system design."

What's more, beyond whatever happened at the appeals court level, no one knew how the Supreme Court might regard these issues should it take the case.

Boies was well aware of the Appeals Court ruling as he posed his questions to Allchin.

In fact, Boies said later, he used the ruling as a road map. In some ways he was grateful to have it, because the appeals court judges had told him what he needed to prove to meet their test.

"On the day it came out, I read it on the plane to San Francisco," where he was to meet with the Justice Department's investigative team. "By the time I landed, I had read it several times and convinced myself it was a good thing because it gave us a roadmap—what the Court of Appeals criteria would be. That was very important."

When he landed and told the San Francisco team of his conclusion, Boies recalled with a grin, "They didn't immediately recognize our good fortune." But in court, he added, "I

seriously degraded the performance of Windows in other important ways.

One part of the demonstration tape showed a slow response when a computer tried to connect to a Microsoft Web page. In the background, a Microsoft narrator intoned, "This shows the performance degradation that has occurred because of running Dr. Felten's program."

But on cross-examination, Mr. Boies challenged the accuracy of this demonstration by showing that the label, or "title bar," identifying the program running on the computer had not changed as it should have if Dr. Felten's program had been run. The title bar indicated the computer was still running Internet Explorer, suggesting that Dr. Felten's program had not been run on this computer at all and that the poor performance was a function of Windows and Internet Explorer, not Dr. Felten's program.

"How in the world could your people run this program when they knew it wasn't accurate?" Mr. Boies demanded. Mr. Allchin insisted that no deceit was intended and that "they probably just filmed the wrong screen shot." He also said he knew from his own tests that the decline in performance from Dr. Felten's program was real in any case.

During the lunch break, Mr. Allchin and other executives made calls to the company's headquarters in Redmond, Wash., to find out what had happened. When they returned to court, Mr. Allchin said he had learned that the computer shown in the tape had in fact been altered by

Dr. Felten's program. But for some reason, he said, the title bar did not change as it should have.

Judge Thomas Penfield Jackson, who is hearing the case without a jury in United States District Court, did not react visibly to any of the exchange. In his own testimony in December, Dr. Felten accused Microsoft of sabotaging his program by redesigning a company Web page so it would not work with computers using the program. The accusation infuriated the judge, who glared angrily at the Microsoft lawyers. Later, in a written filing with the court, Microsoft did not explain how the problem with the Web page had occurred but denied doing anything that would have caused it.

When the testimony had ended today, William H. Neukom, the Microsoft senior vice president for law and corporate affairs, said: "This is a tiny, tiny part of a very long tape. And it doesn't stand for anything more than the fact that things can happen with software."

For his part, Mr. Boies said: "Microsoft says this is some kind of mistake. But we don't know how the mistake occurred. We don't really have an explanation. All we do know is that the tape they put into evidence is not reliable."

In all, Mr. Boies spent less than one full day cross-examining Mr. Allchin, and he barely referred to Mr. Allchin's exhaustive, direct testimony. That led Mr. Murray of Microsoft to declare that Mr. Allchin's "150-page testimony has now gone into the record virtually untouched." He added, "The Government is working very hard to create a mood in the courtroom while we are trying to create a legal record."

But Mr. Boies said he was not concerned about that. "One of the reasons we go into issues of credibility of witnesses is so the judge has a chance to decide who to believe," he said. "All of this is a question of credibility."

With so much of the record in this trial the subject of polar interpretations by the opposing sides, Government officials say, the judge's perception of each side's credibility could prove crucial.

Edward Felten, the Princeton University computer scientist, was on hand to fact-check Allchin's testimony. With him were the former students who had helped write his "removal program." Dr. Felten and his team actually had their own office space adjacent to the government's "war room" in an office building across the street from the Justice Department. And because of a quirk in witness scheduling, Microsoft delivered copies of the Allchin tape a full week before Allchin took the stand. The Felten team pored over them and found all the inconsistencies. They briefed Boies, who offered no particular reaction. The professor and his assistants had no idea whether Boies would even use the material in court.

In the end, Boies used the tapes almost as an afterthought. He completed his cross-examination of Allchin without any reference to the problems on the tape. Then a Microsoft lawyer proceeded through re-direct questioning. Only on "re-cross" did Boies raise the problems with the tapes, producing some of the most spectacular moments in the trial.

When it was all over, however, Judge Jackson was philosophical about Allchin and his tape.

"I never got the impression he was trying to falsify them on purpose," the judge said. "These things happen to trial lawyers. They get sandbagged."

FEBRUARY 3, 1999

Microsoft Marketing Gets No Sale in Court

As soon as the Feb. 3 article about Jim Allchin's ill-fated videotape was published, a former Microsoft employee called to offer his view of what had happened. David Thielen was a senior developer at Microsoft for three and one-half years, and after he left he published an interesting little book entitled "The 12 Simple Secrets of Microsoft Management." The idea behind the book was to pass on to other companies the management style that made Microsoft so successful.

Thielen was a Microsoft booster. But, looking for book promotion, he did provide some perspective on the demonstration problem. It turns out, he noted, that Microsoft put on demonstrations of this sort all the time—dozens of times a year. They were used at trade shows and for smaller sales meetings to show off the capabilities of new products. Over the years, Thielen noted, no one had ever questioned how the tapes were compiled, even though the final products had almost always been pasted together from different takes of tape, and different computers. And if computer industry engineers never noticed any problems, Thielen hypothe-sized, Microsoft had no fears that a bunch of lawyers in Washington would find fault.

But all the previous tapes prepared over the years had been sales documents, not legal evidence. If the company was sloppy about putting them together, it didn't matter; the resulting marketing tool was all that counted.

In a sense, the company carried one of these video sales documents into court. In this case, Microsoft was trying to sell the judge on its version of events. But in Federal Court the rules were different than at the WinHEC conference for hardware developers. As a result, the Microsoft tapes proved to be a precious gift for Boies.

Judge Questions Microsoft Videotape Evidence

The Federal judge hearing the Microsoft antitrust case openly questioned the reliability of video evidence the company had pre-sented in court and called the situa-tion "very troubling."

In a tense, packed courtroom, the Microsoft Corporation suffered its second embarrassing setback in two days, stumbling yesterday and staggering today. A few minutes after the judge's criticism, Microsoft tossed in the towel, with the judge agreeing to recess to let Microsoft regroup and try again on Thursday.

At issue both days has been a videotape that Microsoft has shown in court to try to demonstrate a key defense point—that its Windows operating system and Internet browser are not, as the Government contends, separate products bun-dled together to stifle competition, but a single product blended seam-lessly to benefit consumers.

The Justice Department attacked the video on Tuesday as misleading, saying that one portion seemed to be altered to make Microsoft's point. Today, the department's lawyers focused on a different set of seemingly misleading portions of the videotape. Much of the video concerns the arcane inner workings of software programs, but the more lasting damage to Microsoft's defense could be to its credibility rather than its technical arguments. And that could be crucial to the outcome of the case, especially because so much of the Government's case focuses on private meetings between Microsoft and other companies.

"The court has to weigh the unverifiable recollections of self-interested parties on both sides," said William Kovacic, a professor at the George Washington University Law School. "That is why the credibility of the spokesperson in each case is so important."

The Microsoft spokesman on the stand, James Allchin, a senior vice president, took a drubbing for a second consecutive day. The Microsoft videotape was intended to show that its browsing technology could not be removed from Windows 98 without damaging the operating system. It was to have been a rebuttal of earlier testimony by Edward W. Felten, a Princeton University computer scientist and a Government witness, who said he could disable the browser without harm to Windows.

Microsoft argued that its videotape showed that the Felten approach would cause Windows 98 to slow down and crash when it tried to do certain things. Yet David Boies, the Justice Department's lead lawyer in the case, showed in court that the video showing a computer screen was actually spliced together,

presenting at least two different machines as if it were one machine being put through its paces. The number of icons on the desktop screen varied at different points in the video, indicating different programs loaded on different machines.

Any kind of software incompatibility could cause the problems Microsoft noted, Mr. Boies pointed out; it was not necessarily a result of Mr. Felten's browser-disabling program.

Then, Judge Thomas Penfield Jackson stepped in. While he has asked pointed questions of witnesses previously, he was more direct than he had been in the past.

"How can I rely on this?" Judge Jackson asked Mr. Allchin. "It's very troubling."

"This casts doubt," Judge Jackson added, "on the reliability of the entire videotape demonstration."

Tall, white-haired and soft-spoken, Mr. Allchin allowed that the tape had problems, but not ones that fundamentally undercut his testimony that removing the browsing software hurt Windows. "I'd be glad to bring in a machine and show you," Mr. Allchin told the judge. "This demonstration hasn't turned out very well."

After the court session, Microsoft admitted that it was at fault for producing a flawed tape, but insisted it was an honest mistake. "We make very good software, but we didn't make a very good videotape," said William H. Neukom, the Microsoft senior vice president for corporate and legal affairs.

To straighten things out, Judge Jackson agreed to let Microsoft remake the demonstration video-tape—with Justice Department representatives monitoring the taping—and allow them to show it Thursday morning in court.

Mr. Boies said he did not know whether Microsoft had intentionally made a misleading tape. "But the main point," he said, "was that the videotape was not reliable. This is not public relations. This is not sales. You have to submit accurate evidence, not just something that makes your side look good."

Throughout the afternoon session of the trial, the Government pointed to several internal Microsoft e-mail messages, trying to show that the company had folded its browser into Windows mainly to undermine competition from Netscape.

Microsoft counters that since 1994 it was always the company's intention to put browsing software in its operating system to benefit consumers. Yet the e-mail messages were cast in terms of tactics intended to help Microsoft "win" the browser battle "against Netscape." In one e-mail written on Dec. 26, 1996, Mr. Allchin wrote, "I don't

understand how Internet Explorer is going to win," adding, "My conclusion is that we must leverage Windows."

In another sent to Mr. Allchin in March 1997, Jonathan Roberts, a Microsoft marketing executive, wrote that tightly integrating Windows with the browser would make "Netscape a non-issue—a superfluous product for all but the most committed Netscape user."

When asked about such messages, Mr. Allchin said that Microsoft certainly did compete with Netscape, but the main way it did so was to innovate and improve its leading product, the Windows operating system. At one point, Mr. Allchin noted that words like "tie" and "leverage" are terms used loosely at the company—not with the legal implications of a monopoly case in mind.

Judge Jackson pointed out playfully that "tie" was a term "we use too," though more seriously.

"It's certainly got us in a lot of trouble," Mr. Allchin said of the e-mail language. "This is my first time in court. I'm learning a lot."

FEBRUARY 4, 1999

Microsoft Shows a New Tape And Raises Some New Questions

Trying to stop the damage from a disastrous week in court, the Microsoft Corporation played a new videotaped demonstration at its antitrust trial today.

The 70-minute video showed James E. Allchin, a senior company executive, performing live tests and

then looking into the camera and saying that he had proved his point—that a prototype Government program intended to separate Microsoft's Web browser from the Windows operating system had really done no such thing.

The program just hid the browser,

he showed. Further, he demonstrated that running the program, written by a Princeton University professor and two of his students, disabled some other features in Windows and caused additional problems.

It was Microsoft's second attempt to produce such a tape. In the previous two days, David Boies, the Government's lead lawyer, had gradually pulled the first tape apart, pointing out numerous technical questions and errors, until finally Judge Thomas Penfield Jackson declared Wednesday afternoon that he no longer viewed the original as reliable evidence, at one point calling it "very troubling."

Microsoft asked for and was granted an opportunity to make a new tape. As soon as court adjourned yesterday, a Microsoft spokesman drove to a shopping mall in suburban Landover, Md., and bought six IBM Thinkpad laptop computers at a CompUSA store, for use in the new effort. A film crew was hired on short notice, and the computers were delivered to a conference room at Sullivan & Cromwell, the law firm that is representing Microsoft.

To ensure that the new tape would be viewed as credible, a Government lawyer and the Princeton professor, Dr. Edward W. Felten, along with his two students, were invited to come by at 8:30 P.M. to witness the taping. But they were not permitted into the room for two hours, while the Microsoft team unpacked the boxes and set up the computers—leading to angry concerns that something nefarious was

under way. The taping was not completed until after midnight.

Asked in court today why the Government representatives were not allowed in, Mr. Allchin—normally a low-key, unflappable man—bristled and said, "Sir, I was not involved with that, and it would have been O.K. with me."

Mr. Allchin sat in the witness stand and watched silently as his tape was played. On the tape, he navigated his way into a new computer he did not know and ran up against the same software problems and glitches every computer user encounters.

"O.K., I've got to figure this out, and I don't have my glasses with me," he said matter-of-factly when his screen suddenly went blank. Later, when a Microsoft promotional program popped onto the screen unbidden, complete with a loud gong from Big Ben followed by upbeat jazz, Mr. Allchin looked a bit annoyed and said, "Very nice music, but not tonight."

As he tried to connect to the Internet while the camera watched, the connections often failed, and when one did succeed, it seemed to be agonizingly slow—nothing like the zippy Internet downloads shown in Microsoft's demonstration tape that was played in court on Monday.

"The performance problem you see here has nothing to do with Dr. Felten's program," Mr. Allchin acknowledged at one point.

Judge Jackson, who is hearing the case without a jury, watched the tape silently, often with a bemused expression on his face.

When it was over, Mr. Allchin

demonstrated that after running the Government program he was able to re-enable Internet Explorer through a complex series of changes in the Windows registry file that no normal user would be able to carry out without precise instructions.

Before doing that, he demonstrated that several programs did not work properly on what he called "a Felten-ized machine."

All the problems he demonstrated related to features of the programs that interacted with the Internet. And when Mr. Boies got a chance to question Mr. Allchin again, he immediately asked whether it wouldn't be logical to expect that after the browser had been disabled, "anything that depended on the browser wouldn't work right?"

Mr. Allchin conceded that. And as for the other problems and glitches Mr. Allchin demonstrated, Mr. Boies said: "What Dr. Felten prepared was not a commercial product. It was a concept program. Wouldn't you expect it to have problems? Doesn't Microsoft find bugs in its programs during the normal course of software develop-

ment?" Mr. Allchin admitted that was true.

Microsoft also made public the written testimony of the next witness, William Poole, senior director of business development for Microsoft, who will take the stand on Monday. Mr. Poole's testimony defends the restrictive contracts Microsoft won from other companies doing business on the Internet, requiring them to promote Internet Explorer in exchange for links on the Windows desktop.

The Government charges that these contracts are anticompetitive and illegal, but Mr. Poole calls them "routine cross-licensing agreements, common across many industries."

Mr. Poole also argues that in the end the contracts did not significantly impede the Netscape Communications Corporation, the chief competitor to Internet Explorer. And he adds, the "channel bar," the space on Windows desktop where the links appeared, "turned out to be a commercial disappointment" in any case. It was dropped in Windows 98.

FEBRUARY 5, 1999

Redmond's Aggressive P.R. Machine

Microsoft's public relations managers should have learned a lesson from the Allchin tape debacle, but there was no evidence that they had. Allchin's remedial tape may or may not have been a useful legal tool; there was no way to tell for sure at the time. But it was an extraordinarily effective public relations performance. With a few self-deprecating remarks and humorous asides, Allchin looked human, vulnerable, a sympathetic and appealing figure. As one courtroom observer put it, "Jim Allchin seems like the only guy at Microsoft who didn't drink the Kool-Aid."

Microsoft's typical response to most any challenge was an unyielding, often belligerent rebuttal. But smart political candidates long ago learned that the electorate admires apology, repentance, vulnerability. Candidates willing to display such actions and qualities when necessary were often judged to be honest and trustworthy. Americans like to forgive. Allchin's testimony proved that the same rules applied in a high-profile case. As Allchin's remedial tape was played, the sympathetic mood in the courtroom was palpable.

But Microsoft could not see it. Later that day, the company's minions, like so many chanting Hare Krishnas at an airport, passed out a press release fashioned as the standard Microsoft bludgeon to which reporters had become accustomed. It insisted, "In a live demonstration last night with government lawyers and technical consultants present, Microsoft witness and senior vice president Jim Allchin once again showed that Professor Felten's prototype 'removal' program fails to remove Internet browsing technology from Windows 98, impairs certain Windows functions and breaks software programs developed by independent, third-party companies."

Michael Devlin had the privilege or misfortune, depending on one's point of view, of being scheduled to testify during a break in the most

Michael Devlin

RATIONAL
SOFTWARE
CORPORATION

contentious testimony of the trial to that point. Everyone in the courtroom—judge, lawyers and observers—was so caught up in the theater of Jim Allchin's testimony that no one paid much attention to Devlin. He was on and off the stand in less than two hours—a record in this trial. After he left, no one had much if anything to say, good or bad, about his bit-part performance. The general impression was that Microsoft had wasted a valuable witness slot.

Devlin was president and cofounder of Rational Software Corporation, which sells software tools that help developers write programs and was a close ally of Microsoft.

Microsoft Shows a New Tape, and Raises Some New Questions (continued)

Before Mr. Allchin played his tape today, another Microsoft witness, Michael Devlin, an independent software developer, took the stand for about 90 minutes. In his brief, 27-minute cross-examination of Mr. Devlin, the Government's Mr. Boies barely alluded to direct, written testimony in which the witness had stated that his company appreciated Microsoft's decision to include a Web browser with Windows. Instead he tried to throw Mr. Devlin's motivations for testifying into question by demonstrating that his company was dependent on Microsoft for more than half its business and was at risk of serious financial damage from Microsoft if the company were to decide to make a competing product.

Mr. Devlin acknowledged that, but Mr. Boies never asked him directly if those concerns had played into his decision to agree to Microsoft's request that he testify.

Microsoft made public the written testimony of its next witness—William Poole, the company's senior director of business development, who will take the stand on Monday.

In it, Mr. Poole defends the restrictive contracts Microsoft won from companies doing business on the Internet, requiring them to promote Internet Explorer in exchange for advertising space on the Windows desktop.

The Government charges that these contracts are anticompetitive and illegal, but Mr. Poole calls them "routine cross-licensing agreements, common across many industries."

Mr. Poole also argues that in the end, the contracts did not significantly impede Netscape, and he adds that the "channel bar," the space in Windows where the ads appeared, "turned out to be a commercial disappointment" in any case.

FEBRUARY 5, 1999

Next up for the defense was another Microsoft executive, Will Poole, 37, an earnest, unassuming, businesslike fellow with a thick shock of straight brown hair. Like other Microsoft witnesses, he had sat in the courtroom and watched as David Boies dismembered the previous witness, Jim Allchin, a much more senior executive. And when he sat in the chair, he held no apparent illusions that Boies would not go after him as well. He seldom smiled, and his answers were businesslike—though often rambling, stammering and off-point when Boies was trying to push him into a corner.

Poole's primary mission was to persuade the judge that the con-

William Poole
MICROSOFT

tracts with Internet companies that the government was portraying as evidence of anticompetitive behavior weren't really serious. In the weeks before the antitrust suit was filed in May 1998, Microsoft rescinded many of these contracts. And Poole's job was to convince Judge Jackson that Microsoft had never seriously enforced them anyway and that many companies had not lived up to the contracts' requirements. He tried to leave the impression that Microsoft was a benign, easy-going company that had no interest in threatening anyone. Needless to say, in this courtroom, that idea was not an easy sell.

Microsoft Executive Ends The Day Mostly Unscathed

The biggest news at the Microsoft trial today was what did not happen: For the first time since the company began presenting its defense against Federal antitrust charges last month, a major company witness did not leave the courtroom with his head on a platter.

All through the Government's presentation of its case last year, Microsoft executives counseled patience. When their time came, they promised, they would present a robust, effective defense.

But David Boies, the Government's lead trial lawyer, has forced the first three significant Microsoft witnesses to make damaging statements or to admit embarrassing mistakes, throwing serious credibility questions before Judge Thomas Penfield Jackson.

Today's witness—William Poole, senior director of business development for the company's Windows operating system—managed to hold his own, though Mr. Boies did leave him mumbling and stammering and even backpedaling a few times.

When he returns on Tuesday, he will try to hold his ground while Mr. Boies tries to push him back further.

Mr. Poole oversaw the negotiation of contracts in which Microsoft required Internet companies to limit business dealings with the Netscape Communications Corporation. In exchange, Microsoft awarded the companies advertising space on the opening desktop screen of Windows.

Under questioning, Mr. Poole acknowledged that Microsoft had estimated in 1996 that it could earn about $100 million a year by selling that advertising space but decided to charge nothing. Instead, the companies had to sign binding contracts to promote Internet Explorer and to cease all significant dealings with Netscape.

Mr. Poole said one major company, Intuit Inc., maker of the popular personal finance program Quicken, had approached Microsoft "and asked us to let them use our browser" instead of Netscape's Navigator. Quicken uses links to Web pages for many of its services.

But that testimony contradicted earlier testimony of Intuit's chief executive, William H. Harris. And Mr. Boies displayed an internal Microsoft e-mail from 1996 in which William H. Gates, Microsoft's chairman, summarized for Brad Chase, another senior executive, a conversation with Intuit's chairman at the time, Scott Cook.

"I was quite frank with him that if he had a favor we could do for him that would cost us something like $1 million, to do that in return for switching browsers in the next few months, I would be open to doing that," Mr. Gates wrote. But Mr. Cook was reticent, he said.

A few weeks later, Mr. Chase reported back to Mr. Gates: "I talked to them again today. I just don't think they are prepared to jump this hurdle. I suggested that at least they ship both browsers."

Mr. Poole said he had never seen the e-mail exchange, even though it was entered into evidence many weeks ago.

"Your lawyers didn't show this to you?" Mr. Boies asked.

"I don't remember seeing it," Mr. Poole said.

A Microsoft spokesman later said the company had issued a new and improved version of Internet Explorer between the time Mr. Gates negotiated with Intuit and when Mr. Poole worked out a contract.

With some help from the judge, Mr. Boies also got Mr. Poole to admit that the restrictive contracts with Intuit and others were not standard practices for the company or the industry, as Mr. Poole had asserted in his direct, written testimony.

After Mr. Boies repeatedly posed the question, only to get rambling, off-point responses, Judge Jackson finally interrupted, shaking his head as Mr. Poole set off again, saying: "No, No, No. Try to answer, Mr. Poole. Yes, no or I don't know."

Mr. Boies was in the middle of asking his final question as court ended for the day, challenging Mr. Poole's assertion that "only 4.7 percent of users surveyed stated that they first became aware of a Web site that they now frequently visit through a preconfigured browser setting or start page."

The issue is important because Microsoft and Netscape both ship their browsers with links already preloaded to important, money-earning Web pages.

Judge Jackson adjourned court before Mr. Poole could find the reference he needed in the survey data.

FEBRUARY 9, 1999

Three-Pointers at the Buzzer

David Boies loved to hold a zinger for the end of the day so that the judge and those in the courtroom left with the sense that he'd scored a big coup. This strategy became apparent on the first day of testimony by the first Microsoft

witness, Richard L. Schmalensee. Watching the clock, waiting until the end of the day, Boies announced that he was
asking his last question of the afternoon and picked a line
out of Schmalensee's direct, written testimony where he
quoted from a survey of software companies, known in the
industry as independent software venders.

"In a recent survey of ISV's," the testimony said, "85
percent predicted that Microsoft's integration of Internet
functions into Windows would help their company, and 83
percent predicted it would help consumers."

Boies then asked Schmalensee if he had known that
Microsoft ginned up the survey to give Gates useful material
he could use in testimony at a Senate hearing. Boies offered
as evidence an e-mail Gates had written in which he said: "It
would help me immensely to have a survey showing that 90
percent of developers believe that getting the browser into
the operating system makes sense. Ideally, we would have a
survey like this done before I appear at the senate on March
3rd." And then, as if by magic, that's what the survey found.
Schmalensee was humbled a bit, but not bowed.

Boies's end-of-the-day strategy didn't always make use
of a survey, but he found another for Poole. And so he tried to
trap him, just as he had Schmalensee, at the end of his first
day on the stand. In the end, though, Poole defanged Boies
by asking to study the data overnight. And when Poole came
back the next morning, he offered a blizzard of numbers and
explanations so that the zinger Boies had planned devolved
into a muddy, low-impact discussion of survey methodology.

Executive Downplays Intuit Contract Limits

William Poole, a Microsoft vice president, suggested that a key charge in the Government's antitrust suit was insignificant since it merely dealt with whether customers get to see a dancing Mickey Mouse when they visit a Web page.

Cross-examining Mr. Poole on Monday, David Boies entered into evidence Microsoft's contract with Intuit Inc., the maker of Quicken, the popular personal finance software, which set out the terms for Microsoft's agreement to carry an

Intuit advertisement on the opening screen of Windows.

A condition, Mr. Boies pointed out, was that Intuit and other companies signing these contracts had to agree that some Web pages would present a significant "degradation in appearance" for visitors using Netscape Navigator, the rival Web browser.

In court today, Mr. Poole said that the Walt Disney Company had been the only company to honor the requirement and that Microsoft had made no effort to enforce the stipulation while the contracts were in place.

And the only difference in content on the Disney site, he said, was that a Mickey Mouse cartoon danced across the opening screen for users of Microsoft's Internet Explorer while Netscape users saw no mouse.

The judge chuckled and shook his head on hearing that.

Later, however, Mr. Boies forced the witness to admit that even this enhancement was important to Microsoft. The company had been arguing that features like this would win millions of new customers.

Boies generally picked and chose among the various points in each witness's direct testimony, ignoring vast sections. As a result, as each witness left the stand, Microsoft gloated.

"When the government rested its cross examination, 1,500 pages of testimony went into the record completely unchallenged," Microsoft spokesman Mark Murray said at one such point. It became a mantra.

But Jackson's saw it differently. "Often the testimony they put into the record was simply not to the point," he said later. Much of it recounted Microsoft's many accomplishments, leading Jackson to say: "There is no doubt in my mind that Microsoft is a unique, gifted, efficient and ingenuous organism. But the fact that they do a lot of things right does not give them a license to do anything wrong."

FEBRUARY 7, 1999

John T. Rose of Compaq was a big man in an expensive suit who preened and grinned as he sat in the stands waiting for his turn in the witness chair. He carried himself like a man who knew he was a rich and powerful corporate executive, and thoroughly enjoyed it. But on the stand, it was hard to believe that Rose was the top-of-the-stack executive that his résumé and demeanor suggested. He clearly didn't seem to understand many of the questions he was asked, and he repeatedly said he was wholly unaware of many important actions his company had taken that bore on the case against Microsoft, even when it would have been better for him if he had known. And through it all, even as Boies pummeled him, that grin

John T. Rose
COMPAQ

never left his face. (A short time after testifying, he resigned from Compaq.)

Reporters and other audience members compared his performance to Peter Sellers's role as a clueless simpleton in the movie "Being There." Some speculated that he was acting for the court. And given his résumé, that seemed the most logical explanation. But once again, a Microsoft witness would fail in his mission. Rose was brought to the witness box to demonstrate that Microsoft had loyal partners in the industry. Boies managed to demolish that idea, and Rose did nothing to slow him down. Rose began working for Compaq in 1993 as senior vice president of the desktop personal computer division. He was credited with establishing Compaq's consumer division, which sells the Presario line of desktop computers. Before joining Compaq, Rose had been vice president of Digital Equipment Corporation's personal computing business.

A Government Attack on Multiple Fronts

In his direct written testimony made public today, John T. Rose, a senior vice president of the Compaq Computer Corporation, said he believed that most consumers wanted a computer "with broad functionality that is simple and easy to use right out of the box." He endorsed the idea of giving them a Web browser but added, "It is irrelevant to users whether the feature is incorporated in application or operating-system software."

Mr. Rose also took issue with the Government's assertion that Microsoft had threatened in 1996 to cancel Compaq's license to sell Windows with its computers when Microsoft learned that Compaq was also loading Netscape on its machines.

Mr. Rose said the real problem was that Compaq was deleting some on-screen icons that Microsoft had pre-loaded, including one for Internet Explorer. This was done, he said, as the result of an agreement with America Online. When Compaq restored the icons, Mr. Rose said, Microsoft withdrew its threat.

David Boies, the lead Government attorney, first used Mr. Rose to bolster the Government's assertion that Microsoft is a legal monopoly under antitrust law—a finding that must be made if most of the Government's other charges are to stick.

Questioning from Judge Thomas Penfield Jackson helped Mr. Boies by leading to the central issue of whether Microsoft could raise prices with impunity, a hallmark of the monopolist.

"Is it fair to say there is no commercially viable alternative to the Windows operating system?" the judge asked Mr. Rose.

"That is correct, Your Honor," Mr. Rose said.

Mr. Boies asked him whether it was true that Compaq had not even considered looking for another operating system to replace Windows after Microsoft imposed a steep price increase for Windows last year.

"That is correct," Mr. Rose said.

Then Mr. Boies began a challenge of the central tenet of Mr. Rose's direct testimony: denying the Government's assertion that Microsoft threatened in 1996 to cancel Compaq's license to sell Windows with its computers when Compaq began loading Netscape on its machines.

Mr. Rose said the real problem was that Compaq had separately signed a contract with America Online at about the same time, requiring Compaq to replace the Internet Explorer and Microsoft Network icons in Windows with an America Online icon.

But Mr. Rose said the people who signed that contract did not realize that Compaq had agreed in a telephone call with Microsoft executives a few days earlier not to tamper with those icons.

Mr. Rose said that "there was simply a communication breakdown" at Compaq, and some of the documents Microsoft submitted with his testimony support his story indirectly.

But Mr. Boies showed that some people involved in the first agreement, with Microsoft, were also involved in the second one, with America Online, and he said that it was odd that they did not know of this conflict.

FEBRUARY 16, 1999

Tales of Fear and Loathing of Microsoft

Using internal company documents and sworn depositions at the Microsoft trial today, a Government lawyer depicted the Compaq Computer Corporation, the world's largest manufacturer of personal computers, as so fearful of Microsoft that it repeatedly abandoned software products it preferred in favor of Microsoft's offerings and even passed on information about a competing operating system in violation of a nondisclosure agreement.

"In regard to browsers," one internal memo stated in May 1996, "our goal is to feature the brand leader, Netscape." But in an e-mail written at almost the same time, a Compaq employee wrote, "Microsoft is unhappy with the Netscape icon on the desktop and wants to get it off." He added, "Microsoft's stance to date raises questions of improper use of their monopoly position."

A few weeks later, Compaq signed an agreement making Internet Explorer, Microsoft's browser, the default choice on all Compaq personal computers. That happened even though Celeste Dunn, who was in charge of buying software, had cautioned other executives that to comply with Microsoft's request, Compaq would have to "significantly alter" a line of computers, "revise its business model and jeopardize two profitable, revenue-generating contracts" worth $9 million.

That exchange was just one in a cascade of disclosures that David Boies, the Government's lead trial lawyer, made in court today. They offered an extraordinary look inside the relationship between two powerful companies that are, as one Compaq document described it, "joined at the hip."

Microsoft promises a rebuttal when its lawyers question the witness on Friday.

Tom Siekman, general counsel for Compaq, insisted in an interview that "our relationship with Microsoft is one of equal partners; we are not the weak sister."

Nonetheless, in court today, the testimony of John T. Rose, a Compaq senior vice president, contradicted that of numerous other Compaq employees. He is the only representative of the computer manufacturing industry to appear in court as a witness for Microsoft. Microsoft held high hopes that he would counteract the Government's assertion that Microsoft's main customers—manufacturers of personal computers—fear the company and consider it a bully.

But Mr. Rose seemed generally out of touch. He said he had never seen or heard of most of the contracts, discussions and product proposals that were presented to him. The disconnect was so extreme that at one point Judge Thomas Penfield Jackson noted that Mr. Rose had

disagreed with everything another senior employee had said in a deposition. "And I'm just wondering who speaks with authority for the company," he said.

Mr. Rose insisted that he did.

In the most dramatic disclosure in court today, Mr. Boies asked Mr. Rose if he was aware that Compaq had received confidential product information from Be Inc., a tiny company that makes a niche operating system, and had passed it on to Microsoft in violation of a nondisclosure agreement.

Mr. Rose said he was not aware of this, and Compaq's lawyer, William Costen, leaped from his bench to denounce Mr. Boies's raising the issue in court to "sully the company with this information."

In a telephone interview this evening, Jean Louis Gassee, chief executive of Be, said, "In November, a Compaq executive called me, rather embarrassed, to say that someone had inadvertently leaked some information from us to a company in Redmond," the Seattle suburb where Microsoft has its headquarters. "He was very embarrassed, but my interpretation is that this is a result of the climate of fear Microsoft creates."

Mr. Boies offered several documents suggesting that Compaq's fear of Microsoft was longstanding. A document titled "Microsoft meeting presentation," dated January 1993, postulates Microsoft's "potential reactions" to Compaq's decision to use another company's software for personal digital assistants. "How retaliatory will they get?" it asks, then lists 14 ways Microsoft could hurt Compaq, including "selection and elevation of other" computer manufacturers "as leaders."

Mr. Boies then produced a letter dated three months later in which William H. Gates, Microsoft's chairman, congratulated Compaq's chief executive for selecting "Microsoft as the exclusive supplier of operating system software for your hand-held computers."

What occurred in those three months was not described.

Another e-mail between senior Compaq executives helped to explain why Compaq dropped Netscape Communications' browser for Internet Explorer.

"Microsoft was upset with our internal use of Netscape and initiated a number of activities with Digital Equipment Company and Hewlett-Packard, reducing their emphasis on the Compaq partnership," the executive wrote. Compaq responded, she added, by agreeing to include Microsoft's software for the Internet.

Mr. Boies also presented memos showing that a Compaq executive had agreed in 1997 to make "side agreements" with Microsoft, "given Microsoft's concern that the agreements are defensible" with other manufacturers "and the Department of Justice."

Mr. Boies offered two such agreements signed on the same day and described them as the public agreement and "the real agreement." Details of the two contracts were not disclosed, but Mr. Rose said he was not familiar with either.

Mr. Boies closed today's cross-examination by reading from an e-mail message from a Microsoft official who was the Compaq account manager in 1995, shortly after Microsoft reached a consent agreement with the Government on an earlier antitrust case. In it, Microsoft promised to stop forcing PC makers to buy one copy of a Microsoft operating system for every computer sold and instead charge them only for every computer on which the operating system was installed.

In the e-mail, the Microsoft manager wrote that despite the consent agreement, few manufacturers had chosen to renegotiate their contracts with Microsoft. And if Compaq chose to do so, "it would be a major issue at Microsoft."

Mr. Rose said he had never seen this memo, either.

FEBRUARY 19, 1999

The News According to Microsoft

Media coverage of the trial seldom proceeded as Microsoft would have liked, and that was certainly true on the day Rose first testified. So Microsoft published its own news coverage on its Web site, and generally the articles took a distinctly different tack than the reporting of the mainstream press. It wasn't clear who read the coverage. But here's how Microsoft reported Rose's first day on the stand:

Compaq Executive Confirms That Consumers Have Choice of Browsers

WASHINGTON, D.C., Feb. 18, 1999—A senior executive of Compaq Computer Corp. told a federal district court judge today that his company pre-installs Web browsing software from both Microsoft and Netscape on every personal computer it manufactures, leaving consumers free to choose which browser they want to use and to change their default browser at will.

During cross-examination, government attorney David Boies challenged Rose's assertion, suggesting that Windows 98 still defaults to Internet Explorer even after a user has chosen Netscape Navigator as the default. Rose said he had tested it personally on a new Compaq Presario computer in preparation for his testimony, and found that everything worked exactly as he had testified.

"My legal team purchased one of the new Presarios from Staples, right up the road here, and I went through that process myself," Rose said. "I certified it, set it up, and then I . . . clicked and chose Netscape, and it made Netscape my default browser."

"Mr. Rose, my question is, when you did that, after you had done that, did your Windows 98 Presario computer launch Netscape as the browser every time a browser launched?" Boies asked.

"Yes. Every time I used it there, it launched Netscape," replied Rose, who pointed out that he ran through several functions but didn't attempt to test every possible Internet scenario. "It at times asked me if I wanted to change [the default], and I chose not to. I kept it as Netscape, but I could have changed it back to Internet Explorer with a click of the mouse."

Microsoft Seeks Some Salvage In Courtroom

Burned by a searing cross-examination of a senior Compaq Computer Corporation executive, the Microsoft Corporation and Compaq tried today to regain ground in Federal court, though they may have helped the Government as much as themselves.

At the Microsoft trial on Thursday, David Boies, the Government's lead trial lawyer, used documents from Compaq's files to portray Compaq, the world's largest maker of personal computers, as a fearful vassal of Microsoft.

In one case emphasized by Mr. Boies, an internal document showed that Compaq executives had worried in 1996 about retaliation from Microsoft for their decision to use another company's operating system for hand-held computers. A few weeks later, William H. Gates, Microsoft's chairman, wrote Compaq a letter congratulating the company for instead choosing Microsoft's product, later known as Windows CE.

Today, when Rick Pepperman, a Microsoft lawyer, got a chance to question the witness, John T. Rose, a Compaq senior vice president, he displayed a memo that had circulated within Compaq after the Gates letter had arrived.

It reassured employees that Compaq still had the right to use another company's software if Microsoft was unable to deliver its product, "while keeping our relationship with Microsoft intact." (In the end, Compaq never produced the hand-held computer.)

Microsoft held high hopes for Mr. Rose's testimony. He is the only witness Microsoft recruited from a computer company, and last November, Mr. Gates wrote to "thank Rose for all his trips to Seattle and his willingness to distract a lot of time for the lawsuit."

Part of Mr. Rose's mission was to counter testimony by executives of Apple Computer and the International Business Machines Corporation who portrayed Microsoft as a monopolist and an industry bully.

Mr. Rose was at best only partly successful in his mission. Mr. Boies showed Thursday that numerous employees who reported to Mr. Rose at Compaq both feared and hated Microsoft. But on the stand today, Mr. Rose insisted: "They have a view on some points that doesn't represent the corporate strategy. As a director of the company, I have that strategy. I know what it is." Compaq's relationship with Microsoft has been "bumpy," he said, "but always focused on benefiting customers."

The bulk of today's questions dealt with the central assertion of Mr. Rose's written testimony: that Microsoft's threat in 1996 to stop selling the Windows operating system to Compaq—an act that could have been a fatal blow to the company—was a result of "a communications breakdown" within Compaq.

The Government contends that the threat was made because Compaq was featuring products from the Netscape Communications Corporation on its personal computer. But Mr. Rose said that the real problem was that while one part of his company had removed icons for Internet Explorer and the Microsoft Network from computer screens to meet the terms of a contract with America Online, another part was working out an agreement with Microsoft not to tamper with the icons.

Mr. Pepperman, the Microsoft lawyer, presented documents showing that America Online was trying to enforce a contract requiring Compaq to remove the icons. And he also offered evidence intended to show that Compaq executives did not believe that their agreement with Microsoft prevented them from installing Netscape on their computers.

But Mr. Boies displayed a deposition taken from Celeste Dunn, who was in charge of buying software for Compaq. She said senior Microsoft officials had been informed of the decision to remove the icons in advance and did not object or indicate that it violated any agreements.

Mr. Rose said he did not doubt the accuracy of her testimony, leaving the contradiction unexplained.

Regardless, Compaq did stop installing Netscape on its computers, at least for a while. Mr. Rose said that "there were compatibility problems that eventually Netscape cleared up." But Mr. Boies, when he got another turn with Mr. Rose, presented excerpts from a 1997 deposition in which a Compaq executive stated that the company had stopped installing Netscape because Microsoft had begun including a browser in the operating system.

"That doesn't mention anything about compatibility problems, does it?" Mr. Boies asked

"That's correct," Mr. Rose said, though he also noted that Compaq does install Netscape in its computers today.

FEBRUARY 20, 1999

If Jim Allchin seemed a bad witness at times, Cameron Myhrvold was worse. Allchin in the end came off as an honest, likeable guy who had been caught short as the result of sloppy performances by people working under him. Myhrvold just looked sloppy. He, too, was a likeable, sympathetic witness at first. A big, beefy fellow with an earnest, friendly manner, he won over the courtroom during his first hours on the stand. But Boies quickly caught him in a series of misstatements and contradictions. And by the end of the second day, Myhrvold appeared to have been thoroughly discredited.

Cameron Myhrvold
MICROSOFT

Myhrvold was a vice president in Microsoft's Internet Customer Unit. He was on the stand because from early 1996 to mid-1998, he had been responsible for Microsoft's relationships with Internet service providers, including the companies whose contracts were being challenged in the government's suit. Myhrvold, along with his better-known brother, Nathan, founded Dynamical Systems Incorporated while they were still attending the University of California at Berkeley in the 1980's. Microsoft bought that company in 1986, and both brothers began working for Microsoft that year, though Cameron returned to college briefly to finish work on his degree.

More Peril for Microsoft With Videotape

The Microsoft Corporation once again today found itself in trouble with a videotaped demonstration in Federal court. And while even the Government lawyer who discovered the problem conceded, "I don't mean to imply that this is terribly critical," it adds to a growing body of evidence that the Justice Department is using to throw Microsoft's credibility into doubt.

Last week, Microsoft played a videotape intended to demonstrate the advantages of integrating a World Wide Web browser with its Windows operating system. But over several days, the Government's lead trial lawyer, David Boies, pointed out so many problems and inconsistencies with the tape that Judge Thomas Penfield Jackson declared that he could not view it as reliable evidence.

Today, Microsoft played another tape to demonstrate how much easier it was for a customer to sign up for Internet service on a computer running Windows 98 than it had been on a computer running the older Windows 3.1. On the Windows 98 machine, the sign-up was quite simple and took only about five minutes. On the older system, it took about 17 minutes, including long delays while Internet software was loaded onto the computer.

Microsoft's new witness, Cameron Myhrvold, a vice president in the Internet Customer Unit division, supervised the production of the videotape. As soon as his cross-examination began, Mr. Boies pointed out that the Windows 98 computer in the video was using a faster modem, giving the newer system an unfair speed advantage.

Mr. Myhrvold acknowledged the difference, but added that while using a faster modem "would have been a factor" on the Windows 3.1 machine, "most of the time was spent loading the software."

After the court had adjourned for the day, Microsoft executives scoffed at Mr. Boies's question. Mark Murray, a company spokesman, acknowledged that the Windows 98 machine had used a modem running at 33.6 kilobytes a second, while the other computer used a modem running at 28.8. Of the 12 minutes difference between the operating systems, the modem speed accounted for only 22 seconds, he said.

William Neukom, the Microsoft senior vice president for law and corporate affairs, declared, "The difference in the speeds of the two modems is meaningless, academic."

FEBRUARY 10, 1999

U.S. Hammers At Microsoft's Browser Deals

A senior Microsoft official acknowledged in Federal court today that the company's contracts had prohibited Internet service providers from offering its browser on the same Web page as its main competition because Microsoft executives "thought we would lose in a side-by-side choice."

The admission clearly pleased David Boies, the Government lawyer who elicited it from the witness, Cameron Myhrvold, a vice president in the Microsoft Corporation's Internet Customer Unit division—so much so that Mr. Boies asked the same question four different ways and got the same answer each time.

"Was it true you were trying to prevent Internet service providers from presenting Netscape and Internet Explorer side by side so users could choose?" he asked at one point. Internet Explorer is the name of Microsoft's browser; the Netscape Communications Corporation's Navigator is its principal rival.

"We thought we would lose in a side-by-side choice," Mr. Myhrvold answered, because Netscape was already so firmly established in the market.

In all, it was another bad day in court for Microsoft in its antitrust battle with the Justice Department, which charges that the software giant used a monopoly in personal computer operating systems to achieve a dominant position in Internet software. Hour after hour, Mr. Boies chiseled away at Mr.

Myhrvold's testimony, forcing him to acknowledge incorrect assertions, misleading omissions and deceptive statements. Mr. Myhrvold repeatedly acknowledged that he made misstatements in e-mail memos. He also testified that he disagreed with Microsoft employees whose memos contradicted his own assertions.

As he completed his testimony this evening, it was clear that Mr. Myhrvold's appearance had not helped Microsoft's case. In fact, as Microsoft's defense reached its midpoint this evening, none of its first five witnesses had proved particularly effective advocates of the company's position.

Mr. Myhrvold, a brother of Nathan Myhrvold, Microsoft's chief technology officer, is in charge of the Microsoft division that negotiates agreements with Internet service providers, the companies that give computer users access to the Internet. The Government charges that Microsoft's restrictive contracts with these companies are anticompetitive and illegal. Mr. Myhrvold tried to make the case that the contracts were largely ineffective or benign.

Many of these companies have agreements to be listed in the Internet Referral Service in Microsoft's Windows operating system, which enables users to subscribe to an Internet service posted there. On Tuesday, Mr. Myhrvold insisted that the Government's assertion that these companies had to favor Explorer over Navigator to be included in the service was "absolutely wrong."

But under further cross-examination by Mr. Boies today, Mr. Myhrvold admitted that in most cases the companies had been required to ship Explorer to at least 75 percent of their customers. Mr. Myhrvold added that they were free to stop shipping the Microsoft product if they wanted, in which case they could be dropped from the Windows referral service.

"It's a fairly subtle point," Mr. Myhrvold acknowledged.

Similarly, in his written direct testimony, Mr. Myhrvold pointedly noted that several Internet service providers in the referral service were not shipping Explorer as required, and yet the company had decided not to enforce the contracts. For example, he wrote, "of the copies of Web browsing software shipped by Concentric," a reference to Concentric Networks, a small Internet service provider, "only 17 percent were Internet Explorer." But those figures were for 1997. Mr. Boies entered into evidence a Microsoft document showing that by the first quarter of 1998, 100 percent of Concentric's browser shipments were Internet Explorer.

Mr. Myhrvold repeatedly noted that Netcom, a Internet service unit of ICG Communications Inc. that has a contract with Microsoft, made no real effort to switch customers to Internet Explorer, testifying that one point in 1997—when 10 percent of Netcom's customers were getting the Microsoft product—was "the high-water mark."

But Mr. Boies then displayed a Microsoft document showing that in early 1998 the percentage had risen to 40 percent. Then Mr. Boies offered another Microsoft document showing that Netcom was actually able to control the browser choice of only a small percentage of the people who signed up for its service; most customers were handed to Netcom by computer makers, or by Netscape. That same document showed that Microsoft had won an agreement with Netcom that 90 percent of the customers Netcom did control would switch to Internet Explorer.

To that, Mr. Myhrvold said only that the author of the Microsoft document "was a pretty good salesman." Later, in response to a question from a Microsoft lawyer, Mr. Myhrvold denied a Government assertion that his staff had offered a British division of UUNet, an Internet service owned by MCI World-Com, $500,000 to switch to Internet Explorer. He said he told his staff that "it would not be appropriate to tie payments to shipments of Internet Explorer."

Moments later, Mr. Boies displayed still another e-mail that Mr. Myhrvold had written to a subordinate in Britain in which he said, "I think tying the payment to their shipping of IE is a great idea, though I would not do this formally." Mr. Myhrvold explained that the message had not meant what it said, and he had called the subordinate later to tell him not to tie the two. There was no record of that call, he conceded.

FEBRUARY 11, 1999

100 Ways to Say 'I Goofed'

One tactic was used so often that it almost looked like it had been coached: Over and over again, Microsoft's witnesses explained away contradictions between their current testimony and previous statements with expressions of surprise and the exclamation "Gosh, I was wrong!" Schmalensee, the first witness, used the tactic during his first day on the stand, when Boies presented him with an article he wrote in 1983 that directly contradicted a position he was taking in court. Schmalensee responded, "My immediate reaction is, what could I have been thinking?"

Almost every other witness made similar exclamations. Shown an inconsistency between present testimony and earlier statements, Poole rolled his eyes and said he had been "woefully incorrect." Later in the trial, when Boies showed another Microsoft executive, Brad Chase, an inconsistency between his present statements and earlier writings, he simply explained that "the early estimation was incorrect." And when Boies later trapped him on another point, Chase said: "That is correct. I was incorrect in my deposition."

But Myhrvold took the prize. During his first day on the stand, asked about a contradiction between his assertions in court on downloading browsers and an opposite opinion he had offered earlier, Myhrvold said: "I was fascinated to discover in preparing for this case that I'm actually wrong." But errors were everywhere in Myhrvold's account. Shown one damning document, he said, "This is a draft memo that was never sent." Caught with a contradiction in deposition testimony, he said, "This is a copy of my deposition that does not reflect the errata." Asked about an opinion that contradicted a view offered by another Microsoft executive, Daniel Rosen, Myhrvold said, "Mr. Rosen was wrong." And when he was asked about another statement made previously, Myhrvold said simply, "I would also point out that I think my reasoning here is incorrect."

One morning in court, he turned the "I was wrong" defense on its head when Boies read back the following exchange from the previous day's testimony:

Boies: "Mr. Myhrvold, you know perfectly well that

America Online and everyone else using the online services folder has to commit that 85 percent of the browsers they ship to customers would be Internet Explorer."

Myhrvold: "That's absolutely wrong."

After reading that back from the previous day's transcript, Boies showed Myhrvold a memo showing that, in fact, there was an 85 percent commitment, to which Myhrvold spun the "I was wrong" defense a different way, by saying: "The statement was true, but it was wrong that I knew it."

Brad Chase, a senior Microsoft marketing executive, sat in the front row, watching as Cameron Myhrvold's testimony unfolded. And even as David Boies humiliated Chase's colleague on

Brad Chase
MICROSOFT

the stand, Chase bantered with others sitting beside him, a broad smile on his face. But his salesman's manner—joking, backslapping conviviality—disappeared shortly after he took his place in the witness box and began taking a humbling verbal pummeling from Boies.

Chase, who grew up in the San Francisco area, earned his undergraduate degree from the University of California at Berkeley and a master's degree from Northwestern University's graduate school of management. Before joining Microsoft in July 1987, he was a sales representative for Boise Cascade's office products division.

As Windows marketing chief, he directed the big campaign to introduce Windows 95 with TV commercials featuring the Rolling Stones song "Start Me Up." That campaign changed the way software was marketed, moving it closer to mainstream products like detergent or auto tires.

By the time he took the stand, Chase was already a familiar figure to people following the trial. His name had appeared on numerous e-mail messages introduced by government lawyers. In one, he argued against the idea of giving computer companies greater flexibility to design the opening screen of Windows to feature their own products and services, saying, "Changes like this undermine our whole defense of the Windows Experience."

In Microsoft's corporate reorganization in the spring of 1999, Chase was assigned with another executive to run the new Consumer and Commerce Group.

Government Raises More Questions About Microsoft Demo

At the Microsoft trial today, the Government attacked a key assertion in the company's defense: that bundling a Web browser with the Windows operating system is not anti-competitive because consumers can quickly and easily download a competing browser from the World Wide Web.

That was the central message of a videotape demonstration that lawyers for the Microsoft Corporation played this morning. And, as has become routine in this case, David Boies, the Government's lead trial lawyer, immediately attacked the video as misleading.

Microsoft, he said, had edited out the parts of the demonstration that were difficult and time consuming, leaving the false impression that downloading huge programs from the Internet was a simple, quick and painless operation.

Toward the end of the day, Mr. Boies proposed playing a videotape demonstration of his own. This one, Government officials said, would show the complex steps that an America Online subscriber must take to download the Netscape Communications Corporation's Navigator browser and install it on a computer, mirroring one of Microsoft's edited demonstrations.

Microsoft's lawyers, taken by surprise, asked to study the tape during the weekend, just as the Government has been able to study Microsoft's tapes in advance.

Brad Chase, Microsoft's chief marketing officer, directed the production of today's Microsoft's demonstration and took the stand this morning. And while he held up better under cross-examination than some previous Microsoft witnesses, Mr. Boies accused him of making misleading statements and assertions in his testimony—in addition to pointing out problems with his videotape.

Mr. Boies noted that Microsoft had chosen to edit out the time it had taken to complete the download. After the download began, the videotape's narrator said only, "This will take a few minutes and could take longer depending on your connection," and the tape then cut away. Mr. Chase acknowledged that his staff had been using a high-speed corporate line that would be unavailable to most users. But even with a low-speed line, Mr. Chase said, downloading a program would be faster than driving to a store to buy the software.

Mr. Boies then displayed a memo that Kumar Mehta, another Microsoft employee, had written to Mr. Chase in March 1997, recounting the results of a study conducted by the company. "Almost 60 percent of all surfers never download anything from the Web," Mr. Mehta wrote, "and my sense is that these people are not likely to download anything—let alone a browser that takes two hours to download from the Web."

Mr. Chase said he disagreed with

that characterization and added that Mr. Mehta "was probably being dramatic on purpose." In fact, Mr. Chase volunteered, Netscape announced last fall that 12.4 million people downloaded the company's browser in July and August. But in that attempt to prove that the process was easy, he fell into a trap.

Mr. Boies pulled data from Mr. Chase's own written testimony showing that by last summer, only 6.7 million people in the United States had ever downloaded Netscape and used it as their primary browser.

Mr. Chase then hypothesized that the 12.4 million new users were mostly foreigners, or people who had taken the time to download Netscape but did not use it.

Still, he asserted, "We have had 11 million successful downloads" of Microsoft's Internet Explorer.

But Mr. Boies pounced on that, asking Mr. Chase if he had documentary evidence of this. No, Mr. Chase finally acknowledged, he did not know where his staff had gotten the figure or on what it was based.

FEBRUARY 12, 1999

Tape 36 versus Tape 142

David Boies was having so much fun with Microsoft's videotapes that he began to use the accumulating library of them to show inconsistencies among them.

In several tapes, Microsoft demonstrated the benefits users were supposed to gain by finding a Web browser bundled with Windows. Among the benefits, the tapes said, is that the bundling saves users all of the time and difficulty of acquiring a browser on their own. In one tape, a Microsoft employee describes some of the hassles of installing another browser and adds that these difficulties do not "take into account the set-up time, which for a large number of users is cumbersome and not straightforward."

But then came Chase's videotape and arguments on the stand. Chase tried to convince the judge that downloading an alternative browser was so fast and painless that bundling the browser with Windows couldn't possibly be considered anticompetitive. Of course, Chase made no mention of the earlier, opposite arguments. But when Boies showed them to him, Chase acknowledged: "I do agree it's easier if you get it on your system."

A Government Attack on Multiple Fronts

A Government attorney attacked the testimony of Microsoft's senior marketing executive on multiple fronts at the trial today, and at times the witness's explanations seemed to cause even the judge to question his credibility.

During his two days on the witness stand, Brad Chase, a Microsoft vice president, tried to hammer home one central point: Microsoft's decision to bundle a Web browser with the Windows operating system was not anti-competitive because alternative browsers are easily available. As a result, he argued, if Microsoft's Internet Explorer is gaining market share, that is only because it is a superior product.

This afternoon, David Boies, the Government's lead trial lawyer, introduced a document from Microsoft files prepared last May. Titled "Internet Explorer Marketing Review," it was loaded with statistics, analyses and marketing assessments.

Mr. Boies pointed to one conclusion: Most people who switched to Internet Explorer did so because "it came with my computer," suggesting that the browser was gaining ground largely because it was bundled with Windows.

Asked about that, Mr. Chase explained that the 20-page strategy assessment "was done by a summer intern" and had no standing within the company.

"Do you know where a supposed summer intern got all this information?" Mr. Boies asked, his voice laced with incredulity. Mr. Chase said he did not, prompting Judge Thomas Penfield Jackson to observe that the study appeared to be in the form of a slide show for a meeting, and he asked, "Do summer interns do slide presentations at Microsoft?"

Mr. Chase said it was possible that an intern prepared the show and never presented it. Earlier in the day, Mr. Boies continued to challenge a videotape Mr. Chase played last Thursday that purported to show how easy it was to download Netscape Navigator, the principal competition to Internet Explorer, from the Netscape Communications Corporation. Mr. Boies began the attack last Thursday, noting that the difficult and time-consuming parts of downloading and installing Navigator had been edited out.

Mr. Boies tried to show his own demonstration tape on Thursday to counter Microsoft's. But under the rules of the trial, he had to allow Microsoft 72 hours to examine it.

When Mr. Boies finally played his tape today, he managed to force Mr. Chase to acknowledge that some answers he had given Judge Jackson on Thursday had been incorrect.

Specifically, Mr. Chase had told the judge that an America Online customer downloading Netscape from the service would see a simple, self-explanatory series of screens that makes the process easy. The tape Mr. Boies played today showed that the process was considerably more complicated. Judge Jackson asked several questions along the way indicating that he was confused.

Later, Mr. Boies tried to deflate

Mr. Chase's assertion that Internet Explorer had won the majority of critical product reviews in the last two years. Among other things, he showed the results of a Microsoft tracking poll of professional Web developers, who concluded in the fall of 1997 that "Netscape is still perceived as having the best browser."

Mr. Chase offered the view that these developers used Netscape primarily to check their Web sites to assure that they worked well with Netscape.

The judge seemed puzzled by that explanation and asked, "Is this just speculation, or do you know that for a fact?"

Mr. Chase said several Web developers had told him that.

At midday, Mr. Boies offered what he thought would be an explosive new document, one that a Government official called "a naked attempt at market division."

The document did appear to be just that, but it was so old that Microsoft's lawyer appeared successful in convincing the judge that it was irrelevant.

The document, an e-mail message to Microsoft's chairman, William H. Gates, Mr. Chase and others, was dated March 1990 and was written by Mike Slade, a Microsoft executive who had just returned from a meeting with the leaders of Intuit, manufacturers of Quicken, the popular accounting software.

"I made a fairly surprising proposal to them," he wrote. "Usually we can topple anyone," but "we'd rather not compete with you. So how about this?" Then he suggested that Intuit write software for Apple computers and others running DOS but leave the new market for Windows computers to Microsoft.

He said Intuit's leaders seemed receptive, and "if they were listening carefully, this could have been interpreted as a chance to avoid competition with us."

The proposal is quite similar to one that the Government charges Microsoft made to Netscape several years later, an accusation that Microsoft denies. Mr. Boies said he was offering this memo, despite its age, "because this is something that shows a pattern of anticompetitive behavior." But Mr. Chase said he had no recollection of the document or events surrounding it. And eventually the judge told Mr. Boies to move on to another subject.

After Mr. Chase completed his testimony this evening, William Neukom, Microsoft's senior vice president for law and corporate affairs, asserted that he "hasn't been moved an inch off of the central point of his testimony."

FEBRUARY 17, 1999

The Things You Say

Every lawyer has his own unique strategies, and in a long trial the judge and anyone who attends regularly will over time be able to anticipate his moves. David Boies was no exception. Perhaps his favorite strategy was to find a document or record showing that the witness, or someone related to him, had said something provocative in the past. Boies would read the old statement back to the witness word-for-word, without saying where it came from, and then ask him if he agreed. A theoretical example: Mr. Smith, would you agree that, at the time, you wanted to help Microsoft "bury Netscape six feet under?" To that, under the normal scenario, Mr. Smith would say, "Oh no. I would never say something like that," after which Boies would produce the document quoting him saying exactly those words and ask, "Does this refresh your recollection?"

Some witnesses remain on the stand long enough that they can begin to anticipate this strategy, and Chase was one of those. That led to this exchange:

Boies: Did you have an understanding as to what AT&T's position was, as to how important it was for AT&T to be included in the online services folder?

Chase: Yes. I do recall that AT&T told me that it was important for them to be in the online services folder. That wasn't the only thing they said was important. But they did also tell me that they wanted to be in the online services folder.

Boies: Indeed, it was very clear that they really, really wanted to be in the Windows box, correct, sir?

Chase: I don't recall one way or the other.

Boies: Well, let me ask you to look at government exhibit 179.

Chase: I figured that was going to happen.

Boies: I'm becoming predictable. Now, this is an e-mail from Mr. Dan Steele to you and others dated March 14. And in the next-to-last paragraph, Mr. Steele writes to you that it's very clear that AT&T really, really wants to be in the Windows box. Do you see that?

Chase: Yes, I do.

Microsoft Trial Explores an Odd Alliance

A senior executive of the Microsoft Corporation reported in Federal court today that America Online had, at least for now, renewed its contract to equip its users with Microsoft's Internet browser—even though it is buying the Netscape Communications Corporation, Microsoft's main competitor in the browser field.

The executive, Brad Chase, quickly added that he believed that America Online would abandon Microsoft soon enough, dealing a serious blow to Microsoft's effort to make its browser, Internet Explorer, the industry standard.

Finishing three days of testimony in the Federal antitrust trial against his company, Mr. Chase said he believed that America Online had chosen to stick with Microsoft for the time being in part for political reasons—because the company wanted to influence the outcome of the antitrust case.

"If they switched to Netscape, our market share would drop to 30 percent," Mr. Chase said. That would make Internet Explorer, Microsoft's browser, the underdog and "would be inconsistent with AOL's desire to support the Government in this case."

America Online signed an agreement with Microsoft in 1996 to use Internet Explorer as the default browser for its subscribers. Since those subscribers now number more than 16 million, about 40 percent of the computer users equipped with Internet Explorer are using it in conjunction with America Online.

The motivation for the agreement is a subject of hot dispute at the trial. The Government and a senior America Online executive who testified as a Government witness say the company chose Microsoft, and agreed to limit its members' use of Netscape, because Microsoft dangled irresistible bait: promotion of America Online's service on every personal computer running the Windows operating system.

Microsoft argued again today that America Online actually chose Internet Explorer over Netscape because it was a better product.

The Microsoft-America Online contract expired Jan. 1. But even with the renewal, Mr. Chase testified he believed an eventual switch of browsers was "inevitable." In Securities and Exchange Commission documents that Microsoft submitted as evidence, America Online declared it would create a new browser, working with Sun Microsystems, to compete with Microsoft—and to use with the America Online service.

FEBRUARY 18, 1999

Daniel Rosen
MICROSOFT

Daniel Rosen was the most senior executive at the June 21, 1995, meeting between Microsoft and Netscape. He joined Microsoft in the fall of 1994—after a 14-year career with AT&T—just as Microsoft was really starting to develop its Internet strategy. At AT&T, he'd had a wide-ranging career, rising from a technical staff position at Bell Labs to various management positions overseas to developing a consumer Internet service for AT&T.

The 49-year-old Rosen, who has a Ph.D. in biophysics, is probably a fascinating and bright man. But he often came across in court as
fumbling and ill-prepared. Once, he was forced to retract his own
statement after he was presented contradictory e-mail. Worse, Rosen
himself was the author of the embarrassing e-mail.

In his direct testimony and in documents, Rosen was able to
make some progress with Microsoft's defense that, at the very least,
Microsoft and Netscape executives had left the June 1995 meeting in
Silicon Valley with very different views of what had happened. And a
business meeting where there is honest disagreement about what
occurred is not a clear-cut—and thus not an illegal—proposal to
divide markets.

Yet Rosen's performance on the stand unintentionally seemed to
offer Microsoft a far stronger line of defense: How real a threat could
Microsoft have made at that meeting if this was the guy they sent to
deliver it? Microsoft could have quite convincingly argued that when
it wants to deliver a serious threat, it brings out the heavyweights—
Gates, Ballmer or Maritz—not someone like Dan Rosen.

Microsoft Executive Denies
Key Allegation in U.S. Case

A Microsoft Corporation executive
today denied a key allegation in the
Government's antitrust case—that
the company had both threatened
its main rival in the Internet software business and made it an illegal
offer to divide the market.

In his 90-page direct testimony,
Daniel Rosen, a Microsoft general
manager, called those portrayals of a
June 1995 meeting between executives of Microsoft and the Netscape
Communications Corporation as
"either fabrications or the products
of a fundamental misunderstanding."

Mr. Rosen offered his own
detailed account of the disputed
meeting and the events surrounding
it. The meeting is a pivotal episode

in the Government's suit. After Netscape declined Microsoft's offer to
divide the Internet browser market,
the Government contends, Microsoft embarked on a pattern of anticompetitive behavior intended to
thwart the challenge posed by Netscape.

In his written testimony, Mr.
Rosen, who led the Microsoft team
at the June 1995 meeting, angrily
dismisses those allegations as "misleading," "outrageous" and "rub-
bish"—directly contradicting the
testimony of the Government's
leadoff witness, James Barksdale,
the president of Netscape.

Judge Thomas Penfield Jackson,
who will decide the outcome of this

non-jury trial, must determine which witness is more credible.

Mr. Rosen said that in late 1994 Netscape tried to license its browser to Microsoft and said it would not compete head-on with Microsoft-only to change its strategy and its story later. Mr. Rosen cites an e-mail he received on Dec. 29, 1994, in which James Clark, the chairman of Netscape, stated, "We have never planned to compete with you."

Mr. Clark went on to describe Netscape's browser as "client" software, a way to distribute its technology, but that its main business would be selling Web server software to corporations.

Mr. Barksdale testified that Mr. Clark sent this e-mail in a "moment of weakness," and had not told others at Netscape of his overture. Indeed, Mr. Clark's e-mail ends, "No one in my organization knows about this message."

But Mr. Rosen notes that Mr. Clark's "moment of weakness" lasted at least several days, since he had tried to send it, using an incorrect e-mail address, to another Microsoft executive earlier in the month. Besides, Mr. Rosen said, the Clark e-mail was consistent with conversations he had had during that time with other Netscape executives.

At the four-hour meeting in 1995 at Netscape's offices, Mr. Rosen insists, it was Netscape executives who brought up the issue of the "line" dividing the Internet technology Microsoft planned to put into Windows and Netscape's Internet software that would run on top of Windows.

Microsoft replied that its priority was to "establish Microsoft ownership of the Internet client platform for Windows 95," as Mr. Rosen wrote in an e-mail to William H. Gates, Microsoft's chairman, and other senior Microsoft executives a day after the meeting.

Later in the message, Mr. Rosen wrote, "we discussed sucking most of the functionality of the current Netscape browser" into Windows, confining Netscape's future development mainly to add-ons. Yet, Mr. Rosen reported, "They seemed O.K. with this concept."

In addition, Mr. Rosen said, the Microsoft team suggested that licensing Netscape's browser technology for "the non-Windows platforms might be a reasonable part of a larger strategic relationship."

The Government and Netscape regard these as the ingredients of an illegal market-division offer, while Mr. Rosen says the discussions were "entirely consistent with lawful, and commonplace, business practices."

FEBRUARY 17, 1999

U.S. Attacks Official On Netscape Meeting

The Microsoft executive responsible for dealing with the Netscape Communications Corporation testified today that he did not regard Netscape as a competitor in June 1995. But the Government presented e-mail written at the time in which the witness himself and other Microsoft executives portrayed Netscape as a potentially dangerous rival.

The point is crucial because that meeting between Microsoft and Netscape is a key episode in the Government's antitrust case.

With document after document supplementing his acerbic cross-examination, David Boies, the Justice Department's lead trial lawyer in the case against the Microsoft Corporation, proceeded today with perhaps the most sweeping attack on the credibility of a witness since the trial began last October. Again and again, he tried to point to contradictions between what Daniel Rosen, the witness, was saying today and what he and other Microsoft executives had written and said in the past.

Mr. Boies certainly felt he succeeded. He abruptly cut off his cross-examination in the afternoon as Mr. Rosen repeatedly seemed evasive on the stand, interrupting Mr. Rosen in mid-sentence and telling the judge, "I have no further questions."

Afterward, Mr. Boies explained his tactic on the courthouse steps. "I thought the points about the witness's credibility had been made," he said.

Microsoft replies that Mr. Rosen was simply trying to be precise about highly detailed discussions of software technology and strategy. And Mr. Rosen testified that his belief that Netscape did not intend to compete with Microsoft was based on what Netscape executives told him then.

Mr. Rosen led a team from Mi-

crosoft that met with Netscape executives on June 21, 1995, when the Government contends that Microsoft threatened Netscape and made an illegal offer to divide the Internet browser market between them.

Mr. Rosen testified that at the time he saw Netscape as a potential partner rather than a bitter rival. Microsoft, he added, was trying to persuade Netscape to adopt the underlying Internet technology it was building into its Windows 95 operating system, and then to build software products on top of Microsoft's technology. Yet on May 15, 1995, more than a month before the disputed June meeting, Mr. Rosen wrote an e-mail titled "Internet Direction" in which he described the threat that Internet software posed to Microsoft's control of the basic technology of personal computer software.

"Microsoft currently controls the base and evolution of the desktop platform," Mr. Rosen wrote. "The threat of another company (Netscape has been mentioned by many) to use their Internet World Wide Web browser as an evolution base could threaten a considerable portion of Microsoft's future revenue."

In court, Mr. Boies asked, "Did you believe that at the time you wrote it?"

Mr. Rosen replied, "No sir."

The Microsoft executive added that his memo was a draft document, which he said he had never sent, and that it represented mostly a summary of thinking within Microsoft.

Then Mr. Boies pointed out that the e-mail bore the heading, "Sent:

Monday, May 15, 1995, 12:48 A.M." Mr. Rosen replied that the time in the heading represented when he saved the e-mail on his personal computer and did not necessarily indicate that it had been sent.

But in the afternoon, Mr. Boies presented a Microsoft document list showing that the Government obtained Mr. Rosen's e-mail from Ben Slivka, a Microsoft executive who was listed among the intended recipients of the Rosen message.

"Does that refresh your memory?" Mr. Boies asked.

"Yes," Mr. Rosen replied, "at the least, I sent it to Mr. Slivka." But he added that he still did not believe that he sent the unfinished draft to senior Microsoft executives listed as recipients.

Later in the same memo, Mr. Rosen wrote that Microsoft should try to "strike a close relationship with Netscape" and that Microsoft's goal should be to "wrest leadership of the client evolution from them."

Asked about this passage, Mr. Rosen said that "by wrest, I mean take." But he said again that this referred to underlying Internet software and did not imply trying to push Netscape out of parts of the browser market.

Holding to his testimony that he did not regard Netscape as a rival in

June 1995, Mr. Rosen said that a strategy document written by William H. Gates, the Microsoft chairman, in May 1995 was simply wrong. In the document, "The Internet Tidal Wave," which was widely circulated within Microsoft, Mr. Gates called Netscape a "new competitor 'born' on the Internet" and said Netscape's strategy was to "commoditize the underlying operating system"—a direct threat to Microsoft's lucrative business.

Asked about the Gates document, Mr. Rosen said, "I recall when reading this I thought that Bill was probably wrong."

A team of nearly a dozen Justice Department lawyers took responsibility for the witnesses. Each lawyer took two or three witnesses. And for those witnesses, the lawyers learned all the evidence. They sat in court as Boies cross examined their witnesses, listening for problems or weaknesses that would then be brought to Boies's attention. And so it was with that May 15 e-mail. A couple of the lawyers remembered the document showing where they had obtained the e-mail—from Slivka's computer. Over lunch, they retrieved the document in question, handed it to Boies, and Rosen was undone.

Microsoft Official Concedes That He Erred in Testimony

The Government's lead lawyer accused a Microsoft executive of making up evidence at the antitrust trial today, and, after presenting the

witness with his own e-mail contradicting his statements, forced him to correct his testimony.

The courtroom incident focused

on a matter of timing: when the executive, Daniel Rosen, had known that a software rival was making an Internet browser to run on the Microsoft Windows 95 operating system.

On its own, it is not a central element in the Government's case against the Microsoft Corporation. But the episode is part of the Government's persistent effort to undermine the credibility of Microsoft witnesses.

For Microsoft, the credibility issue has become enough of a problem that Federal District Judge Thomas Penfield Jackson joked that Microsoft's lawyer was embarking on a "heroic endeavor" when he began questioning Mr. Rosen this morning.

It was the second day that David Boies, the Justice Department's lead trial lawyer, and Mr. Rosen had clashed concerning the software giant's intentions and actions at a key meeting with the Netscape Communications Corporation in 1995.

The real fireworks today came after Mr. Rosen said that he did not regard Netscape as a rival in June 1995 and that one of his goals was to "encourage them to write a good browser for Windows 95"—the Microsoft operating system introduced in August 1995.

Far from encouraging Netscape, however, the Government contends that Microsoft tried to persuade Netscape to cede the Windows 95 browser market to it, even though Netscape had long planned to produce a Windows 95 browser.

Mr. Boies asked Mr. Rosen when he had first obtained an advance copy of Netscape's browser for Windows 95. Mr. Rosen said it was not until after the June 21 meeting.

Mr. Boies then presented an e-mail dated May 11, 1995, that Mr. Rosen wrote to another Microsoft executive. It included the notation "Can I borrow/copy the Netscape Win 95 new client they gave us?" The "client" refers to the new Netscape browser.

But Mr. Rosen replied that he never got the test version, which he said did not work properly.

Mr. Boies responded: "You don't remember that, do you? You're just making that up right now."

Mr. Rosen said, "No, I remember it."

"You're sure it was May and not April?" Mr. Boies asked.

Mr. Rosen answered, "Yes."

With that, Mr. Boies introduced an e-mail from Mr. Rosen to another Microsoft executive on April 27 that said: "Do you remember who took the Netscape win 95 browser they gave us during our last meeting? I'd like to get a copy."

Confronted with his own e-mail, Mr. Rosen paused, then said, "I stand corrected."

The Government also introduced as evidence an e-mail written on June 22, 1995, by David Kaiser, an executive at America Online, to another executive of the on-line service, recounting a conversation he had with Marc Andreessen, co-founder of Netscape.

Mr. Andreessen, Mr. Kaiser wrote, told him that at the meeting the previous day, Microsoft offered Netscape a deal: Microsoft would invest in Netscape, take a seat on the board, and Netscape would agree not to compete with Microsoft head-on.

If Netscape accepted, Mr. Kaiser wrote that Mr. Andreessen had told him, it would become "Microsoft's special partner." If Netscape rejected the deal, Mr. Kaiser said in the e-mail, "Microsoft would crush them."

But Microsoft also introduced documents that supported its version of the June 21 meeting. An e-mail written on June 22 by Richard Wolf, a Microsoft executive who attended the meeting, said he did

"not think that they have the intention of competing with us in defining a platform," for underlying Internet software that Microsoft planned to include in Windows 95.

Still, Mr. Wolf added, that "does not mean they will drop a broad-based client," meaning a browser.

After the testimony, William H. Neukom, Microsoft's senior vice president for law and corporate affairs, said: "The record is quite clear. There was no effort by Microsoft to dissuade Netscape from creating a browser for Windows 95. It did and its browser was quite popular."

FEBRUARY 23, 1999

Eric Engstrom, a 33-year-old general manager, took the witness stand to try to refute the Government's allegation that Microsoft's discussions with Apple about multimedia software were an effort to thwart competition by dividing the market between the two companies. Instead, Engstrom said, the talks were merely an effort to settle on some common standards for multimedia software that would benefit consumers.

Eric Engstrom
MICROSOFT

Engstrom was another Microsoft executive with a fascinating résumé. A hacker since high school, with 11 patents to his name, he had no college education but was an avid reader. One book he had read shortly before the trial was "The Feynman Processor," by Gerard Milburn and Paul Davies, which describes applying Richard Feynman's quantum mechanics theories to building computers. He also, according to a Microsoft press release, enjoys "skippering sailboats on world travel adventures and cruising on his Harley."

Engstrom's main accomplishment at the trial was to get off the witness stand after a brief appearance with scant embarrassment, unlike so many of his colleagues.

Microsoft Manager Says Apple Talks Sought Cooperation

Today, Microsoft released the direct written testimony of Eric Engstrom, a general manager in the Web Essentials division of the Microsoft Network. His testimony tries to refute the testimony of an Apple Computer executive and others who said that Microsoft tried to sabotage Apple's Quick Time multimedia software.

In his testimony, Engstrom wrote that the motivation for this talks with Apple executives was to find areas of cooperation between the two companies.

"Contrary to Apple's post-hoc characterization of those communications as threatening and inappropriate," he wrote, "the discussions were undertaken with Apple's full agreement, and involved ordinary efforts to collaborate pm technical issues in a way that would have benefited Microsoft, Apple and end users of computers."

FEBRUARY 19, 1999

Microsoft and Compaq: Quarrelsome Partners Or Master and Servant?

The showdown in 1996—when Microsoft threatened to stop selling the Windows operating system to Compaq Computer unless Compaq also included the software maker's Internet browser—is a central chapter in the Government's antitrust case against Microsoft.

But a look beyond the court documents indicates that that was by no means the first time the software maker that dominates the industry and the largest producer of personal computers had clashed. A dispute between the two companies, over Compaq's plans to become a software player in its own right, was creating tensions as early as 1994.

Understanding the companies' sometimes contentious past is crucial. For in deciding the antitrust case, the court has to make a judgment about the Compaq-Microsoft relationship: Has even the largest personal computer maker been bent to Microsoft's will in ways that stifle competition and harm consumers? Or is the relationship more one of headstrong equals in an often bumpy partnership over the years?

In the fall of 1994, William H. Gates, the chairman of the Microsoft Corporation, was upset about the Compaq Computer Corporation's software plans. Compaq had decided to load a software "shell" on its machines for the home market. Compaq saw the shell—a layer of software that ran on top of Microsoft's Windows—mainly as a way to make computers easier to use.

But a report to Compaq from the consulting firm, McKinsey & Company, noted that the shell could also give the computer maker a measure of independence from Microsoft. The shell, as was later the case with the Internet browser, was software that rested atop the operating system and housed start-up icons for other programs. Such functions would potentially undermine the gatekeeper's role that Windows plays in modern computing and allow Compaq to guide users to software it chose to feature. And at the same time, Compaq was building up its own software development unit in Silicon Valley, eventually staffed with about 150 engineers.

At Microsoft, the Compaq moves were regarded as almost acts of treason by a longtime business partner, posing a threat to Microsoft's control of the desktop screen and a potential assault on Windows, according to a former Microsoft executive, who spoke on the condition that he not to be identified.

"We've got to stop this," the former executive recalled Mr. Gates saying in September 1994.

He was still worried the following summer. In a meeting with executives of the PC chip maker Intel in July 1995, Mr. Gates expressed concern about Compaq's shell software and other moves. "All the things they're trying to do are dangerous," Mr. Gates was quoted as saying, according to notes taken by an Intel executive and introduced as evidence in the Microsoft trial.

Over the years, Compaq has been the most aggressive among the personal computer makers in seeking a measure of independence from Microsoft, even as it is one of Microsoft's closest allies and largest customer. Frequently, Compaq's actions have not fit neatly into the picture of a company in Microsoft's monopolistic grip, constantly seeking favors and ever-fearful of reprisal—the picture the Government tried to paint in court last week when a Compaq executive took the stand as a defense witness for Microsoft.

Yet it is also true that there is an established pattern to the Compaq-Microsoft relationship: Compaq takes an independent path, Microsoft bristles and an accommodation is made.

Compaq removed its software shell as an alternative for the desktop, or main screen, in 1996. The move came after Microsoft tightened contract restrictions on computer makers, but also after the introduction of Windows 95, which made PC's easier to use—addressing the key problem the shell was intended to solve. In 1996, Compaq closed its software development unit. And after being threatened with losing its Windows license, Compaq dropped its plans to remove the icon for Microsoft's Internet browser on the desktop screen for all its machines.

Understanding whether this was business brinkmanship by two equally powerful companies or a demonstration of Microsoft's power to force Compaq to back down is a key to the antitrust case. But it is not an easy determination, judging from descriptions of the Compaq-Microsoft relationship by former Compaq executives and industry executives close to the company. It is a partnership, they say, that rests on mutual dependence and is cemented by money. They agree with John T. Rose, the Compaq executive who took the stand last week, that there has been "significant give-and-take over the years."

Yet they also say that ultimately Microsoft has the upper hand in the relationship because, as Mr. Rose testified, there is no genuine alternative to Microsoft's Windows operating system, but there are many PC makers that are potential customers for Microsoft's software.

Still, no matter what one thinks of Microsoft's market power, most of them also said that having a dominant technology—instead of a handful of competing operating systems—has helped fuel the growth of the industry and drive down prices as consumers, software developers and hardware manufacturers gain the efficiency of working with a single standard.

"Yes, Microsoft is a company with some monopoly capabilities, but we always viewed Microsoft as a partner first," said Gary Stimac, a former senior vice president at Compaq. "And that partnership benefited Compaq tremendously, far more than it ever hurt us."

The Government charges that Microsoft essentially bought its special relationship by giving Compaq a special price for Windows. Judge Thomas Penfield Jackson has kept the testimony on pricing secret by closing the courtroom to the press and public when this confidential business information is being discussed.

But Mr. Rose, the Compaq witness, did testify that it was his company's belief that it got the lowest Windows price in the industry, mainly because it is the largest producer. The Government contends that Microsoft uses the price it charges manufacturers for Windows as a way to reward companies that give favored treatment to a wide range of Microsoft's products and punish companies who do not.

A consultant who worked for Compaq until recently said that Compaq paid about $3 less for each copy of Windows than most of its competitors. Half of that money went straight to Compaq, while the other half went into joint marketing, training and development efforts by the two companies, he said.

It is in the context of the broad relationship with Microsoft, the former Compaq and industry executives say, that the dispute over Internet software must be viewed. Mr. Rose testified that the problem arose because of "a communications breakdown" within Compaq.

Executives in Compaq's consumer division agreed in a deal with America Online Inc. to feature its service and remove the desktop icons for Microsoft's MSN on-line service and its Internet Explorer browser, in return for fees. But Mr. Rose testified that the consumer unit did not realize that more senior Compaq executives had already agreed to include Microsoft's browser and on-line software on the Windows desktop.

According to e-mail introduced in court last week, executives in Compaq's consumer unit wanted to hold onto the America Online deal and the cash it represented. "Some of the discussions inside the company got really ugly," said a former Compaq executive, who insisted on not being identified.

"The consumer group was losing money at the time," the former executive said, "and they wanted the dollar or two per machine they might get from the America Online deal. But that would jeopardize the partnership with Microsoft in which, because of the price discounts, millions and millions of dollars were flowing back and forth to the benefit of both companies."

"In the end," the former executive said, "I believe sanity prevailed."

Microsoft says that Compaq's consumer group simply misunderstood the Windows contract, which treated the browser and MSN icons as part of the operating system and thus not removable.

Whatever their past differences, Compaq and Microsoft are probably more closely aligned today than ever. Compaq increasingly sees its future as moving up the computing food chain, taking the low-cost economics of the personal computer to tackle industrial-strength corporate computing—the traditional bailiwick of mainframes, minicomputers and big machines running the Unix operating system.

To do that, Compaq is betting that Microsoft's industrial-strength operating system, Windows NT, can scale up to handle mainstream corporate computing.

FEBRUARY 22, 1999

(Engstrom testimony continues)

... This morning, the trial had focused on another issue in the suit as a Government lawyer, Phil Malone, cross-examined Eric Engstrom, a Microsoft executive, about whether Microsoft had tried to force Apple Computer out of the market for multimedia software that runs on Windows and had sabotaged Apple's software as part of that effort.

Multimedia software is used to play audio and video clips from the Internet. An Apple executive, Avadis Tevanian, testified last year that Microsoft had designed Windows so that QuickTime, Apple's audio-video software, would not run properly.

Mr. Engstrom said the problem was caused by Apple.

As to the other charge, that Microsoft had tried to push Apple out of the market for multimedia software for Windows, Mr. Engstrom acknowledged that it was true. He had little choice, faced with several e-mail messages from within Microsoft showing that as the company's intent.

FEBRUARY 24, 1999

German-born Joachim Kempin wore his heritage in his bearing, attitude and accent. Most Microsoft witnesses came to trial accompanied

Joachim Kempin
MICROSOFT

by their wives—in many cases probably for moral support, since it quickly became clear that each new witness was likely to come away bruised by David Boies. Not Kempin. He came alone and demonstrated no visible apprehension about what he faced.

Kempin earned his undergraduate degree in mathematics from the University of Hanover, West Germany. He worked for Digital Equipment, National Semiconductor and Apple Computer before joining Microsoft in 1983 as general manager of the company's German subsidiary. He explained the job switch this way: "I left Apple to come to Microsoft because my heart was in software, not just in hardware. I saw the software industry as a bigger opportunity than being the software guy at a hardware company, which is what I'd been."

When he took the stand, Kempin, a 57-year-old senior vice-president, was among the oldest of Microsoft's witnesses.

U.S. Lawyer Questions Message in Videotape

A Government lawyer questioned another videotape demonstration at the Microsoft trial today, but this time the challenge dealt not with the reliability or honesty of Microsoft's tape but with its message.

David Boies, the Government's lead trial lawyer, has successfully attacked several videotape demonstrations Microsoft has played in court over the last few weeks, arguing that they were deceptively edited or did not show what the narrators' contended they did.

Today, as a new witness took the stand, Microsoft played a new tape showing that the company was allowing computer manufacturers

to customize the Windows desktop, the computer screen that users see when turning on the computer. With these customizations, the first screen shows the manufacturers' promotions and advertisements ahead of Microsoft's.

The Federal Government and 19 states offer as evidence of antitrust activities Microsoft contracts prohibiting computer makers from shipping machines with the Windows desktop altered in any way. This requirement, which Microsoft abandoned before the trial even started, is important to the case because the opening screen serves as a gateway to the Internet and to the tremendous profit potential in steering consumers to specific Internet service providers and Web sites.

Microsoft's demonstration today showed that the company was already granting manufacturers the flexibility to change the desktop. Computers being sold by Compaq, Hewlett-Packard, Sony and Acer, among others, were shown with their desktops modified so that they showed Internet sign-up offers and other options, either alongside Microsoft's offers or ahead of them.

Several of these computers also offered Netscape Navigator prominently. The Government charges in the suit that Microsoft has used the monopoly it enjoys with the Windows operating system to prevent computer manufacturers from offering Netscape's browser. Mr. Boies did not challenge the authenticity of the videotape, but he did challenge Microsoft's motivation for allowing the companies to alter the desktop.

"It basically shows how fast the industry is changing as this case goes on," he said.

But Joachim Kempin, a Microsoft senior vice president responsible for contracts with computer makers, responded: "I don't think it has anything to do with this case. I don't think the industry is changing because of this case."

Mr. Boies did show, however, that all the Windows customization in Microsoft's videotape demonstration was still in clear violation of the Windows licensing agreements the companies must sign. But Microsoft gave permission to a dozen companies that asked to make the changes, and Mr. Kempin insisted the same permission would be given to any others that came forward.

Mr. Boies suggested that he did not think it was a coincidence that these exceptions had been granted last spring, just weeks before the Government filed suit against Microsoft. And as a senior Government official noted, "What they give, they can take away if this suit goes away."

FEBRUARY 25, 1999

Microsoft Witness Peppered With Questions From Judge

A Government lawyer and Microsoft's next-to-last witness had been sparring for hours today when the presiding judge asked a few questions of his own that cut to the core of the company's defense. He spoke with a tone of skepticism that had several lawyers at Microsoft's table leaning forward tensely, mouths half open.

The witness, Joachim Kempin, a

Microsoft vice president, had been reciting the same argument each of the company's witnesses had offered over the last several months—that Microsoft had chosen to combine the company's Web browser with its industry-standard Windows operating system because the combination benefited consumers.

He repeated that argument several times as the Government's lead trial lawyer, David Boies, showed him memo after e-mail after document indicating that other Microsoft executives had clearly wanted to tie the browser to Windows to trump their most important competitor, the Netscape Communications Corporation.

"Why do you think integration made it a better product?" Judge Thomas Penfield Jackson asked. His tone, normally amiable when questioning witnesses, was tinged with skepticism bordering on incredulity.

Mr. Kempin gave a familiar response, one that is central to Microsoft's defense. Users get the same graphical interface when they use the computer help system as when they browse the Internet, he said. "And it makes it easier to organize the computer," he said. "There's no difference in the interface between your own files or on the Internet."

But the judge seemed unconvinced.

"You think consumers derive some benefit from knowing that it's on the hard drive or the Internet?" he asked.

"Yes, it's seamless," Mr. Kempin responded.

To which the judge asked again: "Why is that better for consumers?"

Microsoft will rest its case on Friday, and as the judge's questions this afternoon suggested, the trial has not gone well for the company. Again today, Mr. Boies managed to trip up Mr. Kempin and raise credibility questions about his testimony, as has been true of almost every witness who has testified for Microsoft.

Mr. Boies questioned Mr. Kempin for a second day about the company's policies with regard to allowing computer makers to alter the Windows main screen, or desktop, by adding their own software and graphics.

Mr. Kempin said Microsoft developers believed that computer makers were "butchering Windows" with their modifications. Nonetheless, he said, his company has been "very generous" over the years in the changes it had allowed.

But Mr. Boies presented or described memos from executives of computer makers, including Gateway, Packard Bell-NEC and Hewlett-Packard, who were upset about Microsoft's restrictions on changes to the desktop. In 1997, a senior Hewlett-Packard executive wrote, "From the consumers' perspective, we are hurting our industry and our customers." And he added, "If we had a choice of another supplier, based on your actions in this area, I assure you, you wouldn't be our supplier of choice."

Mr. Kempin dismissed this, calling the exchange "nothing but a dispute between two companies looking for the right balance."

As the day wore on, Mr. Boies showed several documents suggesting that the real reason Microsoft was concerned about modifications to Windows was that the manufacturers' screens covered up the icon for Microsoft's Web browser, Internet Explorer. Mr. Kempin said he thought that was wrong but offered no substantiation.

Then Mr. Boies asked whether it

was true that Microsoft had expressed threatening disapproval to computer manufacturers that worked with Netscape. Mr. Kempin responded that the manufacturers "determine their own destiny," adding, "I have a hard time believing we can tell them what to do."

But then Mr. Boies read from a document in which a Gateway executive recalled a conversation in which a Microsoft executive had told him that Gateway's support of Netscape was "a huge issue for Microsoft."

As a result, Mr. Boies asserted, "Microsoft charges Gateway a significantly higher price for Windows than Microsoft charges Dell or Compaq."

Not true, Mr. Kempin said. But then he clarified: Gateway is in fact charged more, he said, but for other reasons that he declined to elaborate.

Mr. Boies read more from the Gateway memo, including an assertion from a Gateway executive that Microsoft's actions were illegal. But before he could finish, the judge took the memo and repeated some of the allegations, asking Mr. Kempin: "How about all these other things? Do you deny all of these, too?"

"This is Gateway's version," Mr. Kempin said. "I have no knowledge of this."

FEBRUARY 26, 1999

Judge Questions Recent Leniency With PC Makers

A year ago, Microsoft forbade most or all modifications by to Windows by hardware manufacturers, a prohibition that contributed to Federal antitrust charges. This morning, as Microsoft's lawyer prompted Joachim Kempin, a Microsoft vice president, to list the modifications Microsoft was now allowing computer manufacturers to make to Windows, Judge Jackson interrupted to ask: "Are all these rights manufacturers now possess a matter of sufferance and grace on the part of Microsoft, or are they expressly written into the contracts?"

Mr. Kempin said some were granted in personal letters to the companies, others in phone conversations—not in contracts.

"So you have chosen to waive or give up certain rights you have in your contract?" the judge asked.

That's right, Mr. Kempin said. The judge's questions appeared to mirror the Government's assertions that Microsoft's new generosity to manufacturers could be temporary—lasting only as long as Microsoft's previous behavior is the subject of antitrust charges.

FEBRUARY 27, 1999

Dangling the Data Bait

Another of David Boies's regular trial tactics collided with Joachim Kempin's personality, but Boies still prevailed. The tactic here was his regular effort to extract numerical estimates from witnesses. He might ask, for example, "What percentage of computer users use Netscape?" To that, the witness would say, "I don't know." So Boies would say, "Just give me an estimate." If the witness still balked, Boies would ask again, "Can't you give me a range?" By the third or fourth such request, the witness would generally comply. And then Boies would try to hang him with the resulting number.

Here's how that strategy worked with Kempin:

Boies: In 1998, of all of the PC's shipped by OEM's, what percentage of those PC's were shipped with Navigator?

Kempin: I personally have never tracked that. I don't know.

Boies: Just give me an approximation.

Kempin: I just say I don't know.

Boies: Can you give me any range at all?

Kempin: I mean, I have not tracked it. I mean, I'm probably too German to say something on this one. And I'm a mathematician and statistician. So, if I tell you it's 20 percent or 80 percent, you know, it's just a wild guess.

Boies: Other than simply giving me a wild guess, can you give me any range or approximation, based on data that you have seen?

Kempin: Data I have here and based on what other people have shipped, maybe it's 20 or 30 percent or something in that range, maybe. But, again, it is not scientific.

Boies then used the estimate to cast doubt on Kempin's assertion that some computer manufacturers were choosing to load Netscape onto their machines. Boies pointed out that in at least one case, Netscape had been driven to pay a manufacturer to do that.

Poor Bob Muglia. He seemed so nice, so earnest. The impression he gave was that he just wanted to do right, set things straight. But cap-

Robert Muglia
MICROSOFT

ping a several-months-long string of embarrassments on the witness stand, Microsoft's
final regular witness was also humiliated in
the chair. In fact, he broke new ground in that
regard; the judge hadn't told any other witness to, in effect, shut up.

By the time Muglia took the stand, everyone in the courtroom was rushing to meet the judge's deadline to complete the testimony phase of the trial by the end of the day Friday. After that, David Boies and Judge Jackson had other trials to which they were committed in March. And another lawyer had made clear that he had a vacation planned starting the following week. So Boies rushed through his cross-examination of Muglia. But as it turned out, he had more than enough time.

Muglia was from Connecticut; his father was an automotive parts salesman. He got his first job at age 15 and had been continuously employed ever since. He earned an undergraduate degree from the University of Michigan in 1981. After college, Muglia worked for the ROLM corporation and joined Microsoft in 1987.

Microsoft Rests Its Case, Ending On a Misstep

After more than five months of testimony, the Microsoft Corporation rested its case today in the Government's landmark antitrust suit, but not before the presiding judge had shouted angrily at the company's final witness and ordered him to stop talking.

Today's incident was yet another blow in several months of missteps and embarrassments as Microsoft has tried to defend itself against Government charges that the company bullied the computer industry and used its monopoly in computer operating systems to the disadvantage of competitors.

The trial is not over; court will reconvene in mid-April for several weeks of testimony from rebuttal witnesses, three to a side. But as Microsoft completed its central case today, six weeks after the Government completed its case, both sides said they were confident of victory.

John Warden, Microsoft's lead trial lawyer, acknowledged that others believed that the Government had "succeeded in undermining our witnesses." But he called this a desperation tactic. "When you don't have the laws or the facts, you try credibility, and that's what I think has driven them to this strategy."

David Boies, the Government's lead trial lawyer, who has tripped up and embarrassed most of Microsoft's witnesses, said he believed that casting doubt on witnesses' credibility was not all that had been achieved.

"They've admitted monopoly power," he said. "They've admitted the absence of competitive constraints. They've admitted raising prices to hurt consumers. They've admitted depriving consumers of choice."

In the witness box today, Robert Muglia, a Microsoft senior vice president, tried to put the best face on his company's relationship with Sun Microsystems, the creator and owner of the Java programming language. The Government charges that Microsoft tried to sabotage Sun because it saw Java as a competitive threat.

Mr. Muglia, who said Microsoft's relationship with Sun was his responsibility, repeatedly asserted that Microsoft was interested in cooperating with Sun. But Mr. Boies presented numerous e-mail messages and memos from senior Microsoft executives, saying in one manner or another that they wanted to defeat Sun.

The combined effect of the memos was to leave the impression that if Mr. Muglia was to be believed, he was either out of touch or naive. And his continued defense of his position, even in the face of a contradictory e-mail from William H. Gates, the company's chairman, set off the judge.

In May 1997, Mr. Gates wrote: "I am hard-core about NOT support-ing" the latest version of Java. Messages in the same string of e-mail from other senior executives made the same statement, but with exclamation points and expletives.

Yet Mr. Muglia tried to make the case that Mr. Gates had not really meant what he wrote, adding, "I don't exactly know what Bill meant by support."

At that, Judge Thomas Penfield Jackson, who is hearing the case without a jury, shook his head and interrupted with an irritated tone, saying: "There's no question he says he does not like the idea of support-ing it. Let's not argue about it."

Mr. Muglia persisted, pleading with the judge, "Can I say one more thing, please?"

But a few seconds after he began what promised to be a long discourse defending his position, Judge Jackson exploded. One hand covering his face, the other held up at the witness, he bellowed: "No! Stop! There is no question pending!"

He then called a recess.

Microsoft spokesmen said they believed that Mr. Muglia needed to keep his answers shorter.

Earlier, Mr. Boies had showed him a Microsoft memo setting out the company's strategy on Java. The first line was: "Kill cross-platform Java by growing the polluted Java market." Sun and the Government accuse Microsoft of creating its own "polluted" version of Java to undermine Sun's version. Microsoft argues that its version is better.

Mr. Muglia said the document was written by a junior employee and was later revised by her supervisor.

Judge Jackson's outburst followed questions he had asked earlier in the day suggesting that he was skeptical of Microsoft's case.

While lawyers warn that it is dangerous to read too much into a judge's remarks, it is also true that judges often pose questions at the end of a trial that are intended to test conclusions they are considering for use in their final ruling.

As the previous witness, Joachim Kempin, completed his testimony, he turned to the next topic of testimony, Java, and offered an eloquent argument for the tenuous nature of Microsoft's dominant position in the industry. Among other threats, he said, Java was such a powerful idea that it could cause "a paradigm shift" that would unseat Microsoft.

That exposed a contradiction in Microsoft's defense. Mr. Muglia, in his written, direct testimony, said Sun's version of Java was so dreadful that Microsoft had every right to create its own version.

Sun's Java, he wrote, "is truly the great equalizing software; it has reduced all computers to mediocrity and buggyness."

At the end of the day, Mr. Muglia described a conversation with Mr. Gates in which Mr. Muglia had told him that Microsoft, which had licensed Java from Sun, could meet its contractual obligations by simply posting Sun's version of Java on Microsoft's Web site, rather than including it in Windows.

Then Mr. Boies introduced a memo in which the company executives charged with doing that described what they had done.

The Java file was posted, one executive wrote, "but there will be no entry index" for it, and as a result a consumer would "have to stumble across it."

"I put it in a directory with 37 other old files," the executive wrote. "In this directory I'd say it's pretty buried."

"Awesome," the other executive wrote back. "Thanks."

Mr. Muglia insisted that he had "said specifically that I didn't want it to be hidden." And he suggested that the hidden copy was just a draft.

But Mr. Boies said simply, "I have no more questions." The trial adjourned.

FEBRUARY 27, 1999

CHAPTER **4**

Bruised and Dazed Between Rounds

In the first long months of testimony, the Justice Department and 19 state attorneys general had clearly presented a compelling case against Microsoft, while the company's legal team and witnesses had stumbled badly.

Time and time again, the government's lead trial lawyer, David Boies, had humiliated Microsoft's witnesses. What's more, the company repeatedly seemed to step on its legal team's defense. Government lawyers offered as evidence documents from Gates or other senior executives stating opinions that contradicted the legal arguments Microsoft was offering in court.

But for all the embarrassments, for all the comments Judge Jackson made that seemed to favor the plaintiffs, Microsoft's lawyers continued to argue that antitrust case law fell in their favor and that all of Boies's accomplishments were mere theatrics, nothing more. His maneuvers played well in the news media, Microsoft argued, but they would mean nothing at the Court of Appeals. And some outside analysts continued to caution that the legal outcome remained uncertain.

"Boies has done an excellent job, but the outcome of this case is still in doubt," William Kovacic, a professor at the George Washington University Law School, said in the spring. "There is enough flexibility in the doctrine of antitrust and enough uncertainty about how the case law applies to a dynamic, high-technology industry like computer software that it could go either way."

As for the judge's supposed tilt toward the government, Microsoft spokesmen liked to point out that during a chambers conference just

after the testimony ended, Judge Jackson had encouraged a settlement by telling the group: "Both sides have taken some hits." Of
course, others suggested that the remark was the sort of innocuous
encouragement lawyers might expect from a judge.

The truth was, Jackson often just didn't believe Microsoft's witnesses. "There were times," he said later, "when I became impatient
with Microsoft witnesses who were giving speeches. They were telling
me things I just flatly could not credit."

But none of the litigants knew that at the time. Judge Jackson did
push them to settle the case during the recess. At first, Microsoft presented the government with a four-page document setting out the
company's proposed terms for a settlement. Among the terms, the
company agreed to relax contract restrictions with Internet service
providers—something the company had already done. Those and a
few other offers impressed no one.

California's attorney general, Bill Lockyer, called the proposal "a
minimalist opening offer that is far from what anyone in our group
would expect to be adequate," adding, "It was a very small offer."
Another government official said of the settlement talks, "The
chances are pretty good that all we're doing is a kabuki dance for the
judge."

The two sides did meet a few times in Washington to talk about
possibly settling the case. And there for the first time, the Justice
Department informed Microsoft that the plaintiffs wanted to break up
the company. After all, they believed they held a strong hand.

"I've never been involved in a case that went as well as this one,"
said Kevin O'Conner, an assistant attorney general from Wisconsin.
And Boies said, "If someone had told me that they would put on a
case that would provide me with as many great opportunities on
cross-examination as they gave me in this one, I probably would have
taken the case for free."

Microsoft made it clear at the outset that the company would not
accept a structural remedy under any circumstances. So on the final
day of these talks, Joel Klein, head of the Antitrust Division at the
Justice Department, gave a 10-minute, oral presentation of conduct
remedies, reading from notes.

They included certain protections for computer manufacturers,
regulations on the pricing of Windows and requirements for publishing certain technical information about Windows. Microsoft officers
listened impassively. They took away a copy of the document, said
they'd think about it and call back.

"There was a clear expectation they would get back to us," said

Richard Blumenthal, the Connecticut attorney general. "But they never did."

But in fact, the state and Federal officials who were prosecuting the case, flush with optimism about the way their case had progressed, were beginning to believe that should they win the case, they would not be happy with any remedy that did not restructure the company in some way.

A senior Federal official said the government, having learned from its past relationship with Microsoft, did not believe any sort of behavioral remedy—contract restrictions and the like that fell short of changing the company's structure or business motivations—would be effective. Behavioral remedies included contract restrictions and the like that fell short of changing the company's structure or business motivations, and they required constant monitoring and intervention—something no one wanted.

Which only left breaking up the company.

The state attorneys general were insistent on a structural remedy. In fact, they'd been researching remedies for more than a year—ever since May 1998, when Kevin O'Connor, an assistant attorney general in Wisconsin, voiced a fear he had just realized: His state and 18 others were suing one of the richest and most powerful companies in America. What would they do if they won?

"It's like the dog chasing the bus," O'Connor had said. "What's he going to do if he catches it?"

The states quickly chartered a remedies committee, and O'Connor was asked to head it. By then he had decided, "We need to change incentives. The remedy has to change their motivations."

Out of that work by the states, the idea receiving the most favor for a while would have forced Microsoft to license the source code for the Windows operating system to several other companies—instantly creating competition in the operating system business. After discussing that for a number of months, the states put the idea to several companies that would be likely bidders. Though these companies were never named, the group certainly included I.B.M., Sun Microsystems and other big companies that already produced operating systems. The states found that none of these companies had any interest in bidding. From their point of view, Windows was too complex and bug-ridden to be workable—and probably too expensive.

"Nobody would buy it," Tom Miller, the attorney general of Iowa, said with a chuckle. So the idea was dropped.

But many of the states—including New York, Ohio, Minnesota

and Utah—had another idea as well. They said they were eager to use provisions in their own laws that would allow them to fine Microsoft for every antitrust "incident." The amount varied—from $2,000 per incident in Kentucky to $100,000 in New York—but there was little if any case law to suggest how an incident would be defined in this context. And levying fines would require additional state litigation.

Officials in several states said they were hoping to establish that every purchase of a copy of Windows constituted a violation, or incident. "With per-violation or per-occurrence, that would be millions and millions of dollars," said Doug Davis, an assistant attorney general in West Virginia. But state officials acknowledged that it was far from certain that the courts would uphold that interpretation.

Microsoft, meanwhile, was working hard to prepare a compelling rebuttal case. Later in the spring, each side would be allowed to present three more witnesses, whose job would be to rebut the testimony of the previous witnesses. And the company's attorneys said the centerpiece of their rebuttal case would be a compelling argument showing that America Online's purchase of Netscape would make the combined company a powerful competitor to Microsoft. What's more, the lawyers said, the AOL and Netscape executives who had testified early in the trial had misled the judge by testifying as if they had not known the merger was in the works.

Boies called all this "a sideshow."

"For the life of me, I don't know what it has to do with the antitrust case," he said. "It's about the monopoly power Microsoft exercises over PC operating system."

Nonetheless, Microsoft subpoenaed reams of documents from AOL, Netscape and Sun Microsystems, a partner in the deal. Microsoft also took depositions from senior AOL executives, including the company's chairman, Steven M. Case, and pressed him on the charges it intended to use in court.

At one point during his deposition, Case looked quizzically at the Microsoft lawyer who was questioning him and asked, "Did I wander into the wrong room?"

A short time before the trial was scheduled to resume, both sides issued their witness lists for the rebuttal phase. And the Microsoft team made it clear that they would rely heavily on the America Online allegations. Among its witnesses, Microsoft said it would call as a hostile witness David Colburn, the America Online executive who had testified for the Government early in the trial. In a court filing, Microsoft said it would challenge "the completeness and candor of prior testimony."

"Our rebuttal witnesses will show that the $10 billion merger of AOL and Netscape completely undercuts the Government's case" by showing that "competition and innovation are stronger than ever in the software industry," said Bill Neukom.

The government, meanwhile, added what promised to be a powerful new witness, Garry Norris, the I.B.M. executive who for several years as director of that company's software strategy division, had been I.B.M.'s chief dealmaker with Microsoft.

At a pretrial deposition taken in Raleigh, N.C., Norris testified that Microsoft had repeatedly raised the price it charged for Windows and had enforced onerous licensing terms in retaliation for I.B.M.'s refusal to stop competing in the market for PC operating systems and applications software.

"Microsoft repeatedly said we would suffer in terms of prices, terms, conditions and support programs, as long as we were offering competing products," he said. As a result, he added, "we were severely disadvantaged in the marketplace."

With the completion of that deposition on May 26, the trial was due to resume in less than a week, and each side said it had powerful new evidence to present.

Gordon Eubanks recalled the telephone call he received in 1999, when Bill Gates asked him to testify as a rebuttal witness for Microsoft. "Bill just asked me to go there

Gordon Eubanks   and explain software and the business,"
OBLIX   Eubanks recalled months after he had testified. "He really believed that if the judge just understood how the industry worked, Microsoft would be all right."

Eubanks certainly had the pedigree for the job. Bearded, balding and affable, he looks like a somewhat older version of the Navy nuclear submarine officer he once was. His manner is straightforward and direct. Trained in computer science, he wrote a compiler—software that translates lines of code written by humans into binary commands that computers can understand—and founded Compiler Systems. His company was bought in 1981 by Digital Research, an early challenger to Microsoft in personal computer operating systems. The rivalry between the two was bitter and resulted in a long-running private lawsuit, which accused Microsoft of anticompetitive practices and was finally settled in January 2000. In the settlement, Microsoft agreed to pay more than $150 million to Caldera, a company that bought the remnants of Digital Research from Novell in 1996. By then, all that remained of Digital Research was the raw material of a law suit.

So Eubanks had once been a Microsoft competitor. Then, he became an industry partner of Microsoft, as the president and chief executive of Symantec, a maker of utility programs like antivirus software, from 1984 to 1999. Like any maker of personal computer software, close and friendly relations with Microsoft were vital to Symantec.

In April 1999, Eubanks became president and chief executive of Oblix, a Silicon Valley startup specializing in software for electronic commerce on the Web. The main venture capital backer for Oblix was Kleiner Perkins Caufield and Byers, which has backed many of Microsoft's leading rivals, including Netscape, Sun Microsystems and America Online. John Doerr, a senior partner at Kleiner Perkins, was one of several Silicon Valley executives with whom the Justice Department spoke regularly.

At Oblix, Eubanks had a complicated relationship with Microsoft, which is true of so many companies in the Internet era of computing. His company's business strategy was a bet on post-PC computing, which relies more on the Internet than on personal computers. Still, Oblix figured it needed Microsoft's technical cooperation because for the next several years the personal computer was likely to remain the main device used to access the Web.

In the trial, the Eubanks testimony was a kind of footnote to the proceedings. He was not a party to any of the meetings between Microsoft and other companies that formed the basis for the allegations in the government's case. He was there as a firsthand witness to the complicated, dynamic tapestry that is the software industry. He was there to support the context that Microsoft wanted the judge to use in shading his judgments on the evidence. To Microsoft, the message of the Eubanks testimony was, "Things are more complicated in this business than the prosecution would have you believe, and, not incidentally, this industry is working just fine."

Again, the intent of the government's cross-examination was to attack the credibility of the witness. That meant trying to portray Eubanks as a Microsoft stooge, beholden to Bill Gates and doing his bidding.

In April 2000, after the government proposed splitting Microsoft in two, Eubanks told *The Times* that he did not think the industry would necessarily suffer as a result. "And potentially, you could get more competition in desktop applications software," he said.

Rebecca Henderson, a professor at the Massachusetts Institute of Technology's Sloan School of Management, cited the Eubanks comment to *The Times* in a paper she filed with the court in support of the government's split-up plan.

The Times piece, of course, goes on to quote Eubanks's saying that while he did not think the government sanctions were necessarily bad, they seemed to be backward looking. "The irony of this," he told *The Times*, "is that Microsoft has never been weaker in recent years. The future is Web-based computing, and that is not where Microsoft's core competence is."

U.S. Hunts for Quid Pro Quo In Microsoft Witness's Actions

The Justice Department's chief trial lawyer in the Government's antitrust suit against the Microsoft Corporation closely questioned a Microsoft witness today about whether he had benefited as a result of his decision to defend the company and to testify in its behalf.

The questioning was one of a series of depositions taking place in preparation for the resumption of the trial in Washington on Tuesday.

Gordon Eubanks, a longtime software developer, who until recently was chairman and chief executive of the Symantec Corporation, frequently responded to the Justice Department lawyer, David Boies, by saying he did not recall details of his communications with Microsoft executives.

Mr. Eubanks, a pioneer in the personal computer industry, once worked for Digital Research, a company that competed with Microsoft in software products, notably operating systems and programming languages. But he has long been a defender of Microsoft, the software giant based in Redmond, Wash.

He is now the chief executive of Oblix, a Mountain View, Calif., software company.

The deposition, which took place this afternoon in a hotel room here in San Jose, began with Mr. Boies asking Mr. Eubanks what William H. Gates, Microsoft's chairman, had said when Microsoft asked Mr. Eubanks to serve as a rebuttal witness in the antitrust trial.

Mr. Boies then referred to a February 1998 E-mail exchange between Mr. Eubanks and Brad Chase, a Microsoft marketing executive, in which Mr. Chase asked Mr. Eubanks to write an opinion piece favorable to Microsoft.

In messages sent on Feb. 21, 1998, Mr. Eubanks said he would be glad to write a newspaper Op-Ed piece supporting Microsoft, and he then asked Mr. Chase if Microsoft would be willing to drop an anti-virus product that competed with Symantec's product from a supplement that Microsoft was releasing for the Windows 95 operating system.

Mr. Boies asked if there was a link between Mr. Eubanks's willingness to write a supportive Op-Ed piece and his decision to raise the question of the inclusion of the competitor's product as part of the Microsoft operating system.

"I understand what you're asking, and the answer is absolutely not," Mr. Eubanks said. He said that the two issues were "disjoint" and that he had consistently discussed the issue with Microsoft executives because he felt strongly that it was wrong for Microsoft, which has a de facto monopoly with its Windows family of operating systems, to "anoint one competitor's product in favor of another."

"Our customers routinely told me that supporting Microsoft was extremely important," he added.

At the outset of the deposition, Mr. Boies had asked Mr. Eubanks if Mr. Gates had asked him to testify to help with "damage control."

"Did he tell you that he wanted to help control the damage and that he felt the case was lost?" Mr. Boies asked.

Mr. Eubanks said he did not recall any such questions.

During the deposition, Mr. Boies and Mr. Eubanks fenced over a quote in a newspaper article in which Mr. Eubanks was reported to have criticized Microsoft's business practices.

Mr. Eubanks said he believed that he had been misquoted.

"I remember consistently telling our employees that our job was to serve our customers and that to get involved in disputes with Microsoft, Apple, Oracle or anyone else was not productive," Mr. Eubanks said.

MAY 28, 1999

After Three-Month Recess, Microsoft Trial Resumes

After a three-month recess and unsuccessful efforts to reach a settlement, the rebuttal phase of the Microsoft antitrust trial opened today with a concerted attack on the previous testimony of the company's chief economic witness.

In the attack, Franklin M. Fisher, a professor of economics at the Massachusetts Institute of Technology, who is testifying on behalf of the Government for the second time, called the economic analysis of Richard L. Schmalensee, his former student and a fellow economist at M.I.T., "ridiculous," "incredulous" and naive.

Both Mr. Fisher and Richard Schmalensee testified at length earlier in the trial on the question of whether Microsoft holds a legal monopoly in personal-computer operating systems—a critical question that will determine what kind of remedies can be applied if the Government prevails.

In his testimony early this year, Mr. Schmalensee tried to make the case that Microsoft was not a monopoly, largely by suggesting that the few, marginal competitors Microsoft now faces, or others, could conceivably become serious challengers in the future.

Mr. Fisher tried yesterday to puncture that argument, saying, "Just because there are unknown future threats does not mean Microsoft doesn't have a monopoly today."

Mr. Boies led Mr. Fisher through a carefully choreographed series of questions during the direct examination—a new practice for this trial. Earlier, witnesses submitted their direct testimony in writing.

Mr. Fisher called several of Mr. Schmalensee's analyses "reasonably confused," adding at one point, in a discussion of market dominance, "I don't think Dean Schmalensee understood this issue."

Later in the day, Mr. Boies led Mr. Fisher through a critical dissection of several charts and graphics that Mr. Schmalensee had offered as evidence. Mr. Fisher argued that in several of them, his colleague had made incorrect assumptions and offered improper numbers, leading to erroneous conclusions.

For example, Mr. Schmalensee had tried to make the case that Microsoft was charging too little for Windows—something a monopolist was unlikely to do. He had then offered a complex economic formula for a realistic price.

But this afternoon, Mr. Fisher said, "he made a big mistake."

Mr. Schmalensee's formula put the average price of a personal computer at $2,000 or $2,500, when, in fact, the average price is now about $950, Mr. Fisher said.

The witness also criticized Mr. Schmalensee's analysis of the market share for Microsoft's Internet Explorer browser, which showed Netscape as a strong competitor. By Mr. Fisher's analysis, Internet Explorer now has about 62 percent of the corporate market compared with 38 percent for Netscape, a unit of America Online.

But in the end, Mr. Fisher said, it did not really matter whether Microsoft had 40 percent of the browser market, or 60 percent or 80 percent.

A central tenet of the Government's case is that Microsoft fought to crush Netscape because Microsoft feared that Netscape's browser could one day be used as an alternative to the Windows operating system. If that happened, Microsoft would lose its crucial advantage, the fact that software developers write programs for Windows first.

"The goal was not necessarily to drive Netscape to zero," Mr. Fisher said. It was, he said, to make sure that Netscape did not maintain a market share that would ever allow software developers to write for Netscape alone. So by that measure, Mr. Fisher said, "Microsoft has already won."

JUNE 1, 1999

Microsoft Attempts to Show
It Had 'Scary' Competition

The Microsoft Corporation once again tried to show in court today that the company was facing potentially lethal competition, even presenting as evidence an e-mail message from one of its employees who called the competitive situation "a very scary thing."

But as a Microsoft lawyer, Michael Lacovara, tried to make the case that the personal computer business was seriously threatened, he first had to get past comments Microsoft's chairman, William H. Gates, made in an interview published by Newsweek magazine last month.

"Predicting the imminent demise of the personal computer has become an annual ritual," Mr. Gates said. "Well over 100 million PC's will be sold this year. That means the world now buys almost as many PC's as color TV's."

Franklin M. Fisher, the Government witness facing cross-examination from Mr. Lacovara today, raised the issue of Mr. Gates's remarks when the lawyer tried to suggest that the operating systems in Sony's new Play Station toy or in the Palm Pilot personal organizer could pose a threat to Microsoft's industry-dominating Windows.

Mr. Lacovara, of the Sullivan and Cromwell law firm, dismissed Mr. Gates's observation, asking, "Isn't that exactly what you'd expect Mr. Gates to say publicly, given the nature of Microsoft's business?"

In preparation for the rebuttal phase of the trial now under way, Microsoft subpoenaed thousands of documents from America Online, Sun Microsystems and the Netscape Communications Corporation about the on-line service's purchase of Netscape and Sun's cooperative role in the new venture.

Mr. Lacovara has not hidden Microsoft's excitement about what it found in those documents, and he entered a few into evidence today to support his assertion that Microsoft faces competitive threats.

One document, prepared last November by Goldman, Sachs & Company, the investment banking firm that managed the Netscape acquisition for America Online, lays out what Goldman took to be "The Strategic Rationale: The Plan."

The first point in the plan said the company could extend Netscape "to be a more comprehensive desktop application, bundling communications and productivity applications to absorb more share of computing time, with the goal of becoming the user's de facto environment."

Mr. Lacovara also entered into evidence an e-mail message from last July describing a meeting between Sun and America Online executives. In the message, a Sun executive said America Online planned to begin using a new browser on its service based on Java, Sun's programming language. This, the Sun executive wrote, will "break the deadly embrace with Microsoft."

America Online, the world's largest Internet service provider, with some 17 million subscribers, has distributed Microsoft's Internet Explorer Web browser with its software since 1997.

Today's courtroom maneuvers were intended to persuade the judge that Microsoft faces competitive threats that could undermine the monopoly position that lies at the heart of the Government's antitrust case.

Several documents were entered into evidence under seal, including every document obtained from America Online, at the on-line service's insistence. But none of the public documents showed that America Online subscribed to any of opinions and plans offered by the documents from Goldman and Sun.

In any case, it was not at all clear that any of it made much of an impression on Judge Thomas Penfield Jackson. After Mr. Lacovara had introduced several of these documents, Judge Jackson calmly asked him to stop, noting that they were "cryptic" and the witness, Mr. Fisher, was not familiar with them.

What is more, Judge Jackson added: "All this is from last fall. It's not clear whether this is current thinking or just wishful thinking."

The larger point Mr. Lacovara offered was that America Online and other companies were trying to counter Microsoft's dominance by offering word processors, spreadsheets, e-mail programs, calendars and other applications as on-line products that work with any operating system.

It was this budding business strategy that a Microsoft employee called "very scary," and Mr. Fisher acknowledged that Microsoft might have reason to be concerned.

"The market is moving under our feet," Mr. Lacovara said on the courthouse steps later.

David Boies, the lead Government lawyer, responded: 'The fundamental issue for us is the operating system monopoly. And that hasn't changed."

JUNE 2, 1999

A Hint of Collegiality

Microsoft's defense gained new energy in the rebuttal round, though the effectiveness of the effort was open to considerable question. After passing the cross-examination duties to six or seven different lawyers in the earlier round, lawyer Michael Lacovara took on the lion's share of duties and generally put on an impressive performance.

Lacovara, who made partner Sullivan & Cromwell at age 33, often spoke admiringly of David Boies, almost as if Boies were a professional father figure of sorts. But soon Boies began occasionally quoting Lacovara in court, asking questions with the precede, "As Mr. Lacovara would say. . . ." Lacovara broke into a broad smile the first time that happened and later said, "You know David means that as a compliment."

Lacovara made his points effectively and with flair, and after one impressive afternoon of questioning Fisher, a reporter congratulated him, saying had done a nice job, though he added, "Considering what you had to work with." Lacovara flinched and said, "you mean it would have been better if we were the ones with the angel on our shoulder?"

The judge appreciated Lacovara's work. In an interview later, he said Lacovara's cross-examination of Fisher was among the most effective moments in the trial. "And they both seemed to be enjoying themselves," he said.

Netscape Chief's Testimony Is Re-examined by Microsoft

The Microsoft Corporation promised it would question the credibility of key Justice Department witnesses during the rebuttal phase of the antitrust trial that began this week, and today a company lawyer introduced several documents that did just that.

The apparent inconsistencies between a Government witness's testimony last fall and subsequent statements out of court caught the attention of Judge Thomas Penfield Jackson—so much so that the judge urged a Government attorney to take account of them in court on Friday.

"There's very interesting information in there, and I hope you will revisit it," he told David Boies, the lead Government attorney. Mr. Boies assured him that he would.

At issue is the testimony last October of James Barksdale, chief executive of the Netscape Communications Corporation, who asserted that Microsoft, through predatory conduct, had so pushed Netscape into a corner that his company could no longer get computer makers to provide its browser with their products.

"That's over half the distribution channel," Mr. Barksdale said on the witness stand, "and we're basically out of it." At another point he said, "I think I've seen numbers around" showing that only about 10 percent of the world's computers come with Netscape pre-installed.

It turned out, however, that just as Mr. Barksdale was testifying, America Online was midway through a review process to determine whether to buy Netscape. As part of that, the investment banking firm Goldman, Sachs & Company was gathering data from Netscape, and one figure Netscape gave the bankers showed that the company's browser was being bundled on 24 percent of the personal computers being sold by the 20 largest manufacturers last fall.

"That's inconsistent, isn't it?" a Microsoft lawyer, Michael Lacovara, asked Franklin M. Fisher, a Government witness on the stand for the third day today.

Mr. Fisher said he thought the statistics in the Goldman documents were simply exaggerated.

Later in the day, Mr. Boies called the problem a minor inconsistency and noted that while Netscape might have been on 24 percent of the new computers, Microsoft's Web browser was on all of them, since it came included with Windows.

Trying to show that Microsoft had not seriously impeded Netscape, Mr. Lacovara introduced another internal America Online document prepared during deliberations over the sale showing that Netscape had reported distributing 160 million copies of its browser in 1998—though Mr. Lacovara, quoting Government figures, said he believed there were only 100 million Internet users worldwide.

"If they believe this document on its face, they'd have to believe there's been big adoption of the Netscape browser" in the last year, Mr. Fisher said. "I don't think they believe it; I don't think you believe it." Mr. Lacovara did not respond.

At another point, Mr. Lacovara presented evidence to support Microsoft's recurring contention that Linux, a free operating system, poses a real threat to Windows. He introduced an e-mail message in which a Microsoft employee complained that Linux was outselling Windows 2 to 1 in certain software stores in Silicon Valley, where Microsoft is not particularly popular.

Judge Jackson scoffed at this, calling the e-mail "a self-serving out-of-court declaration," asking with a laugh and a sarcastic tone: "Can you think of a reason it was forwarded to you?" Then the judge noted that the chart of comparable sales presented with the e-mail did not support the 2-to-1 statement. In fact it showed Windows outselling Linux in these stores. Mr. Lacovara said the 2-to-1 figure came from sales at another store not shown on the chart.

When Mr. Boies got his turn, he entered into evidence interviews with Microsoft executives over the last year, including William H. Gates, the chairman, calling Linux an insignificant phenomenon that did not worry Microsoft. "They've constructed a parallel universe in the courtroom," Mr. Boies declared.

Naked Came the Cookie

Microsoft, like the Justice Department, relied heavily on Internet publications for its defense, printing out pages from other companies' Web sites that offered boasts or promises Microsoft found helpful to its case.

One Web page introduced during Fisher's third day on the stand came from I.B.M.'s site and discussed the company's planned support of Linux. But many Web pages have rotating advertisements, and in many cases the ads that appear on a specific computer are based on information on the computer's hard drive showing what sorts of Web sites the user had visited in the past.

In this case, Lacovara found that the exhibit had been printed with a surprising ad at the top.

"NAKED, NAKED, NAKED!" it said.

Fisher took one look at the top and said, "One does wonder what sort of cookies you have on your machine." The cookie files on a computer hard drive hold the personal information about the user's Web-browsing habits, information that a Web server can check.

The courtroom was lost in laughter, but Lacovara went on to say, "I think I need to make two representations. The first is, this wasn't printed off of my computer. And the second is, the person who printed it did not click on the ad to see where it took him."

Microsoft Trial Data Is Questioned

Trying to defang the Government's antitrust charges against it, the Microsoft Corporation introduced a host of evidence this week to show that the Netscape browser was still healthy and thriving, despite Microsoft's all-out assault on the browser market.

But in a single stroke this afternoon, a Government lawyer under-cut Microsoft's strategy by producing a Microsoft e-mail written in January suggesting that the company had cynically and selectively produced data to support this point of view.

In the e-mail, Greg Shaw, a Microsoft public relations executive, asked others at the company: "What data can we find right away, showing that the Netscape browser is still healthy? The Government is introducing a bunch of data showing Netscape headed down big time and Microsoft way up."

The Netscape Communications Corporation's browser held a commanding lead until Microsoft entered the market with a browser, Internet Explorer, that was tied to the Windows operating system and set out on a campaign to dissuade other companies to work with Netscape. The Government's antitrust case is built on the contention that Microsoft used its dominance in operating systems to bolster its share of the browser market illegally.

"It would help if you could send me some reports showing their market share healthy and holding," Mr. Shaw added.

Later that morning, Robert Bennett, group product manager for Windows, wrote back, saying, "All the analyses have pretty much come to the same conclusion, which is that Netscape is declining and Internet Explorer is gaining."

A half-hour later, Yusef Mehdi, director of Windows marketing, weighed in, saying that he had found one survey showing "us very close on Internet Explorer share" and another that "has Netscape even or even higher."

"This is for the trial," Mr. Mehdi added, "so let's provide the more negative analysts."

As David Boies, the lead Government lawyer, read that aloud, Judge Thomas Penfield Jackson, who is trying the case without a jury, chuckled and shook his head, while Microsoft's lawyers looked grim.

And when Mr. Boies asked the witness, Franklin Fisher, an economist from Massachusetts Institute of Technology, what he thought this said about his analysis of Microsoft's take on the browser war, Mr. Fisher said only: "This document speaks for itself rather louder than most."

In questioning the witness again a short time later, a Microsoft lawyer, Michael Lacovara, heatedly asserted that all the Microsoft executives involved in the E-mail exchange were "marketing and public relations personnel" and that the exchange was "a discussion of trial public relations," not of legal issues. In fact, at one point, Mr. Shaw wrote that the request for market data "is for press purposes."

But it was not the first time Microsoft had been shown to gin up surveys or statistics that would indicate support for the company's view.

In January, Mr. Boies offered as evidence an E-mail message in which William H. Gates, the chairman of Microsoft, wrote, "It would help me immensely to have a survey showing that 90 percent of developers believe that putting the browser into the operating system makes sense." Later, he added, "Ideally we would have a survey before I appear at the Senate on March 3d."

In subsequent E-mail messages, Microsoft employees laid out how they would phrase the survey questions to be sure they elicited the responses Mr. Gates wanted.

Earlier today, Mr. Boies also seemed to take some of the sting out of Microsoft's attack Thursday evening on a previous Government witness, James Barksdale, who was chairman of Netscape. In court last October, Mr. Barksdale asserted that because of what he described as Microsoft's predatory conduct, Netscape could no longer get computer makers to provide the Netscape browser with their products.

"That's over half the distribution channel, and we're basically out of it," he said. But an internal document prepared for America Online at the same time, as part of that company's research for its purchase of Netscape, showed that just over one-fifth of the nation's computer manufacturers were shipping Netscape at the time.

As a result, Mr. Lacovara as-serted that Mr. Barksdale's credibility had been thrown into question, and Judge Jackson expressed interest in that.

Today, Mr. Boies pointed to several passages in Mr. Barksdale's direct written testimony in which he listed all the companies that were shipping Netscape on at least some of their computers and explained precisely what the arrangements allowed. All this detailed information, Mr. Boies and Mr. Fisher both said, showed that Mr. Barksdale was not trying to overstate the depth of Netscape's problem. Judge Jackson did not remark on this development.

JUNE 5, 1999

Half Empty, Half Full, Half True

David Boies was incredulous of Microsoft's cross examination. Even as the company was trying to make the case that Netscape was growing and thriving, he was holding onto the memo showing that the company had cynically manipulated the data. He intended to offer it as evidence as soon as he got the chance. And he knew that Microsoft also had a copy; both sides had access to the other's documentary evidence.

After Boies had entered the document into evidence, deflating that particular line of attack, he commented in the hall, "I don't understand what they are doing. They must be going for one news-cycle testimony. They had to know this other testimony was there."

At the same time, both sides were able to take a single number and use it to make polar arguments over Netscape's claim that it had distributed 160 million copies of the Netscape browser in 1998.

Standing in the courthouse hallway during a break in the proceedings that same day, Boies made the point that the 160 million number proved only that Microsoft had blocked

Netscape from the market. Why else would they have to pass out so many copies of the program?

But John Warden, the Microsoft lawyer, standing on the other side of the hall, had a different take, saying, "I don't see how anyone can make the argument that Netscape was foreclosed when they were able to distribute 160 million copies."

As well as the trial had gone for the government, there seemed to be one voice absent. The personal computer makers, according to the

Garry Norris

I.B.M.

government, were the ones suffering most under Microsoft's boot heel. They were all but captive distributors of Microsoft's products, especially its monopoly product, the Windows operating system.

Still, the march of government witnesses to the stand was a procession of Microsoft's rivals. There were no personal computer manufacturers. The government had tried repeatedly to get a PC maker to take the stand, prodding Ted Waitt, the chairman of Gateway, among others. But all of them eventually declined. Mostly, they told the Justice Department that they were too fearful of invoking Microsoft's wrath. The lone PC maker to take the stand, Compaq, did so on Microsoft's behalf.

The government filled the hole in its case in the rebuttal phase with Garry Norris, who from 1995 through 1997 who had been the company's chief deal maker for PC software. There had been an I.B.M. witness in the main part of the trial, but he was from the software side of the business.

Norris was soft-spoken and matter of fact. He didn't make speeches or folksy asides, as some witnesses had. And the government lawyer who questioned him was Phillip Malone, whose style was similarly low-key. Malone was the quiet hero of the Justice team, a staff lawyer in the San Francisco, who had headed the investigation that led to the suit. "The case that has been presented is Phil Malone's case," David Boies said as the trial ended.

Yet even though the presentational style lacked intensity, the Norris testimony was nonetheless riveting. It was a firsthand account of dealing with Microsoft from the subservient posture of a PC maker. All the power lay on Microsoft's side of the table, as Norris told it, and any sign of independence by a PC maker brought quick retribution.

Norris told his story in graphic detail. Microsoft, he testified, demanded a huge increase in the price I.B.M. would have to pay for Windows 95 to $75 a copy, up from the $9 a copy it paid for the previous version of the operating system, Windows 3.1. When he protested, the Microsoft executive replied, according to Norris, "Where else are you going to go? We're the only game in town."

But Microsoft, for once, seemed to get its side across effectively during the cross-examination. I.B.M. enjoyed a bargain price for Windows 3.1, Microsoft pointed out, because the product was partly based on the joint development work the two companies had done on OS/2, I.B.M.'s personal computer operating system, which never really challenged the success of Windows.

And the price that I.B.M. eventually paid for Windows 95? About $46 a copy, far less than the initial $75 offer. And when Microsoft in late 1997 opened negotiations on a new license for Window 3.1, its opening offer was $62 a copy. But after wrangling, I.B.M. got it down to $19.50. "Pretty good negotiating with the only game in town," noted Richard Pepperman, a Microsoft lawyer.

I.B.M. Executive Describes Price Pressure by Microsoft

A senior I.B.M. executive testified today that the Microsoft Corporation had repeatedly raised the prices it charged the International Business Machines Corporation for its Windows operating system and had enforced other onerous licensing terms in retaliation for I.B.M.'s refusal to stop competing with Microsoft.

"Microsoft repeatedly said we would suffer in terms of prices, terms, conditions and support programs, as long as we were offering competing products," said the executive, Garry Norris, a manager in I.B.M.'s PC division from 1995 through 1997.

In a seven-hour deposition taken here in Raleigh, N.C., today as part of the Government's antitrust suit against Microsoft, Mr. Norris described several instances in which he said Microsoft had followed through with threats so that "we were severely disadvantaged in the marketplace."

Mr. Norris will testify as a witness for the Government when the trial resumes next week. His testimony here today suggested that he will offer compelling new evidence bolstering the Government's case, the core of which is that Microsoft uses its monopoly position in personal computer operating systems to force companies into compliance on other competitive issues. Until now, no computer manufacturer has testified about such threats.

I.B.M.'s willingness to testify is just the latest volley in longstanding antagonism between the two companies. I.B.M. set Microsoft on its course to power and riches in 1980 when it adopted the then-tiny company's MS-DOS operating system for the new PC it was introducing. But the relationship soured as so-called clone makers grabbed huge chunks of I.B.M.'s new consumer and small-business markets by making machines that ran MS-DOS. The operating system then became more important than I.B.M.'s computer design—and eventually, far more profitable.

The final split came in the early 1990's, when Microsoft pulled out of a collaboration with I.B.M. to develop OS/2, a powerful successor to MS-DOS. After both companies had invested several years and many millions of dollars in OS/2, Microsoft decided that its Windows would replace DOS. I.B.M. decided to go it alone with OS/2, and the antagonism Mr. Norris described today resulted largely from I.B.M.'s continuing to offer OS/2 as an alternative to Windows.

Microsoft lawyers conducted today's deposition, and their questions suggested that I.B.M. was in large part to blame for the hostile relationship between the two companies.

For example, Mr. Norris described how Microsoft had stalled I.B.M. for many months in 1995, refusing to sign a licensing agreement allowing I.B.M. to install Windows 95 on its personal computer products until 15 minutes before the launch of Windows 95, on August 24, 1995. As a result, he asserted, I.B.M. was the last computer manufacturer in the world to get Windows 95, putting the company months behind its competitors and costing I.B.M. its position as the largest seller of PCs.

Microsoft also ended up charging I.B.M. more for Windows 95 than it charged other, smaller personal computer manufacturers, Mr. Norris said.

But a Microsoft lawyer, Rick Pepperman, pointed out that at the very time that the two companies were dickering over a license agreement in 1995, Microsoft discovered that I.B.M. had been under-reporting its sales of Windows 95's predecessor, Windows 3.1, by 15 percent, costing Microsoft more than $30 million.

I.B.M.'s resistance to Microsoft's demand for an audit, Mr. Pepperman said, contributed to the Windows 95 license delay.

The problems began, Mr. Norris said, at a meeting in November 1994 at which Microsoft offered I.B.M. lower prices and more cooperation if it would eliminate or reduce shipments of OS/2.

Instead, Mr. Norris said, I.B.M. executives said they intended to step up OS/2 sales and "ship it on as many units as we could."

Mr. Norris said a Microsoft executive told I.B.M. that Microsoft's chairman, William H. Gates, was "surprised and upset" by the decision, and after that, Microsoft was "unresponsive to phone calls and very slow" in supplying advance versions of Windows 95.

But Mr. Pepperman recalled I.B.M.'s ad campaign against Windows 95 asserting that OS/2 was faster than Windows 95 and would crash less often. "Why wait for Windows 95?" I.B.M.'s ads asked.

Mr. Pepperman produced a record of a phone call to senior I.B.M. executives in July 1995 in which Mr. Gates was irate over "I.B.M.'s lack of respect for Microsoft."

Perhaps the most useful testimony for the Justice Department concerned Mr. Norris's contention that Microsoft charged I.B.M. higher prices for Windows as a penalty for competing with Microsoft—exactly the sort of evidence needed to support antitrust charges.

Mr. Norris said Microsoft charged I.B.M. $9 for each copy of Windows 3.1. But after nine months of bitter altercations, the per-copy price of Windows 95 rose to $45.90, boosting I.B.M.'s licensing costs to $220 million a year from $40 million.

Microsoft also insisted that I.B.M. sell 300,000 copies of Windows 95 in the first five months, which I.B.M. said was impossible, or face a 20 percent price increase. In the end, I.B.M. sold only 100,000 copies, and Mr. Pepperman said that Microsoft did not carry out its threat. Instead, Mr. Norris said, the per copy price went up to $46.60, costing I.B.M. $3.5 million more each year.

Mr. Pepperman said that I.B.M. had been given a special price for Windows 3.1 as part of a previous cooperative arrangement. Mr. Norris said that both Compaq and Hewlett-Packard, among other "first-tier companies" paid less than I.B.M. He testified that a Microsoft executive had told him that Compaq paid less "because Compaq doesn't compete with us."

MAY 27, 1999

I.B.M. Official Has Harsh Words for Microsoft

Referring to documents and recalling first-hand experience, an I.B.M. executive today provided the most detailed allegations yet to arise in the Microsoft antitrust trial of how the big software maker wielded its market power to put pressure on personal computer makers to favor Microsoft's products.

The executive, Garry Norris, testified that when he objected to the price and terms under which Microsoft offered its industry-standard Windows operating system to the International Business Machines Corporation, he heard the take-it-or-leave-it arrogance of a monopolist.

Mr. Norris said a Microsoft executive had said to him: "This is the only game in town. Where else are you going to go?"

During a day of friendly questioning from a Government lawyer, Mr. Norris told of Microsoft's using its market power to put pressure on

I.B.M. to reduce its support for competing products, to increase prices and to restrict the freedom I.B.M. had to control the initial screen that users see on its personal computers.

Microsoft denies the allegations by Mr. Norris, a program director in I.B.M.'s networking hardware division, who handled relations between the I.B.M. PC business and Microsoft from 1995 to 1997.

Microsoft says that he is exaggerating what were complex negotiations between two companies that competed in some businesses and cooperated in others. The terms and prices I.B.M. received for Windows, Microsoft says, were the result not of Microsoft's bullying but of business decisions I.B.M. chose to make.

And the Microsoft executive who, Mr. Norris testified, told him that Windows was the "only game in town" insisted that he never made the comment. "Absolutely not—it's not in my character to say something like that," the executive, Mark Baber, who has retired from Microsoft, said in an interview.

Still, the day of testimony by Mr. Norris, unless refuted in cross-examination, appeared to lend new ammunition to the Government's case. Some of his accusations had been made in a pretrial deposition last month, but today's testimony made further allegations and added new details to previous allegations.

And his testimony was backed up by new documents entered into evidence today, including internal I.B.M. memos as well as letters and E-mail between the companies.

"This is some of the most important evidence in the case," said David Boies, the lead trial lawyer for the Justice Department. "It shows Microsoft, once again, going to a competitor and trying to persuade it or pressure it not to compete. This conduct is a clear violation of the antitrust laws."

In his testimony, Mr. Norris contended that Microsoft refused to offer I.B.M. as low a price for Microsoft's Windows operating system as was offered to its leading competitors unless I.B.M. "reduced or eliminated" support for OS/2, I.B.M.'s competing operating system.

In talks before Microsoft's introduction of Windows 95, Mr. Norris contended that Microsoft also said I.B.M. would pay a higher price for Windows if I.B.M. continued to heavily promote the Smartsuite office productivity software, made by I.B.M.'s Lotus division, which competes with Microsoft's Office suite of word processing, spreadsheet and data base programs—a lucrative market that Microsoft dominates.

In July 1995, with the August introduction of Windows 95 approaching fast, I.B.M. was the last major PC maker without a Windows license. Microsoft said it would not sign a Windows deal with I.B.M. until a simmering dispute over past royalty payments had been settled, Mr. Norris contended.

According to Mr. Norris, all these conflicts with Microsoft held a single message—and one that, he said, Microsoft executives delivered to him personally time and again.

"I was told that as long as you compete against Microsoft," Mr. Norris said, "you will suffer in terms of pricing and support."

Even before I.B.M. acquired Lotus in June 1995, Microsoft was concerned about I.B.M.'s support for the Lotus rival to Microsoft's Office.

After the I.B.M.-Lotus deal in 1995, Microsoft's worries about competition from Lotus Smartsuite were heightened. Recounting a dinner meeting with Joachim Kempin, the Microsoft executive in charge of dealing with PC makers, an I.B.M. executive wrote in an internal memo that Microsoft was "definitely worried about Smartsuite being given away and eating into their 'office heartland.'

"There are lots of 'combative' people in Microsoft ready to go to war with I.B.M.," he added.

In July 1995, Mr. Norris testified, Microsoft introduced a new issue into the I.B.M.-Microsoft negotiations over a Windows license—a dispute over royalty fees owed to Microsoft for earlier products, including OS/2, dating back to the days when the two companies were partners in software development.

"I was quite surprised," Mr. Norris recalled. "We never discussed it as being related to the Windows 95 license."

Introduced in court today was a letter written on July 20, 1995, from G. Richard Thoman, who was a senior I.B.M. executive, to William H. Gates, the chairman of Microsoft, complaining that the royalty dispute—the subject of an audit by Ernst & Young—was being linked to obtaining the Windows 95 license.

"This is a complete reversal of Microsoft's prior position," Mr. Thoman wrote.

But Microsoft says it was I.B.M. that first suggested linking the royalty dispute with a Windows license. I.B.M. did eventually resolve the royalty dispute and sign a Windows 95 license with Microsoft, but only minutes before Microsoft rolled out Windows 95 on Aug. 24, 1995. As a result, I.B.M. was not able to have the popular Microsoft product on I.B.M. machines for the surge of Windows 95 sales in the next few months.

The delay, Mr. Norris said, "impacted measurably on our business," resulting in many millions in lost sales.

Mr. Norris also detailed the steadily higher prices I.B.M. has paid in Windows licensing fees to Microsoft, rising from $220 million in 1996 to $440 million last year.

In 1996, I.B.M. was paying $47 for each copy of Windows, according to documents introduced today.

That was several dollars higher than its big rival, Compaq Computer. But Microsoft said that was not out of line with any other PC maker and Compaq's favorable price was explained by a lot of joint software development and technical support work that Compaq chose to do.

Mr. Norris also testified that in 1996 Microsoft imposed a last-minute change in the Windows contract it was then negotiating with

Microsoft, which prohibited it from showing consumers an I.B.M. "welcome screen" before they got to the Windows desktop screen.

I.B.M.'s focus-group research and testing, Mr. Norris said, had found that consumers often found the I.B.M. first screen easier to use than Windows—and would likely reduce the customer-support calls from novice users.

Each customer support call, Mr. Norris said, cost I.B.M. $35. "And three calls to our help center would wipe out the profit I.B.M. made on a consumer PC," he said.

JUNE 7, 1999

I.B.M. Executive Testifies On '97 Microsoft Proposal

At a private meeting in March 1997, a Microsoft executive told I.B.M. that the computer maker would pay a lower price for Microsoft's Windows operating system if it did not ship a competing Internet browser, an I.B.M. executive testified today.

With his handwritten notes of the meeting introduced as evidence in the Microsoft antitrust trial, Garry Norris of the International Business Machines Corporation recounted the meeting and the proposal by an executive of the Microsoft Corporation.

One notebook entry, written in a crimped script, stated that the Microsoft executive said if I.B.M. agreed to "no Netscape"—a reference to Microsoft's main rival in Internet browsing software, the Netscape Communications Corporation—on its machines, then I.B.M. would receive a lower price for Windows.

When a Justice Department lawyer asked Mr. Norris why he wrote three asterisks alongside that entry, he testified, "When he said 'no Netscape,' I thought that was very important."

The Government's case against Microsoft focuses mainly on the software maker's reportedly illegal conduct to thwart the challenge posed by Internet software. In the trial, which began last October, the testimony by Mr. Norris is the first time a PC maker has said that Microsoft proposed tying Windows' price not just to promoting the Microsoft browser but to excluding Netscape's.

A Microsoft spokesman said the company had no information that such an offer was made in March 1997. "Certainly, no such proposal was ever pursued or consummated," said Mark Murray, the company spokesman.

In his second day of testimony, Mr. Norris, who negotiated with Microsoft for I.B.M.'s personal computer division from 1995 to 1997, provided further testimony that Microsoft tried to use its market power to prod PC makers to favor Microsoft products over competing programs.

The currency of Microsoft's approval or disapproval, Mr. Norris testified, is often the complex pricing formula for its industry-standard Windows operating system. The confidential pricing agreements are detailed "market development agreements," or M.D.A.'s, between Microsoft and PC makers. They give PC makers discounts on their Windows price for promoting and supporting Windows in various ways.

In his notes on one meeting, Mr. Norris stated that Microsoft executives pushed hard for shipping Internet Explorer exclusively on its machines. "If not," he wrote, "MDA repercussions."

Still, Mr. Norris acknowledged that I.B.M. did eventually reach an agreement with Microsoft in 1997 to distribute Internet Explorer, and the pact did not include any of the exclusivity that he said Microsoft had proposed. I.B.M. chose to ship both Netscape and Internet Explorer, so it did not try to obtain the M.D.A. discounts, he said.

Microsoft's cross-examination of Mr. Norris began shortly before the lunchtime break. Shortly into the afternoon session, Judge Thomas Penfield Jackson seemed to suggest that Microsoft faced a challenge in trying to refute the testimony of Mr. Norris.

When Judge Jackson raised questions about documents Microsoft wanted to introduce as evidence, a Microsoft lawyer offered to bring to court two people to vouch for the documents—Joachim Kempin or Mark Baber. Both Microsoft executives were mentioned frequently by Mr. Norris as messengers of the effort to get I.B.M. not to ship software that competed with Microsoft.

"If Mr. Kempin or Mr. Baber are called," the judge replied, "there is a lot more they will have to testify about beyond these documents."

The judge then permitted the documents to be introduced. There were three draft proposals for an alliance agreement between I.B.M. and Microsoft, which would have resulted in I.B.M.'s obtaining the same Windows price as Compaq.

The proposals, drafted in 1994, indicated that I.B.M. was being offered increasing freedom to ship and promote other products including its own OS/2 operating system, which competed with Microsoft's Windows.

The first draft proposal said I.B.M. would "primarily promote Microsoft desktop software platforms"—a reference to Windows and Windows NT. A later draft said I.B.M. must be "committed to promote"

Microsoft's software, "but not exclusive to products offered by other divisions of I.B.M."—a reference to I.B.M.'s OS/2.

Throughout his testimony, Mr. Norris said that Microsoft demanded that I.B.M. "reduce, drop or eliminate" its support for OS/2 to obtain the favored price for Windows.

JUNE 8, 1999

Microsoft Trial Witness Undergoes Tough Cross-Examination

Under sharp questioning by a Microsoft lawyer, an I.B.M. executive conceded today that none of the Microsoft contract proposals he read had stated that I.B.M. must stop shipping its OS/2 operating system to get a favorable price for Windows, Microsoft's competing operating system.

But Garry Norris of the International Business Machines Corporation testified that despite the absence of a clear-cut requirement that I.B.M. drop its operating system, the many sales and promotion steps called for in the Microsoft proposal would have had the "effect of killing OS/2 in the marketplace."

The grudging concession and counterattack came during a day of clipped, combative exchanges at the Microsoft antitrust trial between Mr. Norris and Richard Pepperman, a lawyer representing the Microsoft Corporation.

Microsoft is trying to battle back after two days of compelling testimony by Mr. Norris, who handled relations between Microsoft and I.B.M.'s personal computer division from 1995 to 1997. Mr. Norris, the first representative of a PC maker to appear as a Government witness, has contended that Microsoft repeatedly tried to put pressure on I.B.M. to favor Microsoft software and exclude rival offerings—a central theme in the sweeping antitrust suit against Microsoft brought by the Justice Department and 19 states.

The cross-examination by Microsoft was a point-by-point assault on the testimony of Mr. Norris, seeking to refute or at least cast doubt on his allegations. Microsoft's lawyers introduced evidence, including internal I.B.M. E-mail, that sought to portray the company's relations with I.B.M. as the capitalist arm-wrestling of two powerful companies—not as Microsoft playing a bullying monopolist. One I.B.M. memo, for example, said that Microsoft feared that I.B.M. was "out to 'annihilate' Microsoft."

Again and again, Microsoft sought to focus the court's attention on the fact that it did not exclude I.B.M. from shipping competing operating systems, office productivity software or Internet browsers—all subjects of testimony by Mr. Norris. "There were no exclusive contracts, just a lot of hard bargaining by both companies," said William H. Neukom, general counsel of Microsoft.

There were no exclusive contracts, according to the Government, because I.B.M. refused to accept Microsoft's proposals—proposals not made in its written contract offers but verbally in meetings, which Mr. Norris attended and recorded in handwritten notes.

Microsoft's cross-examination, the Government insists, did little to undermine the key point Mr. Norris vividly detailed—that Microsoft used its industry-standard Windows operating system to try to prod I.B.M. to favor Microsoft software over products of rivals.

"Microsoft did link how I.B.M. was treated to whether I.B.M. shipped competing products, and that is the antitrust issue," said David Boies, lead trial lawyer for the Justice Department.

In this nonjury trial, Judge Thomas Penfield Jackson will be the arbiter of how successful Microsoft has been in raising doubts about Mr. Norris's testimony. The judge has shown some impatience with Mr. Pepperman, cutting off some of his questions. And in a private meeting with lawyers yesterday afternoon, Judge Jackson, according to a transcript released today, told Mr. Pepperman, "I'm not sure how much progress you have made so far, but we will leave that aside."

Mr. Norris, who finished his three days on the stand this afternoon, has proved to be a firm and unflappable witness. Today, he often conceded on specific questions, but still went on to make his point.

In one typical exchange, Mr. Pepperman said Microsoft had never refused to grant I.B.M. a license for Windows if I.B.M. shipped Netscape's Navigator browser—a rival to Microsoft's Internet Explorer—on its PC's. True, Mr. Norris replied, but Microsoft executives did tell him that shipping Netscape's product would have "M.D.A. repercussions"—a reference to a marketing development agreement, which links the price of Windows to marketing commitments by a PC maker.

Repeatedly, Mr. Pepperman tried to undercut the allegation by Mr.

Norris that Microsoft had offered I.B.M. a lower price for Windows if it stopped shipping competing software. For example, he asked Mr. Norris to find anywhere in the written contract proposals the requirement that to receive a lower Windows price I.B.M. was required to "drop or eliminate OS/2"—a phrase Mr. Norris had used to describe the proposal.

Mr. Norris said that it was not in those precise words. Chiding the Microsoft lawyer, Mr. Norris said that the phrase he used in his court testimony, though not always in a pretrial deposition last month, was "reduce, drop or eliminate OS/2."

Mr. Pepperman countered, "So is it your testimony that the 'drop or eliminate' are inaccurate?"

Mr. Norris replied in a tone tinged with anger, "I am not changing my testimony."

Microsoft also tried to cast doubt about the accuracy of the handwritten notes of Mr. Norris—crucial evidence in the case. One piece of I.B.M. E-mail described a meeting at which Mr. Norris said Microsoft offered I.B.M. price discounts and other benefits if it stopped shipping Netscape's browser and other competing products. But E-mail on March 31, 1997, from Dean Dubinsky, another I.B.M. executive who attended the meeting, to Mr. Norris and his boss, William (Ozzie) Osborne, did not mention the Microsoft inducement to exclude rival products.

After receiving the E-mail, Mr. Norris explained that he called Mr. Dubinsky, who said he intentionally left the sensitive proposals out of the E-mail. "I'll let you and Ozzie handle that," Mr. Norris recalled Mr. Dubinsky telling him. I.B.M., Mr. Norris testified, refused to agree to the exclusive deal with Microsoft.

JUNE 9, 1999

I.B.M. Negotiator's Testimony Hits Microsoft Hard

The testimony last week of Garry Norris of I.B.M. supplied some of the most absorbing moments so far in the Microsoft trial. His litany of accusations was lengthy and specific—threats and enticements to not compete against the Microsoft Corporation delivered at meeting after meeting. His charges were fleshed out with the dates, places and names, and backed up by his handwritten notes.

Mr. Norris, who negotiated with Microsoft on behalf of the International Business Machines Corporation's personal computer business from 1995 to 1997, was the first representative of a PC maker to testify for the Government. David Boies, the lead trial lawyer for the Justice Department, said the Norris testimony put a "vivid human face" on what he called "some of the most important evidence in the case."

Yet antitrust experts say that the Norris testimony was not a knockout punch on its own and that its legal power may hinge on earlier testimony, in closed sessions, on the prices Microsoft charges PC makers for its Windows operating system.

Big, powerful and itself long a target of Government antitrust suits, I.B.M. was an imperfect object of sympathy as the representative witness for PC makers. Ever since I.B.M. selected Microsoft to supply the operating system for the first I.B.M. PC in 1981, I.B.M. has been out-hustled and outsmarted by Microsoft in the PC business—not the sort of behavior the nation's antitrust laws were meant to prohibit.

The Government, of course, had recognized that I.B.M.'s size, reach and complicated history with Microsoft could be used by Microsoft's lawyers to try to undercut its contentions. For months, the Justice Department had urged other major computer makers to take the stand—and it pushed particularly hard for Ted Waitt, the chairman of Gateway Inc., who ultimately decided against it.

Microsoft's defense, antitrust experts say, may be that I.B.M. was told it would pay a higher price for Windows unless it agreed to "reduce, drop or eliminate" shipments of OS/2, I.B.M.'s competing operating system.

On its face, such an invitation to a competitor to reduce competition would be an antitrust violation, even if the offer were rejected. But the legal standard in such cases, established in a 1984 ruling involving American Airlines, is that the evidence be "uniquely unequivocal"—in the airline case, the evidence was a tape-recorded offer to jointly raise fares.

With Microsoft, there is no such clear-cut evidence. The contract proposals presented in court were a series of suggested discounts on the price of Windows if I.B.M. agreed to certain promotion and marketing efforts on behalf of Windows. No Microsoft contract offer, Mr. Norris conceded, stated specifically that I.B.M. must "drop or eliminate" OS/2. But he insisted that the overall effect of the Microsoft terms would be to "kill OS/2 in the marketplace."

Still, antitrust experts note, it is certainly legal for Microsoft to offer a distributor—as the I.B.M. PC business was—incentives to aggressively distribute its product. If accepting those incentives means featuring Microsoft's Windows over OS/2—made by another unit of I.B.M.—that is mainly a business decision for I.B.M. to make, they say. I.B.M. turned down the Microsoft proposal.

A shrewdly devised offer by Microsoft perhaps, but antitrust experts say it was probably not a violation.

The Norris testimony, however, went well beyond the OS/2 charge. He asserted that Microsoft repeatedly offered I.B.M. better terms and prices for Windows if it favored Microsoft products ranging from so-called office productivity applications to its Internet browsing software. When I.B.M. rejected those proposals, Mr. Norris said, Microsoft charged I.B.M. more for Windows than it charged other major PC makers.

"The strongest Norris testimony was when he recounted the incidents of I.B.M. not using other Microsoft software and then getting punished on the price of Windows," said Robert Litan of the Brookings Institution, who is a former senior official in the Justice Department's antitrust division.

The exception was the Compaq Computer Corporation, which received a significantly lower price, Microsoft says, because it shared in the costs of developing Windows 95—a straightforward business rationale for different terms, says Microsoft, not punishment meted out by a monopolist.

But the Government introduced an I.B.M. document that cast doubt on Microsoft's statement. The document, an internal memo, said I.B.M. believed it paid $5 to $15 more for each copy of Windows it loaded on its machines than did Compaq, Hewlett-Packard or Dell Computer. "I.B.M.," the May 1997 document stated, "currently pays a higher royalty than our leading competitors."

Much of the detailed, company-by-company information on the prices to makers for Microsoft's industry-standard Windows operating system was submitted in previous testimony. To protect confidential commercial information, Judge Thomas Penfield Jackson took that testimony in closed sessions.

If the industry pricing information shows that I.B.M. was paying more than comparable PC makers, the Norris testimony may add more legal ammunition to the Government's case.

"To the extent the Norris testimony fits into the pattern of Microsoft threats and punishment, it is another piece in the puzzle," Mr. Litan, the former Justice Department official, said.

JUNE 14, 1999

Microsoft Lawyer and Witness Wrestle Over Demo Program

With the Government's final witness on the stand in Federal court this afternoon, lawyers for the Microsoft Corporation were obviously eager for an opportunity to mount a demonstration of how it was impossible to remove the company's World Wide Web browser from its Windows 98 operating system.

"The demonstration is so dramatic that I think you will appreciate it," Steven Holley, a Microsoft lawyer, told a clearly amused Judge Thomas Penfield Jackson.

"Mr. Holley really wants to run this program," the judge said with a smile and a shake of the head. So he told the witness, Edward W. Felten, a Princeton University computer scientist, to "click on whatever he tells you to click on," using the laptop computer Mr. Holley had supplied.

At issue was a program that Dr. Felten had written to strip Windows of its Web-browsing capability—something Microsoft insists cannot be done. Central to this antitrust case is the Government's assertion that Microsoft included its Internet Explorer Web browser with Windows to trump its main competitor in the browser business, Netscape Communications, now part of America Online.

When Dr. Felten first appeared as a Government witness in December, he showed that his removal program could easily eliminate the browsing function from Windows. But Microsoft argued that all he had done was to hide it. Microsoft's effort a few weeks later to debunk Dr. Felten's testimony using videotaped demonstrations was riddled with errors and misleading assertions that turned it into a courtroom embarrassment.

Today, Dr. Felten offered a new removal program that he said repaired some flaws Microsoft had pointed up in the original. As required, he had given Microsoft an advance copy of it, and the company again set out to debunk it.

Microsoft representatives bought a Toshiba laptop computer at a local store. They placed it on the witness stand with Dr. Felten, hooked up a phone line and asked him to run his removal program.

Dr. Felten objected, asserting that Toshiba had loaded a dozen additional programs on the machine, including some that offered Internet access. "There's more than one browser on this machine," he said. "My program is not intended to run on this configuration. Whatever behavior Mr. Holley is asking me to create, I don't know what effect all of this will have on it."

Earlier in the trial, this sort of

assertion would have been likely to bring an angry reaction from the judge. But often now, as testimony winds toward a close, Judge Jackson seems simply amused by the foibles of the lawyers and witnesses. So he asked Dr. Felten to proceed, in a manner suggesting that none of it was likely have much effect on the case.

With the browser theoretically removed, Mr. Holley asked Dr. Felten to press the control key and the N key—a combination that brings up a new Window in Microsoft programs. When he did, Internet Explorer appeared on the screen.

Dr. Felten appeared momentarily flustered but recovered quickly, saying: "I don't know what happened; this is a context in which the removal is not supposed to be run. But in any case, you have just demonstrated a bug; that's all."

Mr. Holley gleefully responded, "It's a pretty big bug, isn't it." After a few minutes of back-and-forth, the judge noted, "I think you have both made your points; I don't think further experiments are going to change the minds of either of you."

Outside the courtroom later, David Boies, the Government's lead trial lawyer, said, "If you have two or more browsers on the machine, and you remove one browser, that leaves one or more browsers on the machine."

Mr. Holley countered, "The demonstration would have come out exactly the same way on a virgin machine. None of this changes one teeny-weeny bit the fact that all this guy is doing is hiding the browser."

Earlier today, Dr. Felten had found flaws in many of Microsoft's arguments for tying the browser to Windows, suggesting that Microsoft's behavior often contradicts its words.

Steven C. Holtzman, a Government lawyer, recalled the testimony of James Allchin, a senior Microsoft executive, who said it was extraordinarily important to outside software developers writing programs for Windows to know that the browser was already there so they would not have to ship a copy with their programs.

But Dr. Felten pointed out that half a dozen Microsoft programs, like Money and Front Page, are shipped with Internet Explorer included. Judge Jackson asked him, "Why do they do it?"

Among the tens of million of personal computers in use, Dr. Felten said, many different versions of Internet Explorer are installed—or no version at all. As a result, no software developer—not even Microsoft—can assume it is there.

JUNE 11, 1999

Third Time Is Not a Charm

This was Steven Holley's third try at cross-examining Felten. Each time, he had tried to force the witness to admit that he hadn't really pulled Internet Explorer out of Windows; he had just hidden it. Felten never took the bait; he always managed to dodge or evade, or to answer the question on his own terms. After pushing him on this subject for more than an hour during a deposition a few weeks before the trial resumed, Holley snarled at Felten, "Someday somebody's going to make you answer that question."

Interviewed later, Felten said he could have pulled the Internet Explorer code out of Windows, but that would have been "a man-year of work," time he didn't have. The intermediate option he had, Felten said, was certainly good enough to make the point he wanted to make. And, before the trial, when he told the Justice Department lawyers what he intended to do, they approved.

In court this time, Holley never really pushed the question, hoping that his demonstration with the Toshiba laptop would make the point all by itself. But Felten managed to raise serious questions about it by noting that the laptop had all sorts of additional software already installed. Holley grew quite upset, seeing this as a feeble distraction. And at the end of the day he spoke up to say: "Your honor, in light of this testimony from Professor Felten, I would ask the court to direct him to appear for a demonstration with any machine that he cares to bring with any software that he cares to put on it, and a copy of his Internet Explorer remove program, and we will videotape exactly what we did today, and there will be no difference."

A government lawyer objected. But none of it seemed to matter to the judge. All of this, it appeared, was irrelevant to him at this stage of the trial. He quickly denied the motion.

But Holley's ardor was undiminished. The next day, he staged this very demonstration, on a "virgin machine," in his office for any reporters who wanted to see it. Few accepted the offer. And on the second-to-last day of testimony, he made one final try, interrupting the proceedings to tell the Judge, "As your honor will recall, during Professor Felten's testimony, he suggested that the demonstrations that I took him through in the courtroom would have been different if we were using a so-called virgin Windows 98 machine. And at the end of the redirect—or I guess recross—I suggested that the court instruct Professor Felten to appear, and your honor denied that motion.

"Microsoft then informed the Government that we intended to conduct a demonstration that they were welcome to attend, performed by Michael Wallent, who is a senior program manager at Microsoft. The Government declined the invitation to attend the demonstration, but we conducted it, nonetheless. Mr. Wallent was put under oath. The court reporter prepared a transcript, which was timed so that you can see every second that expires. And we made a videotape of that demonstration, which has been marked for identification as defendant's exhibit 2787."

Once again, the government objected. And the judge sustained the objection, making it clear he still had no interest in the demonstration.

Not to be deterred, Holley then asked to have the tape included in the trial record, even if it wasn't accepted as evidence. That way he could make the same argument to the Appeals Court or the Supreme Court. Judge Jackson permitted that.

Microsoft Puts AOL Witness on Stand

The Microsoft Corporation put its most important rebuttal witness in the Government's antitrust trial on the stand today, a senior executive from America Online, and set out to prove that the on-line service had deceived the judge about its plans to compete with Microsoft.

But the effort proved to be a bust in terms of how it played in court.

By mid-afternoon, the halting, tedious examination of David M. Colburn, a senior vice president of America Online, had put several people in the courtroom to sleep. Finally Judge Thomas Penfield Jackson called Microsoft's lawyer, John Warden, up to the bench and told him he was not getting much if anything out of the questions or the documents Mr. Warden was offering as evidence. Judge Jackson urged Mr. Warden to hurry up and finish.

For weeks, Microsoft's lawyers have been saying they would base a good part of their rebuttal case around their allegation that Mr. Colburn did not tell the complete truth when he testified as a Government witness in October.

Specifically, they said, America Online's plan to purchase the Netscape Communications Corporation was well under way at the time of Mr. Colburn's earlier testimony, and planning documents showed that America Online intended to mount a strong challenge to Microsoft, though Mr. Colburn made no mention of that in his original testimony.

The strategy appeared to be two-fold. Microsoft would challenge "the completeness and candor of prior testimony," the company said in a court filing—raising credibility issues, just as the Government's lead trial lawyer, David Boies, had done with many of Microsoft's witnesses.

The second part of the strategy would be to show that America Online, through its purchase of Netscape, intended to mount a strong competitive challenge to Microsoft, undercutting the Government's assertion that Microsoft holds an unassailable monopoly.

But Mr. Colburn did not cooperate. Today Mr. Warden offered as evidence presumably the best selections from the trove of documents Microsoft subpoenaed from America Online, Netscape and Sun Microsystems, a partner in the deal. Mr. Colburn recognized few of them, however, and quarreled with Mr. Warden's interpretation of almost every one.

Judge Jackson showed little interest.

"I'll admit it," he said with a shake of the hand about one America Online document offered as evidence. "I don't know what's probative in it; I really don't. Without some testimony to give it substance, I don't know what it means."

Earlier, Mr. Warden had displayed documents showing that America Online planned to work with Sun to build a personal computer that used no Microsoft software, thus "breaking the deadly embrace with Microsoft" in the words of a Sun executive.

But Mr. Colburn said the plan went nowhere. It was, he said, intended to create lower-price personal computers, so more people could afford to join the service. But while the planning was under way, computer prices fell sharply, "so the talks are largely dead."

The documents Mr. Warden presented did show that America Online executives, including the chief executive, Stephen M. Case, were concerned about Microsoft. In one, Mr. Case wrote, "Our relationship with Microsoft is strained and will get much worse no matter how we play it." He then wondered what would happen if his company stopped distributing Microsoft's Web browser to its 16 million subscribers and replaced it with Netscape's browser.

But for all the discussion, Mr. Colburn and many of the documents said, America Online finally decided to keep the relationship with Microsoft just as it had been—and to continue using Internet Explorer. The company renewed its contract with Microsoft in January.

Outside the courtroom, a Microsoft lawyer gamely asserted that Mr. Colburn's statements would be useful in later written pleadings, Judge Jackson's lack of interest today notwithstanding.

By shortly after noon today Judge Jackson's attention was clearly flagging as Mr. Warden began another series of questions without looking up at the judge. A lawyer at Microsoft's table quickly sent Mr. Warden a note, and as soon as Mr. Warden read it, he called for a lunch break. The judge readily agreed.

JUNE 15, 1999

Man Without a Country

Everyone was confused about Colburn's place in the courtroom. This time, he was a Microsoft witness, even though he was described as a hostile one. The last time, he had testified for the government.

When he came into the courtroom dressed as always in polished cowboy boots and sporting several days of stubble he and his lawyers began to sit down on the government's side of the room. But a court bailiff corrected them. They had to sit on the Microsoft side. The lawyers got up reluctantly and moved over to the Microsoft side, though they chose to sit two rows back from the Microsoft lawyers.

Microsoft's view of Colburn was equally distrustful. Halfway through his examination of Colburn, Warden said: "Now, I would like the defendant to be . . . the witness to be shown—it shouldn't be 'the defendant'; that was a mishap—the witness to be shown the document that has been marked for identification as defendant's exhibit 2514."

The Judge chuckled at that. So did Colburn.

Microsoft Calls Its Own Character Witness

At its antitrust trial, the Microsoft Corporation today presented its leading character witness, a folksy, plain-spoken industry veteran who delivered a message that pleased Microsoft's lawyers but will surely make its marketing executives cringe.

In testimony that traced his 25 years in the business, Gordon E. Eubanks Jr. portrayed the software business as an entrepreneurial hotbed, fast changing and fluid, where today's dominant company can quickly become tomorrow's also-ran.

And Microsoft is under threat today, Mr. Eubanks said, because the center of gravity in computing is shifting rapidly beyond what he called the "PC centric world" ruled by Microsoft and its Windows operating system.

The key, Mr. Eubanks told the court, is that software programmers are writing more and more programs to run on Internet technology, notably on browsing software, instead of on Windows.

"The momentum of development for writing programs has gone to the browser," testified Mr.

Eubanks, president of Oblix, a Silicon Valley start-up.

The browser comment—though meant to suggest that Microsoft is no entrenched monopolist—supports the Government's case, according to David Boies, the Justice Department's lead trial lawyer. The Government charges that Microsoft illegally moved to thwart competition in the browser market because the browser can serve as an alternative technology to the operating system.

"He made our point—the importance of the browser—and Microsoft's use of its monopoly power to protect its operating system monopoly and to extend its monopoly into Internet software," Mr. Boies said after Mr. Eubanks left the stand.

During his afternoon cross-examination, Mr. Boies attacked the credibility of Mr. Eubanks as a witness, portraying him as a Microsoft ally and dependent. To try to undercut his testimony, the Government introduced documents and E-mail showing that at his current company and at Symantec Corporation, where Mr. Eubanks was chief executive until earlier this year, peaceful accommodation with Microsoft was a priority.

The Government introduced a 1997 agreement stating that Symantec, best known for its Norton Utilities and anti-virus software, would get "early access" to Windows technology in return for agreeing to make Microsoft's Internet Explorer browser its favored, or default, browser and using Microsoft's version of Java, an Internet program-

ming language created by Sun Microsystems Inc.

Presented with a copy, Mr. Eubanks said he was "not aware" of that stipulation in the contract. And a Microsoft lawyer said last night that those provisions of the contract were never invoked.

Under cross-examination, Mr. Eubanks said that he agreed to testify on Microsoft's behalf after he was asked to by William H. Gates, the Microsoft chairman. He also said that Microsoft had asked him to write opinion pieces favorable to Microsoft for the Op-Ed pages of newspapers, and that he had.

The Government also introduced an E-mail from the chairman of his current employer, Oblix, saying the company depended on its relationship with Microsoft, adding, "We need to be totally in bed with them."

The Government even introduced internal Microsoft E-mail suggesting rankings of "friend, enemy or neutral," for software companies. The document came from another antitrust suit against Microsoft, and according to a Microsoft lawyer dealt with a suggested list of companies that might receive royalty waivers from Microsoft. The recommendations were never carried out, he added.

Mr. Eubanks described the software industry as one that lends itself to "natural monopolies" for periods of five to 10 years, but that these dominant companies over the years have all been unseated by the next wave of technology.

"The Government would have you believe that somehow this industry is not working properly," said William H. Neukom, Microsoft's general counsel. "This is a witness for the proposition that this industry is working just fine—that it is highly competitive, innovative and entrepreneurial."

JUNE 16, 1999

Microsoft Presents Last Witness

The Microsoft Corporation's final witness testified today that in his view of the world, the very actions that landed the company in court on antitrust charges have greatly benefited consumers, computer manufacturers and every company that is doing business on the Internet.

Richard L. Schmalensee, dean of the Sloan School of Management at the Massachusetts Institute of Technology, is the last witness in the long-running antitrust trial, and the company is trying to use his testimony to rebut each of the principal charges the Government has raised in the last eight months.

He offered arguments and evidence making the case that nothing Microsoft had done had harmed consumers—an important factor in the case. But in at least one instance, his strategy backfired.

Judge Thomas Penfield Jackson, who is hearing the case without a jury, sat impassively through the morning as Michael Lacovara, a Microsoft lawyer, tossed easy questions at the witness. But the judge stepped in with a telling question as Mr. Schmalensee was trying to demonstrate that Microsoft had not engaged in predatory conduct by including a Web browser with the Windows operating system at no charge.

Mr. Schmalensee was standing before a sketch board presenting theoretical examples of predatory and nonpredatory conduct. In his first case, a company sold a product below cost, driving another company out of business. That, Mr. Schmalensee said, was clearly predatory.

He had moved on to a more benevolent example, when Judge Jackson interrupted him, speaking up for the first time today to ask: "Why isn't what Microsoft did in this case a more egregious example of case one?"

Mr. Schmalensee stumbled for a moment but then said Microsoft gained many other benefits from including a Web browser in Windows. Later he pointed out that in classic economic theory, a predator lowers prices until the competition is weakened or destroyed and then raises them to recoup his lost profits.

But, he noted, Microsoft had not raised prices, even though Government witnesses have said the competition, the Netscape Communications Corporation, has been so greatly weakened that the browser war is over.

Outside the courtroom, Mr. Lacovara said: "He's the final witness, testifying about the whole scope of the case. And our strategy is trying to find out what is on the judge's mind so we can address it."

The last time Mr. Schmalensee took the stand, in January, David

Boies, the Government's lead attorney, suggested that he was Microsoft's "house economist" and compared his testimony in this case with seemingly contradictory arguments he made in the past. The effect was to suggest that Mr. Schmalensee offered whatever opinion suited the need of the moment.

Today Mr. Lacovara tried to turn the tables. He offered as evidence a fat binder of comments, articles and opinions that the Government's economist, Franklin M. Fisher, another M.I.T. professor, had offered over the years. And Mr. Lacovara intended to have Mr. Schmalensee help him demonstrate that they included contradictions.

As Mr. Fisher sat just behind him in the audience, Mr. Boies objected, complaining that it was not fair to try to impeach Mr. Fisher's testimony after he had already left the stand. The judge appeared ready to agree when Mr. Lacovara backed down.

Later, Mr. Schmalensee quarreled with Mr. Fisher's testimony that an economist ought to consider a company's intent when determining whether it was engaging in predatory conduct. That was not proper, he suggested. But Judge Jackson told him, "You know, judging intent is what we do every day. Juries are called on to do it all the time."

At another point, however, the judge seemed to help Mr. Lacovara. The lawyer was trying to make the case that America Online, now that it has bought the Netscape company, was in a position to challenge Microsoft's dominance in browser and operating system software, despite America Online's protestations to the contrary.

He showed a document to the judge and the witness that America Online had insisted be held under seal. But the judge summarily unsealed it, saying there was no justification for the classification.

The document was the text of America Online's presentation to the board of directors for the November meeting at which the board would vote to approve the purchase. And it showed that the company planned to aggressively promote Netscape—even though, in public, America Online executives have said the Netscape business is close to dead.

The company was "willing to spend up to $10 per download" of Netscape "via promotions, contests, incentives and advertising to stimulate downloads," the report to the board said. Mr. Lacovara asserted that America Online would be unlikely to spend that money on a product that was dead.

JUNE 22, 1999

Trial Attachments

Not infrequently Judge Jackson would open the trial with a joke someone had sent him that seemed to have some relationship to the trial, or at least to the computer industry. Everyone tried to read all sorts of messages and intentions into these readings, but most often it seemed likely that there were none. That was certainly true for the joke he offered as this day opened.

"I think, before we get started, I would call your attention to an e-mail that I got that is somewhat dated, but I think it's apropos," he said. "This is a hypothetical letter to Microsoft support:

Dear sirs: Last year I upgraded girlfriend 1.0 to wife 1.0 and noticed that the new program began unexpected child processing that took up a lot of space and valuable resources. No mention of this phenomenon was included in the product brochure. In addition, wife installs itself onto all other programs and launches during system initialization where it monitors all other system activity. Applications such as poker night 10.3 and beer bash .5 no longer run, crashing the system whenever selected. I cannot seem to purge wife 1.0 from my system. I am thinking about going back to girlfriend 1.0, but un-install does not work on this program. Can you help me?

"The response is as follows:"

Dear sir, this is a very common problem men complain about, but is mostly due to a primary misconception. Many people upgrade from girlfriend 1.0 to wife 1.0 with the idea that wife 1.0 is merely a "utilities and entertainment" program. Wife 1.0 is an operating system and designed by its creator to run everything. It is impossible to un-install, delete or purge the program from the system once installed. You cannot go back to girlfriend 1.0 because wife 1.0 is not designed to do this. Some have tried to install girlfriend 2.0 or wife 2.0, but end up with more problems than the original system. Look in your manual under warnings: alimony, child support.

I recommend you keep wife 1.0 and just deal with the situation. Having wife 1.0 installed myself, I might also suggest you read the entire section regarding general protection faults. You must assume all responsibility for faults and problems that might occur. The best course of action will be to push apologize button and then reset button as soon as lock-up occurs. System will run smooth as long as you take the blame for all GPFs.

Wife 1.0 is a great program but is very high maintenance.

Sincerely, Microsoft.

Judge Tangles With Microsoft Witness

A Microsoft lawyer today led the company's final witness at its antitrust trial through the long chain of charges that the Government has thrown at Microsoft through eight months of trial and asked him to rebut each of them.

Not surprisingly, the witness, Richard L. Schmalensee, dean of the Sloan School of Management at the Massachusetts Institute of Technology and Microsoft's expert economist, agreed that there was no substance to any of the charges.

He asserted that the Microsoft Corporation did not hold a monopoly in personal computer operating system software, that it faced vicious and serious competitors charging from every direction. And he said there were no significant barriers preventing other companies from selling operating systems that competed with Windows.

Judge Thomas Penfield Jackson, who is hearing the case without a jury, had nothing to say about most of the testimony. But he grew animated when the discussion turned to the barriers to entering the operating system business.

The Government contends that Microsoft's operating system monopoly is protected by what is known as the applications barrier to entry under which software companies will spend the money to write programs only for the dominant operating system, not for start-ups.

To make the case that the barrier does not exist, Mr. Schmalensee began using an analogy involving competing grocery stores. As he spoke, the judge was shaking his head.

"I have trouble with the grocery story analogy," he said at last. "You have a grocery," and then a smaller, competing market opens. "So you build a mega-market, and the potential competitor is always playing catch-up."

That set off a long discussion of grocery stores as an analogy to Microsoft and operating systems, and Mr. Schmalensee found himself talking about a mega-market that constantly adds features to stay ahead of the competition. "That's what competition is about," he said.

But the judge disagreed. "That's a benevolent despot," he said. "A monopoly."

As the trial nears its end—the last day of testimony is likely to be on Thursday—Judge Jackson seems quite ready to speak his mind, perhaps even show his hand, though David Boies, the Government's lead lawyer, made the point this evening that reading too much into a judge's remarks is dangerous. In any case, most of the judge's remarks have not been flattering to Microsoft.

Late in the day, however, a line of argument pursued by a Microsoft lawyer, Michael Lacovara, seemed to strike a chord. He and Mr. Schmalensee were raising the specter of competition to Microsoft from Web-based applications—software programs like calendars or even spreadsheets that reside on the Web and are used while on line. This, the two of them said, was a serious threat to Microsoft's power.

Judge Jackson asked several questions about the phenomenon, including whether anyone on the Web could get access to his Web-based calendar. Mr. Schmalensee said access would probably require a password.

Finally, the judge, obviously enthusiastic, said, "The concept, to me, sounds very attractive, and I can't understand why" software vendors "aren't writing applications in droves."

That clearly cheered Mr. Lacovara, who has said that he likes to hear what interests the judge so he can address it. With Mr. Schmalensee back on the stand for more discussion with Mr. Lacovara Wednesday morning, it appeared likely that Judge Jackson will hear a lot more about Web-based applications.

JUNE 23, 1999

Expert Witness Questioned on Payments

A Government lawyer began cross-examination of Microsoft's final witness in its antitrust trial today and quickly prompted him to disclose that Microsoft had paid about $250,000 for his testimony and related work.

The witness was Richard L. Schmalensee, dean of the Sloan School of Management at the Massachusetts Institute of Technology and Microsoft's expert economist for the trial. He said that over the last two years he has charged Microsoft $800 an hour for his trial work. In addition, the private company through which he bills Microsoft paid him a $200,000 bonus last year,

double that of the previous year, presumably because of the Microsoft income.

A fee of $800 an hour is not an unusual retainer for an expert witness of this sort. But David Boies, the Government's lead trial lawyer, apparently hoped the disclosure would further his broad effort to impeach Mr. Schmalensee's testimony. The last time Mr. Schmalensee was on the stand, in January, Mr. Boies suggested that he was Microsoft's "house economist."

Expert witnesses are routinely paid for their testimony. And Mr. Boies posed his questions long after the Government's own expert economist, Franklin M. Fisher, another M.I.T. professor, had left the stand, giving Microsoft's lawyers no opportunity to pose similar questions to him. Testimony while Mr. Fisher was on the stand suggested that he, too, stood to profit handsomely from participating in the trial.

Michael Lacovara, a Microsoft lawyer, ended his friendly examination of Mr. Schmalensee this morning with a long series of questions about Web-based applications— software programs that reside on the Web and are used while on line.

He showed several examples of new entrants in this budding market and observed that the trend suggested Microsoft did not have a durable monopoly in personal computer operating systems. Judge Thomas Penfield Jackson, who is hearing the case without a jury, had shown interest in the subject Tuesday evening, saying he imagined software companies were writing these programs "in droves."

This morning, Mr. Lacovara introduced as evidence an Internet news article published just two hours before Judge Jackson's remark, headlined "Web-based applications debut in droves."

"Sometimes, Your Honor, we get lucky," Mr. Lacovara said, and the judge smiled appreciatively.

But when Mr. Boies's turn came, he asked Mr. Schmalensee if it was not true that to use a Web-based application, a user needed a Web browser and an operating system—in most cases, Windows. Mr. Schmalensee reluctantly agreed. The unspoken question was: How does this phenomenon threaten Windows if a Windows computer was needed to use the programs?

In quick succession, Mr. Boies also managed to discredit two charts that Mr. Schmalensee had offered as evidence on Monday and, by implication, to raise questions about the validity of a wide range of statistics the witness had offered as evidence.

The charts were meant to show that the Netscape browser was growing and thriving, despite Microsoft's efforts to crush it. Mr. Boies quickly pointed out that the chart was flawed, the conclusions exaggerated. Mr. Schmalensee, clearly flustered, stammered a bit as he said: "A comparison here suggests there's a difficulty. One of these things is wrong, that's apparent."

Later, Microsoft offered a corrected version of the chart. But then Mr. Boies set about attacking the underlying data. He showed several E-mail messages in which a survey company had told Microsoft that one of the key questions used to derive browser market share was badly flawed, resulting in unreliable answers. But Microsoft had not accepted the company's suggestion to change it.

Mr. Schmalensee said he had not even been aware of the discussion, though the private company with which he is associated was a party to the E-mail dialogue. In any case, the witness said, "I'm not a specialist in writing surveys, and wouldn't have felt competent to evaluate it." Besides, he added, "I don't consider it particularly material."

Then Mr. Boies showed that one key question was so badly designed that 20 percent of the answers were demonstrably unreliable. "A 20 percent figure inconsistency—wouldn't that bother you?" he asked Mr. Schmalensee.

"It would really depend on the exact question asked," the witness replied.

JUNE 24, 1999

But I Digress . . .

David Boies seldom stumbled in his cross-examinations, but over several days he made one recurring mistake. He continually referred to America Online as "American Online." After one afternoon of that, he joked about it, but then he made the same mistake the same day. Then in the afternoon, Boies set out to explain by pointing to a piece of evidence, a document in which market-survey firm called MDC had made the same mistake.

"I now ask you a question that's probably not very relevant to anything other than my reputation," he said to Schmalensee, "but I have been referring in these questions to American Online, and you will note that that comes from the MDC questions, which is not to say that I blame MDC for my prior use of that term, but just that it is not unique."

To that, Schmalensee said: "I'm sorry, is there a question?"

"No," Boies said.

"Okay," Schmalensee responded. And with that small digression, the trial moved on.

Gates Statement Contradicts Microsoft Defense

The absent star made a final appearance in the Microsoft antitrust trial today when a Government lawyer introduced as evidence a comment by William H. Gates, Microsoft's chairman, that knocked the legs from under his legal team's most important defensive strategy.

Mr. Gates has not appeared as a witness at his company's trial. Nonetheless, he has exerted tremendous influence on the proceedings—most often in a manner that helped the Government make its case.

Over the last six months, Microsoft's legal team has mounted a concerted campaign to demonstrate that America Online, through its purchase of the Netscape Communications Corporation, was in a position to mount a strong challenge to Microsoft's dominance of personal computer operating systems.

But today, on the last day of testimony, the lead Government attorney, David Boies, introduced a document that seemed to explode that argument in a single stroke by showing that Mr. Gates did not really believe it. It was an internal Microsoft memo titled Microsoft Competitive Reviews, dated Dec. 15, 1998—about three weeks after the AOL-Netscape deal was announced.

The document includes notes that an unnamed Microsoft employee took as Mr. Gates offered his views on the competitive threat posed by the deal. One note quoted him as saying: "AOL doesn't have it in their genes to attack us in the platform space." In the industry, operating systems are known as "platforms."

The disclosure by Mr. Boies was the most important piece of evidence introduced on the final day. After court had adjourned, Mr. Boies stood on the courthouse steps with Joel I. Klein, the Assistant Attorney General who heads the antitrust division, and expressed broad satisfaction with the case they have presented.

It showed that Microsoft "intimidated, threatened, attempted to preclude," Mr. Klein said. "You name it, they did it. This is a serious, serious competitive problem that

merits a serious solution." Microsoft lawyers did not comment.

In the courtroom earlier, the Microsoft witness on the stand, Richard L. Schmalensee, dean of the Sloan School of Management at the Massachusetts Institute of Technology, dismissed Mr. Gates's comment as barely relevant. "Mr. Gates's judgment is entitled to some weight," he said, "but he hasn't seen the documents I have seen"—the internal America Online documents that Microsoft subpoenaed early this year.

That prompted Mr. Boies to ask him if he was ever willing to consider facts that did not support his position, to which Mr. Schmalensee replied, "Mr. Boies, I don't know if that is a blanket challenge to my ethics, or how to interpret that question."

Later Mr. Boies showed him a contract between Microsoft and Symantec, which makes utility software. It stipulated among other things that if the company used a certain Internet protocol in its product, "Internet Explorer must be set as the default browser."

Microsoft's campaign to force other companies to favor Internet Explorer is at the center of the Government's case. And with the contract on display, Judge Thomas Penfield Jackson asked the witness a question that sounded as if it should have come from the mouth of a Government lawyer.

He asked whether "any of these conditions are, in your opinion, anticompetitive." Mr. Schmalensee said he could not answer. So the judge asked, "Assuming Microsoft is a monopoly, are they anti-competitive?" Once again Mr. Schmalensee said he did not know.

As the day drew toward its close, Mr. Boies introduced several academic papers by Mr. Schmalensee over the years that held opinions contradicting statements he had made in court. Mr. Schmalensee said his views had evolved.

But Mr. Boies's cross-examination seemed to peter out. That was not so for Michael Lacovara, Microsoft's lawyer. Re-examining his own witness, he offered as evidence a news article showing that a small company was about to begin selling an inexpensive product that allows Internet access without Microsoft software.

Microsoft has been trying to make the case that America Online planned to offer such a product, nicknamed the AOL PC, that would pose a competitive threat. America Online executives have denied that.

But Mr. Lacovara offered as evidence a news article that he said had been issued just two hours earlier stating that America Online was in negotiations to buy the company and use its product as the basis for an AOL PC.

JUNE 25, 1999

A Flourish and Fanfare

Boies was famous for saving his best material for the last moment of each day so he could end with a big statement. Everyone assumed he would have saved his very best document for the last moment of the last day of testimony. But he did not. He asked Schmalensee a few uninspired questions about previous testimony, and then just stopped, saying, "Your honor, I have no more questions."

Lacovara tried hard to end his examinations with a flourish. A couple of weeks earlier, he had even apologized when he completed his questioning of Franklin Fisher without one.

"Your honor, that is not going out with a bang," he said then, "but I have no further questions for the witness."

But this time, he was determined, and his introduction of the Internet news story on the AOL negotiations at the very last minute clearly impressed the judge. He raised an eyebrow as the lawyer handed him a printout of the story, then told him with a smile, "Mr. Lacovara, I can't say you haven't brought me current."

With that, the testimony ended, and Judge Jackson addressed the court, telling the lawyers, "All right gentle-

Microsoft was paying for the ads, and at least one now says he would not have signed if he had known the source of the financing.

Greg Shaw, a public relations manager for Microsoft, tonight confirmed that the company had paid for the ads. "We thought this was an important, substantive letter, and we were interested in contributing to making it visible," he said. "In our view, the letter speaks for itself."

During the yearlong public relations war that has been fought in parallel with the antitrust trial, a dozen or more institutes and lobbying organizations have weighed in with advertisements, reports, news conferences or books that offer strong opinions on one side of the case or the other.

Many of the organizations have acknowledged that they were financed by Microsoft, or by its rivals. But the Independent Institute made an extraordinary effort to portray itself as beholden to no one. The institute, based in Oakland, Calif., has written papers and offered opinions on a broad range of political, social, business and foreign policy issues over the 14 years of its existence. Throughout the trial, it has often taken Microsoft's side.

According to its literature, the institute "adheres to the highest standards of independent scholarly inquiry." Its president, David Theroux, describes himself as a scrupulously disinterested academic and adds: "We are not doing contract work. We're independent. Our intention is to do work that holds up to any type of scrutiny."

But internal institute documents show that Microsoft has secretly served as the institute's largest outside financial benefactor in the last year. The documents were provided by a Microsoft adversary associated with the computer industry who refused to be further identified.

Microsoft has mounted an elaborate public relations campaign as part of its trial strategy, to influence public opinion and, perhaps, the trial judge. Much of it is open and above board, but today's admission by the institute suggests that an important part is intended to be secret.

On June 2, the day the antitrust trial resumed for its final month of testimony after a three-month break, the institute ran full-page ads in The New York Times and The Washington Post signed by 240 academics who were said to support the view that antitrust prosecution was harmful to consumers—a key argument Microsoft was making in court. Complemented by a heavily promoted news conference in Washington, the effort received enough attention that David Boies, the Government's lead lawyer in the antitrust suit, referred to it in court on June 3.

Last month, the institute published a book titled "Winners, Losers and Microsoft: Competition and Antitrust in High Technology." The book argued that Microsoft had succeeded in dominating the software industry principally because it makes superior products—another often-voiced theme of Microsoft's trial defense. The company's eco-

men, it has been almost a pure pleasure. Let's keep it that way." He then thanked the support staff, the people who ran the video projectors that displayed all the documents and other material both sides used as evidence.

When court adjourned, lawyers for both sides shook hands with the others, like opposing coaches in a basketball game meeting at mid court to shake hands after the last buzzer has sounded. Amid all that, Boies bumped into Joel Klein, the assistant attorney general who heads the antitrust division—Boies's boss, in this case. Klein had been sitting in the stands watching the last day of testimony, as he had occasionally throughout the trial.

With the nervous laugh that is his hallmark when he's not at the podium, Boies told him, "I haven't quit." Laughing, Klein patted him on the back and said: "No, no. I'm still paying you."

Outside on the courthouse steps, Klein spoke to the reporters who had been covering the trial. Microsoft declined to appear; the company apparently decided that these after-court press conferences were going badly for the company since the reporters generally concluded that Microsoft's statements did not jibe with the evidence that had been presented in court.

Klein said his team had shown that Microsoft "clearly engaged in a broad pattern of illegal behavior" warranting a serious remedy. But he would not say more about that.

The testimony was over, but the trial had many more months of life ahead.

Scholars Say They Were Unaware Ads Paid For by Microsoft

Newspaper advertisements that a California institute presented as independent views supporting the Microsoft Corporation's position in its antitrust trial were actually paid for by Microsoft, the institute said today.

The full-page newspaper ads, published in The New York and The Washington Post Independent Institute last were in the form of a letter by 240 academic experts. prompted news stories and room discussion during the t

The academics were not to

nomic witness at the trial, Richard J. Schmalensee, an economist at the Massachusetts Institute of Technology, cited the book as a source for an important assertion in his direct testimony.

Mr. Theroux has long acknowledged that Microsoft is a dues-paying member of his group, a point that is usually made in news articles about the institute. But he has insisted all along that Microsoft is "just one of 2,000 members" and as such pays a membership fee of roughly $10,000 a year—an inconsequential part of the organization's overall budget that gives the company no special standing. All Microsoft gets for that, he said, is "free copies of our publications, discounted tickets to our events."

He has also maintained that Microsoft had nothing to do with the newspaper advertisements. The ads, he said in the interview, "were paid for out of our general funds."

His letter to economists soliciting participation made no mention of Microsoft.

But, in fact, among the institute's internal documents is a bill Mr. Theroux sent to John A. C. Kelly of Microsoft for the full costs of the ads, plus his travel expenses from San Francisco to Washington for the news conference, totaling $153,868.67. Included was a $5,966 bill for airline tickets for himself and a colleague. Unfortunately, he wrote Mr. Kelly, "the airlines were heavily booked" and "we had to fly first class to D.C. and business class on the return."

Asked this evening about that bill, Mr. Theroux acknowledged that Microsoft had paid for the ad but said it made no difference. "The academic process we use is independent of sources of revenue."

At least one academic who signed the ad disagreed.

"He should have told us," Simon Hakim, an economist at Temple University, said today when told of the financing. "I would not have participated if I had known. It's not right to use people as a vehicle for special interests."

On the other hand, Stan J. Liebowitz, a professor of economics at the University of Texas at Dallas who was one of the authors of the "Winners, Losers and Microsoft" book, said that he, too, had been unaware of the Microsoft payments, but added, "it doesn't matter to me."

Also among the institute's internal documents was an accounting of 337 contributions the institute received for the fiscal year that ended June 30. Mr. Theroux said those donations accounted for 60 percent or 70 percent of the institute's overall budget.

The accounting sheets show that Microsoft contributed significantly more than $10,000 last year—$203,217, in all, the most from any outside individual or organization and about 20 percent of the total outside contributions for the period. (Not counted in that tally was $304,725 that Mr. Theroux contributed to his own foundation.)

SEPTEMBER 18, 1999

Bungled Lobbying Efforts

This was just one of several blunders Microsoft made in attempting to lobby its way out of trouble. Later in the summer, the company lobbied Congress to cut the budget for the Justice Department's antitrust division. That caused people who normally didn't pay any attention to shake their heads. As one *New York Times* columnist wrote, "Think about the arrogance behind that strategy. How would you feel if the biggest company in your town tried to use its influence to slash the funding of your police department, at a time when the police were bringing charges against that company? That's what Microsoft did."

A Justice Department official said: "Even the mob doesn't try to whack a prosecutor during a trial."

Later, Microsoft asked one its consultants, Ralph Reed, the former head of the Christian Coalition, to lobby Governor George W. Bush to take a position against the antitrust case. There was just one problem: Reed was also working as a political consultant for Mr. Bush, already then the likely Republican presidential nominee.

Bush was irritated when he heard about this. Ralph Reed apologized and said his company, Century Strategies, would not lobby Mr. Bush any longer. But as usual, Microsoft was unrepentant.

" 'We think this is a fine resolution to the issue involving Century Strategies and the Bush campaign," Microsoft said. "We will continue to work with Century Strategies and other firms, both Democratic and Republican, to respond to attacks by competitors and to insure that our viewpoint is heard."

As Microsoft awaited the verdict, it also began lobbying shareholders. When the company distributed its annual report in September, two million shareholders also got a letter from Robert Herbold, Microsoft's chief operating officer, urging them to join a lobbying effort to protect what the company called its "freedom to innovate." Loosely translated, that catch-phrase meant freedom to design products however the company chose—including the freedom to bundle other products, like a Web browser, with the Windows operating system.

A Microsoft spokesman said the company's leadership had decided to send the letter to shareholders after the trial was essentially over because the company now viewed "freedom to innovate" as a broader term covering other political issues of interest to the company, like government policies dealing with encryption, software piracy and Internet taxation.

But the "freedom to innovate" Web site, to which Herold's letter directed shareholders, had a different message. It informed visitors that the "freedom to innovate network was formed as a response to the overwhelming amount of correspondence" the company had received "regarding the trial with the Justice Department and other public policy issues."

In the summer of 2000, Microsoft received some news that took the edge off of some of the unflattering news about the company's public relations strategy. First, in early June, a couple of private investigators made a bungling attempt to buy the trash that was being hauled away from the Washington office of a Microsoft-supported trade group, the Association for Competitive Technology. The investigators appeared to be looking for inside information about Microsoft amid the trash.

But building workers refused to sell the trash and complained to the building management. That set off a cascading series of newspaper investigations that, by the end of June, led to the Oracle Corporation, a prominent and aggressive rival of Microsoft. Oracle, it turned out, had hired a private investigative firm that obtained the Independent Institute documents and others that produced unflattering news stories about Microsoft. Working for Oracle, the investigators had also tried to buy the trash from the Association for Competitive Technology, the act that caused the entire effort to unravel.

Lawrence J. Ellison, the chairman and founder of Oracle, defended his company's yearlong spying operation against Microsoft, calling it a "civic duty" similar to investigative reporting by the press.

But Microsoft said: "Oracle apparently believes its business goals are more important than the free speech and privacy of others."

CHAPTER 5

Just the Facts

In an interview near the end of September, Judge Jackson said he wanted the two sides to settle the case. To encourage that, he would deliver his verdict in two parts. Usually a verdict includes findings of fact, which are the judge's conclusions about the factual disputes in the case, and the conclusions of law, the legal analysis and verdict. Judge Jackson said he was going to publish the findings of fact first, with the hope that they would serve as an incentive for a settlement. But he might not have been confident a settlement would actually occur.

A fast-paced trial schedule, he had said, can produce one of two results: a settlement or a war.

"And what we got was a war," he said. "This is like the battle that ended the War of the Roses. That's the way I look at this case, like the fall of the House of Tudor. Something medieval."

At the time, Jackson didn't say how he would rule. But the testimony was over, and he did say he had a problem with a central part of Microsoft's defense—the decision to integrate a Web browser with Windows.

"I am not a fan of integration," the judge said of technology. And he offered as an analogy a 35-millimeter camera: "You have one and you like it, right? You like the convenience of having a light meter built in, integrated, so all you have to do is press a button to get a reading. But do you think camera makers should also serve photographers who want to use a separate light meter, so they can hold it up, move it around?"

Of the trial to that point, the judge said he had been awed by the legal prowess on display in his courtroom. "It's exhilarating to watch," he said in February. "This is a paradigm. You'll never see better."

U.S. Judge Declares Microsoft Is a Market-Stifling Monopoly; Gates Retains Defiant Stance

The judge in the government's antitrust trial against the Microsoft Corporation issued a broad denunciation of the software giant this evening as the first part of his verdict in the landmark case.

The judge, Thomas Penfield Jackson of Federal District Court, said the company had used its monopoly power to stifle innovation, reduce competition and hurt consumers.

"Most harmful of all is the message that Microsoft's actions have conveyed to every enterprise with the potential to innovate in the computer industry," Judge Jackson wrote in his 207-page findings of fact.

"Through its conduct," he added, "Microsoft has demonstrated that it will use its prodigious market power and immense profits to harm any firm that insists on pursuing initiatives that could intensify competition against one of Microsoft's core products."

Judge Jackson's findings of fact clearly show that he found the government's case against Microsoft credible and rejected as "specious," as he stated in one part, virtually all the arguments Microsoft put up in its defense.

The findings are the judge's conclusions about who presented the most compelling and believable case during the yearlong trial that opened in his United States district courtroom on Oct. 19, 1998. As such, they clearly signal how he will rule in his final verdict—the determination of whether the facts as he sees them amount to violations of antitrust law.

Microsoft and the government both reacted quickly after receiving the much-anticipated findings this evening.

The Justice Department was jubilant. "This is a great day for American consumers," Attorney General Janet Reno said. "This case is about the protection of innovation, competition and the consumers' right to choose the products they want."

But Microsoft's chairman, William H. Gates, said: "We respectfully disagree with the court's findings. Microsoft competes vigorously and fairly. Microsoft is committed to resolving this case in a fair and equitable manner." He added that his company "operates within the laws and operates in a way that is great for the people we develop software for."

Mr. Gates's comments followed a

company statement suggesting that Microsoft was already formulating an appeal.

"While we disagree with many of the findings," the statement said, "we are still confident that the law supports us on these points and that the American legal system will ultimately rule that Microsoft's actions were fair, legal and good for consumers."

Neither Microsoft's statements nor those of the Justice Department offered much likelihood of settling the case. Joel I. Klein, head of the Justice Department's antitrust division, said the government would consider a settlement, but only one that "fully and properly addresses" the issues raised in the judge's findings.

"From the very beginning Microsoft has wanted nothing more than to resolve this case," Mr. Gates said. "Getting this behind us would be a very good thing."

The judge, who in years past wrote his decisions longhand, transmitted the document to both sides by e-mail this afternoon. It was made public at 6:30 p.m., after the stock markets had closed.

In after-hours trading, Microsoft closed down more than $4, at $87, compared with its closing price of $91.5625 during the regular session on the Nasdaq.

Microsoft is expected to seek grounds for appeal, should Judge Jackson eventually rule against the company. But Microsoft's lawyers will have to find grounds in law or precedent because the judge's findings of fact are virtually impervious to appeal. Under federal court

rules, appeals courts must give great weight to the conclusions the trial judge draws from hearing the testimony and studying the witnesses as they offer their accounts.

As a result, appeals courts are allowed to challenge findings of fact only if they are "clearly erroneous." And if the judge's verdict is largely based on which witnesses he believed, the verdict stands a better chance of withstanding appeal.

At the outset of his findings, the judge declared that Microsoft "enjoys monopoly power in the relevant market." This is a key assertion because under antitrust laws monopolies cannot engage in practices that would be legal for other companies. The government's charges rested on the assumption that Microsoft has a monopoly in the operating systems market with it Windows operating systems. In a key test for monopoly power, Judge Jackson concluded that Microsoft could charge almost any price for Windows without fear that price increases would reduce demand.

Microsoft expended considerable energy in court arguing that it was not a monopoly. It asserted that a host of small competitors—from the Be operating system to Palm Pilot personal organizers—were long-term threats. But Judge Jackson dismissed those arguments, saying that competition from those competitors was, at the very least, a long way off.

"That day has not arrived, nor does it seem imminent," he wrote of one such claim.

"Microsoft's monopoly power," he concluded, "is also evidenced by the fact that, over the course of several years, Microsoft took actions that only could have been advantageous if they operated to reinforce monopoly power."

From there, the judge ran through each of the charges raised by the Justice Department and the 19 state attorneys general who joined in the suit. In each case, he endorsed the government's charge while rejecting Microsoft's rebuttals.

He found that Microsoft had tried to divide the market for Internet browsing software with the Netscape Communications Corporation in 1995—a key charge in the government's case and a clearly illegal activity under antitrust law. He wrote that other companies had had similar encounters with Microsoft, and "these interactions demonstrate that it is Microsoft's corporate practice to pressure other firms to halt software development" that threatens Microsoft's dominance "or competes directly with Microsoft's most cherished software products."

He found that Microsoft's decision to bundle its Web browser with Windows and give it away free was not, as Microsoft asserted in court, simply an effort to add a desirable feature to Windows.

"Senior executives at Microsoft decided Microsoft needed to give its browser away in furtherance of the larger strategic goal of gaining market share," he wrote. Microsoft, he added, "viewed browser market share as the key to preserving its dominance."

And in one of his most damning findings, Judge Jackson concluded that "Web browsers and operating systems are separate products." Microsoft's key argument was that its browser was simply a feature of Windows, not a separate product.

He turned that argument around on Microsoft by finding that the company had actually harmed consumers by bundling the two products. Consumer harm is a key test in antitrust cases. Bundling the browser with Windows "unjustifiably jeopardized the stability and security of the operating system." With this he meant that including the browser had made the operating system more likely to crash and more vulnerable to break-ins by intruders. "There is no technical justification for Microsoft's refusal to meet consumer demand for a browserless version of Windows 98," he added.

He wrote that Microsoft had threatened and bullied Apple Computer, Intel, America Online and other companies that Microsoft perceived as competitors. In the case of the International Business Machines Corporation, he wrote, "when I.B.M. refused to abate the promotion of those of its own products that competed with Windows and Office," Microsoft's suite of business productivity software, "Microsoft punished the I.B.M. PC Company with higher prices, a late license for Windows 95 and the withholding of technical and marketing support."

"Microsoft's past success in hurting such companies and stifling innovation deters investment in technologies and businesses that exhibit the potential to threaten Microsoft," the judge concluded. "The ultimate result is that some innovations that would truly benefit consumers never occur for the sole reason that they do not coincide with Microsoft's self-interest."

Judge Jackson's final verdict is expected in late December or early January, after which he may hold hearings on possible remedies, if the verdict goes against Microsoft. Proposed remedies could range from relatively minor adjustments in the company's contracts and business practices to more drastic measures like breaking Microsoft's operating system and applications divisions into separate companies.

Antitrust lawyers say they cannot recall another instance in which findings of fact in an antitrust case have been issued ahead of the actual verdict. "I've been at this for 40 years, and I've never heard of anything like this," said Stephen Axinn, an antitrust litigator at Axinn, Veltrop & Harkrider in New York.

Usually the findings are packaged with the conclusions of law—the legal precedents justifying a ruling—and the verdict. But Judge Jackson's decision to separate the findings offers at least two benefits.

"It's potentially a very clever thing to do," said Robert Litan, a former senior official in the Justice Department's antitrust division, now with the Brookings Institution.

For one thing, it will allow Judge Jackson to modify his final ruling if written responses from the litigants suggest to him that he might be standing on weak ground.

Publishing the findings ahead of the verdict also "prompts the parties to try to settle," said Andrew Gavil, a professor at Howard University.

Judge Jackson has repeatedly urged Microsoft and the government to settle the case. Though the two sides have held fitful discussions during the trial, they remain far apart, and most lawyers and analysts watching the case are not hopeful that they will settle, even with today's strong findings in favor of the Government.

NOVEMBER 6, 1999

"A Bolt Out of the Blue"

When weeks after his findings were published, the two sides still had made no move to settle, Judge Jackson decided to appoint a mediator. He would later say that his choice of mediator—Richard Posner, Chief Circuit Court judge in Chicago—had come to him like "a bolt out of the blue."

"I knew," he explained, "that the egos were sufficiently high on both sides that with any ordinary person they would just say: 'So, who are you?' " And when he called Judge Posner, "I was grateful that, one, he would take a call from a district court judge, and two, that he didn't say, 'I have so many things going on I don't have time.' "

Under the arrangement, Judge Posner would brief Judge Jackson on the general status of the talks but give him no information about the substance of the negotiations. The idea was to make sure no one would be concerned that offers made during the mediation would play into courtroom deliberations later, if the mediation failed.

Microsoft Case Gets U.S. Judge As a Mediator

The federal judge overseeing the Microsoft antitrust trial named a mediator today in an effort to bring about settlement talks between the Microsoft Corporation and its accusers: the Justice Department and 19 state attorneys general.

The initiative was wholly that of the judge, Thomas Penfield Jackson, but all sides said they welcomed it.

No settlement talks had been planned before he surprised the Microsoft and government legal teams during a conference in his chambers Thursday by announcing that he planned to name as mediator Richard A. Posner, the chief judge for the United States Court of Appeals for the Seventh Circuit, in Chicago.

In his order, published today, Judge Jackson said that mediation would be voluntary and nonbinding, and that it was up to Judge Posner, "acting in a private capacity," to schedule any talks. None were immediately set.

Judge Posner has written widely and provocatively on diverse topics, notably antitrust law, on which he has shown a libertarian, free-market bent.

Judge Jackson said the schedule for the trial, which calls for a verdict as early as February, was not being altered, meaning the two sides may have as long as 90 days to reach a settlement. Judging from their public statements, they remain far apart.

Judge Jackson's findings of fact in the case, published on Nov. 5, were so heavily weighted against Microsoft that they seemed to leave little room for settlement negotiations. In the findings, Judge Jackson found that Microsoft used its monopoly power to threaten and bully allies and competitors alike, stifling innovation and competition in the software industry.

In a statement issued this evening, the Justice Department said: "Judge Posner is a highly respected jurist. We look forward to meeting with him to discuss the severe competitive problems identified in the court's findings of fact."

Tom Miller, the Iowa attorney

general, speaking for all of the states, said: "We welcome the judge's order. We always have believed in the mediation process."

Microsoft welcomed the news, too, with a different spin: "We look forward to working with Judge Posner to find a solution that is fair to Microsoft, fair to consumers and good for the future of the high-tech industry."

Judge Jackson's announcement, which was made after the markets closed, sent Microsoft's stock up sharply. It ended the trading day at $86 but rose as high as $90.97 in after-hours trading.

Judge Posner comes to the case with no real power beyond the strength of his reputation and the need of both sides to show Judge Jackson that they are being responsive to his initiative. He has no authority to force the parties to reach a settlement, or to impose one.

But lawyers from both sides of the case, and others, describe Judge Posner as a brilliant jurist, among the most respected in the United States.

Daniel R. Fischel, dean of the University of Chicago Law School, where Judge Posner teaches, calls him "the single greatest antitrust scholar and judge of this generation."

President Ronald Reagan appointed him to the court in 1981. At the time he taught law at the University of Chicago—and still does, part time.

Judge Posner is also the author of more than 30 books as well as numerous articles in the scholarly

and popular press. His most recent book, "An Affair of State," published in September, was about the Clinton-Lewinsky scandal.

So, Judge Posner is accustomed to working outside his hours on the bench, as Judge Jackson is now asking him to do for this case. Though he has offered no opinions on the Microsoft case, he has written extensively about antitrust and once offered the opinion, in a law review article, that the AT&T case in the early 1980's was brought "to a triumphant conclusion" by the breakup of the company.

The Seventh Circuit also has an active mediation program, noted one lawyer involved in this case, and one rule prevailing there is that the mediator does not tell the district court judge trying the case what occurred during the talks. That way, if the talks fail because of one party or another, it will not prejudice the judge as he prepares his verdict.

Still, even with that background, coaxing the parties to agree in this case is a leviathan task. Though both sides say they are open to mediation, the plaintiffs are flush with confidence from Judge Jackson's findings, and they are calling for a strong remedy. While Microsoft has said it is open to settlement discussions, it has essentially ruled out most everything the plaintiffs have said they are likely to propose.

The last serious settlement negotiations were held in May 1998, just before the antitrust suits were filed. At that time Microsoft offered concessions that now seem mild. The company told the government that to address a complaint from personal computer makers, it would allow them to customize the opening screen of Windows, Microsoft's dominant operating system.

But when pressed by the government a day later, William H. Gates, Microsoft's chairman, said the company was not willing to consider even that.

Since then, urged on by Judge Jackson, the litigants have held two or three lackluster meetings, most recently last summer, and none of these talks have seemed to go anywhere. Presiding for Microsoft at those sessions was William H. Neukom, Microsoft's chief counsel, along with several lawyers from Sullivan & Cromwell, the firm that represented Microsoft in court.

For the government, Joel I. Klein, the head of the Justice Department's antitrust division presided, accompanied by several other Justice Department lawyers including David Boies, the lead lawyer in court, and one or more state attorneys general. The lineup is likely to be the same for any new talks.

Since the publication of Judge Jackson's findings, the Justice Department and the states have agreed that any remedy or settlement must deal in some way with Microsoft's monopoly in personal computer operating systems—though no agreement has been reached in how that would be done.

Under the mildest proposals that are being discussed, rules would be enacted that would change Microsoft's behavior while allowing the company to keep its present structure.

Stronger solutions under discussion, which Microsoft says it would vehemently oppose, include forcing Microsoft to publish or auction the source code for Windows—so other companies could create competing operating systems—or breaking up the company.

In an interview with Time Magazine last week, Mr. Gates also said he would not agree to any settlement that deprived Microsoft of the ability to add anything it wanted to Windows or that allowed computer makers to alter Windows without Microsoft's permission.

Several state attorneys general have said they would be willing to agree only to one of the stronger remedies, and no settlement is possible without agreement from the attorneys general.

Richard Blumenthal, the Connecticut attorney general, who attended the meeting with Judge Jackson on Thursday, and who will probably be a part of the settlement negotiations, said he was encouraged that the trial schedule "will remain in effect" through the settlement talks "so there will be no delays."

NOVEMBER 20, 1999

U.S. Hires Advisory Firm in Microsoft Case

The Justice Department said this evening that it had hired New York investment bankers to help determine the financial impact of various proposals for restructuring Microsoft or changing its business practices to resolve the antitrust case against the company.

The department said the investment firm Greenhill & Company would "assist the division in analyzing financial aspects of the full range of potential remedies in U.S. v. Microsoft, including conduct and structural relief."

The government and 19 state attorneys general have just begun settlement talks with Microsoft that are likely to continue for the next two or three months, and the government intends to use Greenhill's advice as it devises settlement proposals.

The trial judge's findings of fact last month made it clear that he would rule against Microsoft if no settlement were reached. In that case, the Justice Department would have to prepare a remedy proposal, and once again Greenhill would provide advice.

Remedies under discussion run from forcing Microsoft to change its business practices, so-called conduct relief, to breaking up the company, known as structural relief.

Greenhill & Company specializes in mergers and acquisitions but also offers strategic advice to its clients for "recapitalization and restructurings" and "hostile and defensive strategies," a company document states. The company is led by Robert F. Greenhill, who was a senior executive at Morgan Stanley, then chief executive at Smith Barney before starting his company in 1996.

The Justice Department stressed that hiring the company did not indicate that the department had decided which remedy, or settlement proposal, it would offer. But some proposals would require far more sophisticated analysis than others.

Forcing Microsoft to rewrite certain contracts would not require much financial advice. But requiring it to auction the source code for the Windows operating system—an idea that has been favored by the states—or breaking up the company, would require complicated financial analysis.

Microsoft executives, in arguing against some remedy ideas, have often said the government does not understand the technological and financial implications of the proposals. The company said it had no opinion on today's announcement.

Greenhill & Company bills itself as an expert on technology. Most of the deals it has managed in this area have been on behalf of Compaq Computer, a close Microsoft ally.

DECEMBER 3, 1999

A Contract Clue

While the Justice Department downplayed speculation, officials later said they were surprised that people following the case had not deduced from the contract with Greenhill that the government was intending to break up Microsoft.

Greenhill's job, after all, would be to provide valuations of the new companies.

By now, government officials were firmly persuaded that a breakup would be necessary. Judge Jackson's strong findings of fact had emboldened them, though in public they were still saying they were considering all options.

When the settlement talks with Judge Posner opened in Chicago, the Justice Department put a break-up proposal on the table at the outset. The idea was to divide Microsoft into three companies. One would hold Windows 98, another Windows 2000 and a third everything else, including the company's Office suite of applications programs, Internet businesses and hardware ventures. The government knew this idea was time sensitive. In a short while, Windows 98 would be phased out. So this plan would work only if it were accepted now.

Still, as in the past, Microsoft's lawyers said they would not even discuss break-up plans. So the government negotiators began working on a more modest remedy that would restrict Microsoft's conduct. But their heart wasn't in it.

Microsoft Issues Lengthy Response To Judge in Antitrust Case

Sailing against a fierce head wind, Microsoft delivered the legal arguments today that it hoped would stave off an adverse antitrust ruling, taking issue with a judge's conclusions about the case and restating many arguments that he had already rejected.

Microsoft's 70-page conclusions of law, sent to Judge Thomas Penfield Jackson and published on its Web site after the stock market closed, contend that case law does not support either the government's charges or the judge's findings of fact, published in November. The filing does not, however, directly assail Judge Jackson.

It comes as Microsoft, the Justice Department and 19 state attorneys general enter a critical stage in the settlement talks that have been under way since November in which both sides are to lay out their demands, or concessions. The state and federal prosecutors are expected to ask for a serious structural remedy, perhaps even a breakup of the company, which Microsoft has made it clear it would not accept.

Early in November, Judge Jackson published his findings of facts, in which he portrayed Microsoft as a rapacious monopolist that dedicated considerable resources to maintaining its monopoly by putting potential competitors at a disadvantage. His ruling is most likely to come in March.

The factual findings appeared to make an eventual ruling against Microsoft in United States District Court here all but inevitable. But under the structure set up by the judge, both sides were to file their conclusions of law—the legal arguments behind their cases—after the judge had showed his hand.

The state and federal governments issued their legal conclusions on Dec. 6, and they amounted to a stirring ratification of the judge's conclusions.

Microsoft, on the other hand, said in its filing today that the company "respectfully disagrees with the court's findings and believes they are unsupported by the record." The company added, "Even accepting the court's findings, the plaintiffs have not satisfied the burden under the governing law on any of their claims."

The drift of antitrust case law, legal experts note, has been broadly pro-defendant since the 1980's. In its brief, Microsoft quoted nearly all of it in arguing that the legal restraints on dominant firms are few, giving them much freedom to protect their product designs and copyright. The company liberally cited cases involving I.B.M. and Kodak, two big companies that frequently won private antitrust suits.

But Microsoft also cited a federal appeals court ruling in 1982, in which the court upheld the right of a copyright holder to prevent unauthorized modification of its work. Microsoft contends that its restrictions on how personal computer makers present Windows is an entirely legal defense of its copyright. That 1982 ruling was written by Justice Richard Posner, who is now serving as mediator in Microsoft's settlement talks with the government.

Attacking the government's claims and the judge's findings one by one, Microsoft first tried to rebut the conclusion that it had illegally tied a Web browser, Internet Explorer, to the Windows operating system. The central argument behind that assertion is the same one Microsoft brought to court in October 1997, when the Justice Department first challenged the company's decision to integrate the two products.

Then, and now, Microsoft argued that the browser and the operating system were actually one product—not two products tied together. Following that assumption, which the judge has already said he rejects, Microsoft cited several previous legal cases in which other courts have dismissed tying charges because they have found that only one product was actually involved.

On another charge—that Microsoft worked hard to block Netscape, maker of a competing browser, from the market—the brief appeared to pick and choose from among the judge's findings to highlight those that appeared to support the company's case.

It quoted the judge as saying "Microsoft did not actually prevent users from obtaining and using Navigator." But in the same paragraph, the judge also wrote that Microsoft blocked "the easiest and most intuitive paths" for obtaining Netscape's browser, so that "few new users had any incentive" to install it.

Similarly, while attacking the government's charge that Microsoft sought a monopoly in the Web browser market, Microsoft quoted from the judge's findings as follows: "The evidence is insufficient to find that Microsoft's ambition is a future in which most or all of the content available on the Web would be accessible only through its own browsing software." Microsoft asserted—citing previous case law that hangs on that conclusion— that the conclusion is "fatal to plaintiff's attempted monopolization claim."

But once again, in the same paragraph, the judge wrote: "The evidence does, however reveal an intent" to reduce the number of Netscape users to a point where they are "too few" to be meaningful.

Microsoft rebutted the judge's finding that the company holds substantial monopoly power in the market for personal computer operating systems by repeating the arguments it made in court—the very ones that the judge rejected. As an example, Microsoft wrote that it could not raise or lower output of its operating system at whim—a hallmark of a monopolist—because competitors "could readily expand their output to meet the entire demand."

But the judge found that the niche operating systems Microsoft cited have been unable to convince more than a handful of software companies to write programs for their systems—a fact, the judge noted, that allows Microsoft to maintain its dominance.

The Microsoft filing, antitrust experts say, is partly intended to give Judge Jackson reason to consider a milder legal judgment against the company.

Before this judge, Microsoft "may be trying for a modest defeat instead of a rout," said William Kovacic, a professor at the George Washington University law school. "They have little hope of turning this judge around, but they do want to steer him away from accepting the government's case in toto, and thus chip away at the platform for sweeping remedies against it."

The filing, these experts say, also strongly suggests the line of legal argument Microsoft is likely to take if it loses before Judge Jackson and appeals his ruling. "This is a preview of Microsoft's arguments on appeal," noted Andrew I. Gavil, a professor at the Howard University law school.

Microsoft and the government are each entitled to file rebuttal documents with the judge in the coming weeks. And final oral arguments, summing up the cases both sides have made in their conclusions of law, are scheduled for Feb. 22.

After that, assuming the two sides do not reach a settlement, the judge will issue his verdict.

JANUARY 19, 2000

Microsoft Chided as Antitrust Trial Draws to a Close

Microsoft had its last chance in federal court today to persuade the trial judge not to issue a stinging antitrust verdict against the company.

But the judge, Thomas Penfield Jackson, gave Microsoft little comfort. At one point in today's final arguments, he dismissed a crucial Microsoft defense by comparing the company to John D. Rockefeller's Standard Oil monopoly, the subject of the first major antitrust case, in 1906. That case resulted in a breakup of the company.

"I don't really see a distinction," Judge Jackson said.

The government, in its final argument, said it was "simply impossible to imagine" that the company would not be found to have violated the nation's antitrust laws.

The Microsoft Corporation, for its part, argued that it was impossible to see how the company could be found guilty. "A lot of nothing doesn't add up to something," said John Warden, the company's lead lawyer.

And so the trial drew to a close on exactly the same notes that carried it through 16 months of testimony and argument. The government pressed hard on its broad points, while Microsoft refused to concede even a nit. Today's arguments on the relevant points of law bearing on the case were the last act before a verdict, which will probably be issued in the next few weeks.

The court is likely to hold separate hearings on remedies if, as expected, Judge Jackson rules that Microsoft violated antitrust laws.

A strong verdict against Microsoft could well lead to harsh sanctions against the company, including breaking it up. If, however, Judge Jackson agrees with some of the government's legal contentions but rejects others, the sanctions against Microsoft could be less severe, prohibiting it from some practices but leaving the company intact.

Still, the Justice Department and state attorneys general pressing the case insist that they will not settle for mild sanctions.

"The remedies have to be drastic and far reaching," Richard Blumenthal, the attorney general of Connecticut and one of the plaintiffs, said this evening.

But even as Microsoft and the government concluded this phase of the trial, their representatives were continuing to meet in Chicago in search of a settlement in mediation talks overseen by Richard A. Posner, chief judge of the United States Court of Appeals for the Seventh Circuit. The sides reportedly remained far apart, but government officials noted that the fact they were still meeting at this late date suggested willingness on both sides to reach a settlement.

"We're continuing to work hard with Judge Posner," said William H. Neukom, Microsoft's general counsel.

The debate in court today was

over how legal precedents from industries ranging from ski slopes in Colorado to newspapers in Ohio apply to the facts in the Microsoft case. The government said Microsoft was an old-fashioned monopolist in high-technology clothes. Microsoft responded that computer software—a fast-changing, dynamic, fiercely competitive industry—did indeed have distinctive characteristics, and the courts should tread carefully.

The Standard Oil analogy was just one of several skeptical questions and remarks Judge Jackson aimed at Microsoft's lawyer in court today. Mr. Warden was making the argument that the Windows operating system was protected by a copyright and, therefore, was protected against some of the government's accusations, when Judge Jackson spoke up to say he had a problem with that defense.

"What exactly is covered by copyright?" the judge asked. He then asked whether it was "fee simple"—or absolute—control over code.

"Mr. Rockefeller," the judge said, "had fee-simple control over his oil. I don't really see a distinction."

Mr. Warden responded that the laws were different then, adding that he did not think copyright law was more powerful than antitrust law.

Today's presentations were the final attempts by both sides to try to influence Judge Jackson's thinking. At one point, David Boies, the Justice Department's lead trial lawyer, said Microsoft's business strategy was based on trying to "bribe and coerce" other companies in the computer industry. Mr. Warden dismissed one of Mr. Boies's arguments as "entirely wrong."

The government, according to most antitrust experts, is sitting on a big lead, while Microsoft is trying to limit its losses in Judge Jackson's court while hoping to fare better on appeal. But at one point, Mr. Boies appeared to be trying to embolden Judge Jackson not to worry about appeals by saying: "Try to imagine the Supreme Court ruling that these acts do not violate the antitrust laws. It is simply impossible to imagine that."

Microsoft, on the other hand, seemed to be employing elements of a loss-limitation strategy. Mr. Warden began by saying that Microsoft "respectfully disagreed" with much of Judge Jackson's findings of fact last November, which strongly favored the government's case.

Mr. Warden then went on to tell the judge that his ruling might well shape the ground rules for competition in the entire high-technology economy. And he lambasted the government for its "assault on Windows, which promotes and creates commerce."

The Microsoft case, Mr. Warden noted, focuses on the company's "fights with competitors in a highly competitive, fast-moving industry." And antitrust law, he observed, encourages competition even when that rough-and-tumble competition hurts a company's rivals.

"The law should not be rewritten to prevent Microsoft, or any other company, from competing aggressively," Mr. Warden said.

In the government's view, Microsoft is trying to change the subject with arguments like these. "We don't say competition is a violation of the antitrust laws," Mr. Boies said. "Our allegations here deal with the means by which they compete. They are seriously anticompetitive."

He added that the voluminous court record, including thousands of e-mails, internal Microsoft documents and months of witness testimony, had shown that Microsoft was an arm-twisting monopolist, whose corporate behavior stifled competition and harmed consumers. Judge Jackson's factual findings agreed.

Mr. Boies opened his remarks by emphasizing that the Supreme Court had long recognized that antitrust cases were "especially fact-based cases." And throughout his presentation, he repeatedly made reference to the judge's findings of fact.

But at one point, Judge Jackson asked hard questions of Mr. Boies, too. Antitrust experts say that the government accusation that is most vulnerable is the contention that Microsoft illegally tied its Internet browser to a separate product, its industry-standard Windows operating system.

Judge Jackson questioned Mr. Boies closely on the tying issue. Mr. Boies argued that Microsoft's decision was not really a product design decision but more a mere "bolting" together of the browser and Windows.

In short, Mr. Boies was trying to recast the tying charge as a contract restriction—that is, PC makers who wanted Windows had to take its Internet Explorer browsing software whether they wanted it or not.

Judge Jackson appeared to be skeptical. What about the benefit, he asked Mr. Boies, of the increased distribution of browser technology resulting from Microsoft's decision to fold its browser into Windows? "I can't offset that—one plausible benefit," Judge Jackson said.

Still, Kevin O'Conner, an assistant attorney general for Wisconsin, who represented the states, declared that "Microsoft has used virtually every tool of the monopolist's trade—attempted collusion, exclusionary contracts, tying, predation—in a coordinated scheme to eliminate threats to its monopoly."

FEBRUARY 23, 2000

Training a Mule

In March, the settlement talks with Judge Posner were continuing, so when Judge Jackson read reports in the news media that the government wanted to break up Microsoft, he was distressed.

"I should tell you," he said, "I am not at all comfortable with restructuring the company. I am not sure I am competent to do that. Microsoft is a large and important company, innovative, admirable in a lot of ways. If it ain't broken, don't try to fix it. And it is an engine for the nation's economy. I just don't think that is something I want to try to do on my own. I wouldn't know how to do it, although I am sure there are people who will give me plenty of advice how to do it."

But his findings suggested that the company was broken. So what, he was asked, did he plan to do?

"I like to tell the story of the North Carolina mule trainer," Jackson replied. "He had a trained mule who could do all kinds of wonderful tricks. One day somebody asked him: 'How do you do it? How do you train the mule to do all these amazing things?' 'Well,' he answered, 'I'll show you.' He took a 2-by-4 and whopped him upside the head. The mule was reeling and fell to his knees, and the trainer said: 'You just have to get his attention.' "

"I hope I've got Microsoft's attention." the judge said. "But we'll see."

The judge then offered opinions on a few points in the trial.

Boies's strategy to play the Gates tape on the opening day, Jackson said, was "ingenious, a very effective strategy."

"It set the tone for everything that came after," Jackson said. "Here is the guy who is the head of the organization, and his testimony is inherently without credibility. At the start it makes you skeptical about the rest of the trial. In effect, you put this adverse witness on the stand, and you are saying, 'If you can't believe this guy, who else can you believe?' "

But one flamboyant bit of testimony—Jim Allchin's videotapes—fell flat with the judge.

During Allchin's testimony, Boies pointed out numerous flaws in Microsoft's videotaped demonstration, which the witness had just played. The resulting testimony produced some of the most sensational moments in the trial. Allchin essentially apologized, the Judge told him he found the episode "very troubling," and Justice Department officials were jubilant. It was "a stunning development," said A. Douglas Melamed, deputy chief of the Justice Department's antitrust division.

Looking back, however, Judge Jackson said none of it had really mattered very much. "I never got the impression he was trying to falsify the tapes on purpose," he said of

Allchin. "These things happen to trial lawyers. They get sandbagged."

He had larger problems with the defense, he said: "There were times when I became impatient with Microsoft witnesses who were giving speeches. They were telling me things I just flatly could not credit."

Still, Jackson remained respectful of Microsoft. "There is no doubt in my mind that Microsoft is a unique, gifted, efficient and ingenious organism.

"But," he added, "the fact that they do a lot of things right does not give them a license to do anything wrong."

At the same time, the judge was growing restive. This was a large, important case, and it had been in his hands alone for two years.

"I have been in splendid isolation on this case long enough," he said. "I would welcome another mind studying my work product to see if I am correct or wrongheaded." He said he wanted to move to the remedy phase quickly, immediately after the verdict, if there was no settlement. "I want to bring in other minds as quickly as possible."

Microsoft Said to Offer Plan for Settlement

With two federal judges pressing Microsoft and the government to settle their antitrust case soon, Microsoft presented a formal written proposal today that would restrain some of the company's business practices, officials said.

Lawyers for the Justice Department and 19 state attorneys general were studying the proposal tonight to decide whether it was promising enough to warrant weekend negotiations.

Officials said the proposal included so much technical detail that they could not analyze it quickly, although one also said Microsoft "appears to have come a long way with this, but not as far as I think they should."

Reaching agreement with Microsoft, however, is only part of the plaintiffs' task. They must also agree among themselves.

The Justice Department and the state attorneys general are partners in the suit, and among them hold a range of opinions on what they could accept as a settlement. Some attorneys general believe anything short of breaking up the company would be ineffective, while others do not want to split up Microsoft. But officials said proposals that would restructure the company have not been on the table in the talks.

On Tuesday, Judge Thomas Penfield Jackson, who is trying the case in federal court here, called lawyers from both sides to his chambers to ask for a progress report on the settlement talks, which have been under way since Nov. 30.

The trial is over; all that is left is the verdict. But Judge Jackson is withholding it to give the settlement talks time to run their course. On Tuesday, however, he made it clear that he was not willing to wait beyond next week. And given his findings of fact in the case, published in November, he is almost certain to find Microsoft in violation of antitrust law—prompting the company to offer concessions today that officials said it had not offered before.

Richard A. Posner, chief judge of the United States Court of Appeals in Chicago, who is serving as mediator, has been making similar suggestions of urgency for weeks. Originally he said he wanted to conclude the talks by early February.

Since the meeting with Judge Jackson this week, state and federal officials have been furiously calling, sending e-mail messages and meeting in an effort to agree on a strategy. Many of the attorneys general have been in Washington for an annual meeting that ended today, and while here some of them have met with Joel I. Klein, head of the Justice Department's antitrust division.

But as the attorneys general consider Microsoft's proposal, the states have no central decision-making process for deciding whether it warrants serious negotiation, requiring lots of phone calls and messages to reach a decision.

On Thursday, after reports in The Wall Street Journal and The Washington Post indicated that the pace of settlement talks had increased, Microsoft's stock gained more than 7 percent. Today it closed at $111.6875, down 18.75 cents.

Both state and federal officials said publicly that they would not comment on the talks, and none would describe the proposal in detail. Microsoft declined to comment.

But all of them appear to be keeping their options open to meet in Chicago with Judge Posner this weekend. But they have decided not to meet on Saturday. If government lawyers decide Microsoft's new proposal is serious, William H. Gates, Microsoft's chairman, and Mr. Klein might be expected to join the talks, when they do reopen, perhaps as soon as Sunday or Monday.

Several officials noted, however, that it was not easy to make a decision because of the technical detail in the proposal. The last time Microsoft and the government settled an antitrust case, in 1994, Mr. Gates insisted on one detail—the ability to add new features to the Windows operating system—that seemed unimportant to the government at the time but later proved to be the basis for the current suit, which contends in part that Microsoft illegally combined its Web browser with Windows.

"Our experience with this is not a happy one, not inspiring of confidence," one official said. Several officials said it would take time to analyze the document to make sure it did not include similar potential vulnerabilities.

All of Microsoft's proposals, they said, are for changes in conduct. The company has made it clear, in the settlement talks and in public, that it would not accept a breakup of the company. Breakup proposals, the company has said, are "an extreme and reckless resolution to the government's antitrust suit."

But some government officials think anything short of that would not be effective. As one put it today: "If we don't make fundamental changes, then soon enough we'll be fighting this battle all over again."

And when Mr. Klein met with leaders of the technology industry last fall, asking them for public support of proposed sanctions against Microsoft—without saying exactly what he had in mind—he received something short of enthusiastic responses. Without industry support, a stringent remedy might be hard to enact.

Until now, Microsoft and government lawyers have been meeting separately with Judge Posner in Chicago. One day, the judge would talk to one side, the next day to the other. And then the judge would try to draw the two sides together. If the talks go forward next week, the two sides will probably meet face to face for the first time since their initial meeting with the judge on Nov. 30.

At one stage of the talks early this year, Judge Posner asked the state and federal officials, one by one, for their proposed remedies, and as each official offered his idea, the suggestions were all over the map—from restraining Microsoft's behavior to breaking up the company. Never have all of the parties—the Justice Department and the 19 states—agreed on a common approach.

Among the conduct remedies that have been discussed, officials said, is forcing Microsoft to publish a common price list for Windows so the company could not use prices to penalize or reward computer makers for their level of cooperation with the company.

Another idea would force Microsoft to publish the codes that allow software writers to link their programs to Windows—codes known as applications program interfaces—in a uniform, formal way.

If the settlement talks fail, Judge Jackson's verdict could come within a few days. After that, in a separate proceeding, the state and federal governments will offer a remedy proposal to the judge. For that, the Justice Department and attorneys general will have to agree, because Judge Jackson has made it clear he wants only one proposal.

MARCH 25, 2000

Reading the Judge

At this point, at least one state attorney general, Richard Blumenthal of Connecticut, seemed to be in synch with Judge Jackson on the question of remedies. No matter his own view, he said, "I don't think Judge Jackson will accept a structural remedy. There are too many unknowns. It's too Draconian, too many questions, like who gets what part of which campus. And he's got to be thinking about the Court of Appeals. They are more likely to approve a conduct remedy. It is not so novel, and it is well tied to the facts of the case."

What's more, Blumenthal added, "a structural remedy could involve the judge in years of oversight."

He added, "Others of my colleagues may disagree."

And in fact, at the time, the views of the 19 attorneys general still in the case were all over the map.

Judge in Microsoft Case Delays A Ruling as Mediation Intensifies

The federal mediator in the Microsoft antitrust case has told officials that he may be able to broker a settlement, prompting the trial judge to delay his ruling, which had been due today.

The court-appointed mediator, Richard A. Posner, chief judge of the United States Court of Appeals in Chicago, has laid out an aggressive weeklong schedule of proposals and counterproposals between Microsoft and the Department of Justice. It stipulates that if there is no agreement by next Wednesday, the mediation will end.

But Judge Posner's schedule order immediately caused some state attorneys general to bristle. After reading it, some concluded that they were being left out of the process until the very end.

Although the Justice Department and 19 state attorneys general are partners in the suit, Judge Posner's schedule appears to leave the states out of the discussions over the next week. According to an official who has seen the document, it says that if the federal government and Microsoft agree on a settlement proposal by next Wednesday, the state attorneys general will have two days to ratify it.

"And the states are not going to stand for that," the official said.

Another official noted: "All it takes is for one attorney general to say no, and there's no settlement, and Judge Jackson issues his ruling." Several officials said some hard-line state attorneys general would in fact prefer that because no one doubts that Thomas Penfield Jackson, the trial judge, will find Microsoft in wide violation of federal and state antitrust laws.

But another official said that while the wording of Judge Posner's scheduling order seemed to leave the states out, that was probably not the judge's intent, and the states could be involved if they chose.

By the end of the day it was not clear whether the dispute would be resolved, or how important it ultimately would become. But it did serve as a clear illustration of the divide between these uneasy partners in the case, one that will have to be crossed if a settlement is to be accepted.

The issuing of the schedule does not necessarily indicate that real progress has been made. As late as Monday night, as the judge's document was being distributed, some government officials were saying they thought Microsoft's offer was simply inadequate, though one official suggested that some of the tough talk might simply be a negotiating tactic.

In any case, the written scheduling order is a new strategy for Judge Posner in this case, and one that makes some of the litigants uneasy. They were not expecting such a strong-willed mediator.

Last Tuesday, Judge Jackson called the litigants into his office and told them that they had a week to settle or he would issue his ruling.

Settlement talks have been under way since Nov. 30.

On Friday, Microsoft offered its settlement proposal. Among other ideas, the company offered to provide computer makers a version of Windows that did not include access to Internet Explorer, Microsoft's Web browser. The proposal would apply to present and future versions of the operating system. The company also agreed to charge common prices for Windows so Microsoft could not use pricing to penalize or reward computer makers for their level of cooperation.

But government officials concluded that the offers were riddled with potential loopholes and that they included no mechanisms for enforcement. The Justice Department asked Microsoft for clarification, and Microsoft promised to respond. With that, Judge Posner apparently decided he had enough to keep the process going.

Microsoft's stock has risen and fallen sharply since late last week with the ebb and flow of settlement prospects. Today, with Judge Jackson's decision apparently put off for at least a week, the stock closed at $104.3125, up 25 cents.

The state attorneys general hold a wide range of views about the Microsoft proposal. Several have said they do not believe the changes Microsoft is proposing—even if they are clearly delineated and easily enforceable—are adequate to solve the problem. Some are holding out for a breakup of the company, some officials said without being specific.

State government officials held discussions through the day on nu-

merous issues related to the settlement negotiations, including the
way the states are treated in Judge
Posner's schedule.

Some attorneys general are worried that they might be perceived to
be second-class players in the case.
The Justice Department largely led
the prosecution during the trial,
through the work of David Boies,
the lead trial lawyer. He was so
effective in court that the states
made no effort to right the balance
of power.

But as soon as the courtroom
phase ended, several state officials
said they would insist on playing an
equal role in settlement discussions
or, if the case goes to a ruling, in
proposing court-ordered remedies.
So the wording of Judge Posner's
document, even if it was inadvertent, struck a nerve.

In theory, the states have the
ability to end the partnership with
the Justice Department and pursue
the final stages of the case on their
own. The states filed their own suit
when the Justice Department filed
the federal suit in May 1998. The
two suits were merged for trial.
Still, Judge Jackson has made it
clear he wants to deal with only one
plaintiff. So the states will almost
certainly try to keep the partnership
intact.

But "if this is going to fly, the
states are going to want to add some
things" to the Microsoft offer, one
official said.

Another said Judge Posner's
schedule might not matter in the
end, because "there can be no settlement" without the states.

MARCH 29, 2000

Microsoft and U.S. Unable To Reach Antitrust Accord

After four months, mediation
efforts between Microsoft and the
government were abandoned today,
making it likely that the presiding
judge in the trial will issue his decision in the long-running antitrust
case in the next few days.

The announcement came from
the court-appointed mediator,
Richard A. Posner, chief judge of
the United States Court of Appeals
in Chicago. "The disagreements
among the parties concerning the
likely course, outcome, and consequences of continued litigation,"
Judge Posner said, "as well as the
implications and ramifications of

alternative terms of settlement, are
too deep-seated to be bridged."

Last Tuesday, the trial judge,
Thomas Penfield Jackson, post-
poned a decision in the case to give
the parties one more week to reach
a settlement. In his findings of fact
in the case, issued in November,
Judge Jackson found that Microsoft
had used its monopoly power to
threaten and bully allies and competitors alike, stifling innovation
and competition in the software
industry.

Because those findings were
weighted so heavily against Microsoft, Judge Jackson is expected to

find the company in violation of antitrust laws. The only real uncertainty will be how many of the government's allegations he supports.

The trial, which has gone on for nearly a year and a half, will now consider court-ordered remedies intended to force Microsoft to change its business practices or even restructure the company. With the failure of mediation, Microsoft's hopes of averting a punitive outcome will almost certainly hinge on an appeal.

This evening Microsoft's chairman, William H. Gates, said he had spent "hundreds of hours" on the settlement negotiations, adding: "We went the extra mile to resolve this case, but the government would not agree to a fair and reasonable settlement that would have resolved this case in the best interests of consumers and the industry."

Mr. Gates added: "Ultimately, it became impossible to settle because the Department of Justice and the states were not working together. Between them, they appeared to be demanding either a breakup of our company or other extreme concessions that go far beyond the issues raised in the lawsuit."

The Justice Department, in a statement, said: "We would have preferred an effective settlement to continued litigation. But settlement for settlement's sake would be pointless. We could agree only to a remedy that effectively solves the competitive problems detailed in the court's findings of fact."

Microsoft and the government had been exchanging proposals and counterproposals over the last week,

under a carefully scripted schedule set by Judge Posner. The Justice Department sent its latest proposal to Judge Posner late in the week, and the judge passed it on to Microsoft.

When Judge Posner saw Microsoft's counterproposal, he declared the talks dead.

The 19 state attorneys general, who are partners in the suit, were unhappy both with Microsoft's offer and with the Justice Department's response. This afternoon, before Judge Posner's announcement, one official said the "views of some attorneys general differ" from those of Joel I. Klein, the assistant attorney general in charge of the Justice Department antitrust division. Several attorneys general, this official said, "have severe misgivings about some of the concessions Microsoft has convinced Judge Posner that the governments ought to make."

On Friday, the state attorneys general sent Judge Posner their own set of additional and separate demands, including what they said were stronger terms for enforcing the proposed agreements. Although other participants in the talks disagreed, Microsoft said the additional demands from the states were the death blow to the negotiations.

"The hard-liners won," one Microsoft executive said. The company and the Justice Department, he added, had reached agreement on a number of elements in a possible settlement, though further negotiations were needed. But after the states weighed in with new demands, he said, it became clear that the gap between Microsoft and the plaintiffs was too wide to be bridged.

But one person involved in the talks said Microsoft's response on Friday was "not even close" to the Justice Department proposal. Microsoft, this participant said, insisted on its unrestricted freedom to bundle software—like Internet browsing software—to its industry-standard Windows operating system, which was a crucial element in the case.

Attorney General Richard A. Blumenthal of Connecticut, one of the plaintiffs, said: "We sought common ground, but the differences between us were unbridgeable. We are now ready to return to the courtroom with the same aggressive and determined approach."

Computer industry leaders expressed relief at the news that the talks broke down. For the last two days they had been pressing the Justice Department to toughen its proposed sanctions, which they said would have done little to restrain Microsoft from abusing its market power. The Justice Department, in response, had been telling these executives that they did not fully understand the government's position.

This evening, Ken Wasch, president of the Software and Information Industry Association, a trade group, said: "The Justice Department and the states successfully litigated this case for two years, and now they are going to continue pursuing the goal of restoring competition to the software industry in the courts." He and other executives said they preferred to send the case back to court, where a finding that Microsoft violated the nation's antitrust laws is expected.

Among the major points in the final draft of the proposed agreement put forward by the Justice Department were these:

• Microsoft would be required to establish a uniform pricing schedule for the Windows operating system so the company could not use price discrimination to penalize companies that defy its will.

• The company would be prohibited from tying any of its products to Windows by sales contract, though it would still be free to integrate applications or features into the program.

• Microsoft would be forbidden to strike exclusive contracts with other companies, as it did with Internet service providers who were asked to feature Microsoft's Web browser and no others.

• Microsoft would be required to share technical information about its products without discrimination with any company that had a right to it.

• The company would also be required to disclose the software interfaces that allow programmers to link their programs to Windows.

• Microsoft would no longer be allowed to raise the price of older versions of Windows as soon as a new one is released, a tactic to prompt faster migration to the new version. The company would have to support the old version, and sell it at the same price, for three years.

Computer manufacturers would be allowed to license the source code to Windows so they could modify it, allowing them to change the opening screen users see when they turn the computer on. They could also modify the program to feature a program they prefer, such as a different browser. But Microsoft would disclaim any responsibility for offering technical support for those parts of the program that have been changed, or affected by the changes.

One official said Judge Posner had been receiving e-mail messages and telephone calls from numerous state officials over the last several days, complaining that their interests were being ignored and warning that there could be no settlement without the states' agreement.

Judge Posner, in his statement, noted: "I particularly want to emphasize that the collapse of the mediation is not due to any lack of skill, flexibility, energy, determination, or professionalism on the part of the Department of Justice and Microsoft Corporation." Nowhere did he make mention of the states.

APRIL 2, 2000

CHAPTER 6

Judge and Judgment

When testimony drew to a close, no observer could predict for certain who would triumph. But the one person who had clearly benefited from the proceedings was Judge Jackson. Many people who had followed the case closely agreed that he was administering the Microsoft trial—by far the most prominent and important of his career—brilliantly. Among other things, he won plaudits for innovative procedures that allowed testimony to be completed in less than a year. Most previous major antitrust trials had dragged on for nearly a decade.

Jackson had warned both parties that he wanted to avoid a ten-year trial, like the I.B.M. and AT&T cases. One innovative procedure he employed to speed things along was the taking of direct testimony from witnesses in written form so that only cross examination was carried out in court. This, he said, was a tactic borrowed from a retiring judge, Charles Richey, who had handed off a case to him early on in which that procedure was already in place.

As the trial proceeded, Judge Jackson's knowledge of the computer industry grew; he asked more and more technical questions that evinced an ever-firmer grasp. Still, often, when David Boies and his crew left the courtroom at the end of the day and headed down the steps to the street, they would reflect on the complex testimony of the day, and one would ask the other, "Do you think he understood?"

Later, Judge Jackson chuckled at the question and said that by and large he did understand. And when he was confused, he added, he had bright clerks who were more than literate on the technology, and they would explain anything the Judge didn't get. "We talked all the time," Jackson said, adding that absorbing the issues in the Microsoft case was "a little like learning about aeronautical engineering without being able to fly."

He also grew to be at least a fledgling expert on antitrust law; he read many of the most important precedents, and toward the end of the trial he was able to joust with Microsoft lawyers whose entire careers had been spent in antitrust. Still, he admitted, "I will not represent that I am a seer on these issues."

By the end of the trial, he also had formed clear views about the trustworthiness of the defendant, just as David Boies had hoped he would. Consider for example the testimony of Jim Allchin, the senior executive in charge of the Windows group. With rare unanimity, the plaintiffs had said that Allchin's e-mails declaring that Internet Explorer could not beat Netscape in the market unless it was deeply integrated into the operating system were the most compelling of the case.

"My conclusion is we have to leverage Windows more," Allchin wrote at the end of 1997.

Judge Jackson said those e-mails caught his attention, too. So, from the bench he asked the witness what he had meant by the word "leverage."

Allchin responded: "There's a great opportunity and, boy, we shouldn't miss it."

But the judge didn't buy it. "When Allchin told me that leverage simply meant use it as an opportunity," he said, "that was not credible."

What's more, the judge added, "Microsoft said all along that it was impossible to extricate the browser from Windows. But at three or four points in the proceedings, it was shown that they could." That refuted "their argument that it was integrated. It detracts from their credibility."

He said he found the e-mail and documents subpoenaed from Microsoft persuasive and "corroborative." In addition, he added, "there were many times when an opportunity was given to a Microsoft witness to extricate the company from an unflattering statement that was made in a document, which he did in a manner that just wasn't credible."

Judge Jackson took the air out of another Microsoft claim. By the time many Microsoft witnesses had stepped off the stand, Boies had asked barely a question about the witnesses' written, direct testimony. So Mark Murray, the Microsoft spokesman, would stand on the courthouse steps at day's end and declare: "When the government rested its cross examination, 150 pages of testimony went into the record completely unchallenged." That became a Microsoft mantra. But it turned out to be a hollow boast. In Judge Jackson's view, "Often the testimony they put into the record was simply not to the point."

Above all, Jackson enjoyed the trial.

"I looked forward to every day in court," he recalled with a smile. "This was a trial where I could come to court and be assured no one is going to waste my time. After a while, for example, they learned that I was willing to take a lot of hearsay. So they stopped objecting. That's what happens when you work with skilled lawyers."

During the trial, Judge Jackson once told a group of reporters who happened to share a cab with him that he tried hard to sit Sphinx-like on the bench so that no one could read anything into his expressions. But at that one thing, at least, he failed. Anyone watching could see when he was bored and near nodding off, when he was captivated by the testimony, when he was angry and when he was amused. And while the judge cautioned that no one should read anything into his questions, comments, smirks and shrugs on the bench, the tenor of his behavior usually left little doubt that Microsoft was not winning the day, or the trial.

U.S. Judge Says Microsoft Violated Antitrust Laws with Predatory Behavior

The Microsoft Corporation violated the nation's antitrust laws through predatory and anticompetitive behavior and kept "an oppressive thumb on the scale of competitive fortune," a federal judge ruled today.

The judge, Thomas Penfield Jackson of United States District Court, sided with the government on the most important points in its exhaustive antitrust suit, though he surprised lawyers on both sides by ruling for Microsoft in one area.

The Justice Department and the 19 states pressing the suit contended that Microsoft had hurt consumers by stifling competition in the soft-ware marketplace, particularly at the expense of the Netscape browser. Judge Jackson's findings of fact in the case, issued in November, overwhelmingly supported that view.

Several experts said today's ruling, applying the antitrust laws to those findings, laid the foundation for a powerful remedy. That will be decided in a separate proceeding to begin within a few weeks.

Options range from imposing restrictions on Microsoft's conduct to breaking up the company. Senior government officials close to the state and federal officers who are pursuing the case said many were interested in requesting a breakup, though no decision had been made.

Microsoft made clear it was set for a long fight. Its chairman, William H. Gates, said, "We believe we have a strong case on appeal."

The ruling came just 48 hours after settlement talks collapsed. On Saturday a court-appointed mediator announced that despite four months of mediation and after consideration of almost 20 drafts of a settlement offer, the gulf between the two sides remained unbridgeable.

Judge Jackson issued his judgment at 5 p.m., after the stock markets had closed. But reacting to the failure of the settlement talks and in anticipation of the judgment, Microsoft's stock plunged today, losing almost 14 percent of its value. That helped fuel a broad decline in the Nasdaq composite index, which fell 8 percent.

In his 43-page conclusions of law, Judge Jackson's final judgment on the evidence, the judge wrote that "the court concludes that Microsoft maintained its monopoly power by anticompetitive means and attempted to monopolize the Web browser market," as well as "unlawfully tying its Web browser to its operating system"—all in violation of the Sherman Antitrust Act.

At the same time, the judge ruled that Microsoft's marketing arrangements with other companies to promote its Web browser at Netscape's expense did not have sufficient effect to violate the law.

Microsoft seemed to take little solace from prevailing on that point. Mr. Gates did not even refer to that point when he announced that Microsoft would appeal.

"This ruling turns on its head the reality that consumers know—that our software has helped make PC's more accessible and more affordable to millions," Mr. Gates said.

But Attorney General Janet Reno and other officials seemed delighted.

"Microsoft has been held accountable for its illegal conduct by a court of law," the attorney general said. "We are pleased that the court agreed with the department that Microsoft abused its monopoly power, that it violated the antitrust laws and that it harmed consumers."

Tom Miller, the attorney general of Iowa, said, "Judge Jackson's decision is a broad-based and compelling finding of liability, of law-breaking." Mr. Miller leads the efforts of the 19 states that are partners with the Justice Department in the case.

And another plaintiff, Attorney General Richard A. Blumenthal of Connecticut, said the remedy should be "as far reaching and fundamental as Microsoft's abuse of its monopoly power."

The suit against Microsoft was filed almost two years ago. It accuses the company of using a monopoly in personal computer operating systems to stifle innovation and bully competitors.

The trial opened in October 1998, and from the opening moments, the government presented a case that embarrassed and damaged Microsoft. Then, when the company offered its own case several months later, many of Microsoft's witnesses were humiliated on the stand.

Testimony ended last spring. And when the judge issued his findings of fact in November, he found that Microsoft had "demonstrated that it will use its prodigious market power and immense profits to harm any firm that insists on pursuing initiatives that could intensify competition against one of Microsoft's core products."

With those findings, everyone involved with the case realized that his final judgment—which would be called a verdict in a criminal case— was likely to fall heavily against Microsoft, as it did today.

Still, many lawyers were less certain that the judge would find the company in violation of the provision of the Sherman Act that bears on combining one product with another.

A central conclusion in the government's case—and in the judge's findings of fact—was that Microsoft tied its Web browser to the Windows operating system to gain market share for its browser and put Netscape at a disadvantage.

But a finding of fact does not necessarily lead to a similar conclusion of law, which says that the action violates antitrust laws. That is particularly so in this case because a three-judge panel of the Court of Appeals, overturning an order by Judge Jackson requiring Microsoft to offer a version of Windows without the browser, decided 2 to 1 in 1998 that Microsoft had every right to tie the browser to the operating system, if the company could demonstrate a plausible consumer benefit.

The Court of Appeals judges also

suggested, however, that their opinion might change once they saw the evidence record from a trial. Judge Jackson devoted the largest section of his ruling to defending his judgment of liability on this count.

The Court of Appeals opinion, he wrote, "appears to immunize any product design (or at least software product design) from antitrust scrutiny, irrespective of its effect upon competition, if the software developer can postulate any 'plausible claim' of advantage to its arrangement of code."

He cited several Supreme Court decisions that support his view and called them "indisputably controlling." He concluded: "Microsoft's decision to tie Internet Explorer to Windows cannot truly be explained as an attempt to benefit consumers and improve the efficiency of the software market generally, but rather as part of a larger campaign to quash innovation that threatened its monopoly position."

On other counts, he ruled that Microsoft's campaign against Netscape, as well as its decision to develop its own version of the Java programming language and encourage other companies to use it instead of the authorized version, prevented Netscape and Java from competing on the merits.

"Because Microsoft achieved this result through exclusionary acts that lacked pro-competitive justification," the judge wrote, "the court deems Microsoft's conduct the maintenance of monopoly power by anticompetitive means."

He found in favor of Microsoft on the charge that the company had tried to block Netscape from the market by making exclusive agreements for its browser with computer companies, online services and Internet service providers.

Judge Jackson wrote: "The evidence does not support a finding that these agreements completely excluded Netscape from any constituent portion of the worldwide browser market," as the law requires for a finding of illegality.

But the heavy weight of the ruling was against Microsoft, and it included some extraordinarily damning language in parts.

"Microsoft's anticompetitive actions," he wrote, "trammeled the competitive process through which the computer software industry generally stimulates innovation" to "the optimum benefit of consumers."

Some experts said the ruling made it likely that the government would ask for a remedy that would break up the company.

"It boxes them in," said Robert Litan, a former senior official in the Justice Department's antitrust division who dealt with the department's last suit against Microsoft, in 1994.

In the mediation effort that ended on Saturday, "Microsoft already made it clear that they would not accept a conduct remedy" acceptable to the government, he said. And this suggests that, if one were imposed, the government might face difficult enforcement questions.

"With this strong validation of the case, we now know that only a breakup will address the operating system monopoly" that is at the

heart of the case, Mr. Litan said. He is now with the Brookings Institution and has said he favors breaking up the company into several autonomous parts.

This evening, representatives of both Microsoft and the government said they remained open to the idea of restarting settlement talks. But when the judge's decision was entered, Microsoft's options narrowed considerably.

Judge Jackson's findings of fact in November gave plaintiffs' lawyers who were pursuing private suits against Microsoft useful ammunition for their cases. But the findings had only an ambiguous legal standing without the conclusions of law, entered today.

One of Microsoft's strongest incentives for reaching a settlement before today was that it would have removed the threat of a legal ruling and vacated the findings of fact. But should the litigants reach a settlement in the weeks or months ahead, it is not at all clear that the decision, including its legal conclusion that Microsoft holds a monopoly in personal computer operating system, can be wiped from the records.

"It's an interesting and unsure question," said Andrew I. Gavil, a professor of law at Howard University. "There's no clear precedent for vacating a ruling after it has been issued." But even if Judge Jackson were to agree to vacate his ruling as a condition of a settlement agreement, Mr. Gavil noted that other judges might not feel bound by that.

"Once the ruling is entered, you lose containment," he said.

Mr. Gavil and other lawyers said

they believed private suits against Microsoft would multiply.

"It gives powerful new ammunition to lawyers pursuing class-action cases," said Stephen Houck, who was the chief lawyer for the 19 states that filed suit against Microsoft. He is now in private practice. Mr. Gavil added, "I think we may well see a new wave of them."

APRIL 4, 2000

Flouting the Appeals Court

Judge Jackson came down hardest on the issue of tying the Web browser to Windows—the very issue that had brought him a rebuke from the Court of Appeals in 1998. The appellate court said that Microsoft had every right to integrate new products into Windows, if each new product plausibly presented a benefit for consumers.

Judge Jackson said he was "wounded" by that ruling— and angry, insisting, "It was wrong-headed on several counts." Accepting that ruling, he added, would in essence have meant that the software industry was exempted from compliance with the nation's antitrust laws.

Expedited Appeal Proposed By Judge in Microsoft Case

The presiding judge in the Microsoft antitrust case, meeting with lawyers for both sides in Washington yesterday, said he wanted to put the remedy phase of the case on a "fast track" and consider encouraging the litigants to appeal the outcome directly to the Supreme Court, according to a transcript of the meeting.

One day after he issued his judgment that found Microsoft in broad violation of the nation's antitrust laws, Judge Thomas Penfield Jackson laid out a tight schedule for filings from both parties every 10 or 15 days "under a genuine fast track which would enable us to conclude the remedy phase within 60 days" of Monday, he said.

No decisions were made, and at one point Judge Jackson discussed possibly bypassing the appeals court and encouraging the Justice Department to take the case directly to the Supreme Court, under a law that allows that procedure in antitrust cases of national importance.

"I would be remiss if I didn't tell you that I will be inviting from the government a motion to provide for direct review in the Supreme Court," he said.

Lawyers for both sides raised questions about the various ideas, suggesting that they were not sure what the law permitted.

At the same time, Microsoft faces the threat of a rising wave of consumer class-action cases and other private lawsuits.

During the meeting, Judge Jackson said: "My transcendent objective is to get this thing before an appellate tribunal—one or another—as quickly as possible because I don't want to disrupt the economy or waste any more of your or my time on a remedy if it's going to come back here."

In the remedy phase, the court will decide what penalty, or remedy, is assigned to Microsoft. Ideas range from moderating the company's conduct to breaking the company up.

The judge issued his verdict on Monday, just 48 hours after settlement talks broke down. In his conversations with the lawyers yesterday, he asked them to give him the last offers each side had made in the talks, an idea that both sides resisted. David Boies, the lead government lawyer, noted that offers discussed in mediation talks are often of a different character than those offered to a trial judge.

Both sides were also concerned about making their last offers from the settlement talks part of the public record of the trial, to which Judge Jackson said he would be willing to take them under seal.

No decisions were made, and the lawyers left to discuss the questions with others at the Justice Department and Microsoft.

If the case were sent directly to the Supreme Court, the court could presumably refuse to accept it, thereby sending it to the Court of Appeals for the District of Columbia.

Apart from the appeals process, Microsoft could face a raft of suits from the private sector. With Judge Jackson having ruled on Monday that Microsoft was a "predatory" monopolist that repeatedly violated antitrust laws, private plaintiffs have a far less daunting challenge in suits already filed— and in actions being considered by companies that believe they have suffered from abuse of Microsoft's market power.

"This is now an awfully big invitation to plaintiffs' lawyers," said John C. Coffee Jr., a professor at the Columbia University law school. "We may have reached a point for Microsoft, as there was in the tobacco cases, that basic attitudes have shifted, and a powerful defendant is no longer seen as invulnerable."

Some of Microsoft's leading rivals, and even its biggest customers, could bring private suits, according to legal experts. But they will almost surely hold off, at least until they see what sanctions the courts approve against Microsoft—sanctions that could, among other things, limit its ability to retaliate.

APRIL 5, 2000

Fast Action Sought by Microsoft Judge to Find a Remedy

The judge in the Microsoft antitrust case set a "fast track" schedule today intended to conclude the proceedings and impose a remedy roughly by the end of May. And with that deadline looming, the state attorneys general, the plaintiffs who have favored the strongest remedies, are coalescing around the view that they will not ask the judge to break up the company, several officials said today.

The decision on timing came in a meeting this morning of Judge Thomas Penfield Jackson and lawyers for the government and Microsoft.

"It was an expedited process that everyone agreed on," said Joel I. Klein, head of the Justice Department's antitrust division. The Justice Department prevailed in the case when Judge Jackson ruled on Monday that Microsoft was a "predatory" monopolist that had acted illegally to protect its market domination.

With the fast-track schedule, the judge appeared to drop the idea, discussed at a meeting earlier this week, of immediately urging a review of his conclusions of law by the United States Court of Appeals for the District of Columbia Circuit before he deliberates on a remedy.

In a meeting on Tuesday, the judge told the parties: "We're now entering the remedy phase, and I am very much desirous of having an appellate panel take a look at my work product so far, and would pre-fer if we were able to conclude the remedy phase on a fast track." He did not raise the idea of such a review today, however.

It also remained possible that Judge Jackson might recommend that Microsoft's appeal be filed directly to the Supreme Court once the proceedings in his court are over—another idea he mentioned on Tuesday. Microsoft would almost certainly oppose that because in previous rulings some judges on the appeals court have agreed with some of its positions. For the same reasons, government officials would probably favor a direct appeal by Microsoft.

Under the plan announced today, the state and federal governments must submit their remedy proposal to the judge no later than April 28, and Microsoft is to offer its reply on May 10. A hearing, presumably with witnesses, would begin on May 24.

Though Judge Jackson clearly indicated that he would prefer to receive a single remedy proposal from the state and federal officials—and the parties said they would work hard to comply—he also told them they could submit two if they could not agree.

But Richard Blumenthal, the Connecticut attorney general, who participated in the meeting by conference call, said: "We expect to be working with the Justice Department in the same kind of cooperative spirit" that was in evidence during the trial.

The judge also told the states that they should submit a proposal "preferred by a majority of the plaintiff states"—an important pronouncement because it would not allow a handful of states to hold out for their preferred remedy against the will of the majority.

As one official said last week in the final days of the settlement talks, "All it takes is for one attorney general to say no, and there's no settlement." Presumably, Judge Jackson's instruction would eliminate that threat in the remedy process.

The 19 state attorneys general hold a range of opinions on remedies, and some of them say they believe that only a structural remedy, like breaking up the company, will work, officials said. But a growing number of influential attorneys general now hold the view that breaking up the company is "too radical," as more than one official said today, adding that it might not hold up on appeal.

And, significantly, since the judge has ordered the states to send him only the majority opinion, hard-liners who held out for a stronger remedy would be likely to lose influence.

A remedy that would simply constrain Microsoft's behavior while keeping the company intact would be "more palatable at the appeals level and maybe easier to implement," one official said.

As for "the few cases" of hard-line attorneys general who say they could not accept such a remedy, the official said they could probably be persuaded to change their minds.

A different official who said he was familiar with the views of the hard-liners, said the other attorneys general would "have to show a really bulletproof conduct remedy proposal" to bring them around.

Justice Department officials say they have not made up their minds what remedies to recommend. And Mr. Klein of the antitrust division generally does not disclose his decisions on big issues like this, even to some of his colleagues, until sometime near the deadline, officials said.

Still, serious disagreements arose between the state and federal officials in the settlement talks that ended on Saturday. The federal officials offered behavioral remedies that most of the attorneys general—even those now talking about conduct remedies—considered far too weak.

Two issues most concerned them. The Justice Department proposal would have allowed Microsoft to continue folding new products into the operating system and declaring them to be a part of Windows. Microsoft's management has repeatedly said that was a right it was unwilling to give up.

But state officials said such a compromise would allow Microsoft to continue to use its Windows operating-system monopoly to overpower rivals. This is the very behavior that prompted the present suit, and Judge Jackson, in his ruling, demonstrated clear concern over the issue.

Last week's federal settlement proposal also had no clear enforcement mechanism, several officials said. Under that plan, if a competitor determined that Microsoft was

violating the terms of the settlement, its only recourse would have
been to complain to the government, which could choose to take
Microsoft back to court. For a variety of reasons, few companies would
have been likely to complain—particularly if the November elections
produced a Republican administration less interested in antitrust
enforcement.

A variety of more direct and immediate enforcement ideas have
been discussed, including perhaps
appointing a special court master
with enforcement authority.

In the meeting today, Judge Jackson also dropped an idea he had
offered on Tuesday—that both sides
give him the final offers they made
in the settlement talks as a way to
start remedy discussions. Both sides
had objected to that suggestion.

APRIL 6, 2000

U.S. and 17 States Ask Judge to Cut Microsoft In Two Parts; Serious Curbs Also Sought

Determined to change the rules of
competition in the software industry, the Justice Department and 17
states asked a federal judge today to
break Microsoft into two parts and
seriously restrain its behavior while
the breakup is being carried out.

Federal and state officials, partners in the long-running antitrust
case against Microsoft, said their
approach was intended to encourage market forces to reshape incentives in the software industry. The
two resulting companies, they said,
would have strong motivations to
compete with each other while also
forming new alliances with other
companies and products that Microsoft now shuns.

"Unless effectively remedied,"
the plaintiffs declared, Microsoft's
actions "threaten an enormous toll
on competition and innovation."
Two of the 19 states involved dissented.

Joel I. Klein, the assistant attorney general who is head of the Justice Department's antitrust division,
said that under the proposal, "neither ongoing government regulation
nor the self-interest of an entrenched monopolist will decide
what is best for consumers." Instead, he said, "the marketplace will
decide."

Attorney General Janet Reno
called it "the right remedy at the
right time."

But Microsoft's chairman, William
H. Gates, reaffirmed his company's
determination to fight not only the
proposed remedy but the antitrust
finding. "Breaking up Microsoft
into separate companies is not in
the interest of consumers and is not
supported by anything in the lawsuit," he said. "Dismantling Microsoft would hurt the company's
ability to continue to innovate."

The government's remedy proposal is the culmination of almost
four years of investigation and litigation by the Justice Department
and the states. Microsoft's decision

to include an Internet browser in Windows led to the investigation's start in August 1996. But by the time the case came to trial, in October 1998, it had grown to revolve around Microsoft's operating system monopoly and all of the actions the company has taken to protect it.

After settlement talks broke down four weeks ago, Judge Thomas Penfield Jackson ruled that Microsoft was a predatory monopolist that stunted innovation and harmed consumers.

If the recommendation were enacted by the court and upheld on appeal—far from a certain proposition in both cases—it would be one of the few times in the 110-year history of the Sherman Antitrust Act that the government had succeeded in breaking up a major national corporation. The most prominent were Standard Oil in 1911, and AT&T in a settlement in 1984.

The joint state-federal plan calls for breaking Microsoft into an operating-system company and a second company that would hold everything else, including applications software, like the word processor Word and the spreadsheet program Excel, and Microsoft's Internet properties.

This order would be stayed during legal appeals. But the state and federal officials are also asking the court to impose a group of additional remedies immediately that would restrict Microsoft's conduct. They would be in place for three years after the company was broken up, 10 years if it was not.

Judge Jackson has said he wants to move through the remedy phase quickly and may urge an immediate appeal to the Supreme Court—an idea that Mr. Klein endorsed this evening but that Microsoft opposes. Microsoft has until May 10 to respond to the request, and a remedy hearing is scheduled for May 24. Judge Jackson is unlikely to rule on the request before summer.

The intention of the Justice Department and most of the 19 states involved to seek a breakup of the company had become clear over the last week; state officials who had favored restrictions on Microsoft's conduct began to change their views after they saw that the Justice Department intended to ask for a break up. What was in doubt until today were the specifics of the proposed restrictions on Microsoft's conduct and the number of states that would support a breakup.

In the end, attorneys general from two states—Ohio and Illinois—dissented, saying they believe the government should impose restrictions on Microsoft's conduct first, wait three years and move to break up the company only if those restrictions do not work. And some of the other state officials said they were disappointed that the restraints on behavior had no specific enforcement mechanism.

But Microsoft called the proposal outrageous and unwarranted.

"For months, the government and a handful of our competitors have been repeating that Microsoft should be broken up," Steven A. Ballmer, Microsoft's chief executive, said this evening. "But no matter how many times it's repeated, it's still unreasonable. I remain proud of the work this company does. We do not believe we have violated the law and the Court of Appeals has yet to consider this case."

Senior state and federal officials, disagreed; they said their plan struck the proper balance between strong-armed remedial enforcement and meddlesome government interference in industry.

"This remedy," the document says, "has the best chance of preventing future competitive harms and ameliorating some of the harm already done" while at the same time "it avoids burdensome regulation and minimizes ongoing judicial supervision and involvement. It can be reasonably implemented and will not impair the non-anticompetitive interests of Microsoft or its shareholders."

Under the plan, when the conduct restrictions expire three years after a breakup, the two new companies will be free to pursue their businesses with no government regulation or oversight.

"This decree will not limit Microsoft's ability to add new features to its products or otherwise to innovate," Mr. Klein said. Richard Blumenthal, the attorney general of Connecticut, said it "offers the best hope of restoring competition and reigniting innovation without punishing the company."

The filing includes five supporting affidavits from economists and others. One, Paul M. Romer, an economist at Stanford University, said the proposed breakup was "the most important element of the remedy."

"It will deprive the operating systems company of some of the tools that Microsoft used to limit competition," he said. "It will also create an applications company with the incentive and the ability" to begin licensing software "to competing operating systems."

Carl Shapiro, a business professor at the University of California at Berkeley who served as a consultant to the government in the trial, said the experience of several recent competitive companies and products—Microsoft Word versus Word-Perfect, American Express versus Visa and MasterCard, Nintendo versus Atari video games—demonstrates that "the strongest threat to Windows is likely to come from a company with a strong position in widely used applications software" in the same industry, namely the proposed new Microsoft applications company.

And Rebecca Henderson, a professor of management at the Massachusetts Institute of Technology, said: "Rather than relying on an extensive set of permanent prohibitions that may be difficult to enforce, or which may have undesirable side effects, this remedy will quickly put in place market-based incentives which rely on the firm's basic profit motive to promote competition. It will ensure that the competitive energies of both firms are focused on creating value in the marketplace rather than on evading regulation."

For its part, Microsoft said the proposal was so extreme that it would force the company to ask for extensive discovery and in-court testimony on the remedy. Government officials say that Microsoft's request will require months of hearings and procedures that could stall the case until the next administration takes office. Microsoft denies that.

The White House is taking a hands-off approach to the case. A White House spokesman said today that President Clinton was leaving the decision on remedies up to the Justice Department and had no intention of interfering.

The deliberations over a remedy were long and difficult—especially for the states, which were trying to reconcile the views of 19 independent politicians of both parties and every possible political persuasion.

Lobbying of a small group of holdout attorneys general opposed to the breakup continued until today. But in the end, to the consternation of both state and federal officials, Betty Montgomery of Ohio and James Ryan of Illinois insisted on adding a dissenting addendum to the proposal.

In a statement, Mr. Ryan said he agreed with his colleagues that "the court should impose strong conduct remedies." But he added that "the goals of the litigation can be achieved without reorganization at this time."

Ms. Montgomery, in a statement, said, "A reorganization would be difficult to undo, and its effects would be difficult to predict."

Under the government plan, Mr. Gates, the company's chairman, would have to choose one of the two companies and divest himself of any financial interest in the other. So would the company's two other largest stockholders, Mr. Ballmer and Paul G. Allen, the co-founder.

The plan also includes a long list of restrictions on Microsoft's behavior, generally known as conduct remedies, including these:

• A ban on taking actions against computer manufacturers that choose to feature other companies' software products in place of Microsoft's.

• A requirement that Microsoft allow computer manufacturers to alter the Windows operating system in significant ways.

• A requirement that Microsoft share with other companies any technical information about Windows, including software interfaces, that the system engineers are sharing with other people at Microsoft.

• A uniform price list for Windows.

• A ban on design strategies intended to compromise or disable other programs that run on Windows.

• A ban on exclusive deals with, or retaliation against, other software or Internet companies.

The list is similar to the terms of the last offer the Justice Department made to Microsoft during the settlement talks that ended early this month. Now, as then, it includes no specific enforcement mechanism, a point of contention with some of the states.

If other companies believe Microsoft is violating the agreement, they would be required to petition the Justice Department to open a case and take Microsoft back to court. That is a long and cumbersome process at best, and uncertain as well—though the proposal does give Justice Department investigators the right to enter Microsoft offices virtually on demand. But no one knows how the next administration will regard this suit and enforcement of the ruling.

For that reason, several attorneys general had pushed to include a request for a court-appointed special master who would be given some limited enforcement powers. But the Justice Department declined, telling the states they did not want to burden the proposal with "a lot of heavy-handed regulation," one official said.

The states decided this was not a deal breaker. But Mr. Blumenthal said: "Enforcement remains a work in progress and perhaps best left to the court which, in the end, will have responsibility for oversight and enforcement. It is an obvious area of concern for us."

Both state and federal officials say the states contributed significantly to the final proposal. But it is difficult to assign credit for one proposal or another to one side or the other because the two sides exchanged drafts over several weeks.

But Attorney General Tom Miller of Iowa, who led the states' effort, said the 17 attorneys general were pleased with the end result.

"It is measured relief," he said. "This is a remedy, not a penalty. It is about the future more than the past."

APRIL 29, 2000

A Tangled Path to the Decision to Seek a Split

When it all began two years ago, with the federal and state governments filing their landmark antitrust suit against Microsoft, Kevin O'Connor, an assistant attorney general in Wisconsin, was struck with a numbing fear: What would the plaintiffs do if they actually won the case against one of the richest and most powerful companies in America?

"It's like the dog chasing the bus," Mr. O'Connor said. "What's he going to do if he catches it?"

The answer came Friday. The Justice Department and 17 states asked a federal judge to break Microsoft into two companies that would compete with each other and, they contended, change the rules of competition across the software industry. Today, government officials were relieved, behaving in some ways like a new parent after a long and tortured labor. And that it was.

Over the last few weeks, the Justice Department and 19 states were sometimes in warring camps that reconfigured themselves as events swirled around them. All think it something of a miracle that a vast majority wound up in agreement on a single remedy proposal. (Two attorneys general dissented.)

Within the Justice Department, the job was easier. On Sunday, April 2, the day after mediation efforts broke down, Joel I. Klein, the assistant attorney general who heads the antitrust division, convened his senior aides and polled them on their preferred remedies.

"And everyone said the same thing: ops-aps," said one person with knowledge of the discussion. Ops-aps is the term coined within the department for the proposal to create two new companies, one that would have the Windows operating system and another that would have the applications software, like word processing and spreadsheet programs.

A roughly similar idea had been offered during the settlement talks. But this point of consensus was reached only at the end of a long and bumpy road.

Almost immediately after Mr. O'Connor worried about the dog and the bus in May 1998, the states had agreed to form a remedies committee, which began work well before the trial opened in October 1998. After almost a year of research, consultations with experts and intense internal discussions, they came up with a plan that was presented at the group's annual convention in Washington in March 1999.

The proposal called for forcing Microsoft to auction the source code for the Windows operating system to other companies, which would develop and improve it, creating competition in the operating system business.

The states were not interested in breaking up Microsoft, even though the antitrust trial was almost over and it was clear that Microsoft had put on a miserable defense in court.

Tom Miller, the Iowa attorney general, who was by far the most active of the 19 attorneys general,

said the idea "was somewhere between conduct and structural"— that is, between merely restricting Microsoft's behavior and actually restructuring the company.

But as the states quickly found out, there was one big problem. When they talked to the various companies that might be bidders in the Windows auction, they learned that none had any interest in bidding. The consensus was that the computer code was too complicated, and the price was likely to be too high.

"So we discarded that idea," Mr. Miller said. And another attorney general, Richard Blumenthal of Connecticut, said the government's ability to impeach the credibility of Microsoft executives who testified helped convince him and others about that time that remedies intended to modify Microsoft's conduct probably would not work.

"We saw that there was no moral core to their defense," he said. "It was all bluster and rhetoric, so I came away thinking that it was very risky to believe there would be even a scintilla of credibility on their part" when it came to hoping they would abide by conduct restrictions.

About the time the states were reaching this point in their thinking, Mr. Klein chartered a wide research project on remedies using department staff and academic experts. Over the summer, Justice Department personnel spoke with dozens of computer industry leaders, analysts, venture capitalists, lawyers and others to gauge their views on remedies. Mr. Klein carried out many of the interviews himself.

Some of those consulted were Microsoft allies; others were theoretically loyal customers, and still others were competitors. But "the broad consensus, when you took the competitors out of it, was that Microsoft could and would evade conduct remedies," a person with direct knowledge of the discussions said.

Still no decision was made. But then Judge Thomas Penfield Jackson issued his findings of fact on Nov. 5, declaring Microsoft a market-stifling monopoly, and opinions within the Justice Department began to coalesce. The department began looking for an investment banking firm to help explore the economic ramifications of a breakup or other structural remedy, an official said. On Dec. 2, it hired the New York firm Greenhill & Company.

Around that time, court-sponsored settlement talks opened, mediated by Judge Richard Posner, chief judge for the United States Court of Appeals in Chicago. By the time he asked for remedy ideas early this year, the Justice Department was ready. The department proposed splitting Microsoft into three companies. One would hold Windows 98, and another would have Windows 2000, the new operating system recently released, primarily for big corporate users. A third company would hold the rest of Microsoft's businesses.

This was intended to create immediate competition in the operating system business, and the states joined in advocating the idea. But after a period of discussion, Judge Posner said he had spoken to Microsoft, and the company had made it clear it was not willing even to discuss the proposal. One official said Judge Posner also raised his own objections, saying he believed an appeals court would not look favorably at the idea. "It would arouse tremendous resistance in Congress, allowing Microsoft to rally public opinion against the suit," the official added, paraphrasing the judge.

That breakup proposal was dropped. Instead, the Justice Department, Judge Posner and Microsoft, often represented by its chairman, William H. Gates, fell into intense negotiations over a set of conduct remedies. Judge Posner essentially locked the states out of the process, several state officials said.

As the states got word of the discussions, they grew distressed. They considered the plan under discussion wholly inadequate.

"The states just would not have agreed to it," Mr. Miller said. As a result, he and others said, the attorneys general were relieved when the talks broke down on April 1. But they were also demoralized. The judge had issued a statement praising the negotiating parties but had pointedly failed to mention the states. And Microsoft blamed the states for the failure of the talks—an idea state and federal officials denied.

"Morale was down," Mr. Miller said. But more important, in meetings with the litigants, Judge Jackson had made it clear he wanted to complete the remedy phase of the trial quickly. On April 5 he said he wanted a joint state-federal remedy proposal by the end of the month.

That was three days after the meeting in Mr. Klein's conference room in which the group had reached consensus on the ops-aps breakup strategy (though the department had much work to do on the details of its proposal). But the last the states had heard, the Justice Department was proposing a range of conduct remedies to Judge Posner.

And Harry First, a senior official in the New York attorney general's office, said the states figured "the judge didn't want two different opinions in front of him." The states also believed, "after Justice's performance in the settlement talks, that it was not at all likely they would go for a structural remedy," another state official said, so "we decided we would devise as long a list of conduct remedies as we could."

By mid-April the centerpiece of the states' evolving proposal was three ideas that Mr. Miller called "conduct plus" remedies. The first was to prevent Microsoft from adding new products to Windows unless they were distributed on a separate disk that users could chose whether to install. The second was to require Microsoft to divest itself of Internet Explorer, the Web browser that is part of Windows. It would be put in a separate company. And the third was to require Microsoft to create versions of its package of applications software, Microsoft Office, for other operating systems.

Those ideas and others were proposed at meeting of the attorneys general in Chicago on April 13. All the states but Louisiana attended.

Even the states that opposed structural remedies, notably Ohio and Illinois, seemed to like the ideas. "They seemed pretty interested," Mr. Miller said. So the states prepared a list of conduct remedies, with those three ideas at the center.

At the Justice Department, meanwhile, officials were talking to industry leaders about the ops-aps idea, and other short-term conduct remedies to go with it. Soon after, Mr. Klein took the idea to Attorney General Janet Reno for approval, and she gave it.

In the middle of all this, the states decided to send the Justice Department a copy of their proposal, unsolicited. "We wanted to get it to Justice as soon as we could," Mr. First said. Another official said, "We hoped it would prompt some discussion with them," because so far there had been no substantive contacts.

The Justice Department did not respond substantively even to this, though Mr. Klein did tell Mr. Miller, "I can see you put a lot of work into this," Mr. Miller said.

Work continued on the state plan, but experts consulted by the states began pointing out significant problems with some proposals. For example, what if Microsoft simply reported, a year later, that it had been unable to create a version of its Office software for Linux, another operating system? What recourse would the attorneys general have?

Then, on April 17, Mr. Klein individually called Mr. Miller, Mr. Blumenthal and Attorney General Eliot L. Spitzer of New York. He told them they would be surprised and pleased by the federal proposal.

"It's going to be more aggressive than what you are considering now," Mr. Miller quoted Mr. Klein as saying. One knowledgeable person said Mr. Klein was trying to signal his department's direction without being specific; he was afraid of leaks.

But none drew the conclusion that Mr. Klein seemed to intend. "He didn't convey a whole lot," said Mr. First, who was on the call with Mr. Spitzer. "From my point of view, as we were trying to draft something, it was sort of meaningless."

Mr. Blumenthal said, "The conversation wasn't very specific."

And Mr. Miller said, "I thought maybe he was saying they were going to come up with some proposals in the midrange, conduct-plus sort of things." So the state research continued, but experts and analysts began poking more and more holes in the proposals. "It got very frustrating," one official said.

Finally, on April 20, Mr. Klein convened a conference call with his aides and the same three attorneys general. He told them exactly what the Justice Department intended to propose: the ops-aps idea along with a set of conduct remedies.

"I was somewhat surprised," Mr. Miller said. So were the others. "But the more I thought about it," he added, "I was pleased"—particularly since the states' proposal was rapidly falling apart.

Mr. Miller said he asked Mr. Klein how he had come to his proposal. He said Mr. Klein told him: "We looked at conduct plus, like you did. But we came to the conclusion that it wouldn't work as well as we had thought."

Mr. Miller said the states had come to the same conclusion, "but we hadn't announced it." So the states embraced the federal plan, noting that many elements were identical to their own.

Now all of them have to wait for the decision of the judge. "It's not appropriate to speculate on how he will proceed or how he will rule," Mr. O'Connor said.

But with a chuckle, another official said, "I would bet he'll reach his decision more easily than we did."

APRIL 30, 2000

Microsoft Offers Alternative Plan in Antitrust Case

While continuing to reject the antitrust findings against it, the Microsoft Corporation today offered a series of narrow restrictions on its behavior that it said would be more appropriate remedies than breaking up the company.

Microsoft also asked the judge to throw out the government's breakup proposal immediately, arguing that "the laws and the facts do not support such a radical step."

Microsoft's counterproposal is a four-year plan largely governing its relations with computer makers and software developers.

In its court filing, Microsoft said that if the government's breakup plan were adopted, its employees might "leave the company in droves."

If that were to happen, Microsoft continued, "the company's entire business would be destroyed."

Such passages seemed clearly intended to warn Judge Thomas Penfield Jackson that splitting up Microsoft would be a dangerous gamble to take with a pillar of the nation's high-technology economy.

"We believe there is no basis for the government's unprecedented breakup proposal," said William H. Gates, the company's chairman, "and we are hopeful that the court will dismiss this excessive demand immediately."

The motion for summary rejection was added unexpectedly to the company's formal response to the remedy proposal offered last month by the Justice Department and 17 states. In the motion, Microsoft argued that since the company achieved its monopoly position by legal means, the government had no right "to dismember Microsoft."

After four years of investigation and 19 months of litigation, the Justice Department and 17 state attorneys general proposed on April 28 that Microsoft be broken into two companies. One would hold the Windows operating system, the other everything else, including the Office suite of application programs like Word and Excel. Two of the 19 states joining in the suit—Ohio and Illinois—advocated steps short of a breakup.

Judge Jackson ruled on April 3 that Microsoft was in wide violation of the nation's antitrust laws. But if he chose to break up the company, it would be one of only a few instances the last hundred years when a major national company was broken apart as a result of an antitrust case—and the only one resulting from court order rather than a consent decree.

Next Wednesday, the federal and state governments are entitled to reply to today's filing from Microsoft. And then during a remedies hearing on May 24, both the government and Microsoft will offer arguments in support of their proposals.

In a statement today, the Justice Department said that "Microsoft's proposal is ineffective and filled with loopholes." Among the loopholes, the department added, the proposal would not prevent "attempts to divide markets with competitors; retaliation against personal computer manufacturers and software developers that support non-Microsoft technologies; or tying to require PC manufacturers to ship other Microsoft products with Windows."

And Attorney General Tom Miller of Iowa, who leads the states that are joining in the suit, said: "The remedies proposed are inadequate. These measures would not have prevented the serious violations of law found by Judge Jackson, and they are not adequate remedies to assure that the law is not broken in the future."

In the past, Microsoft's leaders repeatedly said there was a "church and state" separation within the company between the Windows group and the others that develop applications programs like Office.

But in today's filing, Microsoft said: "Cross-pollination between engineers working on different products such as Windows and Office has led to numerous innovations."

It added that the company's success and attendant benefits for consumers "would not have been possible but for Microsoft's unified structure, which enables Microsoft to conceive and implement new ideas that span operating systems and applications."

As part of today's filing, Microsoft offered its own proposed remedies, a collection of rules that would modify the company's conduct, while reiterating its conviction to appeal the case, even if its remedy proposal were accepted.

Many of the company's proposals are similar to those in the government plan, though they are more narrowly focused on specific complaints raised in the trial. Along with the breakup plan, the government wants to impose about a dozen rules intended to moderate Microsoft's conduct.

Microsoft's proposed conduct restrictions fall far short of the government's, and the company explained: "Courts are not authorized in civil enforcement proceedings to punish antitrust defendants. Instead, relief must extend no farther than is necessary to redress the conduct found to be unlawful."

Still, the proposal included several significant concessions. Among them, the company would have to take the following steps:

• Agree not to discriminate in the release of technical information about Windows to outside software developers.

• Allow computer manufacturers to make "non-Microsoft Web browsing software the default browser on a new personal computer."

• Agree not to threaten to withhold a license for Windows from a computer maker featuring products by a Microsoft competitor.

• Enter into no exclusive deals that offer other companies favored treatment in Windows in exchange for agreements to feature only Microsoft products.

• Agree not to condition the release of its software intended for non-Microsoft operating systems, like Apple Computer's, on the other company's agreement not to distribute or promote competitors' software.

The Justice Department complained in its statement that Microsoft's remedies would not "prevent the company from using its monopoly power in the future to engage in the same kind of illegal behavior to crush new innovations." And the department promoted its own plan, saying it would "address the serious violations found by the court" by "stimulating competition and innovation, leading to better products and lower prices for consumers."

Among the government's additional remedy proposals are a requirement that Microsoft, if it adds certain new programs or features to

Windows, sell a version of Windows at a discount with that new feature hidden or removed; a requirement that Microsoft publish a uniform price list for Windows; and a ban on design strategies that are intended to compromise or disable other programs that run on Windows.

Microsoft also offered a schedule for remedy hearings, a sliding scale that calls for longer proceedings if the judge chooses to consider the government remedy proposals that Microsoft considers most onerous.

If Judge Jackson chooses to consider the government's plan to break up the company, Microsoft said it would need six months to prepare for an extensive remedies trial that would begin in early December.

Other options—accepting some parts of the government plan but not others—would bring delays of weeks or months, under the Microsoft plan.

While attending a convention in New Orleans today, Steven A. Ballmer, Microsoft's chief executive, said: "Our company will not be broken up. It will not happen."

Judge Jackson has said he wants to complete the remedy phase by the end of this month. But Microsoft lawyers made clear when Judge Jackson proposed his fast-track timetable last month that the company could not agree until it had seen the government plan.

Microsoft cited one government demand as one justification for its proposed delays: a proposal requiring Microsoft to share technical information about Windows with other software companies that is far more sweeping than Microsoft's plan.

"The need for deliberate procedures is especially strong because much of the intellectual property the government seeks to confiscate relates to products and technologies, such as Windows 2000, that were not even mentioned at trial," one of the company's briefs says. "If the company intends to consider such draconian relief, Microsoft is entitled to address these new issues fully and completely."

Mr. Gates said, "The government's proposal would take away Microsoft's property" even though "Microsoft spent millions of dollars to develop these products."

Throughout the Microsoft documents, the company makes the case that it is a national asset, central to the nation's economy, so that disturbing Microsoft would be unfortunate for both the American people and the economy.

"The public has reaped substantial benefits from Microsoft's development of Windows and other software products," the company said. "Indeed it is no exaggeration to say that the entire United States economy has benefited from Microsoft's efforts. Such benefits would be put at risk were this court to order that Microsoft be broken up into separate companies."

Before the filing, Microsoft's stock fell $1.625, to $66.1875, on the Nasdaq market. In after-hours trading, the shares dipped as low as $65, reaching the company's 52-week low, before rising slightly to $65.50.

MAY 11, 2000

The AT&T Model

Comparing the proposed breakup of Microsoft and the AT&T case of the 1980's, Brad Smith, a Microsoft lawyer, said he saw one big difference.

"AT&T was mostly a national company," he said, "but Microsoft is operating in a global marketplace. If we are replaced as the technology leader, there's no guarantee that our successor will be from this country."

Seventeen years earlier, as AT&T was preparing to spin off its regional telephone companies to resolve that antitrust case, Charles Brown, AT&T's chairman said virtually the same thing. "I guess the competition feels pretty good about it," he said. "The Japanese, primarily."

As the Microsoft antitrust case hurtled toward its conclusion, both sides were drawing on the experiences of AT&T to support their legal and political arguments, though in some cases the references were inaccurate or incomplete. And a few of Microsoft's darkest predictions mirrored arguments that AT&T made 20 years ago—predictions that never came to pass.

The record shows that in the late 1970's and early 1980's, AT&T mounted aggressive legal battles against the government's proposed breakup plan. Innovation would be stifled, research stunted and a precious national resource—the world's best telephone system—would be destroyed, the company warned.

None of that happened.

Of course, there was no certainty that if Microsoft was broken up, its experience, for better or worse, would resemble AT&T's. Still, in invoking the AT&T case to justify some of its arguments, Microsoft was in some instances misstating the record.

Consider Bell Labs, the vaunted research arm of AT&T, and its counterpart at Microsoft, the research division. The government's breakup proposal made no recommendation for how Microsoft's research group would be treated; that was to be decided later.

Nonetheless, Microsoft's brief said: "Research and development organizations are fragile organisms, and the notion that they can be pulled apart with minimal adverse consequences is dangerously naive."

"The one unit of AT&T that remained intact during AT&T's divestiture of its regional operating companies," it adds, "was Bell Laboratories."

AT&T, like Microsoft, argued during its trial that a breakup would damage or destroy the company's research capabilities. But in fact, Bell Labs, formed in 1925, was broken up along with the rest of the company; 7,500 of the lab's 25,000 employees were taken away to form the nucleus of the new Bellcore research lab serving regional telephone companies. AT&T has since spun off Bell Labs; now it is part of Lucent Technologies. And the engineers and executives leading the labs today say they believe they are doing quite well.

"It sure looks to us like we've been just as prolific in the last 15 years as we were in the previous 50," said Michael Jacobs, a spokesman for the labs. "The pace of innovation at Bell Labs today is faster than it's ever been." Bell Labs scientists have won two Nobel prizes in the last 15 years, in 1997 and 1998, compared with four in the previous 50 years. Mr. Jacobs said he believed the prospect of increased competition after the breakup energized the Bell Labs scientists and "fired up" the labs.

Elsewhere in its brief, Microsoft sought to draw a fundamental distinction with AT&T by arguing that "Microsoft is a unitary company," not "an agglomeration of separate operating companies."

As it happens, AT&T made the same argument during its trial. Central to its lawyers' defense was that "the Bell system was so tightly integrated that you could not take it apart without doing enormous damage to the best telephone system in the world," said Philip Verveer, a Washington lawyer who worked for the government during the early stages of the AT&T case.

"They showed that they had a tremendous number of assets in common, and the entire industry was structured around integration"—down to the long-distance toll switches embedded in the local phone switching stations.

Judge Asks Hard Questions About Remedy for Microsoft

The federal judge trying the Microsoft antitrust case raised serious questions today about the government's plan to break up the company, seeming to suggest that he did not think the plan went far enough.

The judge, Thomas Penfield Jackson, praised a brief submitted by a group of computer industry executives—including many of Microsoft's rivals—that called for breaking the company into three parts instead of two, as the government has proposed. He called it "an excellent brief, excellent brief."

With an uncharacteristically determined manner, the judge also bluntly rejected Microsoft's request for months of additional hearings on the remedy for its antitrust violations, telling stunned Microsoft lawyers near the end of the day, "I am not contemplating any further process."

Judge Jackson asked the government to submit a revised version of its remedy proposal by Friday, modified in small ways to reflect answers to questions he asked in court today. And he gave Microsoft 48 hours after that to comment on the form, not the substance, of the revised proposal.

Then, two years and six days after the landmark antitrust suit was filed, Judge Jackson formally closed the proceedings, saying: "The matter is submitted. Thank you, counsel." His ruling on a remedy could come as soon as next week.

On April 3, Judge Jackson found Microsoft in wide violation of fed-eral and state antitrust laws. The next day, he told lawyers for both sides that he wanted to conclude the proceedings quickly. After the government put forward its breakup plan on April 28, Microsoft responded with a request for six months of preparation followed by a new trial.

Microsoft officials were surprised and upset by the decision to close the record today. A few minutes after the hearing adjourned, William H. Neukom, Microsoft's chief counsel, said: "We had sought to have our day in court on remedies, but the judge has decided not to do that. So this case will now be decided at the court of appeals, and we will be raising issues of procedure in our appeal, as well as issues of fact and law."

The Justice Department had no comment.

Almost as soon as the remedy hearing opened this morning, the judge asked questions suggesting his state of mind, though he never explicitly said his ruling would call for a breakup of the company or anything else.

The government's proposal would create one company for Microsoft's operating systems and another company that would hold everything else, including applications software, like the word processor Word and the spreadsheet program Excel, and Microsoft's Internet properties.

Soon after Kevin O'Conner, an assistant attorney general from Wisconsin who represents the 19 states that are partners in the government's suit, began describing merits of the plan, the judge interrupted, saying, "The effect of a bisection will in effect be to create two separate monopolies, with no incentive to interfere with each other's profitability."

He noted that one outsider's brief he received in recent weeks had made that point. He was apparently referring to a plan proposed recently by several prominent academic economists to split Microsoft into five companies, including three competing operating-system companies.

Later, the judge asked David Boies, the Justice Department's lead trial lawyer, about another supporting brief, submitted by the Computer and Communications Industry Association and the Software and Information Industry Association. It proposed dividing Microsoft into three companies, including one that would sell only Internet Explorer, the company's Web browser.

"Rather than reorganizing Microsoft into only a Windows company and a single applications company," the brief said, "the court should supplement plaintiffs' proposed final judgment by separating the Internet Explorer product and personnel into a third, independent company."

Mr. Boies did not criticize the idea in court and said it might hold merit, but added that the government was trying to reduce the complexity of its proposal.

Judge Jackson said: "You talk of the simplicity of implementation of your proposals, but they are any-

thing but simple. I don't think" Microsoft "will be willing to cooperate." He then wondered aloud why the government plan gave Microsoft the responsibility to determine how the company should be divided.

Mr. Boies responded, "We give them the opportunity to do it first, but if they come back with something that simply doesn't meet our requirements, the government will have to do it." The judge nodded.

When Microsoft's turn came to promote its own proposed remedy, the judge asked no questions. And to Microsoft's request for a delay, the judge told a company lawyer: "I find it somewhat ironic that your client believes its travails will end at the court of appeals, and yet wants to spend more time in this court."

John Warden, a Microsoft lawyer, insisted that he found the idea "that we would have some final resolution today really incredible." When another company lawyer made the same point, the judge snapped, "This case has been pending for two years." Later Mr. Warden complained that the government's remedy proposal had been pending for less than a month.

Officials familiar with the government position say Microsoft has known since abortive settlement talks in March 1999 that the government might seek to break up the company. A specific breakup proposal was put on the table during court-sponsored mediation talks early this year. Microsoft refused to discuss the idea at either juncture.

Along with the breakup plan it submitted to the judge, the government proposal includes several temporary rules to alter Microsoft's conduct while the breakup would be carried out. Mr. Warden complained that one of them, requiring Microsoft to divulge technical information on Windows to other software companies, was "confiscatory." It would require Microsoft to turn trade secret over to "all of our fiercest competitors" as well as "pirates and counterfeiters," he added.

A short time later, responding to Microsoft's complaints, the judge remarked: "I ask you if forfeiture is not a traditional, equitable remedy."

As their day in court seemed to be slipping away this afternoon, Microsoft's lawyers hurriedly entered into the record an "offer of proof," which included summaries of testimony that the company would have hoped to offer in further hearings on a remedy.

Among the 16 academic experts, Microsoft executives and others cited in the 35-page brief were Gates and Steven A. Ballmer, the president and chief executive. Microsoft said both would have come to testify. In Mr. Gates's printed declaration, he said the company was working on "a new vision of the future," specifically "making the Internet more useful by creating the first Internet-based platform for software developers." But Mr. Gates added that the "project will be doomed to failure at the outset if Microsoft is split along the arbitrary lines proposed by the government."

Microsoft said the declarations were not ready when it filed its response to the government plan this month. It said it wanted to enter them into the record now so the court of appeals would see them.

Whatever Judge Jackson's comments and actions today might bode, investors did not seem disheartened. Microsoft's stock closed up $2.375, at $65.5625.

MAY 25, 2000

"A Break-Up Is Inevitable"

The day after the hearing, Judge Jackson explained his change of heart. After all, in February he had said he was unwilling to impose a structural remedy. Now, he said, Microsoft's behavior had changed his mind.

"I've been astounded by some of the statements of Gates and Ballmer," he said. Since Jackson's strong verdict against Microsoft on April 3, William H. Gates, the company's chairman, and Steven Ballmer, the president, had repeatedly stated that Microsoft did absolutely nothing wrong. They had also proclaimed they would not change any of the company's business practices.

"I'm in the midst off a growing realization that, with what looks like Microsoft intransigence, a break-up is inevitable," Judge Jackson said.

American jurisprudence values and expects some form of contrition or repentance after a guilty verdict. But there was no hint of those sentiments among Microsoft's leaders, who continued to exhibit in-your-face defiance. That offended Jackson. He certainly did not expect Gates and the others to admit they were guilty and apologize; they intended to appeal, after all. Still, he was surprised by the intensity of their intransigence.

Judge Jackson had frequently expressed respect for Microsoft before the verdict. But the attitude exhibited by Gates and Ballmer had turned him around 180 degrees, convincing him that behavioral remedies would never work and that, therefore, the company had to be broken up.

Microsoft Breakup Is Ordered For Antitrust Law Violations

A federal judge ordered the breakup of the Microsoft Corporation today, saying the severe remedy was necessary because Microsoft "has proved untrustworthy in the past" and did not appear to have accepted his ruling that it had broadly violated the nation's antitrust laws.

"There is credible evidence in the record to suggest that Microsoft, convinced of its innocence, continues to do business as it has in the past and may yet do to other markets what it has already done" to dominate operating systems and Internet software, Judge Thomas Penfield Jackson said in his final ruling in the long-running trial.

Under his order, Microsoft would be broken into separate and competing companies, one for its Windows operating system and one for its other computer programs and Internet businesses. It would also be forced to comply with a long list of restrictions on its conduct lasting three years if the breakup order withstands appeal, and 10 years if it does not.

Microsoft said it would appeal the case to the Court of Appeals, filing the papers within a few days, while the government said this evening that it would try to bypass that court and ask immediate review by the Supreme Court.

While an appeal proceeds, Judge Jackson's order stays the breakup plan, but not the restrictions on the company's conduct. Microsoft intends, however, to ask that the entire order be stayed.

The government charged, and the judge agreed, that Microsoft had used its monopoly in operating systems to put competitors at a disadvantage and stifle innovation.

In surprisingly assertive language, Judge Jackson accepted the government's remedy proposal in its entirety, attaching it to his ruling— utterly rejecting Microsoft's repeated assertions that the breakup plan was "Draconian," "unwarranted" and "bad for consumers, the high-tech industry and our economy."

William H. Gates, the chairman of Microsoft, called the judge's ruling "an unwarranted and unjustified intrusion into the software marketplace, a marketplace that has been an engine of economic growth for America."

"The idea that someone would say that a breakup is a reasonable thing comes as quite a surprise to us," Mr. Gates added. "We have a very strong case on appeal, and we look forward to resolving these issues through the appeals process and putting this case behind us once and for all."

Mr. Gates was in Washington on Tuesday, planning to meet with lawmakers today. Anticipating the ruling, though, he canceled the meetings and hurriedly flew back to Seattle overnight.

Attorney General Janet Reno, smiling broadly, said this afternoon that the ruling "will have a profound impact, not only by promoting competition in the software industry, but also by reaffirming the importance of antitrust law enforcement in the 21st century." And Joel I. Klein, head of the department's antitrust division, said, "Microsoft itself is responsible for where things stand today."

If the judge's order withstands appeal and Microsoft is eventually broken up, it would join a handful of major national monopolies that have been taken apart over the last 90 years as a result of antitrust violations, including Standard Oil, American Tobacco and the Aluminum Company of America.

Tom Miller, the attorney general of Iowa, speaking on behalf of the 19 states that are partners with the Justice Department in the Microsoft case, said the ruling "sends a strong message that no company is above the law." (Two of the 19 states, Illinois and Ohio, declined to support the breakup plan.)

If Microsoft's request for a stay of Judge Jackson's order is rejected, the company must begin complying with the conduct restrictions by Sept. 7 and submit a detailed plan for dividing the company by Oct. 7.

With Judge Jackson's encouragement, the Justice Department announced that it would take the case directly to the Supreme Court, under a 1974 revision to the federal antitrust laws allowing fast-track consideration of significant antitrust cases.

Microsoft opposes the direct appeal to the Supreme Court, preferring to take its case first to the Court of Appeals, which ruled in its favor in a related lawsuit two years ago and reversed a decision by Judge Jackson.

Whether the Supreme Court would even take the case is at best uncertain. Microsoft argued this evening that the suit filed by the states would not be eligible for expedited appeal because the states have no similar law. In that case, the states' appeal would be taken to the Court of Appeals. But state and federal officials said that because the cases were joined for trial, it would make no sense to separate them for differing legal appeals.

The officials acknowledged that the point of law was ambiguous. But Richard Blumenthal, attorney general of Connecticut, said, "Today's victory vindicates and soundly validates our decisions as state law enforcement officers to join this historic action."

If the conduct restrictions are allowed to take effect, computer manufacturers will be allowed to offer customized versions of Windows on their computers in ways they never could before. And future versions of Windows will be offered in a form that allows buyers to accept certain new software features Microsoft chooses to offer—or to decide they do not want them and use a competing product.

It was Microsoft's decision four years ago to tie a Web browser to Windows that prompted the investigation and lawsuits that led to the breakup order today.

Years from now, if the government's remedy plan works as intended, consumers might also begin to see alternate operating systems on sale that are competitive with

Windows. If that occurs, the broad compatibility among personal computers that exists today might begin to erode.

Judge Jackson issued his ruling at 4:30 this afternoon, just after the stock markets had closed. His decision had been widely expected, and investors appeared to have already taken the breakup plan into account. Microsoft stock was up 87.5 cents today, to close at $70.50.

Asked at a news conference today if he had any regrets, Mr. Gates said: "If I look back at anything, I think, perhaps I should have taken the opportunity to go in person and talk about this industry."

Whether Mr. Gates might be called as a witness was a continuing question during the antitrust trial. His halting, obdurate performance in a videotaped deposition proved to be a powerful tool for the government in court.

Though Judge Jackson accepted the remedy plan put together by the federal and state governments, his endorsement was not unequivocal.

He noted that the plan was the collective work of senior state and federal officials "in conjunction with multiple consultants." And, he said, the remedy "appears to the court to address the principal objectives of relief in such cases, namely to terminate the unlawful conduct, to prevent its repetition in the future and to revive competition in the relevant markets."

But even though several experts provided "some insight as to how the provisions" of the remedy might work, "for the most part they are merely the predictions of purportedly knowledgeable people as to effects which may or may not ensue if the proposed final judgment is entered," he added. "In its experience, the court has found testimonial predictions of future events generally less reliable even than testimony as to historical fact."

Microsoft severely criticized the judge this evening for his decision to hold no substantive hearings on the government's remedy proposal. Microsoft said it had been surprised by the scope of the plan and had been unable to respond to it adequately in the six weeks since it was offered.

But in his order today, Judge Jackson retorted: "Microsoft's profession of surprise is not credible. From the inception of this case Microsoft knew, from well-established Supreme Court precedents dating from the beginning of the last century, that a mandated divestiture was a possibility, if not a probability, in the event of an adverse result at trial."

In fact, the government first made plain to Microsoft during settlement negotiations a year ago that it planned to ask for a so-called structural remedy. That was repeated during mediation efforts by a federal judge early this year, though the government offered terms short of a breakup after Microsoft said it would not discuss structural remedies.

The judge also explained why he moved through the remedy phase so quickly, saying that he wanted to pass the case to a higher court as soon as possible for validation, revision or rejection of his decision, "to abort any remedial measures before

they become irreversible as a practical matter."

If necessary, the judge said he could hold hearings later or "modify the judgment as necessary in accordance with instructions from an appellate court."

Judge Jackson noted, with some apparent irritation, that after he ruled on April 3 that Microsoft was in wide violation of the nation's antitrust laws, Microsoft's leaders continued to assert that "the company has done 'nothing wrong' and that it will be vindicated on appeal."

"The court is well aware," he added, "that there is a substantial body of public opinion, some of it rational, that holds a similar view. If true, then an appellate tribunal should be given an opportunity to confirm it as promptly as possible."

Microsoft's continued assertions of innocence were one reason for his ruling, he said. Another was that "Microsoft has shown no disposition to voluntarily alter its business protocols in any significant respect."

A third reason, he said, was that Microsoft "has proved untrustworthy in the past." As an example, he referred to the precedent case he tried in late 1997, after the government accused Microsoft of illegally tying a Web browser to Windows.

In December 1997, Judge Jackson issued a preliminary injunction ordering Microsoft to separate the two products. That was the ruling later overturned by the Court of Appeals.

But "Microsoft's purported compliance while it was on appeal," the judge said today, "was illusory and its explanation disingenuous."

JUNE 8, 2000

Microsoft: After a Rout, Still Fighting

With his final order yesterday in the Microsoft antitrust case, Judge Thomas Penfield Jackson said yes to the government one more time. He has agreed with the government, almost without qualification, on the facts of the case, on the law and now on the harsh remedy of splitting the company in two.

In Judge Jackson's Federal District Court, the result has been not just a defeat for Microsoft but a rout, not a closely fought legal contest but a judicial ratification of the government's case.

Yet the two-year-old case is far from over. And with a year or two of appeals ahead, the chances of Microsoft's ever being broken up are uncertain. Microsoft will try to reverse every element in Judge Jackson's ruling that the company is a monopoly that has repeatedly violated the nation's antitrust laws, stifling software competition and innovation.

The odds against Microsoft's winning outright on appeal are extremely high, according to antitrust experts. But they say that there are legally vulnerable points in the judge's ruling that if reversed on appeal might well enable the company to avoid the drastic sanction Judge Jackson has now endorsed.

"Microsoft is going to try to whittle away at the judge's ruling on appeal," said Andrew I. Gavil, professor at the Howard University law school. "And once you get an incremental erosion of the case, you erode the power of the argument for a breakup as well."

In his order yesterday, Judge Jackson acknowledged that the federal appeals court or the Supreme Court, or both, might disagree with some of his work. Two weeks ago, he surprised both sides in the case and most legal experts when he abruptly ended the court proceedings without a further round of hearings on the government's plan to split Microsoft in two and require a series of curbs on its business conduct.

In his order, Judge Jackson explained that he had moved quickly because, if his findings or legal conclusions are overruled, a higher court might decide on its own remedies or send the case back to him.

After noting that Microsoft contends it will be vindicated on appeal, he wrote: "The court is well aware that there is a substantial body of public opinion, some of it rational, that holds to a similar view. It is time to put that assertion to the test."

So Judge Jackson chose this approach as a way to speed along a case of national economic importance. The alternative, he decided, would be to risk going through two time-consuming sets of hearings on remedies—one based on his legal ruling and one based on a case perhaps scaled back on appeal.

Still, some antitrust experts say that simply accepting the remedies plan from the Justice Department and states suing Microsoft could prove to be a mistake.

"If he's assuming that this case is probably coming back to him anyway, I think that is a safe assumption," said William Kovacic, a professor at the George Washington University law school. "But the danger of his approach is that it increases the chances it will come back to him."

Microsoft's prime target on appeal, antitrust experts say, will be the judge's ruling that it illegally tied its Internet browser to its monopoly product, the Windows operating system, which handles the basic operations on 85 percent of all PC's.

To Microsoft, the tying charge is the heart of the case. If that ruling is upheld on appeal, Microsoft sees a threat to its corporate way of life—its ability to add new software features to its operating system, as it has repeatedly over the years.

In several rounds of settlement talks with the government, Microsoft was willing to change some of its practices, but it stood firm on not allowing any tampering with Windows or letting personal computer makers pick and choose from an à la carte menu of Windows features.

To Microsoft, this stance is not arrogance or hubris—or an antitrust violation, for that matter—but a stand of principle.

"This case, in our view, is about whether we are free to improve our products and whether we can protect the integrity of our most important product, Windows," said William Neukom, senior vice president and general counsel of Microsoft.

Microsoft has argued that Web browsing software should not be considered as a separate product but as a feature in the ever-evolving Windows operating system.

The government contended, and Judge Jackson ruled, that Microsoft had illegally tied its Internet browser, a separate product, to Windows to thwart competition and illegally protect its monopoly. To accept Microsoft's argument, the government said, would amount to granting the dominant software maker an exemption from broad swaths of the nation's antitrust laws.

But antitrust experts note that product-tying charges are tricky, especially when dealing with software, in which the products are rendered in the 1's and 0's of programming code and product boundaries often blur. And a federal appeals court in June 1998 sided with Microsoft in a separate but related case. That court said Microsoft had the right to fold a browser into its operating system as long as it could make a "plausible claim" of consumer benefit.

In addition to the tying charge, Microsoft, antitrust experts say, stands a good chance of getting a reversal on the court's finding that Microsoft made an illegal offer to Netscape Communications to divide the browser market between them. The collusion offer, Judge Jackson ruled, was made during a meeting between executives of Microsoft and Netscape, the commercial pioneer in Internet browsers, in June 1995.

The legal hurdle in attempted collusion cases, antitrust experts say, is fairly high. The crucial case, they say, occurred in 1984 and involved airline executives talking about jointly raising fares in a conversation that was tape-recorded.

Whether the meeting notes, e-mail messages and conflicting witness testimony about the Microsoft-Netscape meeting are evidence that reaches the standard of "clearly unequivocal," established in the 1984 case, is open to question, experts say.

Microsoft is also expected to argue that much of the rest of the case—mainly contracts and practices that the court found to be a "pattern of anticompetitive behavior"—is merely evidence of a company competing aggressively in a dynamic industry, not of an economic outlaw.

"We think this ruling is very vulnerable on appeal," Mr. Neukom said. "We're in the middle innings of a contest that won't be over for another year or two. And the most critical innings are yet to come."

Yet antitrust experts say that the steepest uphill climb for Microsoft on appeal will be to overturn Judge Jackson's determination that the company engaged in an array of illegal acts to protect its monopoly, wielding its market power like a club to bully industry partners and rivals.

"It's the whole gestalt that is a real problem for Microsoft—the court's finding that these are bad guys, who repeatedly acted to stifle competition and not for any efficiency reasons," said Richard Steuer, an antitrust specialist and a partner at Kaye Scholer Fierman Hays & Handler. "That is a lot harder for an appeals court to overturn."

JUNE 8, 2000

Competition: The Fuel of Law

Microsoft's industry adversaries had an enormous stake in the outcome of the suit. The case focused on the conduct of one company that was alleged—and found, by Judge Jackson—to be a monopoly that abused its market power to stifle competition. In bringing suit, the government's stated goal was to restore and enhance competition, the underlying assumption being that consumers would benefit. But the suspicion shared across the Microsoft corporate campus was that the antitrust suit was the result of a successful lobbying campaign by its rivals.

"The view of the team here is that our competitors were losing in the marketplace and they got the Justice Department to help them," said Brad Chase, a senior Microsoft executive who testified at the trial.

That view resonated beyond Microsoft's home in Redmond, Wash., especially among academics who champion the field known as "public choice theory." Some public choice theorists see antitrust as merely a form of regulation in which special-interest groups lobby for advantage, and they regard the Microsoft case as a classic example.

A book about the case was even written from the public choice perspective, "Trust on Trial: How the Microsoft Case is Reframing the Rules of Competition," (Perseus Publishing), by Richard B. McKenzie, a professor at the University of California at Irvine's graduate school of management. McKenzie's thesis is that there was little evidence of monopolistic harm in the Microsoft case—harm, he defines in traditional terms, as raising prices and restricting production. Thus, he concludes, the competitors—the real winners from the suit, he argues—must be behind the lawsuit. He then analyzes the evidence in the case through that prism.

Antitrust, government officials reply emphatically, is law enforcement, and Federal antitrust officials see themselves as the referees of capitalism, not as regulators. They also take issue with the economic theory applied by academics like McKenzie. The Microsoft case was always more about protecting the market for innovation than about prices, noted Daniel Rubinfeld, the chief economist in the Justice Department's Antitrust Division when the Microsoft case was being put together. And certain conventional measures of monopolistic predation, like restricting production, do not really apply to software as they do to other industries. Once a piece of software is designed, the cost of producing each additional copy is nearly zero—a very different economics of production than applies in oil, steel or other physical products.

In their dealings with the Justice Department and the states, Microsoft's rivals may well have been skillful and persuasive. They say they did not try to lobby the government but merely educate the government about the industry, which, of course, is what every lobbyist says. But in the end, the evidence required to win a trial either exists or it doesn't. And the most telling evidence, the prosecutors say, came from Microsoft's own documents and e-mail.

To the people who talked to the government, it did not feel like lobbying. Garth Saloner, an economist at the Stanford University business school, helped draft the Netscape white paper that led the Justice Department to begin its investigation. When originally approached by a Netscape lawyer, Saloner was skeptical. But like so many others who eventually lined up against Microsoft, he came to believe that the company was an economic outlaw.

"In a lot of antitrust work, sure, people want to be on the side they feel is right," Saloner recalled. "But scratch them a little and you get to the practitioner, just working for the client. This never felt like that. The people were passionate. There really was a feeling that Microsoft was a bully that had to be stopped."

U.S. Pursuit of Microsoft: Rare Synergy With Company's Rivals

William H. Gates, the chairman of Microsoft, has no doubts about who is responsible for his company's antitrust woes. During a news conference last Wednesday, hours after a federal judge ordered that Microsoft be split in two, Mr. Gates spoke pointedly of the "competitors that have been behind this lawsuit."

What part did Microsoft's rivals play? The competitors, to be sure, played a crucial role throughout the investigation, litigation and sanctions phase of the suit by the Justice Department and 19 states. It was, in fact, a 222-page white paper written in the summer of 1996 by lawyers for Netscape Communications, Microsoft's main rival in the market for Internet browsing software, that caught the attention of Joel I. Klein, head of the Justice Department's antitrust division, and prompted him to order an investigation.

At the trial, a procession of competitors—representing Netscape, Sun Microsystems, America Online and others—testified against Microsoft. And in the months and weeks before the government presented its proposal in April to break up Microsoft, industry executives—some rivals, some not—were shown or read individual sentences and paragraphs in drafts of the remedies plan by government lawyers, who then asked if the provisions seemed sensible.

The scale of the antitrust case, including the extent of consultation with industry rivals, was extraordinary, government officials acknowledge. But the methods employed were not: Despite all the information and interpretation given to the government from other companies, industry executives and government lawyers say the Justice Department kept its own counsel as it sifted evidence and built its case.

The government charged, and the court found, that Microsoft is a monopoly that has thwarted competition and innovation. Some of the evidence came from competitors, but much of it came from Microsoft's e-mail and internal documents.

"The industry's role in a case like this is as a resource—a source of ideas, comments, facts and analysis," said David Boies, the Justice Department's chief trial lawyer. "But the government brought the Microsoft case because the evidence was there. And the most powerful documents were ones created by Microsoft itself."

Yet, to bring and win the Microsoft suit, the government had to build a relationship of cooperation and trust with the industry. When the investigation started in 1996, there was skepticism in Silicon Valley—home to many of Microsoft's rivals—about the wisdom of working with the government.

A consent decree with Microsoft that the Justice Department signed in 1994, and that a court approved a year later, had mainly focused on a modest change in Microsoft's licensing practices. In Silicon Valley, the consent decree was regarded as a slap on the wrist that did nothing to loosen Microsoft's control of computing. So, many companies were reluctant to cooperate with the government and risk angering Microsoft.

To meet with the Justice Department, some industry executives insisted on strict conditions to ensure anonymity. Late in 1997, the chief executive of a Silicon Valley company agreed to meet only at a hotel suite in Washington—not at the Justice Department's offices—and only with a promise that any notes of the meeting could not mention him or his company, recalled Daniel Rubinfeld, former chief economist in the department's antitrust division.

The chief executive did eventually agree to send a senior member of his management team to testify in the Microsoft trial, which began in October 1998.

Indeed, that kind of visible industry support—sending witnesses to testify in a high-profile, high-pressure trial—was needed to present a convincing case in court. And Justice Department officials stressed that point in meetings with industry executives. "They did say repeatedly that if you don't stand up and take this on, neither will we," recalled William J. Raduchel, a former senior executive at Sun Microsystems who is now chief technology officer of America Online.

Yet throughout the case, the government and Microsoft's competitors had a delicate, often wary relationship, according to both prosecutors and industry executives.

And no wonder. The Justice Department's antitrust division receives a steady stream of complaints from companies about their rivals. Much of this proves untrue or exaggerated upon investigation, prosecutors note. And the government's policy is not to inform anyone in advance about whether it will take action.

Several industry executives who cooperated in the prosecution described dealing with the Justice Department as "speaking through a one-way mirror." The government officials asked questions, and they answered. That approach, apparently, remained consistent—from the initial investigation, right through to consulting on the proposed remedies.

One executive recalled being asked to comment on the government's sanctions plan. "It was, 'Does this sentence make sense to you,' or 'If the following rule were in place, do you think PC makers would choose operating systems other than Microsoft's Windows,'" the executive said. "But you never quite know what they're up to. I had no idea they were going to propose breaking Microsoft in two."

Mr. Raduchel, who spoke with Justice Department officials several times in the last few years, remarked: "I really believe that you can't lobby them. But what you can do is educate them. They gradually came to realize that seemingly arcane details of software really do matter."

The education process did take time. It took the government investigators a while to appreciate the legal significance of a meeting in June 1995 between Microsoft and Netscape executives, for example, even though the Justice Department received a detailed account of the meeting two days after it occurred.

The account came in a letter to the department from Gary L. Reback, a lawyer representing Netscape, who described how Microsoft had used access to its industry-standard Windows operating-system technology to threaten Netscape. He also attached notes of the meeting taken by Marc Andreessen, co-founder of Netscape, which strongly suggested that Microsoft had made an offer to Netscape to divide the market for Internet browsing software—an offer that, if proved, was a violation of antitrust law.

That June 1995 episode eventually became an accusation in the government's suit against Microsoft, one that Judge Thomas Penfield Jackson accepted as a fact and ruled to be illegal. Yet at the time, word of the meeting did not set off alarm bells in Washington.

"You have to understand that back then, the Internet was just starting to take off," said Roberta Katz, the former general counsel of Netscape, "and people other than techies did not understand the Internet or software. The troops at Justice, understandably, had a lot of learning to do."

And Netscape certainly helped. "My whole approach," Ms. Katz said, "was to get to the point where they really understood what was going on. After that, if the government did anything or not was obviously up to them. And they totally held their cards closely. There was never a time when the Justice Department let us know what they were going to do."

The Netscape white paper in August 1996 helped get things started. Despite its dull title, "White Paper Regarding the Recent Anticompetitive Conduct of the Microsoft Corporation," the paper often reads more like a book than a legal document. Indeed, its 222 pages are formatted and laid out like a book, with attractive typefaces and chapter headlines like "A Fork in the Road" and "Microsoft's Fear: The Threat to Its Desktop Monopoly."

The Netscape white paper was never made public, but it was passed to some industry executives and state attorneys general, in addition to the Justice Department. An industry executive allowed a reporter for The New York Times to read parts of the document. It was written mainly by Mr. Reback and Susan Creighton, then both lawyers at Wilson Sonsini Goodrich & Rosati in Palo Alto, Calif., with contributions from Garth Saloner, an economist at the Stanford University business school.

The Netscape document includes a litany of accusations against Microsoft. These were backed up with e-mail messages that Netscape had received, from personal computer makers and others, about Microsoft's actions.

But the one assertion that really interested Mr. Klein, the Justice Department's antitrust chief, was that in June 1996 Microsoft had threatened to cancel Compaq Computer's license to use Windows unless Compaq stopped featuring Netscape's browser over Microsoft's. To Mr. Klein, this seemed to be evidence of Microsoft's selling its Windows operating system to PC makers on the condition that the manufacturers also take the Microsoft browser. To him, the threat violated the 1994 consent decree and raised broader antitrust issues about the company's behavior.

Microsoft has argued that its browsing software should be considered part of Windows—one product, not two, and thus not an antitrust violation. In June 1998, a federal appeals court agreed with Microsoft in a related case. But after reviewing the evidence, Judge Jackson ruled that Microsoft had illegally tied two products.

The government pursued some accusations in the Netscape white paper and set others aside. Over all, though, the legal and economic theory in the Netscape document is remarkably similar to the themes laid out in the government's suit two years later. The core of the case the Justice Department lawyers presented at trial was that Microsoft had illegally maintained its monopoly by engaging in a broad pattern of practices intended to stifle the competition posed by Internet software.

"This is, at bottom, a very simple case," the Netscape white paper stated. "It is about a monopolist (Microsoft) that has maintained its monopoly for more than 10 years. That monopoly is threatened by the introduction of a new technology (Web software) that is a partial substitute—and, in time could become a complete substitute for the monopoly product."

The Netscape white paper also pointed toward a broader public-policy issue surrounding Microsoft. Personal computers were the way people got onto the Internet and thus, the paper asserted, Microsoft's industry-dominant Windows operating system could give the company a gatekeeper's control of the flow of information and electronic commerce in the future.

"There is no reason to believe," the Netscape document warned, "that Microsoft's monopoly power will be confined to a single industry."

That broader message resonated beyond the software industry, and eventually led executives in other industries to raise concerns about

Microsoft with the government. Andrew Steinberg, who was then general counsel of Sabre, the computerized airline reservations system, recalled traveling through Silicon Valley early in 1997. Sabre had recently begun a travel Web site, Travelocity, and Microsoft had a competing site, Expedia. Mr. Steinberg was told of the Netscape white paper, and he obtained a copy from Netscape.

Reading the document had a "profound effect" on him, recalled Mr. Steinberg, who is now an executive vice president of Travelocity. "It struck me that this was a serious threat to competition over the Internet and the future prospects of our company."

Other industry executives had similar worries about Microsoft's power and its potential use of that power. Executives from many companies expressed such concerns in meetings with the Justice Department—Including those from Time Warner, Disney, Sabre, General Motors and Palm, according to people who attended or knew of those meetings.

Further white papers were produced. Netscape updated its original document, and then provided still another with a more detailed focus on e-commerce and media over the Internet, "Access Denied: Microsoft's Strategy for Overriding Consumer Choice." The other companies that sent white papers to the government included Apple Computer, Sabre and the makers of speech-recognition software, according to people familiar with those documents.

The suit the government brought against Microsoft was based on accusations about what Microsoft had done, rather than what it might do. But the government has said it took action partly to protect innovation in the future and to keep the Internet open to competition.

"The role of the browser as the gateway to the Internet was significant to bringing this case," said Mr. Boies, who presented the case against Microsoft in court for the Justice Department. "It's what made this case important."

JUNE 12, 2000

Conclusion

Why did Microsoft do so badly in court? How could this unprecedented engine of success have not only lost the case but also gone down in such a rout? At the outset the adversaries had seemed well matched.

"Microsoft and the government were the perfect opponents," Boies observed. "The government has some power, but Microsoft has at least as much. Anyone else facing either one of them would be overmatched."

But over the months, the balance shifted heavily in favor of the government. In fact, Microsoft's problems began well before the trial opened in October 1998. It misjudged the legal trouble that its own e-mail and other documents could create. It chose not to reach an out-of-court settlement when the sanctions it faced were a wrist-slap compared with the breakup plan it would eventually face. In court, Microsoft's defense stumbled repeatedly. And with each misstep, the government was emboldened.

The plaintiffs assembled and then presented their case with ever greater confidence, continually broadening it to embrace a far richer array of charges than the issue that started it all—incorporating a Web browser in the Windows operating system. As the case progressed, the government presented evidence to show that Microsoft had bullied partners and competitors alike, halting or attempting to stifle innovations that threatened its Windows monopoly. And as the allegations spilled out in court, Microsoft was increasingly on its heels, arguing over and over again that all the government had really shown was that Microsoft was a rough-and-tumble competitor, not an economic outlaw.

Lawyers who fought Microsoft, and others looking back on it all, ascribed the company's loss to a corporate personality failing, a form of myopia. It was a common theme among the postmortems offered by several of the company's antagonists.

"They are a prisoner of their own world view," said Stephen Houck of the New York Attorney General's office. "They just had no idea whatsoever how all of this would play in public and in court. And they let Gates set the tone for the trial with that take-no-prisoners approach."

Richard Blumenthal, attorney general of Connecticut said, "The problem was Microsoft's mindset: 'We know better than everybody else.' I think that culture permeated all preparations for the trial."

As Attorney General Tom Miller of Iowa saw it, "The general strategy of denial, denial, denial never works for anybody in court. It always fails badly."

And A. Douglas Melamed, deputy head of Justice Department's Antitrust Division, said, "I have a sense that the Microsoft team was so convinced of the correctness of their view, and of the law and their story, that they didn't come to understand as well as they might have how the story could be told by the plaintiffs."

But it was Judge Jackson who summed it up most simply: "I suspect Microsoft is not an easy client to work for. But I think Microsoft didn't take this matter seriously enough."

The view of the case from the Microsoft campus in suburban Seattle remained steadfast: Things had come to this pass not because of corporate myopia or arrogance, but because the company had taken an unflinching stand of principle. The case against Microsoft, said William Neukom, the company's general counsel, was fundamentally about the company's decision to include Internet software in Windows and then, due to judicial error, it expanded into a "monopoly broth" lawsuit that attacked Microsoft's business practices in general.

As the case headed toward appeal, Microsoft refused to give any ground or admit mistakes. The tide would turn on appeal, and the company would be vindicated, Neukom insisted. He talked of the case being in its "middle innings" with another year or two to play out. The company had taken its stand, he said, to protect the integrity of its most important product, Windows. "To defend that principle," he declared, "we are willing to withstand the short-term pain, which is considerable."

Epilogue

Almost before the ink had dried on Judge Jackson's order to break up the company, Microsoft filed a motion asking for an immediate stay on his entire remedy order. The company argued that imposing the remedies immediately would "inflict grievous and irreparable harm on Microsoft, its 35,000 employees, its millions of shareholders, its thousands of business partners and tens of millions of consumers around the world who rely on Microsoft's products."

It seemed a pro forma act. Everyone, including Microsoft's leaders, assumed unsurprisingly that Judge Jackson would deny the request to stay the order he had just entered. But, though not everyone realized it at first, by filing the motion, Microsoft was pursuing a clever legal strategy, trying to out maneuver both the judge and the Justice Department.

Back in early April, the judge had told both sides during a chambers conference that he wanted to send the appeal of the case directly to the Supreme Court. He reasoned that the case was having a direct effect on the nation's economy; the NASDAQ index had taken a sharp dive on word that Microsoft might be broken up. And a little-used law known as the Expediting Act permitted direct appeals of Federal antitrust cases "of general public importance in the administration of justice."

A corollary, unstated benefit of a direct appeal for Judge Jackson and for the Justice Department was that the Appeals Court had often overturned Jackson's rulings, most particularly his 1997 order that Microsoft unbundle the Internet Explorer browser from Windows.

Precisely because Microsoft had previously prevailed in the appeals court, the company vociferously opposed direct appeal to the Supreme Court, whose views on the issues were not known. Microsoft wanted its case sent to the Court of Appeals. And that's where the stay request came in. As soon as Judge Jackson denied the request, Microsoft was entitled to take it to the Court of Appeals.

True, the stay request was not the full legal appeal. But once one court was engaged in the case, judging the stay request, it would seem to make little sense to get another court involved.

The Justice Department saw through the strategy rather quickly. Microsoft might get a part of the case into the Appeals Court before the government could get its request up to the Supreme Court because, for the moment, the department was hamstrung. The law said Justice could not petition Judge Jackson to invoke the Expediting Act until Microsoft had filed its Notice of Appeal, a one-page document simply noting that the company intended to appeal. And, not surprisingly, Microsoft had not chosen to file that yet.

Government lawyers quickly drew up a brief informing the judge that Microsoft was trying to undermine his direct-appeal strategy. Picking up on that, on June 13 Judge Jackson informed Microsoft in a one-page order that "the court reserves ruling on Microsoft's motion" of a stay pending appeal "until such time as a timely notice of appeal is filed."

But that simply set off a flurry of late-afternoon legal maneuvering. Microsoft did file its notice of appeal that afternoon, but almost simultaneously the company filed a stay request with the Court of Appeals—even though Judge Jackson had not yet acted on the stay request before him. The Appeals Court accepted Microsoft's stay request immediately and with some eagerness, it seemed, to get a piece of the most important legal case of the time. The judges issued a remarkable order saying that the entire court, minus three judges who had recused themselves, would hear the case "in view of its exceptional importance." In almost every other case, only a three-judge panel would hear an appeal, and the full court might get it after that. The judges were so eager to get involved that their order was entered even before Microsoft's lawyer showed up at the clerk's office with the stay request, apparently realizing from newspaper reports that he was coming. When the Microsoft lawyer handed over his motion and turned to leave, a court clerk stopped him, saying, "Oh, I have something for you," and handed over the court's order.

Microsoft's 39-page stay request provided an outline of the company's appeals strategy. (To win a stay of the remedy, the defendant must provide information to show that he has a reasonable chance of winning the larger case on appeal.) Microsoft's brief said Judge Jackson had committed "an array of serious substantive and procedural errors that infected virtually every aspect of the proceedings."

The brief restated many of the substantive arguments Microsoft had made in the past, but for the first time it also included specific criticism of Judge Jackson, both of his trial procedures and of the judgments he had made based on the evidence. It accused Judge Jackson of having failed to give Microsoft due process and of issuing findings without citing evidence or legal precedents to justify them.

In harsh, censorious language, the brief complained that the judge's findings "do not contain a single citation to the record, making it impossible to ascertain" their "purported basis." It said the court "erroneously imposed extreme and punitive relief" that "bears no relation whatsoever to the antitrust violations found."

It noted that the judge "signed plaintiffs' final judgment as ultimately proffered without a single substantive change." And in an elliptical complaint, it observed that Microsoft had "the largest market capitalization in the world" until "the court entered its findings of fact."

"At trial," the brief added, "the district court largely suspended application of the Federal Rules of Evidence, admitting into evidence numerous newspaper and magazine articles and other rank hearsay." (Though the brief failed to mention this, many of the newspaper and magazine articles, perhaps even the majority, had been offered into evidence by Microsoft.)

The brief concluded that if Judge Jackson's remedy was carried out, "the public will suffer serious and far-reaching harm."

Hours later, the Justice Department entered its request with Judge Jackson for direct appeal to the Supreme Court. And over the next week, the defendants and plaintiffs exchanged daily argumentative briefs on the direct-appeal request and on Microsoft's stay request before the Court of Appeals.

Finally, on June 19, 2000, the Appeals Court said it would hear Microsoft's stay request on a fast-track schedule—a schedule that would immediately be suspended if the case was certified to the Supreme Court.

Then two days later, Judge Jackson surprised everyone. As expected, he issued the certification to the Supreme Court, cutting off the Court of Appeals. But at the same time, he unexpectedly issued a blanket stay of his entire remedy order—the very order he had signed just two weeks earlier.

Of course, the breakup order had already been stayed until the appeals could be complete. But the behavioral remedies—the restrictions on Microsoft's business practices, ranging from the features of its software to its relations with customers and rivals—were to have taken effect in just 11 weeks. Now none of the steps he ordered in his remedy would go into effect for a year or longer, even if they were upheld.

Microsoft was jubilant; for weeks the company had been arguing that the conduct restrictions would damage the company, perhaps irreparably.

The Justice Department tried to put the best face on the order, though unquestionably it was a blow. The department lauded Jackson for referring the case to the high court but added, "Given the district court's decision to stay the remedy during the appeal process, the direct appeal to the Supreme Court is of particular importance to the national interest."

The department's true view was revealed in a brief the department had filed with the judge earlier in the day, arguing for a direct appeal. It said; "In an industry Microsoft vigorously characterizes as fast-paced and quickly changing," any delay "would undermine the ultimate value of the remedy to correct the harmful results of Microsoft's anticompetitive actions and to restore competition."

Still, over the next few days, everyone began to see positive sides to the order. But the real winner, it turned out, was Judge Jackson. For months, he had been expressing discomfort about the fact that he alone was making all the judgments in this important case.

"So far, I am the one decision maker," he said in a late-February interview. "I would derive some comfort if I could call on someone else's intellect to assist me."

As a result, on April 4, the day after he found Microsoft in broad violation of state and Federal antitrust laws, the judge told the litigants that he intended to "sever the liability and the remedy" and to encourage appeal of his verdict before imposing a remedy. But both Microsoft and the government told him they did not think that was allowed under the law, so Judge Jackson reluctantly backed down.

Still, with his stay on remedies, Jackson accomplished the same thing. Now a higher court would have the opportunity to rule on the merits of the case—"the liability," as Judge Jackson had put it—before even thinking about the remedy.

The government, too, found a silver lining. Microsoft had repeatedly argued that Judge Jackson had made a serious procedural error by failing to give the company a full hearing before imposing his remedy. Even some of the plaintiffs believed that a higher court might side with Microsoft on this question. But now the court would have no reason to consider this issue until the very end, if at all.

"It takes all the steam out of Microsoft's due-process argument," said Blumenthal, the Connecticut attorney general. "Now Microsoft will have a full opportunity to present their views on remedies" to the high court.

Robert Litan, a former senior Justice Department official now with the Brookings Institute, said Judge Jackson "looks more even-handed, and now there's no need for a higher court to admonish him over the remedy-hearing question."

Another official said, "If they had sent the case back down to him for hearings because of errors in the remedy phase, it kind of adds a bad flavor to the whole thing."

Still, some government officials worried about what Microsoft might do "with nobody watching," as one official said. And no matter what happened, that was likely to be the case for many months.

Judge Jackson's order started a clock. Under the normal rules, Microsoft would have 60 days to file a brief with the Supreme Court offering its arguments on the direct-appeal question. After that, the Federal and state governments would have 30 days to reply. But the Justice Department quickly announced that the litigants had agreed to shave a month off that schedule, meaning that the last brief would be filed in late August. After that, the Supreme Court could decide whenever it chose.

After two years of trial, Judge Jackson's final order sent the anti-trust case sailing into an uncertain future.

Chronological Index
of New York Times *Articles*

Index